BV
4501.3
.B676
2012

$50 $\underline{00}$

The Bloomsbury Guide to Christian Spirituality

The Bloomsbury Guide to Christian Spirituality

Edited by

Peter Tyler and Richard Woods

BLOOMSBURY

LONDON · NEW DELHI · NEW YORK · SYDNEY

First published in Great Britain 2012

© Peter Tyler and Richard Woods, with the contributors, 2012

The moral right of the author has been asserted

No part of this book may be used or reproduced in any manner whatsoever
without written permission from the Publisher except in the case of brief
quotations embodied in critical articles or reviews. Every reasonable effort has
been made to trace copyright holders of material reproduced in this book, but if
any have been inadvertently overlooked the Publishers would be glad to hear
from them.

Bloomsbury Publishing Plc
50 Bedford Square
London WC1B 3DP

www.bloomsbury.com

Bloomsbury Publishing, London, Berlin, New York and Sydney

A CIP record for this book is available from the British Library.

ISBN 978-1-4411-8484-9

10 9 8 7 6 5 4 3 2 1

Typeset by Newgen Imaging Systems Pvt Ltd, Chennai, India
Printed and bound in Great Britain

Contents

Contents

Introduction: What is Christian Spirituality?

Peter Tyler and Richard Woods

Recent attacks on religion by well-publicized scientists and journalists have at least in one important respect gone wide of the target, for spirituality continues to flourish and is claimed as the 'heart' of religion by many of its defenders. Historically, the term 'spirituality' had religious, indeed Christian, provenance and meaning. Today, however, religion and spirituality not only fail to refer to the same general set of meanings and values they once shared, but a clear distinction if not antagonism exists between them in the mind of many, perhaps especially the young.

As early as 1980, an astute observer could write,

> The broadest way to think of spirituality as the word is used by some recent writers is to think of it as a heuristic, or analytical, concept. In this sense, *spirituality* is a word used by contemporary writers when they are discussing those aspects of human life which are seen by their subjects, or interpreted by their observers, as intentionally related to that which holds unrestricted value. *Spirituality* in this sense may be used to discuss phenomena not generally considered 'religious'.[1]

It may be argued, of course, that the often-heard slogan, 'I'm spiritual but I'm not religious', indicates not only youthful frustration in being unable to find meaning in either the sterility of fundamentalism or the rigidity (or irrelevance) of the organized churches but also a deep longing for spiritual life among the young in particular. Moreover, while church membership and attendance are in decline, not to mention vocations to the monastic and active religious communities (excepting fringe and reactionary groups), interest in yoga, Zen and Sufism is burgeoning, as is that in Native spiritualities.

In recent years, the perceived gap between religion and spirituality attracted the attention of several observers (see Fuller 2001, Locklin 2005), as it surfaced both a troubling situation for the churches and also required a deeper understanding of the contemporary spiritual quest. It raised, moreover, the fundamental question, 'what do we *mean* by "spirituality"?' The present volume may be considered an effort towards addressing that question, particularly in regard to the relationship between Christianity and spirituality, not least in its interface with the spiritual traditions of other religions.

A Brief History of a Word

With roots in the Middle Ages, the term *spiritualité* first came to prominence during the seventeenth century in French literature. Safe from the implications of the 'mysticism' that was arousing suspicion among both Catholics and Protestants, *spiritualité* came to suggest what had been known as 'devotion': a life of methodical prayer and active service distinct both from 'mere' theology or doctrine and also from fanaticism.[2]

In English, *spirituality* originally referred to the properties and influence of the church as distinct from those pertinent within civil society. Gradually, the connotation of non-materiality (if not immateriality) came to predominate, especially in the post-Cartesian period. Eventually, the term acquired the full range of its present meanings.

The contemporary and more secular understanding of 'spirituality' seems to have risen in practice, particularly in the nursing profession where the term appeared in a number of journal articles in the 1970s. In 2000 an important study collated 16 definitions from recent sources, most of them works on nursing and medical care. Few hinted of religious provenance, but most expressed some kind of 'transcendent' element.[3]

The question this poses is whether the long tradition of Christian spirituality will be sufficiently flexible and welcoming to embrace within its ambit the rising elements of Asian and indigenous spiritualities, ecological and cosmological concerns, women's experience and expectations and even globalization as we face the coming decades and an unfolding century. Perhaps the greatest threat to traditional spirituality is the strident challenge presented by science and technology, whose spokesmen blithely dismiss religion as a whole as delusional, harmful and retrograde, although some, such as E. O. Wilson, exhibit a very well-defined and engaged 'atheist' spirituality.

The Return of Religion

Thus, while much ink has been spilt in recent years in defining Christian spirituality and what distinguishes it from other spiritualities, in many respects the question is unanswerable. Perhaps the best way of approaching it is to look at the rich diversity of Christian tradition and practice so that hopefully we may then draw conclusions as to the nature of this vibrant, eternally shifting and kaleidoscopic religion. This will be our approach in this volume. However, before embarking on this journey it is worth recalling some of the excellent scholarship of the past few decades that has seen a renaissance of interest in Christian spirituality as a subject of serious academic study. This renaissance has gone hand in hand with a popular groundswell of interest in spirituality, perhaps at a time when religious institutions take a battering from without and within. David Tacey in a now classic article (Tacey 2003) described this outpouring as the 'rising waters of the Spirit' that occurs every few centuries.[4]

In this article the Australian academic suggests that we are in the midst of what he terms a 'spirituality revolution'. He describes it as 'the emergence of the sacred as a leading force in contemporary society' which is not to be confused with 'the rising tide of religious fundamentalism':

Spirituality and fundamentalism are at opposite ends of the cultural spectrum. Spirituality seeks a sensitive, contemplative relationship with the sacred and is able to sustain levels of uncertainty in its quest because respect for mystery is paramount. Fundamentalism seeks certainty, fixed answers and absolutism, as a fearful response to the complexity of the world and to our vulnerability as creatures in a mysterious universe. (ibid.: 11)

At various times in history, Tacey suggests, the stream or hidden river of spirituality rises and falls according to its own mysterious rhythms. We live in one such time when a rising tide of spirituality is emerging on all sides. This affects all of us in society – the churches, politicians, education and the realm of pastoral care, – 'cure of souls', as it has been called. There are numerous responses to this rising tide of spirituality. One such, fundamentalism, has already been mentioned as the grasping after illusory (usually religious) certainties as a bulwark against the uncertainities of a faith or 'higher power' that challenges all our strongly held habitual beliefs. Tacey characterizes the choice between fundamentalism and authentic spirituality as that between 'conscious intimacy and unconscious possession' (ibid.: 12).

As will become clear throughout this book the rich and diverse tradition of 2000 years of Christian spirituality has evolved a path or way between this Scylla and Charybdis of fundamentalism and cold mechanistic reductionism. But it now faces a third possibility – religionless spirituality.

Humans are clearly made for the spiritual, and the spiritual realm is part of what it is to be human. Yet, as the excesses of fundamentalism(s) show, there are dangers lurking within the realm of the spirit and we must approach it with due caution and respect.

In the pages that follow we will trace the evolution of this 'method' or 'way' as it has evolved throughout Christian history. In a perceptive series of articles in the late 1980s and early 1990s Archbishop Rowan Williams reflected on how Christian spirituality, and the mystical tradition in particular, could be seen as a series of reactions to the original foundational inspiration of the Gospel narratives (See Williams 1983, 1984, 1991). In these essays he suggests that Christian spirituality, or, as he would prefer to call it, the 'contemplative enterprise or discipline' should be seen as teleological in the sense that through Christian contemplation and practice the believers have 'the image of Christ formed' in them. In this understanding, Christian spirituality, especially its more 'mystical elements', becomes shorthand for,

> The deepening and habitual awareness of loss, recovery and transformation in relation to the paschal focus of Christian commitment . . . the capacity for radical liberty and trustful responsibility in the face of a world of senseless pain and oppression, the bearing of a darkness which challenges all our desires and projections, in the confidence that we are taken into a (deeply paradoxical) relationship with the source of all meaning, an elusive – if not entirely effable – union with 'the Father'. (Williams 1984: 209)

The aim of Christian spiritual practice becomes then for Williams the process whereby we are brought closer to the *persona Christi* which we hold in potential. Later, on writing about St Teresa of Avila, he emphasizes the 'reformative' or 'generative' element of Christian spirituality. In this sense *spirituality* in general becomes the means whereby we return to the original 'charism' of a religion – whether that be in the life or teaching of a charismatic founder such as Mohammed or Gautama Buddha, or the generative terms of a religion such as Judaism or Hinduism.

However, in contrast to many other world religions, Williams emphasizes that the complexity of the Christian foundational story makes Christian spirituality by definition far more complicated, rich and diverse than the spiritualities of many other religions. Christian spirituality is able to reflect any one of a number of elements from the foundational story of Christianity:

> There is the story of God's becoming human, the story of that humanity itself, and the story of the establishing of the community in faith in Easter and Pentecost. What is it that needs to be recapitulated? The movement out from heaven and back to it? The pattern of the incarnate ministry? Jesus's path to the cross? The disciple's experience of the resurrection? (Williams 1991: 156)

In the pages that follow we shall explore many forms this Williamsian 'refoundational Christian spirituality' has taken. We will see how different individuals have modelled themselves on Christ and by this recapitulation of the life of Christ in their lives have assisted this 'refoundation' of the charism of Christianity in their communities, circumstances and worlds. What will emerge is the enormous flexibility and diversity of Christian spirituality and how this 'refoundational charism' can adapt itself across continents, ages and people of staggering diversity. The richness and variety of Christian spirituality that emerges suggests that Christianity as a religion has a rich and diverse future ahead of itself. However, we shall leave that question open to the final chapter when we shall return to the subject of 'Whither Christian Spirituality'?

In the writing and compilation of this book we would like to acknowledge many and varied inspirational people who have helped bring this enterprise to success. Chief among these must rank Robin Baird Smith of Bloomsbury whose idea the book originally was. Without his unfailing enthusiasm and support the book would have floundered many times. The colleagues who have contributed to the volume have shown undiminished support for the project and we salute their perseverance, professionalism and profound knowledge. Many colleagues and friends have supported the project through thick and thin. In particular, Peter Tyler would like to thank the staff of the School of Theology, Philosophy and History at St Mary's University College, Twickenham, London, especially the Head of the School, Dr Anthony Towey, for giving Dr Tyler study time to complete the work. During that time he was particularly enriched by visits to the ashrams and monasteries of Southern India where the staff and students of Christ University, Bangalore, were exceptionally kind and hospitable. Finally he acknowledges once again the unlimited help and support of his family and that of Ashish Deved and family, Fr James McCaffrey OCD, Julienne McLean and David Stones, Br Patrick Moore and Joanne Mosley.

Fr Richard Woods likewise owes a great debt of gratitude to colleagues at Dominican University, particularly Dean Jeffrey Carlson of Rosary College of Arts and Sciences, Prof Hugh McElwain, director of the theology department and the other members of the department whose forbearance enabled him to devote time and energy to the project. He wishes to express especial thanks to Dr James Halstead OSA, DePaul University, Dr Daniel Helminiak and Mr Steven Plane for their unfailing and generous assistance.

Notes

1 Jon Alexander, OP (1980), 'What Do Recent Writers Mean by "Spirituality"?', *Spirituality Today* 32, 3: 254.
2 See Chapter Four by Sr Benedicta Ward, below.
3 David Aldridge (2000), *Spirituality, Healing, and Medicine: Return to the Silence.* London and New York: Jessica Kingsley Publishers, pp. 27–8. See also Mary Elizabeth O'Brien (2011), *Servant Leadership in Nursing: Spirituality and Practice in Contemporary Healthcare.* Sudbury, MA: Jones and Bartlett, Publishing; and *Spirituality in Nursing: Standing on Holy Ground.* Sudbury, MA: Jones and Bartlett, Publishing (4th edn, 2010).
4 See also David Tacey (2004), *The Spirituality Revolution: The Emergence of Contemporary Spirituality.* New York and East Sussex: Brunner-Routledge.

Bibliography and Further Reading

Aldridge, David (2000), *Spirituality, Healing, and Medicine: Return to the Silence.* London and New York: Jessica Kingsley Publishers.

Fuller, Robert C. (2001), *Spiritual but not Religious: Understanding Unchurched America.* New York: Oxford University Press.

Locklin, Reid (2005), *Spiritual but Not Religious? An Oar Stroke Closer To the Farther Shore.* Collegeville: Liturgical Press.

Sheldrake, Philip (2007), *A Brief History of Spirituality.* Oxford: Wiley-Blackwell.

Tacey, D. (2003), 'Rising Waters of the Spirit', *Studies in Spirituality*, 13, 11–30.

— (2004), *The Spirituality Revolution: The Emergence of Contemporary Spirituality.* New York and East Sussex: Brunner-Routledge.

Williams, R. (1983), 'The Prophetic and the Mystical: Heiler revisited', *New Blackfriars*, 64, 330–47.

— (1984) 'Butler's *Western Mysticism*: Towards an Assessment', *The Downside Review*, 102, 197–215.

— (1991) *Teresa of Avila.* London: Continuum.

Part I
The Building Blocks

1 The Origins of Christian Spirituality in the Temple Tradition

Margaret Barker

Introduction

Christian worship, theology and lifestyle derive from the temple, not from the temple that Jesus knew, which John saw as the harlot and the burning city (Rev. 17.1–6; 18.1–24), but from Solomon's temple, destroyed first by king Josiah's purges in 623 BCE (2 Kgs 23) and then by the Babylonians in 597 BCE and 586 BCE (2 Kgs 24–5). People remembered the original temple and longed for it to be restored. The second temple[1] was very different from the first: old men wept when they saw it (Ezra 3.12); and for centuries people said that the full glory of the LORD had not returned. The symbolic furnishings, seen and understood only by the high priests because they alone could enter the holy of holies (Num. 4.1–15),[2] were missing from the second temple. The anointing oil, the seven-branched lamp, the fire, the Spirit, the cherubim and the ark containing the manna and the high-priestly staff would be restored only when the Messiah rebuilt the true temple.[3] When the Christians described Jesus as their great high priest (Heb. 4.14), the Messiah, they would have expected him to restore the true temple. Jesus said he would destroy the temple and build another, it was claimed at his trial, and so the high priest asked him: 'Are you the Messiah, the Son of the Blessed?' (Mk 14.57–61). Peter exhorted the Christians in Asia Minor to become the living stones of the new temple, the royal priesthood, called from darkness into the marvellous light of the divine presence (1 Pet. 2.4–10).

The New Testament presupposes the world view of the original temple, which represented the cosmos, both the visible and the invisible creation. The proportions of the temple, and of the desert tabernacle on which it was modelled (Exod. 25–40), represented the revealed order of creation, and any alteration was rebellion against the divine plan. It was distortion, the literal meaning of the biblical term 'iniquity', and the second commandment warned that the LORD would allow 'distortion' to affect subsequent generations if they followed false gods (Exod. 20.4–6). The LORD revealed the order of creation to Moses on Sinai when he was within the cloud for six days. He was told to build the tabernacle to represent what he had seen (Exod. 24.15–16).[4] David received from the LORD a plan of the temple, which he gave to Solomon (1 Chron. 28.11–19), and an angel revealed to Ezekiel the correct measurements for the temple to be rebuilt in Jerusalem. The people would then be ashamed of their 'iniquities' and restore their social order as they restored the temple (Ezek. 43.10). John saw the angel measuring the heavenly city, which was itself a huge holy of holies (Rev. 21.15–17).

Solomon's Temple

In Solomon's temple, the key proportion was 2:1, which is found in traditionally built Western churches. The outer hall, the holy place (the 'nave'), was twice the length of the inner sanctuary, the holy of holies (1 Kgs 6.16–17). The two were separated by a curtain known as the veil of the temple, which was woven from four fibres: white linen for the warp, and red, blue and purple wool for the weft. It represented matter: the linen was earth, the red was fire, the blue was air and the purple was water. The fabric was 'skilled work', *chosheb*, but nobody is certain what that word meant (Exod. 26.31; see also Josephus, *Jewish War* 5.212–13). The same fabric was used for the outer vestment of the high priest, which was *chosheb* work woven with gold (Exod. 28.5–6). Since the veil represented matter, the high priest's vestment did too; it was the symbol of the glory of the LORD veiled in matter, that is, the LORD incarnate.[5] Thus the veil of the temple tore when Jesus died, and Hebrews describes the flesh of Jesus as the veil of the temple (Mk 15.38 and parallels; Heb. 10.20). The *Infancy Gospel of James* says that Mary was weaving a new veil for the temple when she was pregnant. Gabriel spoke to her as she was spinning wool for the veil, the scene in the Annunciation ikon.[6]

The high priest represented the LORD on earth. He wore the four letters of the sacred Name on his forehead,[7] and people knelt before him when he emerged from the temple (Sir. 50.11–17). In the first temple, when the king was a high priest 'after the order of Melchizedek', he was declared at his enthronement to be the 'son' of the LORD, which meant he was his earthly manifestation (Pss 110.4; 2.7). He sat on the cherub-throne of the LORD in the holy of holies and was worshipped as the LORD.[8] He was anointed with the perfumed oil, which represented oil from the tree of life,[9] and this gave him Wisdom. His eyes were opened, and all his senses were transformed. He became a holy one, a son of God and a son of Wisdom.[10] He was marked on the forehead with X, the ancient mark of the name of the LORD, and was anointed on his eyelids to show that his spiritual eyes had been opened.[11] The oil was the sacrament of Wisdom, the gift of the Spirit that transformed the human mind (Isa. 9.1–3), and so John reminded the Christians: 'You have been anointed by the Holy One and you know all things' (1 Jn 2.20). John also saw the throng in heaven who had the Name on their foreheads, because the X was the original mark of baptism (Rev. 14.1).

This way of thinking was abandoned in Jerusalem during Josiah's purges, when tradition said that the oil was 'hidden away', but it was written into the story of Eden, where the human pair chose the tree of knowledge rather than the tree of life and its oil. It was also remembered in the many legends and traditions about Eden, preserved in books that did not become part of the Old Testament but were used by the first Christians. How they were preserved and transmitted is not known, although one broken text among the Dead Sea Scrolls tells of 'teachers who had been hidden and kept secret'.[12] The story of Ezra restoring the scriptures after the destruction of the temple implies something similar. In a trance he dictated 94 books, but the Most High told him to make only 24 of them public. The other 70 were to be reserved for the wise because they contained understanding, wisdom and knowledge (2 Esd. 14.47). Although this story is 'set' in the fifth century BCE, it is a thinly veiled account of how the canon of Hebrew scriptures was determined at the end of the first century CE. It is a warning that many significant books are not found in the Old Testament. Further, people remembered as late as the fifth century CE that many first-temple priests had fled during Josiah's purges and gone to 'Arabia' (Jerusalem Talmud *Ta'anit* 4.5). Other people had fled to Egypt and settled there (Jer. 44.1). Presumably they took with them the religion of the original temple. The history of Jerusalem found in 1 Enoch says that just before the original temple was burned, the priests there abandoned Wisdom and lost their spiritual sight, and then the people were scattered. Those who restored the temple were not true to the original tradition; they were apostate.[13]

The Temple and the Cosmos

The temple represented the cosmos, and all temple worship concerned the relationship of the creation to God – praise, thanksgiving, asking for forgiveness and invoking his presence. Erecting the tabernacle or temple re-enacted the process of creation,[14] and each stage represented one day of creation as described in Gen. 1. The beginning of creation, separating light from darkness, corresponded to setting up the outer tent; the firmament made on the second day was represented by the veil; the plants on the third day by the table for plant offerings – bread, wine and incense (Exod. 25.23–30); the lights of heaven on the fourth day by the menorah, although this was a complex symbol and also represented the tree of life; fish and birds on the fifth day and the animals on the sixth by the altar of sacrifice; and Adam, the last to be created, was the high priest.[15] The visible world was thus the temple where human beings were the priests. 'Adam' (the name simply means a human) was put into Eden to 'serve' it and to 'preserve' it, two Hebrew words which also meant to lead worship in the temple and preserve the teachings. After six days, God rested on the seventh, the Sabbath, showing that when the creation was complete and 'very good', nothing more was made. The goal of creation was not more and more, but sufficiency, completion and rest.

Adam the high priest was created as the image of God on earth, and so there was no statue in the temple in Jerusalem. People worshipped God by their treatment of other human beings[16] and by their care for the creation. Genesis says that Adam was created from dust, but began his real life when God breathed into him (Gen. 2.7). Other books say he was clothed with garments of light which were woven from wisdom and cut from the glory of God,[17] and the Dead Sea Scrolls Community prayed that they would regain the glory of Adam and learn again the knowledge of the Most High.[18] The angels wore these garments of glory, as did the high priest when he entered the holy of holies. They were made of fine white linen, and angels were known as 'men in white'. The Christians put on white garments after baptism, because they too became angels, and the earliest baptism rites are very similar to those for making a high priest.[19]

Adam the high priest was forbidden to take the fruit of the tree of knowledge of good and evil – secular knowledge – but all the other trees were permitted, including the tree of life which was the symbol of Wisdom. Satan, described as 'the deceiver' (Rev. 12.9) because he made false knowledge look attractive, persuaded the human pair to eat the forbidden fruit, and they discovered the consequences of secular knowledge: materialism and reductionism. They lost their garments and knew they were naked; the LORD made for them instead garments of skin, which means mortal bodies (Gen. 3.7; 21). They discovered they could not eat from both trees and became no more than the dust from which they had been made. They were banished from the presence of the LORD and left Eden. The story of the New Testament is about returning to Eden, regaining the garments of glory and standing again in the presence of the LORD, seeing his face (Rev. 22.4).

The Holy of Holies

The purpose of the tabernacle/temple was to have a holy place where the LORD would dwell in the midst,[20] and so at the heart of the temple and its world view was the holy of holies. 'Holy' and 'holy of holies/most holy' in temple discourse are not just a matter of degree: 'holy' means that something or someone has been made holy, but 'holy of holies' means that the object or person is actively holy and can impart holiness. The holy anointing oil was the exception because it imparted 'most holiness' and could make any anointed object or person 'most holy'. Thus the tabernacle furnishings were anointed and became 'most holy', as did the high priests.[21] The holy of holies itself was the source of holiness, the state of the glory of the LORD, and anyone entering was transformed into a holy one, an angel, a son of God. This transformation, later called *theosis*, was how the temple understood resurrection. John emphasized: 'We have beheld his glory', and Jesus described himself as the one who had been consecrated (anointed) and sent into the world as Son of God, that is, as the true high priest (Jn 1.14, 10.36). In some sense the lost oil was restored, since no high priest in the second temple was anointed. In temple discourse, an anointed one (a Messiah) was by definition resurrected.

The Genesis creation story calls the holy of holies Day One, not 'the first day' because it was beyond time and was the ever-present source of all life. It was the state of pre-created light and unity (*Genesis Rabbah* III.8), the throne of the LORD around which Isaiah and John saw the heavenly powers praising the Creator (Isa. 6.1–3; Rev. 4–5). This was the kingdom, and everything taught about the holy of holies became Christian teaching about the kingdom of God. There was no division nor distinction there (Gal. 3.28), all were holy ones (i.e. 'saints') and servants before the throne. John described the heavenly city as a huge holy of holies, a golden cube that needed no created light (Rev. 21.23), where the servants saw the face of God and had the Name on their foreheads (Rev. 22.3–5). The Jewish statement of faith 'The LORD our God is one LORD' (Deut. 6.4: the Shema') became the basis of Christian unity. In Hebrew, 'God' is a plural that can also mean 'angels', and so the unity of the angels in the LORD became the unity of the Christians in the LORD. Jesus prayed for his disciples 'that they may be one even as we are one' (Jn 17.11).

The unity of Day One underlies and binds together in one system everything in the visible creation. The prophets saw this vision, and the sages warned that when people lost sight of it, everything disintegrated.[22] The temple term was 'seeing the face/presence of the LORD',[23] and the high-priestly blessing was 'May the LORD bless you and keep you: May the LORD make his face shine on you and be gracious to you; May the LORD lift up his face on you and give you peace' (Num. 6.24–6, my translation). Such anthropomorphism was a sensitive issue, and so some Hebrew texts were later pronounced differently: at a temple pilgrimage, according to the old calendars, all men saw the face of the LORD, but this became 'shall appear before the LORD'.[24] It was forbidden to explain this blessing (Mishnah *Megillah* 4.10) or even to translate it,[25] but the Psalms retain the older form, praying for the face of the LORD to shine (Pss 67.1; 80.1, 3, 7, 19). 'Hallelujah' also means 'Shine, LORD'. Jesus said the pure in heart would see God (Mt. 5.8), and John described the baptized before the throne, 'seeing his face' (Rev. 22.4).

Angels

People on earth were able to learn something about God from the angels (the Hebrew word means 'messengers'), who were themselves part of the glory and unity of God. The song of the angels symbolized the harmony of all creation centred on God, and when people on earth praised the Creator, they joined with the angels in their music and became part of the great pattern of the Creation.[26] This is why Christian liturgy is sung, 'with angels and archangels and all the company of heaven'. The harmony and wholeness, *shalom*, of creation were maintained by the obedience of the angels, and humans had to be obedient to God if they were to preserve the creation. Some angels – known as the sons of God – rebelled against God and brought their heavenly knowledge to earth[27] but without the law of God. They corrupted the creation by teaching secular knowledge – 'the knowledge of good and evil' – which fragmented and destroyed. Theirs was a deceptive, false covenant, offering a 'freedom', that led only to death and decay. Paul taught that Christians were the (new) sons of God who were to free the creation from these bonds of decay (Rom. 8.12–23) and restore the covenant of *shalom*, and in Revelation, John learned that faithful Christians would again eat from the tree of life and be restored to Eden (Rev. 2.7; 22.14).

Covenant

The whole creation – earth and heaven – was bound in a network of bonds known as the eternal covenant and the covenant of peace.[28] Everything – the visible natural world, human society and the invisible world of the angels – was part of one system created by God. The bonds held everything together and joined the visible world to the LORD at its centre. Any action which broke the bonds was by definition, 'sin', and so human conduct could and did destroy the system. Sin could be deliberate or through ignorance; the effect was the same. Thus one of the key roles of the priests, who represented the angels, was to teach about right conduct. Breaking away from God was not liberation but rebellion and deprivation, losing touch with the source of life and renewal. The mystics described the holy of holies as 'the mystery of existence' and 'the mystery of becoming'.[29] When the bonds of the covenant were broken, the whole system collapsed; because of human sin, the stars fell from the sky, the sun lost its light, the earth shook – the familiar pictures of the apocalypse (Isa. 24.4–6 is the earliest text).

The pattern of creation was determined by God and described as the statutes, the 'engraved things'. When earth was in harmony with the divine statutes, the natural world and human society enjoyed 'justice' and 'righteousness', words describing the state of wholeness, *shalom*, when the covenant of peace was unbroken (Isa. 32.1–20). The exact measurements, proportions and roles of everything were planned by God, and these were known as the 'mysteries' of the creation. They were not simply cosmic dimensions, but even included fair dealing in weights and measures (Ezek. 45.9–12). Perpetual progress was not part of the picture; the aim was to keep everything in harmony with the Creator's plan. This was the context for the Sabbath commandment, to rest because the Creator had rested (Exod. 20.11), and the Lord's Prayer: 'Thy Kingdom come', which means 'Thy will be done on earth as it is in heaven.'

The eternal covenant was repaired by 'atonement', when the temple/creation was purified from the effects of sin (described as pollution), and recreated. The covenant bonds which bound the visible creation and joined earth to heaven were renewed. Atonement involved repentance and self sacrifice to renew and restore everything that had been damaged: the creation, human society and the sinner's relationship with God. Atonement restored the covenant of peace when both the causes and the effects of sin were removed, and the process was known as 'making righteous'. 'Righteousness', *tsedaqah*, and 'making righteous' were key concepts: in the writing of Paul they became 'justification', *dikaiosune* and 'justify', but the covenant context was the same.

The day of atonement was part of the new year celebration, when the earth was cleansed and the covenant of peace was restored. The ritual involved two identical goats[30] which were designated by lot. One 'for the Lord' and one 'for Azazel' is the usual translation. Origen, who worked with Jewish scholars in Caesarea in the early third century, implied that the Hebrew meant 'as Azazel' not 'for Azazel', and so also 'as the Lord'.[31] The sacrificed goat *represented the Lord* and the other, the 'scapegoat' represented Azazel, the chief of the fallen angels, banished to the wilderness bearing the people's sins. The high priest took the blood of the sacrificed goat into the holy of holies, offered it there and then emerged, sprinkling various parts of the temple to cleanse and reconsecrate them. The ritual of atonement meant the Lord pouring out his life to take away the effects of sin, to restore the creation and renew the covenant. The ritual of making righteous, *tsedeq*, was performed by a high priest named *tsadoq* (Zadok), the one who makes righteous, the Righteous One.

The covenant of the last supper was this covenant of peace, and in early Christian writings, the great majority of references to the last supper and atonement recognize that the day of atonement, not Passover, was the context for Jesus' words and actions. There are many covenants in the Old Testament: with Noah, with Abraham, with Moses and with David (Gen. 9.16, 15.18; Exod. 24.8; 2 Sam. 7.12–16), but none deals with the 'putting away of sin' (Mt. 26.28). At the last supper, Jesus the Lord described the wine as his blood of the covenant, poured out for 'the putting away of sins', and Peter described him as 'the Holy and Righteous One . . . the Author of life' (Acts 3.14–15).

The writer to the Hebrews explained that the new Melchizedek did not use a goat as a substitute, but offered his own blood, 'thus securing an eternal redemption' (Heb. 11–12).

Wisdom

When Adam and Eve rejected the tree of life, they rejected Wisdom. She (not it) was the Lady of the original temple. One of her symbols was the tree of life (Prov. 3.13–18), the source of the oil that anointed the messiahs and of the fruit that nourished them. Wisdom gave her children the anointed knowledge that bound all creation in harmony to the Creator and maintained righteousness. The command to Adam, 'subdue the earth and have dominion' is better translated 'bind together the earth and rule it in peace'. This command to the unfallen Adam with his garment of Wisdom was to uphold the covenant of *shalom*, and so the early Christians hymned the second Adam as 'the image of the invisible God, the first-born of all creation . . . and in him all things hold together' (Col. 1.15, 17).

So much of the Wisdom tradition has been lost, but fragments remain and something of the Lost Lady can be recovered. She was the main victim of Josiah's purge in the seventh century BCE, and the scribes who collected and compiled the texts that became the Hebrew scriptures were often the spiritual heirs of Josiah. In the era of the second temple, the 'men of the great synagogue' determined the meaning of the texts,[32] and a group of 'correcting scribes' were authorized to remove 'blasphemy' from the texts,[33] but they had to work within certain limits: setting letters in a different order, substituting one letter for another that looked or sounded similar, pronouncing a word differently. Traces of the Lady are often found in communities beyond their influence. The Greek translation of Proverbs describes her as the Lady who holds all things together in harmony and as *the* Virgin who bears Immanuel;[34] the great Isaiah scroll found among the Dead Sea Scrolls describes her as the Mother of the Lord.[35] On his spirit journey, the prophet Ezekiel saw the glory of the Lord in the temple, by the seat of the statue of 'the image of jealousy that provokes to jealousy'. Remove one silent letter from 'jealousy', and the Lady reappears: 'the statue of the Lady who creates', a title for the mother of the sons of God, that is, of the angels, the hosts of heaven, the stars. This title was known in the neighbouring culture of Ugarit.[36] Ezekiel said that this was the same as his vision of the chariot, the mysterious wheels within wheels (Ezek. 1, 10), when he must have seen the Lady leaving the temple.

One of the symbols of Wisdom was the tree of life, represented in the temple by the menorah, a stylized almond tree (Exod. 25.31–7) whose seven lamps represented the lights of heaven. The perfumed oil from her tree was copied by Moses as the anointing oil. This tree, and all that it represented, was the

'Asherah' that Josiah removed from the temple and destroyed (2 Kgs 23.4). Although there was a menorah in the second temple,[37] it was not the true menorah. How the later menorah differed is not known, but the true menorah was one of the missing items to be restored by the Messiah, and John did see the tree of life in the holy of holies (Rev. 22.1–2). The Messiah, her son, was known as the Branch (Zech. 6.12) who would rebuild the temple. Jeremiah, a witness to Josiah's purges, saw a rod of almond in his call vision – presumably the almond in danger – and the LORD said he was watching over his work. Jeremiah was to be his prophet against the kings, princes and priests in the land, those endangering the almond (Jer. 1.4–19).

Another of her symbols was bread. The refugees in Egypt told Jeremiah that they had venerated the Queen of Heaven with incense, libations and loaves to represent her,[38] and that she had protected the city. The editors of the Hebrew scriptures were hostile to the Lady and implied that she was an alien diety. Papyri from a Jewish community in the south of Egypt, however, show that they did worship a female diety with a Semitic name, presumably the Lady they had brought with them. They worshipped only with incense, wine and cereal offerings until they were ordered by Jerusalem to observe the Passover sacrifice.[39] There had been a table in the temple for incense, libations and loaves (Exod. 25.23–30), but nothing is said of its role in temple ritual. The bread, however, was called the shewbread, literally, 'the bread of the presence'. Whose presence? Wisdom fed her children with the bread of understanding and the water of Wisdom (Sir. 15.3), and the earliest eucharistic prayer outside the New Testament gives thanks over the bread for the life and knowledge made known by Jesus (*Didache* 9). The process of making the bread was kept secret (Mishnah *Yoma* 3.11), but the ritual implied that it acquired holiness while resting in the temple for seven days (Mishnah *Menahoth* 11.7). Then it was eaten by the high priests on each Sabbath as their most holy food; they were nourished with holiness (Lev. 24.5–9). Those who complained that the second temple lacked the essential furnishings also complained that the bread offered there was not pure.[40] The early Christians understood that the bread of the Eucharist was the pure bread of the presence restored, the bread of Wisdom (Mal. 1.11 cited in *Didache* 14 and Justin, *Dialogue with Trypho* 41).

At the last supper, Jesus took the two elements of the Passover meal that represented the two temple rituals exclusive to the high priests: the atonement blood that renewed the eternal covenant, and the bread of the presence that nourished them with holiness. These became the Eucharist. The earliest known Marian devotion shows that the imagery and titles of the Lost Lady were given to her as the Mother of the LORD. John saw her restored to her place in the holy of holies, giving birth to her son who was set on the throne in heaven (Rev. 12.1–6), and the titles in the great Akathistos Hymn and in the Litany of Loreto can all be traced back to Wisdom, the Lost Lady of the temple.

Notes

1 Restored after 520 BCE.
2 See also Origen *On Numbers*, Homily 5.
3 Babylonian Talmud *Horayoth* 12ab, Jerusalem Talmud *Ta'anit* 2.1, *Numbers Rabbah* XV.10.
4 The six days of the vision became the six days of Gen. 1, the beginning of the books of Moses.
5 Simeon of Thessalonike, *On Prayer* 41: 'The priest wears sacerdotal vestments to signify the incarnation'.
6 *Infancy Gospel of James* 10–12.
7 Exodus 28.26, which should be translated 'a plate of pure gold, engraved like the engraving of a holy seal belonging to the LORD.' See *Letter of Aristeas* 98 and Philo, *Life of Moses* 2.114. The four letters YHWH were formerly voiced as Jehovah, but now as Yahweh.
8 1 Chron. 29.20, 29. Most English versions have '(The people) worshipped the LORD *and* did obeisance to the king' but there is only one verb in the Hebrew. The people worshipped the LORD-and-the-king.
9 *Clementine Recognitions* 1.45–6. Dionysius, *Ecclesiastical Hierarchy* 472C–485B.
10 Thus Philo, *On Flight* 109, who said the Logos, the LORD, was the son of Wisdom his mother.
11 Ezek. 9.4, the 'mark' is the ancient letter *tau*, X. The X on the high priest, Babylonian Talmud *Horayoth* 12a.
12 The translation proposed in F. Garcia-Martinez, ed. (1998), *Discoveries in the Judean Desert* 23, Oxford: Oxford University Press, p. 229.
13 *1 Enoch* 93.8–9. *1 Enoch* was considered scripture by the early church, but then fell out of use. It was rediscovered by the European church in the late eighteenth century when James Bruce, exploring Ethiopia, found it in the Old Testament of the Ethiopian church. Fragments have been found among the Dead Sea Scrolls.
14 L. Ginzberg, *Legends of the Jews*, vol. 1, Philadelphia, 1909, p. 51.
15 Compare the order of Gen. 1 and Exod. 40.16–33. The text of Exodus is dislocated in places, but the ancient pattern can still be seen, as too in the *Benedicite*.
16 Hence the words of Jesus, Mt. 25.37–40.
17 *Genesis Rabbah* XX.12; *The Teaching of Silvanus*, from the Coptic Gnostic Library VII.4.89–91.
18 Dead Sea Scrolls *Community Rule* column IV.
19 See my book *Temple Themes in Christian Worship* (2007), London: T&T Clark, pp. 106–7.
20 Exod. 25.8. The Greek text here has 'that I may be seen in the midst'.
21 Exod. 30.29–31. An illustration is found in Hag. 2.11–13, where the prophet taught that uncleanness was contagious but simple holiness was not.
22 Prov. 29.18, is, literally: 'Where there is no prophetic vision, the people unravel'.
23 Hebrew *panim*, a plural noun, means both face and presence.
24 Exod. 23.17; 34.23; Deut. 16.16. There are many other examples.
25 Some Aramaic translations (Targums) left these verses in Hebrew.
26 Rev. 4.8–11 shows the early Christian context.
27 The myth of the fallen angels is found in *1 Enoch* 6–11, but is assumed by Gen. 6.1–8.
28 Gen. 9.12–17 and Isa. 54.10, both in the context of Noah, show that the eternal covenant and the covenant of peace were synonymous.
29 For example, in the Dead Sea Scrolls *Community Rule* column XI.
30 Lev. 16, with additional details in Mishnah *Yoma*.

31 Origen, *Against Celsus* 6.43
32 Babylonian Talmud *Nedarim* 37b.
33 S. Levin (1978), *The Father of Joshua/Jesus*, New York: SUNY, *passim*.
34 The Hebrew of Prov. 8.30 is an otherwise unknown word *'amon*, which the Greek rendered as *harmozousa*, the lady who holds together in harmony. *The* Virgin (not *a* virgin) is an ambiguous Hebrew word, but the Greek remembered its significance and used *he parthenos, the* Virgin.
35 The Isaiah Scroll, 1Q Isaᵃ has 'Ask a sign from the mother of the LORD your God' at 7.11; whereas the current Hebrew has 'Ask a sign of the LORD your God.' This involves changing the letter *aleph* to *ayin*.
36 Ezek. 8.3: Hebrew *hqn'h*, jealousy, and *hqnh*, lady who creates.
37 Depicted on the arch of Titus among the loot taken to Rome after the second temple was destroyed in 70 CE.
38 Jer. 44.19. 'cakes bearing her image' is literally 'to represent her'.
39 B. Porten (1968), *Archives from Elephantine*. Berkeley: University of California Press.
40 Mal. 1.6–12; *1 Enoch* 89.73 says that the priests who had lost their spiritual sight offered polluted bread.

Bibliography and Further Reading

Barker, M. (2003), *The Great High Priest. The Temple Roots of Christian Liturgy*. London: T&T Clark.

— (2007), *Temple Themes in Christian Worship*. London: T&T Clark.

— (2011), *Temple Mysticism. An Introduction*. London: SPCK.

Murray, R. (1992), *The Cosmic Covenant*. London: Sheed and Ward.

2 The Origins and Scope of Biblical Spirituality

Gerald O'Collins

If spirituality is understood as a way to God and of living in relationship with God, what role have the Scriptures played in furthering a progressive union with God through prayer and a particular lifestyle? How has the Bible affected and shaped living in response to God who is revealed in Jesus Christ and who has graced us with the Holy Spirit?

Any acquaintance with Christian history shows how from the outset the inherited Jewish books and 27 further books written by followers of Jesus have proved indispensable for the Christian spiritual life. An article on biblical spirituality could examine how the Scriptures formed a path to God for St Augustine of Hippo, St Simeon the New Theologian, St Hildegard of Bingen, St Francis of Assisi, St Ignatius Loyola, St Teresa of Avila, St John of the Cross, St Thérèse of Lisieux and many other outstanding examples of Christian discipleship. How far were their lives and teaching moulded by the Bible? A similar, if wider but more demanding, project could investigate the ways the Scriptures have over 20 centuries entered the worship and lives of baptized men and women. How has 'ordinary' Christian Spirituality proved to be recognizably biblical? These two approaches would, in a different but related fashion, be concerned with the 'reception history' of biblical spirituality or the effective impact (*Wirkungsgeschichte*) of the Bible on two millennia of Christian experience of God and discipleship. This present chapter will, however, focus on the biblical texts in themselves and highlight some major themes and figures (in particular, the psalms, Jesus himself, Paul's letters and John's Gospel). Almost every page of the Bible sheds light on what the journey to God involves. We can hardly do more than sample the extraordinary wealth of what they offer for Christian Spirituality.

The Jewish Scriptures

Christian Spirituality has been persistently nourished by the Jewish Scriptures. The liturgy and the divine office would, for instance, be unthinkable without the inspired and inspiring psalms. It is no accident that Augustine developed some powerful spiritual insights in his *Expositions of the Psalms*: for instance, his reflections on the unique beauty of Christ when commenting on what we know as Psalm 45. Before examining what the psalms contribute, let me first draw attention to something at the heart of the spiritual life: our image of God.

The Jewish Scriptures record a progressive purification of their image of God. The Israelites moved from a vision of God as a tribal deity who could order the total destruction of all the inhabitants of town after town (Deut. 2.31–3.7) to a true image of God who loves and cherishes all people, which we find in Second Isaiah, Jonah and other later traditions and books. The earlier passages maintain, however, their spiritual value by warning against the constant human temptation to create a savage deity in our own image and likeness. National interests and security, or at least perceived national interests and security, have continued to encourage human beings and their leaders to picture God as ferociously 'with us' but 'against them' and so justify 'taking out' enemies on a large scale.

The Ten Commandments reflect a very 'spiritual' understanding of YHWH and begin by excluding any idols: 'You shall not make for yourself an idol, whether in the form of anything that is in the heaven above, or that is on the earth beneath, or that is in the water under the earth. You shall not bow down to them and worship them' (Exod. 20.4–5; see Deut. 5.8–9). Idols are dismissed as mere 'gods made with human hands, objects of wood or stone that neither see, nor hear, or eat, nor smell' (Deut. 4.28; see Isa. 44.9–20; Jer. 10.1–16). Neither true nor life-giving, idols do not offer a path to the real God. The biblical rejection of idolatry has not lost its spiritual relevance; Christians, no less than other men and women, can lapse into worshipping such new idols as wealth, status and health.

Named as 'the God of Israel' (Exod. 24.10), the tribal God, who had encountered Abraham and Sarah, the ancestors of the Israelites, and inaugurated a special relationship with them, delivered the people from captivity, gave them the great gift of the law (Torah) (Deut. 6.1–25; Ps. 119), and entered a communion of covenanted life with them. As a 'holy nation' (Exod. 19.6), they were drawn near to God and called to a life of holiness through observing God's commands: 'You shall be holy, for I the Lord God am holy' (Lev. 19.2). Centuries later this call to holiness and complete loyalty 'to the Lord your God' (Deut. 18.13) would be echoed by Jesus: 'Be perfect, as your heavenly Father is perfect' (Mt. 5.48).

The Jewish Scriptures record numerous public and private prayers – in particular, the psalms, which have always fed Christian spiritual life in its common worship and personal prayer and which mainly fall into two classes: hymns and laments.

Focusing on what God has done as creator (e.g. Pss 8, 19, 104) and victorious deliverer (e.g. Pss 66, 98), the *hymns* give voice to what individuals and the community at large believe: 'It is good to give thanks to the Lord, to sing praises to your name, O Most High' (Ps. 92.1). Beginning and/or ending with the words 'halelu-yah (Praise the Lord)', clusters of psalms (Pss 105–6; 111–13; 115–17; 146–50) demonstrate how praising God was highly significant for Israelite devotion. To drive home this theme, the Book of Psalms closes with six psalms that praise God as creator and saviour. Psalm 150 forms a fitting climax, and runs through the instruments of an ancient orchestra to tell everyone and everything: 'Praise the Lord!'

Whether individual (e.g. Ps. 3) or communal (e.g. Ps. 44), *laments* invoke God, describe some distressing experience(s) and appeal for divine help. With its opening 'cry of abandonment', uttered by Jesus on the cross (Mk 15.34), Psalm 22 moved from personal lament to praise in the context of Temple worship and a vision of God's future rule over all the nations (O'Collins 2007, 140–8). Jesus' cry encouraged Mark and the other evangelists to borrow language from this psalm when they told the story of his suffering and death. What was originally a psalm of lament and thanksgiving became *the* passion psalm, feeding Christian meditation on the crucifixion of Jesus.

During the early centuries of Christianity, many believers understood the psalms as Jesus speaking to the Father, and they joined Jesus in his prayer to God. For instance, they imaginatively associated themselves with Jesus by confidently praying in distress: 'In you, O Lord, I seek refuge; do not let me ever be put to shame; in your righteousness deliver me' (Ps. 30.1). In the company of Jesus, they expressed their yearning for the face of God: 'As a deer yearns for flowing streams, so my soul longs for you, O God. My soul thirsts for God, for the living God' (Ps. 42.1–2). As well as praying *with Jesus to the Father*, they used the psalms to speak *about Jesus to the Father*. The longest psalm (Ps. 119) meditated with great joy and thanksgiving on the gift of God's law, the Torah that identified Israel as God's people and set them on the path of life. Since it was so long (176 verses), that psalm spoke not only of God's 'law' but also introduced various synonyms for law: 'decrees', 'promise', 'word(s)' and so forth. Since Jesus was 'the goal of the law' (Rom. 10.4), early Christians thought of his name when they sang or recited Psalm 119: 'I rise before dawn and cry for help; I put my hope in your word [Jesus]. My eyes are awake before each watch of the night, that I may meditate on your promise [Jesus]' (Ps. 119.147–8). Using this and other psalms to pray about Jesus to the Father, as well as consciously praying with Jesus to the Father, Christians found in the psalms a vivid and appropriate language to express their religious feelings and to move ahead in the journey of faith.[1]

Contemporary Christian Spirituality normally involves the psalms, albeit in a variety of ways. Any spirituality will remain desperately impoverished if it attempts to abandon the psalms for public and private prayer.

Before leaving the Jewish Scriptures, let me select for a brief mention five out of numerous further items that illuminate and promote the Christian way to God. First, God met people where they were. A herdsman and dresser of sycamore trees, Amos was neither a 'professional' prophet nor a member of a guild of prophets when God called him to prophesy to the people of Israel (Amos 7.14–15). Over and over again God chose seemingly 'ordinary' men and women and made them mediators of divine revelation and salvation. 'Come as you are' sums up the divine dealings in biblical history and beyond.

Second, an adage that proves itself in the sinful and graced lives of Christian believers, 'God writes straight with crooked lines', had already verified itself repeatedly in the story of the chosen people. There are, for instance, crooked lines in the list that Matthew provides of Jesus' forebears (Mt. 1.1–17). David committed adultery and murder on the way to acquiring Bathsheba as his wife and the mother of his successor Solomon (2 Sam. 11.1–25). We are dealing here with the key figure in Jesus' family tree; King David provided Jesus with royal lineage. This made David essential for Matthew's three groups of fourteen names; fourteen is the sum of the numerical value in Hebrew of the three letters in the name 'David' (DWD). David confessed: 'I have sinned against the Lord' (2 Sam. 12.13). But he also continued to trust that God would 'write straight' by carrying through the promise to make David's dynasty everlasting (2 Sam. 7.1–29). In and through Jesus, the Son of David par excellence, God did just that.

Third, Job, Proverbs and other wisdom books picture the universal concerns of individuals in a world created by God. As well as mysterious sufferings (above all, in the case of the innocent Job), there are blessings that come from the God who cherishes and seeks out all human beings. In comparison with the New Testament (where, apart from the Gospels and the Letter of James, sapiential themes barely surface), the Jewish Scriptures offer a rich storehouse of wisdom literature (O'Collins 2008, 54–63, 230–47). A wise way of living should characterize the existence of Christians. Their spiritual life, as St Teresa of Avila, St Frances de Sales and other classical teachers of spirituality have insisted, should be a wise life.

Fourth, St Ignatius Loyola stood out for stressing the 'discernment of spirits' and for helping people to let themselves be led by the Holy Spirit. His teaching reached back through the history of Christian Spirituality to St Paul: 'test everything, hold fast to what is good' (1 Thess. 5.21; see 2 Cor. 13.5). But the challenge of discernment had surfaced centuries earlier through the need to distinguish between true and false prophets. Criteria came not only from the fulfillment of prophecies (e.g. Jer. 28.15–17; Deut. 18.22) but also, and even more, from loyalty to the inherited faith (e.g. Deut. 13.2–5; 18.19–22) and from present lifestyle (e.g. Jer. 23.9–40; 29.21–3). This ancient biblical tradition dealt with a specific issue, how to discriminate true from false prophets. Yet two of its criteria, loyalty to their inherited faith and a morally acceptable lifestyle, retain their significance for Christians who practise serious discernment in their spiritual lives.

Fifth, St Paul (Rom. 4.16–25) and, much more, the Letter to the Hebrews (11.4–12.2) recommended finding and following a cloud of witnesses to faith. Hebrews listed by name some heroes and heroines of faith, before speaking in general of those who suffered heroically and finally reaching Jesus, the supreme exemplar of a faithful life. Paul and Hebrews encourage Christians to find role models for their spiritual lives by also attending to Abraham, Sarah and other shining examples to be found in the Jewish Scriptures.

Jesus and Christian Spirituality

John's Gospel provides a lapidary account of what Christians find in the crucified and risen Jesus: he is their 'way', their 'truth' and their 'life' (Jn 14.6). Faith in Jesus, reception into his Church through baptism and sharing in the sacrificial meal-fellowship he instituted at the Last Supper shape the basic contours of their existence. Every celebration of the Eucharist involves hearing the Gospels, which confront them with a constant challenge to their spiritual existence coming from the birth, life, ministry, suffering, death and resurrection of Jesus. The liturgical year of the Church draws its content from his story: the annunciation, the nativity, episodes from the infancy narratives, his baptism, the ministry, the transfiguration, Jesus' entrance into Jerusalem on Palm Sunday, the events of Holy Week that led to his crucifixion and burial, his Easter appearances, the ascension and sending of the Holy Spirit. Thus the Gospel stories of Jesus underpin the public worship that feeds and enlightens the Christian way of living. The changing seasons of Advent, Christmas, the Epiphany, Lent, Holy Week, Easter and Pentecost sustain a feeling of human life moving through sacred time to a final meeting with God through the glorified Christ. This liturgical spirituality is inseparable from a biblical spirituality that recognizes in Jesus the heart of the matter.

In the *Spiritual Exercises*, St Ignatius Loyola inculcated a 'Gospel spirituality' that finds its origins and whole scope in the earthly history of Jesus. After the introductory 'first week' of the *Exercises*, through the second, third and fourth 'weeks', Ignatius presented the Christian way of life as a discipleship that is utterly Gospel-centred and Jesus-centred. The remarkable mystical experiences that he and others, like St Teresa of Avila, enjoyed never led them to move away from a path to God that leads through the story of the earthly Jesus and, in particular, his (1) teaching and (2) example.[2]

Teaching

In his *parables*, those simple-sounding yet amazingly profound stories, Jesus shows us how the final kingdom of God takes shape among us. Much more than mere picturesque illustrations, his parables question us, challenge the normal standards and securities of our lives, call for our whole-hearted response, and invite us to walk in radically different ways. The personal power of God is setting things right in our world. We should acknowledge that sovereign power and Jesus as the Lord of the kingdom are already present in our midst.

Jesus' parables reveal a new world and a new way of living. They do so through language and pictures that seem quite familiar and 'ordinary', even if at times he gives his storyline unusual and even extraordinary twists: for instance, in parables about the Labourers in the Vineyard (Mt. 20.1–15) and the Dishonest Manager (Lk. 16.1–9). Jesus brings in women searching for lost property or preparing dough for the oven. His stories present a lazy judge, a merchant searching for precious jewels, a traveller robbed and left for dead, servants waiting up all night for their master to return. These parables take us into the mind and heart of Jesus. They let us glimpse his vision of the world.

These stories answer our questions: What is God like? And how is God dealing with us in these 'last times'? Jesus' parables hold out to us his vision of the incredible generosity of our heavenly Father. Through his stories, Jesus wants to share his insights with us and gently coax us into opening ourselves to God's final rule over our lives (O'Collins 1999).

From some points of view, Jesus did not change very much in the area of *morality* and seemed to keep the best of Jewish teaching. He built on an existing moral tradition by upholding the Ten Commandments (Mk 10.19) and following the prophets in stigmatizing social injustice, especially the failure to act lovingly towards those like Lazarus who suffer and are in terrible distress (Lk. 16.19–31). But Jesus went so far, according to one tradition, to make the final judgement depend simply on our practical concern for the hungry, the sick, prisoners, homeless persons and others in great need (Mt. 25.31–46). This involved Jesus in teaching something no prophet ever taught. He identified himself with the hungry, the sick and others in terrible distress. Moreover, his table fellowship with the pariahs of society took Jesus beyond anything prophets ever taught or practised.

Jesus also broke new ground by linking the commands to love God and to love our neighbour (Mk 12.28–34). Here he maintained some central moral teaching he had inherited from the Jewish Scriptures, but innovated by putting together into one love command the hitherto distinct commandments to love God (Deut. 6.5) and to love one's neighbour (Lev. 19.18).

Jesus also introduced something startlingly new by teaching love for one's enemies (Mt. 5.41–8). Here we reach what have been called 'the hard sayings' of Jesus: 'love your enemies'; 'do not resist an evildoer'; 'do not refuse anyone who wants to borrow from you' (Mt. 5.38–42). These and other hard sayings embody heroic ideals that go beyond any commonsense morality that might be established on reasonable grounds. A dramatic example comes from what Jesus said to someone who had invited him to a meal: 'When you give a luncheon or a dinner, do not invite your friends or your brothers or your relatives or rich neighbours. . . . But when you give a banquet, invite the poor, the crippled, the lame, and the blind' (Lk. 14.12–13). Such a practice obviously went well beyond the call of duty and what would have seemed reasonable to any 'ordinary' good person. It was not simply that such hard sayings spoke out against a self-centred policy in life. They were part and parcel of a new life of discipleship that gave total allegiance to Jesus himself. After announcing his coming suffering and death, he added: 'if any want to become my followers, let them deny themselves and take up their cross and follow me' (Mk 8.34).

Jesus endorsed the Ten Commandments, which exhort us to do what in any case is morally good and to avoid what in any case is immoral. But he went further to inculcate the heroic morality and spirituality involved in becoming his disciples. He encouraged his listeners to change their moral perception of the world and to do so by accepting a permanent relationship with him – in other words, by accepting a relational, instead of a self-regarding, sense of their moral and spiritual identity and so asking: *'whose* am I?' rather than *'who* am I?'

If we look to Jesus for specific instructions about behaviour, we find that he forbade certain types of action. He condemned, for instance, retaliation or paying back in kind those who have harmed us (Mt. 5.38–42). Yet he appears to have taught little about specific issues of human behaviour, and obviously offered no complete moral and spiritual code. What he did was to inculcate certain attitudes and dispositions, and left it to his followers to work out the detailed consequences. Take the parable of the Good Samaritan. The lawyer who provoked Jesus into telling the story asked the question 'who is my neighbour?', because he wanted to 'justify himself'. He was concerned to establish his right to eternal life by specifying (or having Jesus specify) exactly his duty towards his neighbour and then by proving that he had carried it out. In that case, he would be shown to be 'righteous' or acceptable to God. But, instead of engaging in such specifics, Jesus gave an example of helping another human being whom he might come across in great distress, and added: 'go and do likewise' (Lk. 10.29–37). As far as Jesus was concerned, our neighbours are any human beings who desperately need our help, no matter who they are in their ethnic, national or religious identity. If we share Jesus' general vision of the world and hear his call to be 'perfect as your heavenly Father is perfect' (Mt. 5.49), we will set no limits to our goodness since God's goodness knows no limits.

Example

Three themes serve to summarize the unique *example* of holy living Jesus offered: (a) his constant communion of prayer with his loving Father;

(b) his single-minded devotion to the service of the divine kingdom and (c) his unswerving obedience to his mission he had received, despite the mortal danger into which it brought him.

As regards (a), in the post-Easter situation his disciples came to realize that his human life had transposed to the earthly level an eternal relationship with the Father within the life of the Trinity. In the midst of overwhelming and exhausting activity, he never failed to take time to commune in prayer with 'Abba' (e.g. Mk 1.35). Naturally he wanted those who, through doing God's will, became his brothers and sisters in God's new family (Mk 3.31–5) to turn constantly to the Father in prayer. He taught them the Lord's Prayer (Mt. 6.9–13) and encouraged them to practise persistent prayer (Mt. 7.7–11).

As regards (b) and (c), serving the kingdom involved Jesus in struggling with the demonic forces of a counter-kingdom and 'the evil one', supremely active 'in the time of trial' (Mt. 6.35). The message of the kingdom involved a period of crisis and distress that would move towards 'the day of the Son of Man' (Mk 13), the restoration of Israel (Mt. 19.28), the banquet of the saved (Lk. 14.15–24) and the salvation of the nations (Mt. 8.11–12). Thus the arrest, trial and crucifixion of Jesus dramatized the very thing that totally engaged Jesus, the rule of God which was to come through a time of ordeal.

Where Jesus preached the kingdom, Paul preached the crucified and resurrected Jesus. For the apostle, Jesus was the human face of God, albeit a crucified and risen face. Let me turn now to the apostle Paul and six of the many spiritual themes we can glean from his letters.

Paul and Christian Spirituality

First of all, Paul offers a spectacular example of someone who encountered Jesus and allowed that experience to transform his life radically. For the apostle, 'knowing Jesus Christ my Lord', who had suffered, died and was raised from the dead, was a treasure of 'surpassing value'. Paul longed to suffer like Christ and with Christ because he had the sure hope of being raised from the dead and living with Christ forever (Phil. 3.8–11). A passionate love for Christ possessed Paul and he wanted to share that love with as many others as possible. Paul had seen the beauty of God on the face of Christ (2 Cor. 4.6), and the beautiful Christ had taken over the apostle's existence. 'For me', Paul declared, 'living is Christ' (Phil. 1.21).

Second, that union with Christ involved the apostle's ministry being marked by 'affliction' (2 Cor. 6.4–5; 11.23–7) and being 'crucified with' Christ (Gal. 1.19; 6.14). But Paul's 'weaknesses' or hardships reveal the power of God (2 Cor. 12.9–10) and the apostle's share in the mystery of Christ, who 'was crucified in weakness, but lives by the power of God' (2 Cor. 13.4).

Third, Paul set going a central theme of Christian Spirituality, the imitation of Christ: He told the Corinthians: 'be imitators of me, as I am of Christ'

(1 Cor. 11.1). This imitation was no superficial matter. It cut deep by entailing bodily sufferings that replicate the death of Christ. But these sufferings 'make visible' the life of Christ (2 Cor. 4.11).

Fourth, the apostle highlights the spiritual significance of both Baptism and the Eucharist. Baptism involves dying with Christ to sin, being buried with him and rising to 'walk in newness of life' (Rom. 6.2–11; see Col. 2.12–13). By partaking in the Lord's Supper, the baptized participate in the blood of Christ (1 Cor. 10.16). They are joined with the risen Christ and with one another in an extraordinarily intimate union: 'we who are many are one body, for we all partake of the one bread' (1 Cor. 10.17).

Fifth, Paul treasured the holiness of all the baptized. They form the sanctuary of the Holy Spirit (1 Cor. 3.16–17; 6.19) and the body of Christ, in which individual gifts should serve the unity and well-being of the whole community (1 Cor. 12.4–31). Yet Paul knows how sinfulness can spoil this holiness: divisions within the community (1 Cor. 1.10–4.21), the case of a man living with his stepmother (1 Cor. 5.1), sins of fornication (1 Cor. 6.12–20), drunkenness, failure to feed the hungry (1 Cor. 11.21) and other moral defects. Even if we lack a full and accurate picture of all that was going wrong in the Corinthian church, nevertheless, the reproaches coming from Paul in 1 Corinthians, along with other letters, challenge illusions about a hypothetical golden age of Christianity that practised heroic ideals on all sides. From the outset the Church suffered from scandals and divisions. The Book of Revelation, with its opening letters to the seven churches, joins the apostle in testifying to the mixture of holiness and sinfulness that has characterized Christianity from the beginning (Rev. 2.1–3.22). The Gospels also repeatedly imply and even frankly point to deplorable conduct to be found in the early communities; even prophets, exorcists and miracle-workers could do evil and fail to follow the will of God (Mt. 7.15–23). Thus other New Testament witnesses converge with Paul in warning us that our way to God through Christ can never hope to be supported by a perfect community but must always contend with scandalous failures.

Sixth, Paul insists that the life of grace is a totally gratuitous gift of God, the unmerited favour of being saved in Christ through faith (Rom. 3.23–5). The divine initiative stands behind the whole process of salvation. The new life of grace has its source in the crucified and risen Jesus and its immediate cause in the Holy Spirit. The twofold relationship to the Son and the Spirit transforms those who are justified and makes them adopted sons and daughters of the Father (Rom. 8.12–17; Gal. 4.5–7).

As the closing exhortations of Paul's letters (and 1 Corinthians throughout) testify, God's free self-gift calls for a personal response through conduct worthy of God's children. Nevertheless, the apostle remains steadfastly aware of the priority of God's call and initiatives, trusting always that God who began the 'good work' will 'bring it to completion by the day of Jesus Christ'

(Phil. 1.6, see 2.11). No 'do-it-yourself' affair, from beginning to end Christian spiritual life depends on divine grace.

Johannine Spirituality

Arguably the Fourth Gospel represents the highpoint of biblical spirituality. Let me close by limiting myself to three wonderful themes. First, decades of loving reflection on the story of Jesus and prayerful experience of him gave rise to this Gospel. It came out of prayer and very easily leads back into prayer. As Evagrius Ponticus (d. 399) remarked, the right posture for reading the Fourth Gospel is leaning on the breast of Jesus like the beloved disciple. This Gospel nourishes contemplative communing with the Lord.

Second, right from Chapter One, the reader of the Fourth Gospel is introduced to the theme of personally 'remaining' in or 'abiding' (*menein*) with Jesus. Andrew and his companion want to know where Jesus is 'staying'; after 'coming' and 'seeing' where he is 'staying', they 'stay' with him that day (Jn 1.38–9). The verb *menein* conveys more than the superficial meaning of stopping or hanging around somewhere. The two men initiate a relationship of 'staying/abiding' with, and, in fact, 'in' Jesus. He will be disclosed to them as the 'true vine' in whom they will allow themselves to be incorporated (Jn 15.1–11 – a passage that uses the key verb *menein* ten times).

Third, Chapters 14–16 of John's Gospel offers the most extensive biblical treatment of what it is to be 'taught' and 'guided' by the Holy Spirit. 'Sent' in the name of Jesus (Jn 14.26), the Spirit will lead the disciples on the right path to God, the heart of the spiritual life.

Notes

1 On the Christian use of the Psalms, see also Chapter 21 'Christian Spirituality and Judaism'.
2 See also Chapters 13 'Ignatian Spirituality' and 10 'Carmelite Spirituality'.

Bibliography and Further Reading

Barton, S. C. (1992), *The Spirituality of the Gospels*. London: SPCK.
Bouyer, L. (1968), *A History of Christian Spirituality*, vol. 1, *The Spirituality of the New Testament and the Fathers*, trans. M. P. Ryan, London: Burns & Oates.
Byrne, B. (2010), *Galatians and Romans*. Collegeville, MN: Liturgical Press.
O'Collins, G. (1999), *Following the Way: Jesus Our Spiritual Director*. London: HarperCollins.
— (2007), *Jesus Our Redeemer: A Christian Approach to Salvation*. Oxford: Oxford University Press.
— (2008), *Salvation for All: God's Other Peoples*. Oxford: Oxford University Press.

3 The Mystical Tradition

Bernard McGinn

Introduction

The scholar of mysticism Henri Bremond once wrote: 'In short, it is not possible to ignore the mystics without disowning one's self'.[1] The mystical element in Christianity, understood in the broad sense as the effort to attain a deeper and transforming consciousness of God's presence, is an essential feature of the Bible, as well as the church's teaching. The mystical element is always present in the action of the Holy Spirit in the lives of believers, while the historical development of that element forms the mystical tradition, that is, the accumulating wisdom of the mystical teachers that often began in oral instruction, but that came to be enshrined in the mystical classics that have nourished the faithful over the centuries. The purpose of this overview is to provide a sense of the development of this tradition.

The term 'mysticism' is a modern creation, originally pejorative, but since the nineteenth century widespread in both academic and popular discourse. In Christianity, *mustikos/mysticus* (literally, 'hidden') has mostly been used as a qualifier, not a substantive, so to speak of the mystical element, or the mystical tradition, is doctrinally more traditional and correct.[2] The word does not occur in the scriptures, but by the second century AD/CE Christians such as Clement of Alexandria were using 'mystical' to indicate the hidden dimension of Christian beliefs and practices, the inner depth where God was to be found as a transforming presence. The most frequent use of *mustikos* was in the phrase 'mystical sense, or understanding' of the Bible. On the surface, the text of the Bible often seems opaque, sometimes even contradictory or immoral, but Christians believed that God is always present in the depths of the words He addressed to humanity. A spiritual, or mystical, reading could bring the believer past the surface letter into the saving realities within. The early Christian master of mystical interpretation, the Alexandrian Origen (d. 254), described the aim of interpretation as writing the meaning of the sacred scriptures on the soul (*On First Principles* 4.2.4), a process that he compared to '. . . galloping through the vast spaces of mystical and spiritual understanding' (*Commentary on Romans* 7.11).

The Christian sacraments also had a hidden or mystical meaning. To the outsider, baptism was only pouring water, the Eucharist eating bread and drinking wine, but to the believer these rituals brought saving contact with God. The early Christians adopted the Greek word *theôria* (Latin, *contemplatio/speculatio*), that is, gazing on supreme reality, to describe the goal of their belief and practice. 'Mystical' was therefore also applied to 'contemplation' to indicate that Christian prayer should aim at seeing God, who is invisible to the eyes of flesh. Finally, about AD/CE 500, an Eastern monk who called himself 'Dionysius' (after the person mentioned in Acts 17.33) wrote a treatise *On Mystical Theology*. For Dionysius mystical theology was not an academic teaching about God, but a total way of life in which God is approached through prayer and liturgy by way of 'naming God' (i.e. using the positive names given in scripture) and also by 'un-naming God' (i.e. negating terms pertaining to created reality to point to God's utter transcendence). The goal of this upward striving, or 'anagogical', process was so that a person can be '. . . supremely united [to God] by a completely unknowing inactivity of all knowledge' (*On Mystical Theology* 1.3).

'Mystical understanding', 'mystical sacraments', 'mystical contemplation' and 'mystical theology' show that the mystical tradition has deep roots in Christian history. These activities characterize the lives of the 'contemplatives' or 'spiritual persons', those who seek a direct contact with God in and through the open and manifest practices of Christian life. The great contemplatives of the mystical tradition, both in the patristic and medieval periods, were convinced that all the baptized were called to this deeper life, though individuals would realize it in different ways depending on their gifts and stations in life.

Scripture and Experience

Christians considered the Bible as *the* 'mystical' book, in the sense that although the scripture taught many things about sacred history, moral behaviour and the like, it was first and foremost the place where God could be found. The God revealed in the Bible was the God made flesh in Jesus Christ – the Christological reading of the Bible was the interpretive key that unlocked its mystical meaning. This meaning was found not only in the New Testament accounts of Christ's life in the Gospels and in the teaching of the Epistles, but also in the Old Testament, especially the Psalms, seen as the prayers of Christ and His body the church, and the Song of Songs, read as the revelation of the love between Christ and the church and Christ and each soul. The bedrock of the mystical tradition in Christianity is scripture read Christologically and mystagogically (i.e. as leading to transformation in God). For the first 1,000 years (c. AD/CE 200–1200), most of the literature that constitutes the mystical tradition was directly exegetical in the sense that it involved interpreting the Bible for the Christian community through catechesis, homilies and extended commentaries for the spiritually advanced.

In the twelfth century, in the midst of a series of sermons commenting on the Song of Songs, the Cistercian mystic Bernard of Clairvaux (d. 1153) told his monks, 'Today we are reading in the book of experience' (Sermon 3.1). Obviously, Bernard did not intend his audience to give up reading the Bible. What he meant was that seekers after God needed to make use of both the biblical inner message and their own interior experience to advance on the road to contemplation and union. In the centuries that followed, appeals to the book of experience became strong in the mystical tradition, as seen in the growth of accounts of inner visions, locutions (hearing the divine voice within), descriptions of uniting with God, etc. Writing out of the book of experience is mostly autobiographical in nature, so some modern interpreters have restricted the mystical tradition to first-person narratives about union with God. This is misleading because Christian mystics never forgot the Bible. Even those who expressed their teaching in autobiographies, visionary narratives and diaries did not base their authority on what God had personally revealed to them, but rather sought to show the conformity between the teaching of the Bible and the church and their inner experience.

The search for a deeper sense of God's presence was not seen so much as a state of perfection attainable in life, but as a process, or a journey, begun here, but only to be completed in the permanent vision of God in heaven (*visio beatifica*). This is one reason why so many mystical authors present accounts of itineraries, or stages, on the road to God. These itineraries are many and need not be thought of as mutually exclusive; they are different ways of providing sketches, handbooks, road-maps of pathways through the inner terrain of the soul in its search for God. If the final goal is the vision of God in heaven, this still left room for many ways of conceiving the partial goal sought in this life. The most popular form of language was speaking about being united with God. The term 'mystical union' (*unio mystica*) was actually rarely used in the mystical tradition, but general union language was frequent. Union was fundamentally Christological, becoming one with Christ, as suggested by the Johannine references to being engrafted into Christ (e.g. Jn 15) and the Pauline motif of being *en Christo*, 'in Christ' (e.g. Gal. 2.19–20, 4.19), as well as the model of sexual union found in the mystical reading of the Song of Songs. To become one with Christ, the God-man, was to be united with the second person of the Trinity, and since all three persons are one God, union language in Christianity frequently took on Trinitarian dimensions. Two major paradigms for understanding union are found in the tradition. The first often cites a Pauline text, 1 Cor. 6.17 ('The one who adheres to the Lord is one spirit . . .'), to argue that the created spirit never loses its own essence in union, but attains a state of loving conformity with the Divine Spirit – a union of wills. Some mystical teachers went further, asserting that on some level (not on all) there was a complete merging, or identification, with God, an identity based on Christ's prayer, '. . . that they all may be one, as you Father are in me and I am in you, may they be one in us . . .' (Jn 17.21).[3]

Along with union language there were many other forms of expressing the transformative consciousness of God taught in the mystical tradition. Another prominent motif was that of seeing, or contemplating, God, which often appealed to the passage, 'Blessed are the pure of heart for they shall see God' (Mt. 5.8). Again, there were various ways of understanding how God might be seen, from physical appearances, through imaginative visions, to purely intellectual beholding of incommunicable divine truth. The mystics sought to distinguish between the preliminary vision given here below and the final vision of heaven, and there was much debate over a number of issues, such as whether the invisible God could ever *really* be seen in God's self or was visible only through 'theophanies', that is, manifestations of his nature. Another way of expressing the goal of the mystical itinerary was deification (*theosis/deificatio*). Given that humans were made in God's image and likeness (Gen. 1.26), Christian teachers viewed growing conformity with Christ as becoming like God, even coming to share in the divine nature (e.g. 2 Pet. 1.4) through a process of divinizing love. Closely allied with deification was the notion of birthing, being born again as a child of God (e.g. Jn 3.5; Gal. 3.26; 1 Jn 3.2). The birthing motif was taken even a step further when some mystics reasoned that just as Jesus was born both physically and spiritually from a human mother, Mary, so too believers could come to share in her privilege by bringing Christ to birth spiritually in their lives.

The Tradition of Negation

Finding God in the depths of the soul is most often viewed today in positive terms as coming to a deeper knowledge of God and finding complete joy and fruition. The mystical tradition, however, shows that the negative dimension of the search for God is at least as important as the positive. It is possible to distinguish three forms of negativity in the history of Christian mysticism.[4] The first is apophatic, or negative, theology, that is, the argument that God is better known by unknowing than by knowing, because all our knowledge is based upon categories taken from creatures. Though rooted in Platonic philosophy, apophatic unsaying also appealed to the mystery of God proclaimed in scripture (e.g. Isa. 45.15: 'Truly, you are a hidden God'). Many mystical teachers (Gregory of Nyssa and 'Dionysius' in the patristic period; Marguerite Porete and Meister Eckhart in the Middle Ages) emphasize that although we cannot do without some positive (cataphatic) naming, negation (apophatic, stripping-away) is higher and brings us closer to God. A second form of negativity concerns the will more than the intellect. The Gospel command to give up all things and follow Christ (Mt. 19.21ff.) gave rise to forms of self-denial and asceticism that were seen as preparation for mystical contact with God, but such stripping-away reached a new level in Eckhart and later mystics who taught that exterior abnegation was not as important as total detachment from the self, all created things and even all practices that sought to 'gain' God. These teachers held that we must learn to give up our created will, and even our 'God' insofar as God is the aim of *our own* thoughts and desires. The third form of negation involves the experience of dereliction and affliction, even damnation. Imitating Christ on the cross in his utter abandonment by God ('God, my God, why have you forsaken me': Mt. 27.46), some mystics have spoken of the sense of torture and betrayal felt when God withdraws himself as a necessary, even central, aspect of the mystical path. All three of these forms of negativity involve the kind of paradoxes that are an integral part of the mystical tradition: we know God best by unknowing; we find God by relinquishing him; God is present even when he abandons us.

The mystical tradition involves many other issues concerning the relationship between God and the human person. Only three other central concerns can be discussed here: (1) the interrelation of love and knowledge; (2) the role of extraordinary modes of consciousness, such as ecstasy and (3) the relation of love of God and love of neighbour as reflected in Christ's command – 'You shall love the Lord, your God, with your whole heart, your whole soul, and your whole mind, . . . and love your neighbor as yourself' (Deut. 6.5; Mt. 22.37–9).

Love and Knowledge

Knowing and loving are the fundamental operations that characterize the human person made in God's image and likeness, which is why humans strive to know and to love God to the extent that they are able. On the basis of texts such as Paul's hymn about love in 1 Cor. 13 and 1 Jn 4.16 ('God is love, and those who abide in love abide in God, and God abides in them'), the mystics insisted that love has a superior role in the path to God – God can never be adequately known by human concepts, but love as unceasing desire participates in the infinite love that is God. Nevertheless, as many mystics averred, nothing can be loved unless it is known, so knowing, especially the knowledge gained in faith, cannot be neglected. The mystical teachers spent a good deal of time reflecting on the respective roles of love and knowledge in the path to God (loving and knowing as *means* to God), as well as on the ways in which both loving and knowing are present in uniting with God or seeing God, that is, knowing and loving as *ends*. Different ways of conceiving of the interrelationship of knowledge and love emerged. What might be called the standard model held that both activities were necessary, though love was superior. The love by which God is attained both in this life and the next, however, would draw up our own knowing into a higher form of non-conceptual and connatural knowing of God, as expressed in the formula *amor ipse intelligentia est*, 'Love itself is a form of understanding'. Some mystics, especially in the late Middle Ages, held that human knowing might be useful on the lower levels of the ascent to God, but such knowing needs to be cut off at the higher stages so that God can be attained in what was called the *apex affectus*, the 'height of affectivity'. Some of the most apophatic mystics insisted that all modes of human knowing and loving must be let go. As Meister Eckhart put it: 'Some teachers claim that the spirit takes happiness from love; others claim it takes it in seeing God. I say, however, that it takes it neither from love nor from knowing nor from seeing' (Sermon 39).

Altered States

Mystical teachers often spoke about forms of what we call altered states of consciousness, modes of awareness that change and even negate our usual sense of the world and self-presence. Prominent among these is 'rapture', or 'ecstasy', a loss of ordinary consciousness in which the sense of time and space fall away. Such states are found in many religious traditions and are mentioned in the Bible (e.g. Pss 30.23, 67.28; Acts 3.10, 10.10). Paranormal physical manifestations are also recorded about some mystics, phenomena such as inedia (not eating for long periods of time without loss of health), levitation (rising in the air) and stigmata (the appearance of the wounds of Jesus on the body).[5] At one time, rapture and paranormal phenomena were seen as miraculous signs of the authenticity of a person's claims to union with God, but the teaching of the mystical masters denies this. Even visionary mystics who experienced raptures and visions and manifested some of these paranormal conditions, such as Julian of Norwich and Teresa of Avila, held that such things were secondary to the deep inner consciousness and love of God that could not be seen but was manifested in a more loving life. While accounts of visions of God and the heavenly world, descriptions of ecstatic states, and even stories about paranormal gifts, are part of the mystical tradition, they are peripheral rather than central. This is why many mystics insist that God can and should be found in ordinary, everyday consciousness as an awareness of the divine depth in all things.

Love of God and Neighbour

What is central for the mystics is love of God and love of neighbour. Attaining union with God, seeing God in contemplation, being deified and the like are modes of expressing the total love of God commanded in the scriptures. This single-minded love of God was often described as the 'contemplative life' (*vita contemplativa*), but such a life of complete dedication never precludes the obligations of loving service of the neighbour, often spoken of as the 'active life' (*vita activa*). Indeed, the only *real* proof of the purity of a person's love of God is demonstrating that love to others. Many mystics believed that the active and contemplative styles of life were so different that a person could only practice them in succession: being totally absorbed in God in loving contemplation (the higher life) had to yield to loving service when the needs of the neighbour became pressing. Other mystics, however, taught that the most advanced contemplatives could reach a state where action and contemplation were one. They could be, in a phrase used of Ignatius of Loyola, *in contemplatione activus* ('Active in the state of contemplation').[6]

A fundamental characteristic of the mystical tradition is its variety. This long tradition cannot be reduced to a single approach, or measured by one yardstick. Hans Urs von Balthasar once declared that 'Truth is symphonic', and the mystical tradition is a good illustration of how many different instruments or melodies can be united to form a harmonic whole. A good way to understand the historical development and richness of the mystical tradition is to see it according to a kind of geological model in which different strata, or layers, build upon earlier manifestations in their historical unfolding.

Monastic Mystical Tradition

The earliest layer can be called 'monastic', not because Christians ever thought that the spiritual elite of monks and nuns were the only folk who could reach union with God, but because monasticism as a special form of religious life provided the context, the training ground and the institutional repository for mysticism as an inherited tradition. This layer, which was dominant from c. AD/CE 200 to about AD/CE 1200, provided the foundation for much that was to come. Its first great spokesman was Origen of Alexandria, referred to above. Although he was not a monk in the formal sense, Origen's dedication to ascetical and contemplative practices, as well as his numerous writings, were mined by mystics for centuries. By the fourth century AD, when the Roman Empire was converted to Christianity, the ascetical impulse led to the beginnings of the monastic life in the proper sense, first in Egypt and then across the Mediterranean world. There were two main forms: the eremitical, or hermit, life lived by individuals who fled society in order to find God in the solitude of the wilderness (e.g. Antony of Egypt, d. 356), and the coenobitical life of monks in community under a rule. Evagrius of Pontus (d. 399), who was deeply influenced by Origen, was the first mystical theologian of the monastic life. Through his disciple John Cassian (d. 435) this form of mystical thinking also migrated to the West. Many of the great mystical teachers of the ancient church, both in East and West, were bishops in charge of urban congregations, including figures such as Gregory of Nyssa (d. 395), Ambrose of Milan (d. 397), Augustine of Hippo (d. 430) and Gregory the Great (d. 604). These episcopal leaders preached the message of attaining deeper awareness of God to a wide audience, but it is significant to note that all of them had either lived as monks or been influenced by the monastic ideal.[7]

The Eastern (Orthodox) and Western (Catholic) sides of Late Antique Christianity began to drift apart in the early medieval period (c. AD/CE 600–1200), but this did not seriously affect the role of monasticism as the basic home for the teachers of the mystical tradition. In Orthodox Christianity, monks like Maximus the Confessor (d. 662) and Symeon the 'New Theologian' (d. 1022), carried on the Greek patristic tradition of seeing all theology (true speech about God) as essentially a mystical teaching. In the Latin West, strained by the collapse of the Roman Empire, monasticism remained a force for stability, but did not produce much original teaching until the twelfth century, when the Cistercian reform of the Benedictine order led to an outpouring of mystical teaching in figures like Bernard of Clairvaux and his friends, William of Saint-Thierry (d. 1148), Aelred of Rievaulx (d. 1167) and Isaac of Stella (d. c. 1170). Equally important for the mystical tradition was the contribution of the Victorine order of canons, priests living a monastic life in the Abbey of St Victor at Paris. The Victorines combined the contemplative teaching of monasticism and the new academic theology of the cathedral schools, soon to become the first universities. Victorines such as Hugh (d. 1140), Richard (d. 1173) and, finally, Thomas Gallus (d. 1246) wrote treatises on contemplation and commentaries on the Bible and mystical classics, such as the writings of 'Dionysius' that were important textbooks for centuries to come. These were by no means the only mystical authors of the twelfth century, but they were the most important.

The New Mysticism

Around AD/CE 1200 a major shift occurred in Western Christian mysticism. Changes in society and the church provided a context in which the second major layer of Western mysticism was born, the 'New Mysticism' of the late medieval and early modern periods (c. 1200–1650). In society, increasing urbanization and the growth of the middle class, as well as spreading literacy and the beginnings of vernacular literatures, were part of the background to this new stage. In the church, the papacy's emergence as the centre of ecclesiastical power and the arbiter of religious reform was important. A rapidly changing society no longer found the enclosed monastic life lived far from urban centres as the prime spiritual ideal, so new forms of religious life appeared that advocated the 'apostolic life' (*vita apostolica*) of poverty and preaching of the Gospel throughout the world. The most important of these movements were the mendicant (i.e. 'begging') orders of Franciscans and Dominicans originating in the early years of the thirteenth century, and the contemporary spread of 'beguines', small groups of women living a pious life but not under a formally approved rule that involved cloister, or enclosure from the world. Both the mendicants and the beguines produced paradigm figures of the new forms of mysticism (e.g. Francis of Assisi, d. 1226; and Mary of Oignies, d. 1213).

This new mysticism was characterized by several features. First, there was a 'democratization', that is, a renewed insistence on the fact that the call to find God must be addressed to all Christians and not restricted to a spiritual elite. Second, we can note a 'secularization' in which new forms of religious life, as well as preaching and teaching, moved out of the cloister into the world, especially the urban centres of Europe. These processes were accompanied by a 'vernacularization' as mystical teaching and writing began to move away from the learned Latin and into the developing vernacular languages of Western Europe. Although a good deal of mystical writing was still done in Latin, the shift to the vernacular allowed for experimentation with new genres and new forms of expression. Finally, the wider appeal and use of the vernacular were important in giving women a greater opportunity to engage in teaching and writing about their inner experience of God. From the thirteenth century on, women began to play a major role in the story of the mystical tradition. Along with these positive features came others that portended difficulties. Fears of mystical error had already surfaced in the early church, but from the latter part of the thirteenth century signs of tension between the clerical guardians of orthodoxy and mystical teachers became more evident. The neuralgic flash points were many, often involving views of union with God, the role of interior annihilation, forms of prayer and obedience to ecclesiastical authority. The debates were to continue for centuries.

During the thirteenth and the fourteenth centuries the mendicants and the beguines produced many mystics. Among the beguines the Dutch Hadewijch of Antwerp (c. 1250), the German Mechthild of Magdeburg (d. c. 1280) and the French Marguerite Porete (d. 1310) stand out. It is significant that these three wrote in the vernacular and also that Marguerite Porete was executed as a heretic for her mystical teaching. In the Franciscan order, there were both male mystics, like the scholastic master Bonaventure (d. 1274), and women, such as the tertiary (laywoman following a Franciscan way of life) Angela of Foligno (d. 1309). The great age of Dominican mysticism was the fourteenth century which witnessed the mystical preaching of Meister Eckhart (d. 1329) and his disciples, Henry Suso (d. 1366) and John Tauler (d. 1361). There were also mystics among the enclosed Dominican nuns of Germany, although the most famous female Dominican was Catherine of Siena (d. 1380), a laywoman following the Dominican lifestyle. During these centuries, however, there were important mystical teachers who did not belong to the mendicants or beguines, such as the Dutch Augustinian Jan van Ruusbroec (d. 1381), the English anchoress Julian of Norwich (d. c. 1415) and later the Italian laywoman Catherine of Genoa (d. 1510).

The split of Western Christendom at the Reformation had effects on the mystical tradition, but did not produce a new major level or stage. The essential aspects of the New Mysticism continued to be developed in various ways. It has sometimes been claimed that the Reformers were opposed to the mystical element in Christianity, but the reality is more complex. Martin Luther (d. 1546) was not a mystic, but was influenced by some mystical themes, and the Lutheran tradition produced mystics such as Johann Arndt (d. 1621). Aspects of late medieval German mysticism helped shape the thought of some of those called the 'Radical Reformers', such as Valentin Weigel (d. 1588). Mystical writers and poets were also found in seventeenth-century England among both Puritans and main line Anglicans. The sixteenth and seventeenth centuries were most noted, however, for the powerful mystical teaching found in Spain and in France. In Spain the Franciscans and Augustinians produced mystics, but the greatest figures belonged to the reform wing of the Carmelite order, notably Teresa of Avila (d. 1582) and John of the Cross (d. 1591). The seventeenth century was the Golden Age of French mysticism, with figures like Francis de Sales (d. 1622), Pierre de Berulle (d. 1629) and Marie de l'Incarnation (d. 1672), an Ursuline missionary to Canada.

Crisis and Renewal

The late seventeenth and early eighteenth centuries saw the beginnings of the third great layer in the story of the mystical tradition, what can be called the time of the crisis of mysticism. This crisis, which led to a serious break in the tradition and a marginalization of mystical teaching, was born from factors both internal and external. Internally, the debates about the dangers of mystical heresy that originated in the thirteenth century reached a culmination in the struggle over and condemnation of what was called 'Quietism', the alleged errors of those who so stressed interior annihilation and devotion to the 'prayer of quiet' that they were accused of abandoning the ordinary practices of the Christian faith and perhaps even of the moral law. A Spanish priest resident in Rome, Miguel de Molinos, was condemned for such errors in 1687, and in the 1690s France was convulsed by the theological debates between the powerful J.-B. Bossuet (d. 1704) and François Fénelon (d. 1715), who supported the controversial mystic Madame Guyon (d. 1717). Bossuet and his allies engineered a papal condemnation (albeit mild) of Fénelon's views in

1699 and from then on fear of Quietism effectively squashed much mystical teaching in Roman Catholicism. At the same time, however, there was also external criticism of the mystical tradition from the regnant Enlightenment philosophy that reduced God to a distant celestial 'clockmaker' and ridiculed the idea that humans could reach union with God in this life.

Despite a few notable figures (e.g. J.-P. de Caussade, d. 1751), the eighteenth and nineteenth centuries, at least in the West (but decidedly not in Orthodox Russia), can be spoken of as the nadir of the mystical tradition. The so-called mystics were characterized more by their paranormal experiences than by any serious teaching, and an understanding of mysticism as constituted by private psychological states dominated. It was only in the twentieth century that a renewed interest in the richness of the mystical tradition undertaken by scholars from different disciplines began to show that the mystical element in Christianity was far richer and more important than its marginalized status in the church would indicate.[8] This academic revival was strengthened by the appearance of original mystical teachers (e.g. Thérèse de Lisieux, Teilhard de Chardin, Simone Weil, Thomas Merton) whose witness and insights are helping nourish a revival of the mystical tradition at the outset of the third millennium.

Notes

1 Bremond, H. (1930), *A Literary History of Religious Thought in France*, Vol. II: *The Coming of Mysticism*. London: SPCK, p. 432.
2 Bouyer, L. (1980), 'Mysticism/An Essay in the History of a Word', in R. Woods (ed.), *Understanding Mysticism*. Garden City: Doubleday, pp. 42–55.
3 On these two models, McGinn, B. (1996), 'Love, Knowledge and *Unio mystica* in the Western Christian Tradition', in M. Idel and B. McGinn (eds), *Mystical Union in Judaism, Christianity, and Islam*. New York: Continuum, pp. 59–86.
4 McGinn, B. (2009), 'Three Forms of Negativity in Christian Mysticism', in J. Bowker (ed), *Knowing the Unknowable*. London: I. B. Tauris, pp. 99–121. See also Sells, M. A. (1994), *Mystical Languages of Unsaying*. Chicago: University of Chicago Press and Turner, D. (1995), *The Darkness of God. Negativity in Christian Mysticism*. Cambridge: Cambridge University Press.
5 On paranormal states, Thurston, H. (1952), *The Physical Phenomena of Mysticism*. Chicago: Henry Regnery.
6 See Chapter 13 on Ignatian Spirituality.
7 See Chapter 6 on Monastic Spirituality.
8 Important twentieth-century scholars of mysticism include Friedrich von Hügel, Evelyn Underhill, William James, Henri Bremond, Joseph Maréchal, Jacques Maritain, Albert Schweitzer, Karl Rahner, Michel de Certeau and Hans Urs von Balthasar.

Bibliography and Further Reading

De Certeau, M. (1992), *The Mystic Fable. Vol. One, The Sixteenth and Seventeenth Centuries*. Chicago, IL: University of Chicago Press.

Haas, A. M. (2004), *Mystik im Context*. Munich: Wilhelm Fink.

Harmless, W. (2008), *Mystics*. New York, NY: Oxford University Press.

McGinn, B. (1991–2012), *The Presence of God. A History of Western Christian Mysticism*. 5 vols to date. New York, NY: Crossroad.

McGinn, B. (ed.) (2006), *The Essential Writings of Christian Mysticism*. New York, NY: Random House.

McIntosh, M. A. (1998), *Mystical Theology: The Integration of Spirituality and Theology*. Oxford: Blackwell.

Maréchal, J. (1927), *Studies in the Psychology of the Mystics*. London: Burnes, Oates & Washbourne.

Underhill, E. (1911), *Mysticism: A Study in the Nature and Development of Man's Spiritual Consciousness*. London: Methuen.

Von Hügel, F. (1908), *The Mystical Element of Religion*, 2 vols. London: James Clarke and Co.

4 The Spirituality of the Desert Fathers and Mothers

Benedicta Ward

Introduction: What is 'Spirituality'?

The use of the term 'Christian spirituality' for material relating to the Desert Fathers and Mothers presents problems in itself as 'Spirituality' is not a word the monks of the desert would have recognized, nor indeed is it a traditional Christian word at all. Its earlier use in the plural, 'spiritualities', referred to spiritual jurisdiction as opposed to temporal jurisdiction, the 'lords spiritual' as opposed (and how often literally opposed) to the 'lords temporal'. *Spiritualité* has, of course, undergone a later transformation and in its French form there is a very good chance that *un spirituel* will be someone who is witty, lively, mad or even drunk. Indeed, the twentieth-century use of the word 'spirituality' seems vaguely gnostic, if it means the non-material aspect of things, as in the 'spirituality of the motor bike', the 'spirituality of progress', 'the spirituality of electronics': a passive use of the phrase, referring to human reaction to these objects. A more active use of the phrase is current in 'the spirituality of culture', and this is closer to the use I want to make of the term in relation to the desert fathers and mothers. To see the prayers and desires and aspirations of people of the past within their context can be extremely illuminating for understanding inner motivation in the lives of the individuals concerned. In the nineteenth century the word was used to describe a field of study earlier called ascetical theology, and/or mystical prayer. By 'spirituality', then, I mean what people have thought and said and done and prayed in the light of the Spirit of God.

It seems that anyone reading about the desert fathers and mothers could use this approach. In their earliest records very little is said about prayer but their spirituality can be seen in lives lived not only in times of prayer. Because prayer is basic to their whole lives, their direct comments on prayer are brief and astringent. For instance, Agathon said:

There is no labour greater than prayer to God. For every time someone wants to pray, his enemies the demons want to prevent him, for they know that it is only by turning him from prayer that they can hinder his journey. Whatever good works a man undertakes, if he perseveres in it he will attain rest. But prayer is warfare to the last breath.[1]

When some monks asked Macarius how to pray, he replied:

There is no need to speak much in prayer; often stretch out your hands and say, 'Lord, as you will and as you know, have mercy on me'. But if there is war in your soul, add, 'Help me!' and because he knows what we need, he shows mercy on us.[2]

Most telling of all is this acted parable of prayer, linking it with Pentecost:

Lot went to see Joseph and said to him: 'As far as I can I say my little office, I fast a little, I pray and meditate, I live in peace as far as I can, I purify my thoughts; what else can I do?' Then the old man stood up and stretched his hands towards heaven. His fingers became like ten lamps of fire and he said to him, 'If you will, you can become all flame'.[3]

Most succinct of all is this Gospel-style of advice about prayer from Paul the Great: 'Keep close to Jesus'.[4]

These comments can be expanded to discover more about their spirituality from indirect sources, but first of all, who were they?

Who were the Desert Fathers and Mothers?

The term 'desert fathers and mothers' is a parallel to the term 'fathers of the church', which means the major theologians of the early church whose writings were the origin of Christian doctrine; the 'desert' fathers and mothers refers to equally influential people, who were not in the towns but in the desert, who were not analysing or writing about Christian doctrine but living it. Both kinds of 'fathers' were monks, that is *monos,* those vowed to celibacy, to live without a human partner of any kind for life. This central fact of celibacy belongs to the long tradition of asceticism as a human reaction to divinity. Christian monks did not invent celibacy or monasticism; both are older and part of the natural reaction of humans towards the divine which was further expressed by silence, solitude, fasting, keeping vigil and following a disciplined lifestyle. The desert fathers and mothers adopted all these customs; they did not invent them: they were not the first monks. In fact, the older way of monasticism is Buddhism, but in the early centuries of the Christian era for

43

the first time the monastic life was placed under the lens of the Gospel and there are records of Christians undertaking this monastic way of life as a way of following Christ.

How are they Known About?

The written records of them that survive show that they lived in Egypt, Syria and Cappadocia in the fourth century. They are not known through their own writings like the fathers of the church; they were almost all illiterate though there were at least two scholars among them, Evagrius and John Cassian, who wrote about and analysed desert life and thought later. The desert monks themselves are best approached through the eyes and ears of those who knew them, in small recorded sayings or accounts of actions. Such storytelling about what people had seen and heard reminds us of the way of the Gospels discussed in an earlier chapter. Christ did not write books; like Him the monks were seen and heard by others who then either passed on what they knew orally or wrote some of it down in collections called *apophthegmata* ('sayings').

Their way of life was caught not taught, but it is a long way from the strong oral and visual communication of the early centuries to today's reading and writing culture. In order to know them as friends and companions in the way of following Christ, it is necessary today to read about them. Oral tradition is not now at all the strong way of communication it was for them as most modern memories are defective and untrained, so that written texts are essential.

The accounts of the desert were written in Greek, Latin, Syriac and later in dialects of Coptic and were known by oral transmission throughout the Middle Ages in both the east and west of Europe. Nowadays since not so many people find understanding ancient languages easy, there are translations into modern languages such as English, French, Italian and German of the earliest accounts of the desert. There are also accounts of the lives of some desert fathers, as in Athanasius' *Life of St Antony* and there are letters such as those of Antony, Amoun, Barsanufius, John and Jerome. Later they could also be known through the precepts of monastic rules like those of Pachomius and Basil; and there was monastic theology later in the writings of John Cassian and Evagrius.[5]

These accounts show that some of the desert monks lived in communities, while some lived as complete solitaries, others in a mixture of both ways, as solitary disciples grouped round a respected hermit. There are also records by visitors to the desert, pious tourists, those who wanted to see this way of life for themselves: the Spanish nun Egeria; the Roman widows Paula, Eustocium and Melania; seven monks from Palestine; John Cassian and Germanus – all visited Egypt and recorded what they saw.[6] In fact in the fourth century, the desert dwellers became immensely popular and thus provided the format for Christian virtue for centuries.

Why should they be included in a guide to Christian Spirituality?

It is possible to retain a narrow focus on present needs and interests but it is also possible to be changed and expanded by contact with others in the past. With the hermits of the first days of Christianity, it is especially fruitful to get close to them and listen to them by reading about them in translations, or to look behind the translations to the Greek, Latin, Coptic texts, even to the manuscripts behind the printed words. Their lives of prayer can be seen in the context in which they lived, and it is possible to understand the influence they have always had.

There are four stages in any true learning: first, to want to know; second, to stand back and see the topic as it truly was for its initiator; third, cautiously to put questions to it and finally to allow the past its own integrity and leave it unchanged. This particular form of spirituality is best understood through the second of these stages: to see what they did and said themselves in their own context. It is important to look honestly at these writings, without distorting them by beginning with present day concerns. But having seen them as they were, modern questions can then be posed. It is a way of making friends with the past. The best sources for such friendship are the *Sayings* because they are simple and direct records, not the systematic approach that comes later.

The first people to be involved in this way of life were laypeople, not clergy. These were not professionals nor intellectuals, just very ordinary men and women. They were grown ups, not children, young people doing something daring and new. They were not high-class mystics but sinners, and over them all was the cross of Christ. Their lives had been by no means virtuous: robbers, murderers, prostitutes, as well as the peasants of the villages. They were not clever or educated; few of them could read the scriptures though they all knew a great deal of them by heart so that their prayer arose naturally out of the fact that they had physically absorbed the bible texts. They were not interested in church services or sacraments; some of them were not even baptized until after they had lived as monks for years. While the hermits who lived in Nitria and Scetis could attend the liturgy on Sundays, solitary hermits might be without the Eucharist for years. Even services of the church were regarded as rather secular: if you only pray at those hours, they said, you are not really praying; a true person of prayer has prayer always in their heart. The completeness of giving of the self to God, with heart, soul and mind found in the early church especially among the martyrs, now after the peace of the church and its increasing secularization, continued among the monks who had moved into deserted places, far from towns. Martyrdom and eschatology were main themes in the early church: they said at their Eucharist 'let grace come and this world pass away'[7] and they were formative also for the desert dwellers. Such an eschatalogical perspective is found in this vignette:

> It was said of Arsenius that on Saturday evening preparing for the glory of Sunday he would turn his back on the sun and stretch out his hands in prayer towards the heavens till once again the sun shone on his face.[8]

The way of life of the hermits became a major influence on the way Christians prayed and lived but in itself it was not the whole of Christianity. In fact, it was only possible because other Christians were doing it differently elsewhere; all ways of human living could become part of the new kingdom, as John Climacus wrote:

> God is the life of all free beings. He is the salvation of all, of believers or unbelievers; of the just or the unjust; of the pious or the impious; of those freed from the passions or of those caught in them; of monks or those living in the world; of the educated or the illiterate; of the healthy or the sick; of the young or the very old. He is like the outpouring of the light, the glimpse of the sun, or the changes in the weather, which are the same for everyone without exception.[9]

Their Way of Life

Just as others tried to combine Christianity with human ways of living in the world, so the desert elders tried to combine Christianity with the specific monastic and ascetic way of life, which was so often linked with dualism and negativity. To the monks, to be 'in the church' did not mean entering into a building or becoming a minister of any kind: to 'be church' was to become the body of Christ. They were not, therefore, at all churchy, not because they despised or distrusted the church but first because many of them in the desert had little contact with the establishment and secondly because those who had were convinced that their life in the body of Christ was to be interiorized; the desert, the place of solitude within, was where reality was faced. What they faced in solitude was of course themselves, that central battleground of all the passions, and much of their literature is about this, described as a fight with inner demons. Understanding failure, despair, that sense of non-identity, was their central work. The only requirement for entry into the desert-style of prayer and life was a call of God and awareness of need, transformed into a great longing and desire. While their external way of life seemed extraordinary their inner concerns were common to all mankind.

The desert fathers and mothers can be seen and known through stories about them and by sayings which were not just remarks remembered by chance. One of the most frequent requests made to the desert elders was to 'speak a word'. This word was not advice, rebuke, or continued analysis, but a sacrament through which God would give to the recipient all that she was truly asking for. This was the same pattern as that which they encountered in the Gospels: 'That which we have seen and heard and our hands have handled declare we unto you' (1 Jn 1.3). This simplicity of personal encounter makes the hermits deeply significant today because they were not trying to instruct or analyse but to live in Christ, and therefore receive the life of the Trinity.

Among Christians, the things that belonged to the ascetic tradition could seem negative, but for these new monks renouncing the world took on a positive aspect. They chose to live on the limits of human life, not out of fear or dislike of the flesh but out of love. Their silence was not a dislike of talking but a reaction to hearing the voice of Christ and wanting to listen to him; their choice of solitude was so that they could walk more closely with the Lord; they fasted because they fed in inner food and did not need much earthly food; they waited so eagerly for the coming of the Lord that they did not want much sleep. This kind of positively chosen life in God was not a matter of strain and effort but of lived faith, relying on Christ, seeing not what was given up but what drew them forward. This inner work was available for all and was very simple if not easy. It was fundamentally a human response to the call of God.

In linking monastic practices with the Gospel it is easy to see how the monks followed the first commandment to love God: 'Jesus said to the lawyer, "You shall love the Lord your God with all your heart and with all your soul and with all your mind"' (Mt. 22.37). Their whole lifestyle emphasized that God is here and now or else he is nowhere. But how did they keep the second commandment and promise: 'You shall love your neighbour as yourself' (Mt. 22.39)?

Criticism of the Desert Hermits

With regard to this, then as now, two kinds of criticism were levelled at hermits: first, there is the criticism of humanists that the solitaries were abandoning years of effort by which humanity had shaped itself through literature, art, architecture, beauty and learning – all seemed thrown away by these wild people and the arts of living together abandoned. They were seen as haters of mankind:

Squalid fugitives from light . . . Driven by furies, out from men and lands, a credulous exile skulking in the dark, thinking, poor fool, that heaven feeds on filth; himself to himself more harsh than the outraged gods, a worse creed this than ever Circe's poison, men's bodies then turned bestial, now their souls.[10]

This description of uncivilized human beings is taken from the pre-Christian world of monasticism. That such conduct could be adopted by Christians seemed a contradiction to the ways of the normal, pious Roman citizen and his hard-won culture. This was especially dangerous when theology was involved. Such ascetic living could be linked to heresy. Moreover, the monks were not subtle theologians and they could indeed get it wrong. It is this background which caused Athanasius to stress in his *Life of St. Antony* so much about doctrine in the post-Constantinian church with its responsibilities for doctrine, sacraments and behaviour. He was presenting a defence against those who assumed all monks to be heretics but it was also a warning to the monks themselves. They needed to be careful about belief and its expression; they were living very much like the early church, but this was a new age and presented new challenges and new dangers.

Secondly, there is the criticism of hermits by monks who lived in community. The criticism of Basil and the monastic bishops took the form of the criticism, 'Whose feet do you wash?':

Life lived in common with others is more useful than solitude . . . the Lord girded himself and washed the feet of his disciples in person. Whose feet will you wash? Who will you care for? In comparison with whom will you be last if you live by yourself?[11]

In seeing how the hermits responded to this, it is possible to discover deeper levels of their spirituality. First of all they agreed they would say that they were sinners, not worthy or strong enough to live with others. God in his mercy had called them apart to limit the damage they might do to others and to make them ready for unity with all in heaven. Their solitude was in fact a part of their love of others. One might answer the humanist argument by pointing to the fact that out of the solitude and stillness of the desert came the new forms of Christian civilization; and Basil himself agreed that there was value in a mystical sense in the life of solitude. A disciple of his, Evagrius, wrote that 'a solitary is one who is separated from all and united to all'.[12] The Christian hermit went apart from civilization at the call of God, and in doing so met the world at the deepest level within himself.

In fact, humans are never entirely alone. There will always be somebody wherever the monk goes. For instance, a monk thought he would leave his cell since he had become discouraged and thought he was making no progress there: somewhere different might make life easier. But as he was putting on his sandals to go, he saw a demon beside him also putting on sandals to go with him. However far a person flees there will always be himself. This sense of being *yourself* is significant in the desert because of the mysterious connection between all humanity, so that whenever someone allows the evil in his heart to be touched by mercy, even though one is in total physical solitude, all humanity is changed.

Individuals and Communities

But what about the other solitaries? It is a curious irony of solitary life that it attracts others. Antony the Great, 'the first to know the utter desert'[13] after 20 years alone in a tomb, found a crowd of disciples waiting for him outside; he fled to the inner mountain to try and avoid them but they followed. There are several stories of the secret saint who avoided being recognized by the visitors who came to find him. When Mary the niece of Abraham returned to life in total solitude after living in a brothel in the city, she wept in her cell and her prayers and tears were so wonder-working that many came to be near her.[14] So there were always others to relate to, and for all there was always the 'great cloud of witnesses' (Heb. 12.1), those who have died and are alive on the other side of Christ and were constantly known by prayer and praise.

There are also some stories about practical living in the desert where care of others had to be exercised in daily life in several ways. First there was care for each other in need, especially for the sick and dying. Secondly for newcomers who became disciples and were welcomed to live in the same way permanently. Finally, there was their attention to visitors. Here, for example, is a description of their combination of solitude and communion, isolation and fellowship:

> This place was called Cellia because of the number of cells there, scattered about the desert. Those who have already begun their training in Nitria and want to live a more remote life, stripped of external things, withdraw there. For this is the utter desert, and the cells are divided from one another by so great a distance that no-one can see his neighbour nor can any voice be heard. They live alone in their cells; there is a huge silence and a great quiet there. Only on Saturday and Sunday do they meet in church and then they see each other face to face as men restored to heaven.[15]

Their way of living together as solitaries encapsulated some great themes of the Gospel: for instance, they had total respect for one another, and therefore there was true freedom for each. No one was forced to undertake such a way of life – it was always a free choice which they respected in one another:

> Some monks came to see Poemen and said to him. 'When we see brothers who are dozing during liturgy, shall we rouse them so that they can be watchful?' He said to them, 'For my part when I see a brother who is dozing, I put his head on my knees and let him rest'.[16]

This freedom also meant that they did not judge one another, a central theme in all their lives:

> They said of Macarius the Great that he became as it were a god upon earth because just as God protects the world, so Macarius would cover the faults that he saw as if he did not see them, and those which he heard, as if he did not hear them.[17]

This story was told to emphasize non-judgement about the African, Moses the Black, one of the most revered of the hermits:

> A brother in Scetis committed a fault. A council was called to which Moses was invited, but he refused to go. Then they sent someone to him saying, 'Come, everyone is waiting for you'. So he got up and went. He took a leaking jug filled with water and carried it with him. The others came out to meet him and said, 'What is this, father?' The old man said to them, 'My sins run out behind me, and today I am coming to judge the errors of another'. When they heard this they forgave the brother and said no more to him.[18]

Another story illustrates the non-judgement theme applied to non-monks:

> Mios was asked by a soldier whether God would forgive a sinner . . . The old man asked him, 'Tell me, my dear, if your cloak were torn, would you throw it away?' 'No', he replied, 'I would mend it and wear it again'. The old man said to him, 'Well, if you care so much for your cloak, will not God show mercy on his own creature?'[19]

It was an exacting way of life but a free one and just as they did not judge one another, they did not order each other about:

> A brother asked Poemen, 'Some brothers live with me; do you want me to be in charge of them?' The old man said to him, 'No, just work first and foremost and if they want to live like you, they will see about it for

themselves'. The brother said to him, 'But it is they themselves, father, who want me to be in charge of them'. The old man replied, 'No, be their example, not their legislator'.[20]

The way the monks lived with each other determined how they behaved towards those who came to join them. Newcomers were not children but young adults who were making a responsible choice to the call of God, therefore there was respect for the integrity of each. Interference with each other would be destructive of both monks and newcomers. They allowed others to come and let them follow as Christ led. Thus there could develop a pattern of spiritual relationship that was entirely personal and genuine in which an experienced monk would be seen as the father of a newcomer, not in modern terms as his 'spiritual director' but as a living companion, whether they met often, rarely or even not at all. There was a basic assumption that the Christian has no father but the Father of the Lord Jesus Christ who has called men and women His brothers and sisters and the duty of the 'soul friend' (to use the expressive Irish term for this relationship) was: to disappear. The face of Christ and not the face of the Father was what mattered; they knew how easily projections of their unconscious selves could be put onto the father so that he could seem to them either an angel or devil; what mattered was that behind him was God, to whom the heart related.

Conclusions: Facing Brokenness and Failure

The hermit who was truly dying daily into the life of Christ became a new Adam in a newly created earth. 'Desert' itself denoted death, barrenness and loss, but as Christ changed the death of the cross into new life, so the hermit made his inner and outer desert a new world. Then he could relate to all creation, naming the animals, enjoying them, not dominating and using them. In the desert, the hermits experienced the restoration of all creation. There are stories about this new relationship, in which hermits cared for and were respected by lions, donkeys, crocodiles, hyenas and gazelles.

Vital to the whole spirituality of the desert was this sense of an inner contact running through all creation. The formation of a new world was not done by power and domination or by human ability of any kind. It was done by each facing brokenness and failure, not by self-centred success. The monks' pattern was Christ who emptied himself and became the servant of all. The definition that the monk had of himself was always the same: he was created by God but he was also a sinner, of no use, the most needy and weakest of all. Outsiders said other things and praised them as people who persistently loved God and through receiving the love which is God, transmitted it to others. Visitors saw that the hermits served Christ who washed their feet constantly in forgiveness and through them those who joined them, those who visited them, those who persecuted them, those they met and so the whole world. They were described as those by whom the world was kept in being. Just as trees make oxygen to purify the atmosphere, so praying people were seen as trees of the spirit. Antony said 'My life and my death is with my neighbour; if we win our brother we win God, if we cause our brother to stumble we have sinned against Christ'.[21]

The reality of the desert was in its recognition of the simplicity of being made in the image of God, a creature before the Creator, and realizing in one-self both this glory and at the same time the shame of being a sinner before God the Saviour, asking him daily with thankfulness and love to have mercy, to recreate all in the love which is the Spirit. The solitary was always wounded, always rejoicing, in an inner desert which blossomed and made him open to all. Antony, the father of solitaries, saw this way of life as open to all:

> Do not be afraid to hear about virtue and do not be a stranger to the term. For it is not distant from us nor is it external to us; its realization lies within us and the work is easy if only we want it. The Greeks leave home and cross the seas in order to gain an education, but there is no need for us to go away on account of the Kingdom of God nor need we cross the sea in search of virtue. For the Lord has told us, 'The kingdom of God is within you'. All that is needed for goodness is that which is within, the human heart.[22]

Notes

1 *Sayings of the Desert Fathers* (1975) (hereafter '*Sayings*'), trans. by Benedicta Ward, Mowbrays and Cistercian Studies, Agathon 9.
2 *Sayings*, Macarius 19.
3 *Sayings*, Joseph of Panephysis 7.
4 *Sayings*, Paul the Great 4.
5 For translations see bibliography.
6 Many of the sayings mention visitors to the desert, the most famous of which were John Cassian and Germanus.
7 *The Didache* (1976), trans. J. B. Lightfoot. Grand Rapids, MI: Baker Book House, p. 27.
8 *Sayings*, Arsenius, 30.
9 Climacus, John (1982), *The Ladder of Divine Ascent*, trans. Colm Luibheid and Norman Russel, intro. by Kallistos Ware. London: SPCK, p. 74.
10 Rutilius Namantianus, *De Reditu Suo*, 11, 519ff. Trans. by Helen Waddell (1936), in *The Desert Fathers*. Constable, p. 22.
11 Basil the Great: *Longer Rules*, Rule 7; trans. by Augustine Holmes (2000), in *A Life Pleasing to God*. London: Darton, Longman and Todd, pp. 73ff.
12 Evagrius Ponticus, *The Praktikos & Chapters on Prayer*, trans. by John Eudes Bamberger (1981), Kalamazoo: Cistercian Studies, no. 124.
13 St Athanasius, *Life of St. Antony*.

14 Benedicta Ward (1987), *Harlots of the Desert, A study of repentance in early monastic sources.* Mowbrays and Cistercian Studies. 'Life of Maria' p. 100.
15 *Lives of the Desert Fathers* (1980) (hereafter *'Lives'*), trans. by N. Russell, with monography by Benedicta Ward. London: Andrew Mowbray and Kalamazoo: Cistercian Studies, p. 67.
16 *Sayings*, Poemen 92.
17 *Sayings*, Macarius 32.
18 *Sayings*, Moses 2.
19 *Sayings*, Mios 3.
20 *Sayings*, Poemen 124.
21 *Sayings*, Antony 9.
22 Athanasius (1950), *Life of St. Antony*. Trans. Robert Meyer, London, p. 37.

Bibliography and Further Reading

Primary Sources (English Translations)

Athanasius (1950), *Life of St Antony*, trans. T. R. Meyer, New York: Paulist.
Cassian, John (1994–6), *Institutes and Conferences*, trans. Boniface Ramsey, New York: Paulist Press.
The Desert Fathers (1936), trans. Helen Waddell, London: Constable.
Sayings of the Desert Fathers (1975), trans. Benedicta Ward, Kalamazoo, MI: Cistercian Publications/Oxford: AR Mowbray (rev. edn, 1984).
Lives of the Desert Fathers (1980), trans. Norman Russell, with monograph by Benedicta Ward, Kalamazoo, MI: Cistercian Publications/Oxford: AR Mowbray.
Wisdom of the Desert Fathers (1986), trans. Benedicta Ward, Oxford: SLG Press.
Harlots of the Desert: A Study of Repentence in Early Monastic Sources (1987), Benedicta Ward, Oxford and Kalamazoo, MI.
The Desert of the Heart (1996), trans. Benedicta Ward (Selections), London: Darton, Longman and Todd.
The Wisdom of the Desert (1999), trans. Benedicta Ward (Selections), London: Lion Press.
The Desert Fathers: Wisdom of the Early Christian Monks (2003), trans. Benedicta Ward, London: Penguin Classics.

Commentaries

Brown, Peter (1971), *The World of Late Antiquity*. London: Thames and Hudson.
Burton Christie, Douglas (1993), *The Word in the Desert and the Quest for Holiness in Early Christian Monasticism*. Oxford: Oxford University Press.
Chadwick, Owen (1968), *John Cassian: A Study in Primitive Monasticism*. Oxford: Oxford University Press.
Gould, Graham (1993), *The Desert Fathers on Monastic Community*, Oxford Early Christian Studies. Oxford: Oxford University Press.
Stewart, Columba (1998), *Cassian the Monk*. Oxford: Oxford University Press.
Williams, Rowan (2004), *Silence and Honeycakes: The Wisdom of the Desert*. London: Lion.

Part II
Schools of Spirituality

5 Augustinian Spirituality

Martin Laird

Introduction

Rome's Church of Santa Maria del Popolo is best-known today for its cache of Caravaggios. But in the thirteenth century, long before the Caravaggios arrived, the Church of Santa Maria del Popolo was the site of an extraordinary gathering of Italian hermits.

In March 1256, Pope Alexander IV convoked this gathering in order to unite into a single religious order various groups of Italian hermits, the majority of whom already followed St Augustine's *Rule* (Gutierrez 1984, pp. 23–41; Andrews 2006, pp. 71–90). In 1244 Pope Innocent IV had already united a group of hermits into one religious family (known today as the Little Union). These hermits (chiefly Tuscan) soon spread from Italy into France, Germany, England and beyond. But what emerged from the convocation called by Pope Alexander IV in 1256, referred to today as the Grand Union, was a new entity. A single Order gathered from yet more groups of Italian eremitical congregations (most of whom already followed the *Rule* of St Augustine) all united by the *Rule*, under the leadership of a single Prior General, and given the name the Order of Hermits of St Augustine, with its own protector, Cardinal Richard Annibaldi.

This new Order, called into being by the Church, was ranked among the four great mendicant Orders traditionally listed as the Franciscans, Dominicans, Augustinians and Carmelites (Gutierrez 1984, p. 52; Andrews 2006, p. 69). The Augustinians soon enjoyed wide expansion throughout Europe, especially in the great university cities such as Bologna, Salamanca, Paris, Oxford and Cambridge.

The *Rule* of St Augustine (written around 397) was one of the most ancient monastic rules in the Latin west and followed already, for example, by the Canons Regular of Prémontré, the Canons Regular of the Lateran, as well as by the Dominicans (among others). The Order of St Augustine, newly emerged from the defining shape given it by the Church at the Grand Union of 1256, mounted a robust claim that the bishop-monk, St Augustine of Hippo, was uniquely their founding father and that they themselves were the legitimate heirs of St Augustine's monasticism in a way that other religious Orders following the *Rule* of St Augustine could not claim. While this claim has been contentious among scholars of the history of the Order (Gutierrez, 1984, p. 14; Saak, 2002), certainly this Order of St Augustine looked to St Augustine alone as their founding spiritual father.

In this same Church of Santa Maria del Popolo, now amid its great cache of Caravaggios, the Order of St Augustine gathered on 26 March 2006 to celebrate the seven hundred-fiftieth anniversary of the foundation of the Grand Union. In his address to the Augustinians there present, as well as to all Augustinian nuns and friars throughout the world, the Prior General of the Order of St Augustine identified three defining character-istics of the way of life of the reputed heirs of Augustine's monastic ideal: (1) the spirituality and thought of St Augustine; (2) the Order's eremitical–contemplative experience and (3) the life of apostolic fraternity developed and lived in the context of the mendicant movement. Moreover, these defining characteristics should not be thought of as three separate charac-teristics but as a threefold unity. Indeed the harmonious integration of this threefold unity gives the Order of St Augustine its originality and identity (Prevost 2007, p. 25).

The Spirituality and Thought of St Augustine

It is indeed a challenge to present in the space of this chapter a complete over-view of the thought and spirituality of the most eloquent and prolific author in Late Antiquity. While St Augustine never wrote a treatise on the spiritual life as such, all of his works are saturated by a vision of the spiritual life of the Christian, a vision born of Augustine's own experience (Cipriani 2009, p. 5). This chapter shall therefore focus on those defining elements of Augustine's spirituality that bear especially closely on the development, identity and spir-ituality of the Order of St Augustine – interiority, common life and service to the Church.

Interiority

No single author in the Western church has provided the Christian tradition with such a rich resource of language to express the heart's deepest long-ing for the triune God. From his encounter with the living God, incarnate in Jesus and proclaimed by Sacred Scripture, St Augustine provides a language of deep intimacy with God. Many call this the language of interiority. This term 'interiority' does not imply a narcissistic turning in on oneself. In fact it is the liberating *antidote* to any such self-centredness; for, in the Augustinian tradition, interiority unfolds in God and therefore embraces the entire crea-tion. One of St Augustine's most famous expressions of his understanding of interiority is found in *Confessions*: 'You are closer to me than I am to myself'

(*Confessions*, III (vi), 11, p. 43). This phrase has become so woven into Christian spiritual discourse that it is usually not even attributed to St Augustine.

St Augustine was always a Christian in search of God. Even before his baptism by St Ambrose in 387, Augustine sought the living God with 'the eye of the flesh' and sought God 'by means of that eye' (*Confessions*, III (vi) 11). That is to say, St Augustine's search for God was skewed by his search for fame, reputation and careerism as a teacher of rhetoric and speechwriter for the Emperor (not to mention his membership of the Christian sect known as the Manicheans). Listening to the preaching of St Ambrose of Milan, however, revealed to St Augustine that his previous escapades in the search for the Living God were all spiritual nonstarters. The preaching of St Ambrose finally led to St Augustine's baptism by St Ambrose into the 'Great Church', and gave birth to the insight that what is necessary for the Christian life is the awakening of an inner eye: 'What is called for in the Christian life is "the healing of the eye of the heart, with which God is to be seen"' (Sermon 88.5).

Moving back to Roman North Africa, and now monk priest and bishop himself of Hippo Regius, St Augustine's discovery in his own spiritual life leads to a key theme in his understanding of interiority: it is a question of returning to the heart. This theme is largely inspired by Isa. 46.8, and puts a definitive stamp on his spirituality, expressed, among many other places, in Sermon 102, 2: '"Go back, therefore, to the heart" (Isa. 46.8), and if you are believers, you will find Christ there; he himself is speaking to you there. Yes, here am I, shouting my head off; but [Christ], in silence, is doing more teaching.' The one who seeks the living God returns to the heart, one's innermost depths, having been led to these depths, often through years of fruitlessly seeking God in various *cul de sacs* of careerism. The search will inevitably lead to yet more anxiety-ridden grasping for God who is already within us and who has already found us from all eternity: 'You were within me Lord, but I was outside myself' (*Confessions* X, xxvii, 38).

St Augustine has a way of expressing our transparent intimacy with God as lived out with all who seek communion with God. The communion of mind and heart in God is at once deeply personal and at the same time deeply ecclesial; nor is it limited to those living together in the monastery. Indeed the outstanding characteristic of Augustinian Spirituality is entering the spaciousness of an unshakeable paradox: self-forgetful contemplation of the indwelling mystery of the Triune God and a deeply ecclesial communion with all who seek the face of God (Ps 26). These two are one. For Augustine, the interior journey finds its consummation not in ourselves but in God.

The passage from Isa. 46.8, 'return to your heart', serves as a consistent refrain and foundation to Augustinian Spirituality: 'Go back, therefore, to the heart (Isa. 46.8), and if you are believers you will find Christ there; he himself is speaking to you there . . . in silence' (Sermon 102, 2). 'God is delight',

Augustine claims in his famous *On the Trinity*, 'and those who are faithful rest in God, called home from the noise that is around us to the joy that is silence. Why do we rush about searching for God who is already here at home within us? If only we would be with God'.

There are times, in fact, when St Augustine, now a monk-bishop, arrives at the conclusion that one should only speak if one's duties require it. In an intriguing commentary on Psalm 139, he says 'Why do you want to speak and not want to listen? You are always rushing out of doors, but are not willing to return into your own house. Your teacher is within . . . It is inside that we listen to the truth' (*Commentary on Psalm 139*). He goes on to say in this same commentary that we should speak only when our office requires it. Indeed it appears that there is a certain primacy of interior silence in the writings of the Bishop of Hippo: 'God is delight and we who are faithful rest in God, called home from the noise that is around us to the joy that is silence. Why do we rush about searching for God who is already here at home within us? If only we would be with God' (*On the Trinity*, 8.7.11). Perhaps there is no more powerful statement of this as when St Augustine concludes his famous *On the Trinity* with a prayer: 'if only I spoke when preaching your word and praising you . . . Deliver me, God, from the barrage of words, which I suffer from inwardly . . . My thoughts are not silent even though my voice is' (*On the Trinity*, 51; translation altered slightly).

Augustinian Spirituality has unshakeable foundations in the Indwelling Presence; as a result he is acutely aware of how too much speaking can drown by its din a deep listening to Christ who is speaking within; in silence, Christ is doing more teaching (*Letter* 102, 2).

Common Life

One would expect him to enjoin on his monks perpetual silence, eschewing all opportunity to speak. But in fact St Augustine takes quite a different view of the matter when it comes to his monks disposing themselves to service of the Church. St Augustine's *Rule* begins, 'The following precepts we order you living in the monastery to observe. The main purpose for you having come together is to live harmoniously in your house, intent upon God in oneness of mind and heart' (*Rule* 2–3). While these precepts characterize how the friars should live among each other, St Augustine always conceived this communal search in unity of mind and heart intent upon God as the foundation of the many monastic communities he founded. However, he never *opposes* this common search for God in contemplation to apostolic service to the Church.

In Letter 48, 2 St Augustine politely rebukes Euxodius, the abbot of the monks of Capraria, because they seemed to be doing exactly that. And so St Augustine writes, 'Do not prefer your peaceful withdrawal to the needs of the Church' (*Letter* 48, 2). As in *The City of God* Augustine expresses this dynamic integration of contemplation and apostolic service:

> A man ought neither to lead such a contemplative life that in his leisure he does not consider the welfare of his neighbors, nor to lead so active a life that he does not seek holy leisure; the demands of love take up the proper task. If one does not impose this burden on us, we have the time free to perceive and contemplate the truth; but if this burden is placed on us, we must take it up as charity demands. (*City of God*, 19, 19, in Zumkeller, p. 339)

For St Augustine's communities (and in his own life) there is a strong preference for the contemplative life, 'a life that cultivates the inner eye whereby God may be seen', but not in such a way that a response to the needs of the Church is rejected.

Service to the Church

As a fourth-century monk-bishop Augustine attempted to cultivate his conviction of the primacy of contemplation, but never in such a way that he ignored or compromised the legitimate needs of the church, the duties and call of charity and the privileged burden of service to the Church. Let it be clear, however, that service to the Church, as he makes clear in the *City of God*, is not at the cost of the *otium sanctum*, that holy leisure necessary for giving oneself entirely to contemplation. Nor is this dedication to the *otium sanctum* of contemplation pursued out of neglect of the privileged burden of charity and service to our neighbour. St Augustine's negotiation of this dynamic and integrating paradox of contemplation and apostolic service led him to one of his most succinct expressions of the self-forgetful service to God in contemplation at the heart of a Church in need of labourers in the pastures of service: '*inde pasco, unde pescor*' / 'I nourish you with what sustains me' (Sermon 339, 3).

The Order's Contemplative–Eremitical Experience

History has not been generous, either textually, archaeologically or otherwise, in allowing us to trace the fate of Augustine's monastic foundations after the Vandal invasions of Roman North Africa. We can legitimately say that some made their way to Italy. But what happened to them? And then there is always Charlemagne and his insistence that all monasteries follow the *Rule* of St Benedict. There is in fact a paucity of indisputable historical evidence that directly connects St Augustine's monastic foundations from the fifth century to the rise of communities following the *Rule* of St Augustine by the early twelfth century (e.g. the Canons Regular of Prémontré in 1120). Moreover, history witnesses to the rise of different groups of hermits in Italy, who claim to be the legitimate heirs of Augustine's monastic legacy. After a few monastic disputes with older religious communities who made the same claim (a view significantly contextualized and critically nuanced by Saak, 2002), the Order of Hermits of St Augustine came out of the brawl as the outright winner as the legitimate heirs of Augustine's monastic legacy. At the same time, the Order acquired its place among the great mendicant Orders (Franciscans, Dominicans, Augustinians and Carmelites), all of whom were responding to the wider social movement from feudalism to the rise of the city. This now officially mendicant Order of Hermits of St Augustine responded to this restructuring of society by moving into the cities throughout Europe and exercising pastoral care of souls. The monasteries of the mendicant orders were typically built just inside the city walls to keep, so to speak, one foot in the desert and the other in the city in service of the pastoral care of the many people who had moved from the shifting social life of a feudal society to the rising life in the urban centres of Europe. One clear example of this (among many) is found in the community of friars in the Tuscan town of San Gimignano. Even today this Augustinian monastery opens onto the life of the city of a still vibrant twenty-first century, mountain-top town, and yet at the same time the back of this monastery forms part of the old city walls of the town.

Even though the Order committed itself to embody its new charism and mission to the pastoral care of souls, requiring a move from the countryside into urban centres, it did not abandon its eremitical roots entirely. It kept communities in the countryside for those friars who felt called to witness to the ecclesial solitude that characterized the pattern of Jesus' own prayer life of routinely going off to a desert place to commune with the one he called 'Abba'. In fact, the Augustinian Jordan of Saxony (c. 1299–c. 1380), who in many ways created the spirituality of the Order (Gutierrez, 1984, p. 94), describes this succinctly in his *The Life of the Brethren*:

> We can infer from what has already been said that anyone may depart to the wilderness from a house of common life and embrace the anchoritic state. So long as this is done to obtain the fruits of a better life and with the permission of one's superior, for we have shown that the anchorite's state is more perfect. (79)

The Order's history reveals many who lived out the ecclesial charism of solitude within the Order. The Englishman William Flete, confessor to Catherine of Siena, left England to respond to this charism in the forested solitude of the Monastery of Lecceto outside Siena (now inhabited by the Italian nuns of the Order) (Hackett 1992, pp. 61–71).

According to Ann K. Warren this tradition remained alive in the Order for centuries. She gives us the names of friars such as Robert Barrett who lived as solitaries dedicated completely to the life of contemplation and pastoral counselling in the context of the fourteenth-century English anchoritic movement up to the reforms of Henry VIII. The Augustinian monasteries at Tickhill, Droitwich and Northampton featured among such Augustinian communities who supported this charism among those friars called by God to express the charism of ecclesial solitude alongside these communities of conventual life (Warren 1985). Names of other Augustinians have been lost due to the henrician reforms that featured, among other things, the dissolution of the monasteries and the destruction of the great bulk of their archives (ibid., p. 289).

The Life of Apostolic Fraternity in the Context of the Mendicant Movement

Whether the Augustinian charism of religious life is lived out in the context of an explicitly conventual life (what Jordan of Saxony called the cenobitic life) or is lived out in the call to ecclesial solitude, buried in the heart of the Augustinians as a response to the Gospel being read out and preached to Christian communites, each of these expressions of the Order of St Augustine are expressed in its *Rule*: 'The main purpose for your having come together is to live harmoniously in your house, intent upon God in oneness of mind and heart' (*Rule*, chapter 1). Irrespective of this plurality of expressions of one single charism, which nourishes both the life of the Order and the wider Church, contemplation is the nexus that draws together the contemplative and therefore apostolic life in service of the universal Church.

Among the Order's most famous Augustinians who give witness to the inextricable unity between the call to contemplation and the charism of apostolic service, is the life and preaching of the learned Spanish Augustinian, St Thomas of Villanova (1488–1555), who remains until today the patron of studies in the Order (Back 1987).

For St Thomas of Villanova, contemplation is the doorway to the apostolic life. This is a consistent theme in his preaching, whether to the friars of the Order, whom he served for many years as superior, or to the diocesan clergy whom he served as bishop of the important See of Valencia (Back 1987). St Thomas of Villanova wrote and preached of contemplation as the doorway to apostolic life. He writes for example:

Exercise as best you can in contemplation, even if you achieve little. For without it you will accomplish nothing, nor will you be able to live the active life. Contemplation is needed to protect you and give you wings so that you may exercise yourself in the active life. Otherwise you will remain without either of the lives, like a fruitless tree. (*Plática y aviso al religioso*, VI, 506–7, *The Works of St Thomas of Villanova* (1994), vol. 1)[1]

St Thomas of Villanova does not view contemplation as the opposite end of the spectrum of the 'active life'; rather contemplation creates the *possibility* of the active life.

Not only does contemplation provide access to the contemplative life, but the cultivation of solitude in the context of community life creates the viability of the active life. Thus, St Thomas preaches:

First [Christ] makes use of solitude . . . Solitude is a tremendous help, for those occupied with activities, those in the commotion of agitation, do not feel injuries or wounds; . . . they do not even notice it. But when those who are alienated from themselves, when they regather themselves, separate themselves from commotion in a place of prayer, will see their wounds . . . When someone is in silence and calm, he is on careful watch. In the same way the person who is in calm and solitude senses an evil thought or evil desire and pushes it out of his heart. (Thomas of Villanova, First Sunday of Lent, Sermon VII, *Works* 3, p. 75)

St Thomas' most powerful statement of contemplation as the ground of the Augustinian preacher's efficacy is rooted in his conviction that a considerable amount of time devoted to contemplation should ground the friar's preaching to the people of God:

Do not ascend the pulpit, I beg you, without studying your subject and giving it mature consideration beforehand . . . Above all, you must give at least two hours entreating God in the silent contemplation of divine things. (First Conference on Tuesday after the Second Sunday, quoted in *Propers of the Order of St Augustine. Offices of Augustinian Saints and Blesseds in the Liturgy of the Hours*, p. 125)[2]

St Thomas' understanding of the ground of the apostolate in the interior silence of contemplation is not merely something which he discovers on his own. Indeed there is a cloud of saints and sages who likewise discovered this. While certainly he discovered this in his own life, centuries earlier his confrère Jordan of Saxony, OSA, described the dynamics of silence in the common life of the friars. Jordan of Saxony remembers a speech from a former Prior General (Alexander of Sant' Elpidio), who reminded the Augustinians that the Holy Spirit inspired Augustinians to cultivate 'certain times and places in the monasteries and religious houses where silence should be observed. From this silence peace of mind is born'. The silence of which Jordan of Saxony speaks is not turned in on itself, 'but through silence a brother begins to cultivate and practice justice . . . . On the other hand, from the breakdown of silence arises disturbance of mind . . . quarrels are born, strife' (Jordan of Saxony, 1993, *Life of the Brethren*, p. 375).

For the Augustinian firmly grounded in the Order's tradition, silence is revealed to be something dynamic and integrated into the way of community life. Silence is generative of the peace of mind that is born, not as the opposite of turmoil, but as the developmental ground of both turmoil and tranquility. It gives birth to justice and resolves our problems and anxieties. In light of the dynamic silence that creates and fosters community and its overflow into the service of the people of God, one of the most influential among the Priors General of the Augustinians in the twentieth century, Theodore Tack, OSA, makes the claim (to some, outrageous) that 'the community is the very first apostolate which must concern every one of us Augustinians without exception. In other words, the community in itself is an apostolate of the first order, indeed our primary apostolate' (Theodore Tack 1979, pp. 151–2). In many ways this statement served as the pole star of the Order's rediscovery of its life and spirituality as it negotiated the renewal of religious life after the Second Vatican Council.

Conclusion

In light of what has been presented in the course of this examination of the spirituality of the Augustinians, it is easy to see why the Augustinians are considered 'the most contemplative among active orders and most active among the contemplative orders' (Bellini 1987–8).

For the Augustinians, contemplation is neither something tagged on to apostolic service nor something that stands in tension with the need to be harmonized with apostolic service. For the Augustinians contemplation is the fertile ground and creative possibility of service to the people of God. For this reason (and many more) the *Constitutions of the Order of St Augustine* insist that according to St Augustine (and indeed the great thrust of the tradition of the Order) the Augustinian 'ought to be dedicated essentially to a holy leisure with which his only ambition is to love God. . . . This holy leisure should not make us forget the love of neighbor, because love of God and neighbor form an indivisible unity in the thought of St Augustine' (*Constitutions*, 5). This fundamental dedication to 'holy leisure', a term St Augustine uses to describe a life of contemplation, bears apostolic witness to what the Augustinians give to the Church and the world:

> Gathered together as a community, the first service that we render to the Church and humanity as religious is witnessing to the experience of our

encounter with God through his Word and the events of history. This encounter occurs always when we freely recognize the presence of God who creates us and draws us unceasingly to himself. (*Constitutions*, #80)

Finally, what distinguishes the Augustinians from the other mendicant orders? This is no better stated than by the historian of spirituality, José Maria Moliner:

Unlike the friars of St Francis, the Augustinians sought the fullness of love not through poverty but through love itself. The Dominicans sought the love of God through the apostolate, the Carmelites through contemplation, and the Augustinians through love; of the four mendicant Orders only the Augustinians seek God directly without intermediary. Augustinians love in God the reality of unity wherein multiplicity is resolved, and union with God for them is something more than spiritual marriage; it is the transformation expressed by St Paul when he cried that he did not live but Christ lived in him. (José Maria Moliner, 1961)

Notes

1 Trans. M. Boulding (Villanova, PA: Augustinian Press).
2 Washington, DC: Augustinian Liturgical Committee, 1976.

Bibliography and Further Reading

Andrews, Frances (2006), *The Other Friars: Carmelite, Augustinian, Sack, and Pied Friars in the Middle Ages*. Woodbridge, UK: The Boydell Press.

St Augustine (1992), *The Works of Saint Augustine: A Translation for the 21st Century*. Hyde Park. New York: New City Press (translations altered slightly).

Back, Siegfried (1987). *The Pelican: A Life of St. Thomas of Villanova*, trans. Matthew J. O'Connell, Villanova, PA: Augustinian Press.

Bellini, Pietro OSA (1987–8), 'Our Roots', *Augustinian Heritage*, 33(2–3), 161–78.

Cipriani, Nello OSA (2009), *Molti e uno solo in Cristo: La spritualita di Agostino*. Rome: Citta Nuova (Translation my own).

Counihan, Cyril OSA (1983), 'Contemplation and Augustinian Common Life', *The Tagastan*, 29(1), 39–68.

Gutierrez, David OSA (1984), *History of the Augustinian Order*, 5 Vols, Vol 1. part I. *The Augustinians in the Middle Ages 1256–1356*, Villanova, PA: Augustinian Historical Institute.

Hackett, Benedict OSA (1992), *William Flete, OSA and Catherine of Siena: Masters of Fourteenth Century Spirituality*, trans. Arthur Ennis OSA. Villanova, PA: Augustinian Press.

Jordan of Saxony OSA (1993), *The Life of the Brethren*, trans. Gerard Deighan, Villanova, PA: Augustinian Press.

Lawless, George OSA (1987), *Augustine of Hippo and his Monastic Rule*. Oxford: Clarendon Press.

Martin, Thomas OSA (2003), *Our Restless Heart: The Augustinian Tradition*. London: Darton, Longman and Todd.

Mary, Agatha SPB (1991), *The Rule of Saint Augustine: An Essay in Understanding*. Villanova, PA: Augustinian Press.

Moliner, José Maria (1961), *Historia de la literatura mística en España*. Burgos: El Monte Carmelo.

O'Rourke, Benignus OSA (2010), *Finding your Buried Treasure*. Liguori, MO: Liguori Publications.

Prevost, Robert OSA (2007), *Acta Ordinis Sancti Augustini*, 57, pp. 24–7 (Translation my own).

Rano, Balbino OSA (1994), *Augustinian Origins, Charism, and Spirituality*. Villanova, PA: Augustinian Press.

Saak, Eric (2002), *High Way to Heaven: The Augustinian Platform between Reform and Reformation, 1292–1524*. Leiden: Brill.

Tack, Theodore OSA (1979), 'Augustinian Community and the Apostolate', in *Living in Freedom under Grace: Augustinian Spirit and Spirituality in the Writings of the Popes and Priors General (1953–1978)*, Rome: Curia Generalizia Agostiniana, pp. 151–2.

— (1988), *If Augustine were Alive: Augustine's Religious Ideals for Today*. Staten Island, NY: Alba House.

St Thomas of Villanova (1994), *Collected Sermons*. Villanova, PA: Augustinian Press.

Warren, Ann K. (1985), *Anchorites and their Patrons in Medieval England*. Berkeley: University of California Press.

Zumkeller, Adolar OSA (1986), *Augustine's Ideal of the Religious Life*, trans. Edmund Colledge OSA. New York, NY: Fordham University Press.

6 Monastic Spirituality

Laurentia Johns

Introduction

It is perhaps surprising that in highly secularized Europe at the start of the twenty-first century, two films about monks should have proved phenomenal box office attractions. But 'Into Great Silence',[1] the 3-hour – almost wordless – portrayal of Carthusian life, and 'Of Gods and Men',[2] the story of the Trappist martyrs of Tibhirine (d. 1996), are just two of the more prominent peaks on the landscape of interest in the monastic life which has been emerging over the past half century, attested, for example, by the burgeoning of retreats, monastic literature and various forms of new lay associations. In 2008, Benedictine Oblates (men and women who live the spirit of the Rule of St Benedict in everyday life), outnumbered monks and nuns by several thousands.[3]

What makes monastic spirituality so compelling to our age? In trying to offer some thoughts on this question, no attempt will be made to give a systematic history of monasticism (on which many studies already exist).[4] It should also be stated from the outset that the author is a Benedictine nun, and so writes from a faith perspective and, while hoping to include all those who take the Rule of St Benedict as guide and inspiration, cannot speak with any authority on the Carthusian[5] and Cistercian[6] traditions or the new expressions of communal monastic living which emerged in the twentieth century, for example at Taizé, Bose and the Fraternities of Jerusalem.[7] Rather, this chapter aims to identify some general monastic 'impulses' which have shaped a recognizable monastic 'movement' (mostly lived by monks and nuns) which in turn has given rise to a distinctive monastic spirituality (lived also, and in increasing numbers, by people outside monasteries). This spirituality may be briefly described as one of the heart, marked by a search for inner unity and balance; Christocentric, scripturally based, essentially practical; to some degree perceived as independent of institutional structures; characterized by an openness to the other expressed in hospitality, and therefore able to bridge divides within Christianity while reaching out to those of other faiths and none. The life, writings and death of the Trappist monk Thomas Merton (d. 1968) seem to embody many of these currents of monastic spirituality as well as fuelling its development, and may even provide an approximate dating for the moment when the more traditional monastic movement began to 'morph' into a spirituality. For while 'guests have never been lacking in monasteries', as the sixth-century Rule of St Benedict (RB) notes,[8] and throughout the subsequent centuries there has been a close symbiosis between monastics and other laypeople[9] at both the spiritual and economic levels (see, for example, the patronage-for-prayers exchange typical of the Middle Ages); and while further, there have been numerous experiments in living a quasi-monastic life in the world, ranging from Nicholas Ferrar's at Little Gidding in the seventeenth century to Dietrich Bonhoeffer's underground seminary at Finkenwalde during the Second World War, not until the second half of the twentieth century did the phenomenon of people taking selected elements of monasticism into their own spiritual lives become sufficiently prevalent as to warrant its own chapter in a guide such as this.

Early Monastic Impulses

Monasticism predates Christianity. Both Hinduism and especially Buddhism have strongly monastic characteristics: distinctive dress, diet and some form of life commitment usually lived out in separation from mainstream society in pursuit of the absolute, for which sake a range of ascetical practices is embraced. But even some indigenous cultures exhibit what we might label 'monastic' features: communities of virgins are known to have existed in Peru under the Incas and also form part of the traditions of the Iroquois of North America.[10]

The existence of a universal monastic archetype which informs the struggle of all seekers, whether or not they are monks or nuns in a formal sense, has been expounded by Raimundo Panikkar.[11] Consciously or otherwise, individuals flocking to see our monastic films may have been driven, at some deep level, by such a primordial force towards the transcendent. When, as in the Christian tradition, the transcendent is believed to be a Trinity of persons forming one Godhead whose characteristics the seeker is thought to reflect, the nature and context of the search for unity cannot but be marked by a certain ambiguity with which the very word 'monastic' is loaded. For St Basil of Caesarea (d. 379), a strong proponent of community life, to apply the word *monastikon* to Christian life of any sort was a nonsense.[12] *Monos*, from which 'monastic' is derived, carries at least two strands of meaning. The original Greek could mean 'simple' or 'unified' as well as the more familiar notion of 'one', 'single' or 'alone'. At times, both meanings seem to come together, as for example when used to translate *īhīdāyā* ('holy single ones'), for those early Christians in Syria who chose to remain celibate for the love of Christ, initially in their own homes. In other words, staying 'single' for Christ was a positive, single-minded choice made for love which drew the individual into a bond of communion. Thus the term 'monastic' would later be applied to men and women living in communities as well as to those pursuing a more eremitical path as hermits, while always remaining part of the wider Body of Christ, the Church. So while the idea of the monk as isolated monad seeking the absolute alone is not totally off the mark, such a notion narrows the scope of the concept and can lead to stereotyping or even caricature.[13] Yet the resilience of the 'monos' word into our own day[14] does suggest its power to evoke something of the universal monastic archetype outlined above, that irreducible 'I' which constitutes at least a part of the human condition wired to seek unity with the divine in a single-minded search, or to use another monastic phrase, to seek 'purity of heart'. It may be helpful, then, to think of the 'monos' tag more in terms of the nature and intensity of this search and its goal of unity than about a specific state of life. Adherents of Christian monastic spirituality today are drawn from the ranks of the married as well as the celibate, and both always within a wider context of community relationships.[15]

The Jerusalem Community: Primary Impulse

All roads on the monastic spirituality map lead back, not to Rome, but to Jerusalem, to the early community of believers[16] in Christ described in the New Testament Book of Acts.[17] Comprising initially the apostles and a small band of Jesus's close followers, including his mother, Mary, and the women disciples, this group met regularly to pray and, galvanized by the gifts of the Holy Spirit at Pentecost, began to attract large numbers of converts:

> These remained faithful to the teaching of the Apostles, the brotherhood, the breaking of bread and the prayers . . . All who shared the faith owned everything in common; they sold their goods and possessions and distributed the proceeds among themselves according to need. Each day, with one heart and mind, they regularly went to the Temple but met in their houses for the breaking of bread. (Acts 2.42–27)

This proto-Christian community, characterized by a life in common, the pooling of resources, shared prayer at intervals throughout the day (after the pattern of the Jewish Temple services) and bound together by commitment to the mandate of Christ to live out the Gospel precepts of love of God and of neighbour, forms both the primary impulse for, and the model of, all subsequent monastic endeavours. For example, in the fifth century, St John Cassian (d. 435) in seeking to 'market' desert monasticism to monasteries in Southern France, holds up as an example the primitive Jerusalem community[18] and, by the same token of apostolic authenticity, names Alexandria (perhaps founded by St Mark) as the seed-bed of monastic life in Egypt.[19] A century after Cassian,

St Benedict makes a similar connection in his Rule: 'when they [monks] live by the labour of their hands, as our fathers and the apostles did, then they are truly monks'.[20] Monastic reformers in the high Middle Ages claimed the same pedigree, defining monastic life as a realization of the apostolic life: the *vita apostolica*.[21] So when, for example, Rupert of Deutz (d. 1129) describes the apostles themselves as 'monks', although he is using a cart-before-horse style anachronism, the logic is nonetheless apparent.

Inherent from the start in the early Church are tensions as to how this new Gospel way of life should be lived: implicit tensions between, for example, the demands of a stable life of prayer and of missionary activity or, as became clear early on, more explicit tensions between the exigencies of preaching and of charitable work.[22]

Martyrdom, another key strand informing the monastic impulse, resolves these opposing pulls in an act which combines the self-offering of prayer with a powerful witness[23] to Christ's Gospel values of non-retaliation[24] and can therefore be seen to be both missionary/apostolic as well as stable/contemplative.[25] 'The blood of the martyrs is the seed of Christians'[26] as Tertullian (d. 225) wrote, and he might have added, 'the seed of the monastic impulse'. Traditionally, monastic life has been called a 'white' or bloodless form of martyrdom. In the story of the martyrs of Tibhirine is thus embedded a double-strength symbol of lives given for God and neighbour – perhaps another clue to the power of this film.

From Impulse to Movement

By the time St Athanasius (d. 373) wrote his best-selling *Life of the Desert Father, St Antony the Great of Egypt* (often styled the Father of Monasticism) in the middle of the fourth century, knowledge of this 'new [monastic] life'[27] had spread throughout the Mediterranean from Spain to Italy as well as into North Africa: the disparate monastic impulses had become a movement, a widespread, discernible trend of people consciously quitting conventional bonds of family, society and culture to seek God in a life of withdrawal (*anachōrēsis*), simplicity and poverty. By 'movement' is not implied any centrally organized, premeditated enterprise but rather a grass-roots phenomenon, rising up simultaneously in centres like Egypt, Syria and Asia Minor, and gaining momentum as if by gravitational attraction. Both in geographical extent and sheer numbers involved (thousands went into the Egyptian desert) it is difficult for the modern mind, conditioned perhaps to think of the monk as an isolated marginal figure, to conceive of such a groundswell. Certainly there is paradox in a mass movement seeking 'withdrawal' on such a scale. Perhaps the interest in monastic spirituality we see in our day gives an inkling of this earlier force and points to similar underlying causes. While this phenomenal blossoming of the monastic movement in the fourth century cannot be adequately accounted for or explained by any single cause,[28] that very many, if not all of the individuals caught up into the swell of monastic living in these early centuries were responding to a call from God, cannot be ruled out.

The Rule of St Benedict

The chances are very high that anyone (including our filmgoers) who comes into contact with monastic spirituality today will do so either directly or indirectly through the lens of the Rule of St Benedict (RB), a mediaeval document of incalculable importance in the shaping of the culture initially of Europe and subsequently of the Americas, Australasia, large parts of Africa and even of Asia (though the Rules of St Basil have generally been more prevalent in the East). The influence of the RB can be seen outside the specifically religious sphere, extending, for example, to agriculture (the Cistercians in particular, through extensive sheep farming, changed the face of vast tracts of land in Northern Europe) and even to academia as monasteries were primary centres of learning (the monastic cowl has influenced the traditional academic dress of universities). Written in Latin by Benedict when he was abbot of Monte Cassino in Italy in the first half of the sixth century (and originally therefore for monks),[29] the Rule distils, in fewer than a hundred pages, three centuries of monastic wisdom from the desert tradition as conveyed to the West mainly by St John Cassian, as well as the teachings of other monastic founders such as St Augustine (d. 430) and St Basil. Thoroughly Biblical (about half the Rule is made up of quotations from scripture), it synthesizes these more obviously monastic sources with works of Church figures such as St Cyprian (d. 258) and the fifth-century pope, St Leo the Great (d. 461),[30] while always presenting the Gospel of Jesus Christ as the monk's supreme guide.

For their part, the three Benedictine vows[31] distil the spirit of the Rule. Unique to Benedictines, the vow of stability binds monastics to a particular community for life. The spiritual value underpinning this vow, stability of heart, clearly has something to offer our society where any sort of commitment seems difficult to sustain. The vow of obedience, common to all Western religious orders, is really about listening (in Latin 'to obey' and 'to listen' share a common etymology), about openness of heart. Stability and obedience converge in the third vow, also specifically Benedictine, and practically impossible to translate: *conversatio morum*, a promise to live the monastic life in all its demands and to let that life change you. The three vows interrelate: a difficult obedience may tempt a monk or nun to want out, but stability binds them to the task of conversion (*metanoia*, change of heart).

Within a generation of its appearance, the RB was described by Pope St Gregory the Great (d. 604) as 'remarkable for its discretion and clarity'.[32] This, together with its all-pervading humanity (provision is made for all manner of human weakness from particular dietary needs to outbursts of aggression), has contributed to the document's survival and diffusion. Becoming normative in the ninth century for monasteries within the Empire of Charlemagne, the Rule had spread to England even earlier, thanks largely to the influence of St Wilfrid of York (d. 709). Subsequent monastic reforms in England in the tenth century ensured that the Benedictine ethos became ever more closely woven into the fabric of society, especially through the monastic cathedrals, institutions peculiar to England.[33]

A key factor in the spread and survival of the RB is its flexibility. While firm on essential precepts: nothing is to be preferred to the love of Christ; the kingdom of God is to be sought first; peace is to be the monks' quest and aim,[34] Benedict gives considerable scope for the arrangement of the details of everyday life: clothing, meal-times, psalm-schemes may and should be adapted to suit local needs. The very diversity which such flexibility in living the Rule has encouraged makes it virtually impossible to describe a single 'Benedictine Spirituality'. What is more feasible, and will be attempted here, is to discern common elements which bind together those who find in the Rule of St Benedict an inspiration for living the Gospel, whether they be monastics of more missionary Congregations such as St Ottilien of Tutzing or the English Benedictine Congregation; those whose mission is lived out mainly within the monastery (while its influence extends beyond) such as members of the Solesmes or Subiaco Congregations or those trying to incarnate Benedict's version of monastic spirituality in the world.

Some Common Elements in Ways of Living the Rule of St Benedict

Concise, clear and adaptable as the Rule is, these qualities alone – which, after all, are shared by any good recipe book – cannot account for its far-reaching influence throughout 1,500 years. It is rather as a guidebook to sanctity that this text owes its place as a classic of Christian Spirituality, and which has increasingly recommended it to seekers outside the formally vowed life of the monastery.[35] Written originally for those more consciously searching for God, it speaks in every age to the deepest yearnings of the human heart, though in our day seekers may not be so aware of exactly what they are seeking, and are as likely to be drawn by a perceived need for 'peace', 'space' or 'sanctuary' rather than that desert place fundamental to monastic spirituality and in which prayer – a personal encounter with God – can be nurtured.

Creating Space for Encounters with God, Neighbour and Stranger

The genius of the Rule is the way it makes the lofty goal of communion with God attainable, or rather, by a combination of outer observances/structures helps form in the practitioner those dispositions which facilitate the reception of God's gift which is the Holy Spirit, leading to inner integrity, unification and peace.[36] The primary common element, then, in any spirituality claiming to be Benedictine/monastic (in the West at least, and bearing in mind the history sketched above, the two are virtually synonymous) must be this desire for God, made concrete in a disciplined life of personal prayer, fostered by periods of withdrawal (*anachōrēsis*) and silence. The names of Dom John Main (d. 1982) and Dom Laurence Freeman are among the most well-known in channelling this river of contemplative prayer outside monasteries, following in the slipstream of Father Augustine Baker (d. 1641), the renowned monk of the English Benedictine Congregation whose treatises on prayer were written for both monastic and layfolk outside monasteries and continue to inspire both today.[37] In this space carved out by prayer may also be situated Benedictine hospitality, an openness to the stranger and the basis for all dialogue. Again our Tibhirine martyrs exemplify, to the highest degree, such openness growing from prayer. Bl. John Paul II captured this facet of monastic spirituality in a memorable passage:

> In the heart of the Church and the world, monasteries have been and continue to be eloquent signs of communion, welcoming abodes for those seeking God and things of the spirit, schools of faith and true places of study, dialogue and culture for the building up of the Church and of the earthly city itself, in expectation of the heavenly city. (*Vita Consecrata*, 6)

Shaping Lives

Benedictine life is famously ordered and structured (RB 15 even indicates when 'alleluia' should be said). This reflects not so much an obsessive preoccupation with tidiness but rather imitation of a God who brings order out of chaos[38] and who has placed humankind in an ordered cosmos (the Greek original implies an ordered world). St Benedict devotes 12 detailed chapters in his Rule to the arrangement of the worship of the community, the *Opus Dei* (Work of God), and it is this regular corporate worship – liturgical prayer – which is often regarded as the distinctive trait of the Benedictine: nothing is to be put before the Work of God.[39]

Rooted in the Jewish Temple worship[40] and heavily weighted, in the tradition of the desert monastics, towards psalm singing/recitation, on one level these regular pauses for worship spaced throughout the day (a practice shared, of course, by those of the Muslim faith) respect the natural rhythms of sunrise, midday and sunset. But the main purpose in Christian monasticism is a Christocentric one: in conjunction with the Eucharistic celebration, to recall and celebrate the life, death and resurrection of Jesus Christ and to incorporate each monk/nun/oblate more deeply into Christ's Paschal Mystery. Thus the whole Benedictine year and timetable revolve around Easter, of which Sunday is the weekly remembrance and the morning service of Lauds the daily one. Those who try to practise these hours of liturgical prayer tend to find such prayer a helpful counterbalance to the pace of modern life in which work can so easily dominate and even 'leisure' has the tendency to become frenetic.[41] Above all, worship restores the right relationship between creature and Creator.[42] At the start of the Third Millennium, and in keeping with their heritage as stewards of the land, Benedictines across the globe are taking seriously the environmental challenges of our day.[43]

Grounded in the Word of God

Monastic spirituality is essentially pragmatic. How can any Christian Spirituality so grounded in the Word which became flesh at the Incarnation be anything else? In a spirituality marked by a profound interrelationship between exterior observance and interior disposition, ideally, as RB 19.7 states, monastic minds (for 'mind' read 'heart') and voices should be in harmony: a symbol of how the interior and exterior should mesh in all fields of action. But Benedict was a realist, and while no Pelagian,[44] accepts, in the spirit of the desert tradition, that holiness is a task to be worked on while always a gift. Significantly, one of the editorial changes he made to the fifth-century Rule of the Master[45] which formed the template for his own Rule, was to rename the chapter on 'The Spiritual Art' as 'The Tools for Good Works' (RB 4).[46] Silence, fasting, vigilance, prayer, moderation in all things, can and should be actively cultivated. At the end of chapter 7 'On Humility', which concludes the more specifically spiritual section of the Rule, we see the other side of the equation: a pen portrait of the monk whose outward appearance has been gradually transfigured by the inner working of the Holy Spirit so that he appears free from fear, an incarnation of real love.

The compass of this chapter does not allow for a detailed treatment of the whole gamut of monastic practices and attitudes.[47] Instead, one overarching monastic attitude: reverence, and one practice: *lectio divina,*[48] will be taken as paradigmatic.

Reverence

Although it is possible to classify some parts of the Rule as more spiritual than others, it is axiomatic of the Benedictine ethos that there is no unbreachable divide between the material and spiritual and that 'in all things, God should be glorified'.[49] A profound reverence for God (the Old Testament 'fear of the Lord') and all creation, including one's fellow creatures, permeates the Rule and both engenders and springs from an attitude of humility: truthful respect for the created order so that even the 'mundane' tools and utensils of the monastery are to be treated with the same care as sacred altar vessels.[50] Such a sacramental view of created matter extends also to time – another created construct – and includes a healthy regard for personal needs, especially those of the most vulnerable. Drawn up in an era when slavery was the norm, the Rule upholds the essential freedom and dignity of the human person in a way that is no less necessary in the twenty-first century where the enslaving forces may be more subtle, including, for example, the pace of modern life, the pressures of too much or too little work and of the media, both old and new.[51]

Lectio Divina

Taking a broad sweep over the past half a millennium, certain 'moments' may be discerned when a particular monastic practice seems to have had a particular influence on broader tracts of the Church in response to currents in society at large. Thus, the twin engines of contemplative prayer and commitment to conversion to Roman Catholicism which marked the refounded English Benedictine Congregation during the seventeenth century can be seen as responses fitting a time of crisis and persecution, while the mid-nineteenth/twentieth-century Gothic revival, characterized by a reflowering across the Church, largely under the influence of monastic persons,[52] of mediaeval practices such as plainchant, was clearly in step with the re-establishment in Europe, after the revolutionary upheavals of the eighteenth century, of more traditional values and institutional forms which had been proscribed. We may be too close to events of our own time to reach an accurate assessment but it is perhaps not fanciful to see *lectio divina*, as the monastic practice which the needs of our age seem to be drawing to the fore. Certainly, there can be no doubting the veritable explosion of publications,[53] internet resources, conferences and retreats on the subject over the past 20 years.[54]

Predating monasticism, exposure to the 'voice' and words of God is as ancient as the Jewish and Christian revelations themselves, while to hear and to read the Gospel proclamation is constitutive of Christianity. What in Benedict's day was simply a part, albeit a significant one, of the monk's day, has today almost become a spirituality in its own right.[55] Notable for this is the Manquehue Apostolic Movement founded by José Manuel Eguiguren in Chile in 1977 and which has since spread to other parts of the world. The Movement, which grew out of Benedictines, links since cemented by a juridical bond, has developed a whole way of life based around *lectio divina* usually done in groups.[56]

The regular, attentive, prayerful listening to the Word of God, both as proclaimed publicly in the liturgy and inwardly appropriated by personal reading, *lectio divina* is not so much a technique as an attitude, or rather, a cluster of attitudes which can be seen as a nexus of monastic spirituality's main features: a respect for silence and that openness to 'the other' already mentioned which presupposes humility, docility and a willingness to be challenged. The

Word of God acts as a lamp, lighting up the dark areas of the heart and gradually purifying and illumining them. Together with prayer and the sacraments, the practice of *lectio divina* helps, over time, to refashion in the practitioner the likeness of Christ, the Word himself. The ancient craft of refining precious metals by removing surface dross until the face of the refiner appeared on the metal's surface captures something of this mysterious inner process.[57] As the antithesis of so many of the aspects of life in the West – the overwhelming speed of computer technology, the perceived need to 'master' information as well as informational overload – the practice of *lectio divina* may be working as an antidote to some of the more negative aspects of contemporary culture. At a deeper level still, should we be surprised that a world created through the Word of God[58] and evangelized through the preaching of the Word should, in what many claim to be a post-Christian era, be reinvigorated for evangelization, reevangelized or even evangelized for the first time by that same Word? In an age marked by increasing social fragmentation, isolation and interior psychological breakdown, the power of the Word of God to effect interior healing and to draw people together can surely be considered a factor in assessing the current attraction to monastic spirituality as a whole and to *lectio divina* in particular.

Conclusions

All the above yet begs the question: is there anything predicated of monastic spirituality which does not apply to Christian Spirituality as a whole? Is the 'Benedictine' attitude to created matter outlined above really any different from the sacramental theology of the Church? What is particularly distinctive about monastic spirituality? A perceptive observer[59] has noted of Benedictines (and therefore, *mutatis mutandis,* of all living under the influence of the Rule) that they farm but are not professional farmers, teach while not being primarily teachers, run parishes but are not, in the first place, parish priests. He goes on to suggest that their primary purpose is to bear witness to the transcendence of God. Benedictine monastic spirituality absolutizes nothing but God. The balance, moderation, sense of proportion which characterize the Rule of St Benedict derive fundamentally from placing everything else in relation to the one absolute: God alone. This harks back to the 'monos' imperative which, as we have seen, finds its roots in the human heart and the Early Church.

Are we to see, then, in the rise of monastic spirituality nothing more – nor less – than a reclamation by the lay faithful of that integrated, community-based, generative, whole-of-life-embracing way of living the Gospel which marked the earliest followers of Christ?[60] Significant sections of monastic rules such as the Rule of St Benedict seem to derive from pre-monastic, early Christian sources. For example, RB 4 resonates strongly with the earliest known Christian rule of life *The Didache* and sections of the Prologue of the RB are thought to have been initially baptismal catechesis material.[61]

Is the spread of monastic spirituality to be viewed as the outworking of the monastic charism through the Church as yeast leavens dough? Parallels might be drawn with the 'greening' of mainstream politics/society from an initially smaller band of more extreme environmentalists. If so, are we to expect the emergence of newer forms of a more intense monasticism – another flight to another desert? Or will a new era of martyrdom serve to test the authenticity of current adherents of monastic spirituality?[62]

In his classic book *After Virtue*[63] philosopher Alisdair MacIntyre stated that the West was awaiting a new – and probably very different – Benedict to rescue it from the current Dark Age. Perhaps what the rise in monastic spirituality indicates is that the monastic wisdom enshrined in the original Rule of St Benedict is sufficient for the task if taken up in new ways and contexts, new contexts which can, however, continue to draw inspiration from traditional expressions of monastic life when lived with the same degree of faithfulness as that shown by the Tibhirine martyrs.

Notes

1 Philip Gröning, 2005.
2 Xavier Beauvois, 2010.
3 c. 26,000 Benedictine Oblates (2008), Source: International Benedictine Oblates' Website, www.benedictine-oblates.org/mondo-en.php.
   Benedictine monks, c. 7, 700 (2005); nuns and sisters, c. 15, 400 (2006). Source, *Benedictine Yearbook, 2011*. Combined monks & nuns = c. 23, 100.
4 M. De Dreuille OSB (1999), *From East to West: A History of Monasticism*. Leominster: Gracewing; P. King (1999), *Western Monasticism: A History of the Monastic Movement in the Latin Church*. Kalamazoo: Cistercian Studies 185; For England & Wales, D. H. Farmer (ed.) (1980), *Benedict's Disciples*. Leominster: Fowler Wright.
5 The Carthusian Order was founded by St Bruno in 1084 at la Grande Chartreuse, near Grenoble, France.
6 The Cistercian Order was founded at Citeaux, France, by Robert of Molesme, Alberic of Citeaux and Stephen Harding in 1098.
7 The now worldwide Taizé movement was founded at Taizé in France by Br Roger Schutz in 1940. The Monastic Community of Bose, North Italy, was founded by Enzo Bianchi in 1965. Both are international and ecumenical. Br Pierre-Marie Delfieux founded the Monastic Fraternities of Jerusalem in Paris in 1975. All three emphasize dialogue and peace.
8 RB 53.16. All references to the Rule of St Benedict, unless otherwise stated, are from *RB 1980: The Rule of St Benedict in Latin and English with Notes*, (1980), ed. Timothy Fry OSB. The Liturgical Press: Collegeville.
9 The monastic state itself is lay as opposed to clerical. The picture is complicated by the fact that some monks are also priests.
10 See Joseph-François Lafitau SJ, *Customs of the American Indians Compared with the Customs of Primitive Times* (1974–7), Fenton and Moore (eds). Toronto: The Champlain Society. See also 'Christian Spirituality in America' below.

11 R. Panikkar (1982), *Blessed Simplicity*. New York: Seabury Press. See also chapter on Hinduism and Christianity in this volume.

12 See St Basil's Longer Rule 7, pp. 139–43 in A. Holmes (2000), *A Life Pleasing to God*. London: Darton, Longman and Todd.

13 An example of this misperception of the monastic state is found in the well-known and otherwise insightful passage from E. M. Forster's novel, *Howards End* (1910):

> 'Only connect the prose and the passion, and both will be exalted, and human love will be seen at its highest. Live in fragments no longer. Only connect, and the beast and the monk, robbed of the isolation that is life to either, will die' (p. 188, Penguin version).

> Possibly monastics have not always been very good at portraying themselves as 'connected' parts of the wider body of the Church.

14 'Monos' is the name of a centre for the study of monastic culture and spirituality launched in Britain in 2004. Lay-led, it espouses the so-called new or secular monasticism lived by people outside monasteries.

15 For more on the etymology of *monos,* see RB 1980, op. cit., pp. 305–13.

16 The term 'Christian' was first used at Antioch. See Acts 11.26.

17 See Acts 1.14; 4.32–5; 5.12–16.

18 See Conference XVIII: 5 and Conf. XXI: 30 in *John Cassian: The Conferences,* trans. and annotated by Boniface Ramsey OP (1997). New York: Newman Press.

19 See Book 2: V, 1 in *John Cassian: The Institutes,* trans. Boniface Ramsey OP (2000). New York: Newman Press.

20 RB 48.8

21 See, for example, St Nilus (d. 1005) of Grottaferrata, St Romuald (d. 1025/27) and the Camaldolese hermit monks and St John Gualbert (d. 1073) of the Vallombrosians, Florence.

22 See Acts 6. The tension can also be found in the Gospel where Christ calls his disciples both to be with him *and* to go out to preach the good news – on one level mutually exclusive demands. See Mark 3.13.

23 The Greek original means both 'witness' and 'martyr'.

24 See Mt. 5.38–42.

25 The relationship between consecrated life and mission is more integrated than perhaps generally considered. Pope Pius XI, in making the enclosed contemplative Carmelite St Thérèse of Lisieux a patron of missionaries, highlighted their essential unity. See also Pope John Paul II, *Vita Consecrata*, para. 25:

> 'The sense of mission is at the very heart of every form of consecrated life. To the extent that consecrated persons live a life completely devoted to the Father, held fast by Christ and animated by the Holy Spirit, they cooperate effectively in the mission of the Lord Jesus and contribute in a particularly profound way to the renewal of the world'.

26 Apologeticus, 50.

27 St Augustine uses the term 'new life' on first hearing of St Antony. See his *Confessions,* Book VIII, 6 which also indicates how the *Life of Antony* was instrumental in the diffusion of the monastic ideal.

28 For a useful summary of possible reasons for the growth in monasticism, ranging from persecution to tax evasion, see Burton-Christie, D. (1993), *The Word in the Desert*. Oxford: Oxford University Press, pp. 3–7.

29 Women have followed the Rule of St Benedict from earliest times. The notion that monks live in monasteries while nuns inhabit convents is only partly correct. Nuns

who follow the monastic way live in monasteries; sisters of the Apostolic Orders which blossomed in the nineteenth century live in convents (or since the Second Vatican Council often in small houses in the community) though technically the term *conventus* refers to the gathered community members of a religious order and applies as much to male as to female religious: thus 'conventual' duties for both monks and nuns.

30 See especially RB 49.
31 RB 58.
32 St Gregory the Great, *The Dialogues*, Bk II, 36.
33 See Farmer (1980), 6–10.
34 See RB 4.21 and 72.11; RB 2.35; RB Prologue, 17.
35 See Jamison, C. (2006), *Finding Sanctuary: Monastic Steps for Daily Life*. London: Weidenfeld & Nicolson, published in the wake of the BBC television series, 'The Monastery'.
36 Enzo Bianchi defines the goal of the monastic life as the acquisition of the Holy Spirit. See 'The Holy Spirit in monastic life' (2002), *Cistercian Studies Quarterly*, 37(2), 153–66.
37 A conference held at Abergavenny in 2000 to mark the quatercentenary of Fr Baker's conversion drew large numbers of people from a broad spectrum of backgrounds. See *That Mysterious Man*, (2001), ed. M. Woodward. Abergavenny: Three Peaks Press.
38 See Gen. 1.1–5.
39 RB 43.3.
40 See Chapter 1 by Margaret Barker.
41 For more on 'space' in the RB see chapters 20, 48 and 53.
42 Some see the conscious re-establishment of humanity's role as the priestly voice of creation as the most profound, long-lasting and effective 'green' insurance policy. While this 'priestly' vocation is perhaps more clearly articulated in the Orthodox tradition, there is also something deeply Benedictine about it (cf. RB 31.10). See John Zizioulas, 'Proprietors or Priests of Creation?', given at the Baltic Symposium in 2003: www.rsesymposia.org/themedia/File/1151679350-Pergamon.pdf, and Chapter 7 by John Chryssavgis in this volume.
43 See 'Benedictines and the environment' by James Wiseman OSB in *The Benedictine Year Book 2009* and 'Stanbrook moving on' by Scholastica Jacob OSB, pp. 39–42 in the 2010 edition of same publication.
44 Pelagius (end of fourth to mid-fifth centuries) may have been a British monk. His teaching on the relative weightings of grace and human effort in the economy of salvation has traditionally been thought to underplay grace.
45 For more on the relationship of the RB and the Rule of the Master (RM) see *RB 1980*, op. cit., pp. 70–3.
46 The contemporary spiritual writer, Mary Margaret Funk OSB, has made use of the 'tools' analogy in her works, for example, *Tools Matter for Practicing the Spiritual Life* (2004). London: Continuum.
47 For a more extensive treatment of monastic practices, see Charles Cummings OCSO (1986), *Monastic Practices*, CS 75. MI: Cistercian Studies.
48 Literally 'Holy Reading'. A slow and meditative digestion of a spoken text.
49 RB 57.9. This phrase has also become significant in Ignatian Spirituality, see Chapter 13.
50 RB 31.10.
51 For more on Benedictine attitudes to work see Dollard, K., A. Marrett-Crosby OSB, T. Wright OSB (2002), *Doing Business with Benedict*. London: Continuum.

52 See contributions of Benedictines, Dame Laurentia McLachlan, Dom Pothier, Dom Mocquereau, in *In a Great Tradition,* by the Benedictines of Stanbrook (1956). London: John Murray, ch. 7.

53 Some of the more notable contributions include, M. Casey OCSO (1996), *Sacred Reading.* Missouri: Liguori; D. Foster OSB (2005), *Reading with God.* London: Continuum; M. M. Funk OSB (2010), *Lectio Matters.* London: Continuum.

54 A conference on *lectio divina* organized by the Lay Community of St Benedict and held at Worth Abbey in July 2009 filled the spacious auditorium of the school theatre. The participants came from all walks of life, mostly lay, and spanned a wide range of ages.

55 In the Rule there is no separate chapter on *lectio divina* which falls within RB 48 'On the daily manual labour', while 'listen readily to holy readings' is a tool of good works, RB 4.55.

56 See *The Benedictine Year Book 2006* for an article on the Manquehue Movement by Jonathan Perry.

57 Cf. Mal. 3.3

58 See Gen. 1; Ps. 33. 6; Jn 1.1–3.

59 Timothy Radcliffe OP (2001), 'The Throne of God', address to the World Congress of Benedictine Abbots in Rome September 2000, pub. in *I Call You Friends,* Continuum.

60 One of the earliest names for the followers of Jesus was 'people of The Way'.

61 See *The Rule of Benedict* (1994), notes and commentary by G. Holzherr, translated Glenstal. Dublin: Four Courts Press, pp. 28–31.

62 If such an era has not already begun. Figures released in 2011 by the Organization for Security and Cooperation in Europe state that every year 105,000 Christians are killed because of their faith, that is, a martyr every 5 minutes.

63 A. MacIntyre (1981), *After Virtue.* London: Duckworth.

Bibliography and Further Reading

Bianchi, Enzo E. (2002), 'The Holy Spirit in monastic life', in *Cistercian Studies Quarterly,* 37, 2.

Boulding, M. (2010), *Gateway to Resurrection,* London: Continuum. See esp. ch. 5, 'Monastic Journeying'.

Casey, M. (1996), *Sacred Reading: the Ancient Art of Lectio Divina.* MO: Liguori.

Cummings, C. (1986), *Monastic Practices.* MI: Cistercian Studies.

De Waal, E. (1984), *Seeking God: The Way of St Benedict.* London: Collins.

Foster, D. OSB (2007), *Deep Calls to Deep: Going Further in Prayer.* London: Continuum.

Grimley, A. and Wooding, J. M. (2010), *Living the Hours: Monastic Spirituality in Everyday Life.* London: Canterbury.

Jamison, C. (2006), *Finding Sanctuary.* London: Weidenfeld & Nicolson.

Leclercq, J. (1961), *The Love of Learning and the Desire for God.* New York: Fordham.

RB 1980: The Rule of St Benedict in Latin and English with Notes (1980), ed. Timothy Fry OSB, Collegeville: The Liturgical Press.

7 Orthodox Spirituality

John Chryssavgis

Introduction

Recently, I was privileged to accompany His All-Holiness Ecumenical Patriarch Bartholomew on one of his annual pilgrimages to Cappadocia, a region in central Anatolia of Turkey, where geology and theology merge to create a spectacular exhibit of awe and beauty. The exaggerated and extraordinary rock formations offered a unique insight into the breadth and depth of the Orthodox Christian spiritual world view as informed by iconography, liturgy and prayer. From St Basil the Great (330–79), who was bishop of Cappadocia in the fourth century and shaped the liturgical canon as well as the monastic rule of the early Eastern Church, to St Arsenios Hadzis (1840–1924), who was a simple parish priest in Farasa and profoundly influenced the revival of Mt Athos in the twentieth century, through the centuries this region boasts a myriad of saints, martyrs, ascetics and righteous men and women, who have generated a distinctive piety and spirituality.

A New Heaven: Through the Lens of the Icon

Perhaps the most overwhelming experience of Orthodox iconography was the visit to the 'dark church' (or *karanlik kilise*), located in the Göreme open-air museum, which has been on the Unesco World Heritage List since 1984. As the darkness of the sixth-century cave church inevitably surrendered to the dim ray of candlelight, an entire world opened up with the magnificent eleventh-century Byzantine frescoes, probably painted by imperial artists of the time and arguably paralleling the elegant artwork of Haghia Sophia and Chora Monastery.

Indeed, a monk praying inside the 'dark church' would be unaware whether it was night or day outside, just as he would not comprehend whether he was on earth or in heaven, 'being caught up to the third heaven, whether in the body or out of the body, only God knows' (1 Cor. 12.2). This monk would have shared the same experience as every Orthodox Christian that enters a church in the twenty-first century. He would have beheld the world through the lens of the icons, the most striking and immediate impression for anyone entering an Orthodox church. For the icon is a touchstone of Orthodox Spirituality.

Icons are precisely the way Orthodox Christians perceive the world and evoke the presence of grace. In the words of St Basil: 'The honor attributed to the icon transfers directly to the prototype'.[1] The vision and veneration of an icon become an immediate and intimate encounter between the believer and the depiction, reflected in the mysticism of the solitary burning of a candle and the movement of the dense cloud of incense that fill every Orthodox church.

An icon, then, offers new insights into heaven and earth, God and world. Without icons, we remain self-centered, shut out from the breadth of heaven, bereft of any communication with the beyond. We are inexorably locked within the restricted confines of our individual interests, without access to the world of mystery. The icon opens up a fuller, spiritual vision; it offers a 'different way of life', as an Orthodox Easter hymn professes.

The icon restores the sacred covenant between ourselves and God. It aspires to the inner, eternal vision of all people and all things. It reconciles heaven and earth. It dismisses any objective distance between this world and the next, between material and spiritual, between body and soul, time and eternity, creation and divinity. Beyond the spoken and written word, the icon proposes the language of the kingdom. Indeed, when a eleventh-century monk in the 'dark church' recited the words of the fourth-century Nicene Creed – 'I expect the life of the age-to-come' – he would undoubtedly have recognized how the 'end times' (or *eschata*) inform the present times, how the 'omega' gives meaning to the 'alpha', how this world is intimately related to and properly interpreted through the heavenly reality. The myth about heaven's existence would have dissolved; the lie that heaven is elsewhere would have been exposed.

There are two ways in which an icon achieves this. The first is through its powerful and profound personal perspective. All icons depict faces in full, frontal view, with two eyes always gazing back at the beholder, even when the saint pictured is facing to the side. Faces in Orthodox icons are traditionally frontal, all eyes receptive of and susceptive to divine grace. 'I see' signifies 'I am seen', which in turn implies that I am in communion. The second way is through the dimension of light, which 'knows no evening', according to another Orthodox hymn. Thus, events depicted in the nighttime are no darker than events portrayed in the daytime. The icon of the resurrection is no brighter than the icon of the crucifixion.

The lens of the icon also informs us that we are but a small detail of the world around us, that we are not mere or passive spectators in time and the universe, that we are *in* the world, though not *of* the world (Jn 17.14 and 16). Thus, we are no longer afraid of the world (Jn 16.33), we no longer feel threatened or as strangers in the world and are active participants in the world.

Finally, although a medieval monk standing at prayer inside the 'dark church' may not have been deeply instructed on the eighth-century iconoclastic controversies surrounding religious images, he would, nevertheless, definitely have been deeply informed about the inseparable connection between theology and iconography. Indeed, the doctrine of the incarnation – the conviction that 'the divine word assumed human flesh' (Jn 1.14) – lies at the very heart of Orthodox iconography. It is the teaching that, in Christ, the uncreated God acquires a human face; it is the assurance that God is 'Emmanuel, which means in our midst' (Mt. 1.23).

In Orthodox theology, doctrines are signposts, or icons – pointers on the journey towards heaven. This is why doctrine is sometimes referred to as symbolical, as a symbol of the word of God. Doctrine is a 'logical icon' of the living God, a doxological expression of a mystical experience. It is no wonder that, for the Orthodox, the *lex credendi* is inseparably connected to the *lex orandi*. And it is hardly surprising that St John of Damascus, the foremost champion of icons, would claim: 'We do not change the everlasting boundaries set by our fathers, but we keep the tradition as we have received it'.[2] His treatise on icons is regarded as a standard in the Orthodox Church, where the educated scholar and the unsophisticated believer alike appreciate the silent energy and authority of the icon. In fact, there are certain 'silent' doctrinal traditions, never formally defined by conciliar acts, which are preserved and respected with 'the same force and honor' by Orthodox Christians as an explicit dogmatic formulation.[3] One such tradition is the liturgy.

Mystery and Transfiguration: The Sound of Liturgy

What the icon accomplishes in space and matter, the liturgy achieves in time and song. The liturgy is precisely the way Orthodox Christians celebrate the world and embrace the presence of God through communion. The singular purpose and goal of liturgy, 'the one thing that alone is necessary' (Lk. 10.42), is the 'hymn of entry'[4] into the kingdom of heaven. It is neither purely ceremonial nor exclusively mystical. It is the conviction and celebration of 'God in our midst'. Liturgy moves beyond the vision of the icon to the voice of the word. It transcends the eye to the ear, which in turn welcomes the annunciation of the divine word.

When it comes to the sacrament of liturgy, even the word 'mystery' means 'something which cannot be described in words', rather than something into which we are initiated. It is the awesome experience of standing on hallowed ground (Exod. 3.5). This is why there is darkness; this is why the prayers are recited silently; this is why the altar space is often invisible – although the 'dark church' reflects the architectural style of early Christianity, with the low icon screen revealing the altar but in fact concealing the bishop's throne, which consists of small, low seating on the right-hand side inside the altar.

In the liturgy, heaven and earth coincide and merge. The future kingdom becomes present reality and not just distant hope. Much like the icon, the liturgy becomes a foretaste of the age-to-come, at once heaven and home. The liturgy is the ground on which everything made sense. It is the air breathed by John, when on the not too distant island of Patmos he wrote: 'I, John, was in the Spirit on the Lord's Day . . . and I saw a new heaven and a new earth' (Rev. 1.10). Whether in the glorious imperial edifice of Haghia Sophia in Constantinople or in the humble volcanic excavation of the 'dark church', the experience would have been identical: a tangible, albeit mystical revelation and reflection of the *eschaton*.

Yet, it is not an otherworldly experience. A monk at liturgy in the 'dark church' would not feel disconnected from the world. This is what he would have learned from the great liturgical interpreters who lived in the surrounding Asia Minor: Germanos of Constantinople in the eighth century, Theodore the Studite in the ninth century, Symeon the New Theologian in the tenth century and Theodore of Andida in the eleventh century. To him, liturgy was informal and familiar; it would have primarily felt natural and not supernatural, everyday instead of esoteric, normal rather than paranormal. In the context of liturgy, there is no need to philosophize about the existence of God or the meaning of life. In liturgy, we know God and we love life. The only genuine expression is gratitude, the deeper significance of the term 'eucharist'.

Moreover, the liturgy is not disconnected from society because it seems as if the entire world is present, attendant, prayerful. As the fourth-century Archbishop of Constantinople and author of the most popular Orthodox liturgy, John Chrysostom (349–407) observes: 'Those in heaven and those on earth form a single festival, one choir'.[5] What impressed me most about the beauty of that 'dark church' in Cappadocia was not the splendid iconography or the classical architecture, but the sense that this church was filled – almost stiflingly – with the company of countless others, 'a cloud of witnesses' (Heb. 12.1), the overwhelming majority of which were invisible. In the words of the Liturgy of St John Chrysostom: 'Hosts of archangels, tens of thousands of angels, the many-eyed cherubim and the six-winged seraphim . . . the prophets, apostles, preachers, martyrs, confessors, ascetics, and every righteous spirit perfected in faith', including the anonymous monk kneeling in the corner of that 'dark church'. It is in a similar setting that Peter once said to Jesus on Mt Tabor: 'Lord, it is good to be here' (Mt. 17.4).

This communal aspect of worship is central to Orthodox Spirituality. The liturgy is never predominantly the sum of gathered individuals. It is the spacious roominess of divine love and mercy. In fact, this is precisely what the Greek term for 'forgiveness' signifies. *Synchoresis* has very little to do with remorse or guilt; rather, it implies being in the same space with everyone. The liturgy teaches us the alphabet of grace, where we welcome God's love and in turn embrace others with compassion. This is why the eleventh-century liturgy in that isolated cave church of Cappadocia affected the whole world, every generation and every nation. The liturgy is never simply for inner consumption but always for cosmic transfiguration. Standing at the centre of the temple during the liturgy, the Orthodox deacon exclaims: 'Let us stand in goodness'.

The emphasis on 'goodness' in Peter's exclamation on Mt Tabor and in the Orthodox divine liturgy echo the opening chapter of the Book of Genesis: 'God saw everything that was made, and indeed it was very good' (Gen. 1.31). The liturgy is certainly no escape from the world; instead, like icons, it invites the world to become an organic part of heaven. Moreover, like icons, the liturgy offers a refreshing revelation of a new, enlarged creation, which is transformed to the last speck of dust. In the end, Orthodox Spirituality is not so much an exotic introduction to the world of icons and liturgy but a vision of and initiation into a world where divine beauty and sacredness are discerned everywhere. For if God is not visible in creation, then neither can God be perceived in icons or worshipped in liturgy.

A New Earth: The Beauty of the World

I had always suspected the close connection between the natural environment and the eternal kingdom; but never had the intimate association between geology and spirituality appeared so conspicuous as when I contemplated the iconic caves of Cappadocia. Part of the reason we have disconnected this world from heaven lies in the fact that we are no longer respectful pilgrims in this world; we have been reduced to mere tourists, indifferent to the consequences of our attitudes and actions. Yet, the Orthodox spiritual tradition promulgates a world imbued by God and a God involved in this world. Indeed, Adam's original sin lies precisely in the refusal to perceive how God deeply penetrates and extensively permeates all of creation. As such, we can dare to speak of the sacredness – or even the sacrament – of creation.

This primeval spirituality, or 'Genesis worldview', is tangibly apparent in the spectacular white 'fairy chimneys' and stark 'cone-shaped' rock formations in Cappadocia. Surrounded by these colossal natural geological structures, it is easy to imagine what St Maximus the Confessor in the seventh century called 'cosmic liturgy'.[6] This is what led St Isaac the Syrian in the same century to speak of 'a merciful heart, which burns with love for the whole of creation – for humans, for birds, for the beasts, for demons – for all of God's creatures'.[7] In the late nineteenth century, Fyodor Dostoevsky revealed the same intuition, when he wrote in *The Brothers Karamazov*: 'Love all God's creation, the whole of it and every grain of sand . . . If you love everything, you will perceive the divine mystery in things'.[8]

There is a dimension of art and beauty in the world; and our vocation is precisely to discern this sacred perspective. This means, however, that whenever we narrow life to ourselves – to our concerns and our desires – we neglect our vocation to reconcile and transform creation. And whenever we reduce our religious life to ourselves – to our concerns and our desires – we forget the function of the liturgy to implore God for the renewal of the whole polluted cosmos. A spirituality that remains uninvolved with outward creation is ultimately uninvolved with the inward mystery, too. Our relationship with this world determines our relationship with heaven. The way we treat the earth is reflected in the way that we pray to God.

However, we have ignored the sacred dimension – broken the sacred covenant – between heaven and earth. We have become indifferent to our sacred connection with all people and all things. We are called to repentance for the way we have treated creation, for the disconnection between the prehistoric rock formation of Cappadocia and contemporary environmental disasters. Christian Spirituality has long emphasized the individual or social implications of sin. It is time now to expand the concept of sin to incorporate the effects of our actions and abuses on the natural creation. It is Ecumenical Patriarch Bartholomew, who has repeatedly remarked: 'To commit a crime against the natural world is a sin'.[9] In the eighth century, John of Damascus claimed: 'The whole earth is a living icon of the face of God'.[10] The truth is that we are less than human without God, less than human without each other, and less than human without creation.

People often refer to the current crisis as 'ecological', which is fair insofar as its results are manifest in the ecological sphere. Yet, the crisis is not first of all about ecology. It is about us as human beings; it is a crisis about the way we imagine our world. We are treating our planet in an inhumane, godforsaken manner because we perceive it this way. If, as Gerard Manley Hopkins said, 'the world is charged with the grandeur of God',[11] it behooves us to claim solidarity with the earth and its living creatures. Therefore, before we can effectively deal with environmental issues, we must convert our world view. Otherwise, we are dealing only with symptoms. It is essential that we stop to reflect. In his now classic article, titled 'The Historical Roots of our Ecological Crisis', Lynn White, Jr. (1907–87), a distinguished medieval historian, already suspected this truth – although in some ways neither he nor subsequent scholars have elaborated on it. He wrote: 'The Greek saint contemplates; the Western saint acts . . . The implications of Christianity for the conquest of nature would emerge more easily in the Western atmosphere'.[12]

What is crucial here is a discipline of voluntary frugality. That is the way of humility, of treading lightly on this planet. We have learned not to treat people like things; it is time we learned not to treat also things like mere things. If we are guilty of relentless waste, it may be because we have lost the spirit of simplicity and sharing. The challenge is: How do we live in such a way that promotes harmony and not division? How can we acknowledge 'the earth as the Lord's and all the fullness thereof' (Ps. 23.1)? How do we live in such a way that reflects our spiritual values, that communicates gratitude and not greed? How can we recognize in other people faces – or icons – and recognizing in the earth the very face of God? Because if we do, then we will perceive the same awe in every corner of the planet as we behold in the wonder of Cappadocia. If we do, then we will hear the ocean groan, and notice the grass grow and feel the seal's heart beat. Then we will see the earth as God saw it on that sixth day, when, 'indeed, it was good'.

Spiritual Connections: Solitude, Silence and Sharing

What attracted early monastics to the Cappadocian caves were the solitude and the silence. Both of these distinct qualities are vital to Orthodox Spirituality. While the classics of the spiritual tradition may not always be very precise in the distinctions that they draw, yet, they underline the importance of taking time to examine the various aspects of the soul and the particular principles that govern them. In our age of instant communication and immediate gratification, we seem to know less about ourselves, and about the motives behind our actions, than any other subject. Yet self-knowledge is the heart of solitude and the basis of silence.

Somewhere on that long trail between childhood and adulthood, many of us have lost touch with the vital skills that permit us to know ourselves. Perhaps part of the problem is that we have set impossible goals, which can only be met by angels. The spirituality of the Cappadocian desert taught the early monks that perfection is for God alone; we are called neither to forego nor to forget our imperfection. The fragility and vulnerability of life itself reveals the priority of confronting and embracing our inner desires and personal weaknesses. The truth is that God may be discerned in the very midst of these tensions and trials.

Indeed, those who sought refuge in the rock formations of the region appreciated the fact that, unless we take the radical step of surrendering familiar connections and concepts through an act of extreme renunciation – whereby we enter the foreign territory and learn to speak the foreign language of solitude – then we cannot begin to articulate the language of the soul. For, solitude is what allows us the time and the space to become alert to others and ourselves. Unfortunately, however, we tend to confuse self-knowledge with self-absorption. Curiously, while we encourage the need for knowing and loving others, we less frequently reward knowing ourselves in solitude.

Knowing why we do what we do facilitates the awareness also of why other people do what they do, and in the end the acceptance of other people as they are. Narcissism, then, is not too much self-knowledge but rather insufficient knowledge of our true self. People who are self-absorbed and self-centered normally suffer from too little rather than too much self. We often seek intimacy by facing in the wrong direction. Instead of looking inwardly, we turn outwardly towards others.

So the isolation of solitude becomes the first step towards any intimacy or communion with other people. Intimacy begins from within; and it reflects the inner world of the soul. It is the solid ground from which we are able to reach others, even God Himself. Ultimately, the degree to which we are able to acknowledge and accept others will be limited to the degree that we can understand and tolerate ourselves. We are more united to each other through our weaknesses and shortcomings than through our strengths and successes.

In the solitude of the cell, through temptations and tensions, the monastic becomes painfully aware of what is lacking. There, the hermit is haunted by the absence of love and yearns for the depth of communion. The cell symbolizes the safe haven of the soul, which one never leaves and where one can always willingly return in order to discover more and more of the authentic self, irrespective of how painful an ordeal or how agonizing a struggle this may be. Such a discovery through solitude eventually becomes a fountain of healing.

Embracing solitude in the loneliness of the cell (or the soul) means knowing what you think, understanding how you behave and finally accepting others without the need to defend oneself. It is assuming responsibility without the least sense of self-justification. It is the source of vulnerability and openness. Solitude reminds us that the soul is not a conflict-free zone where we can evade or ignore the perils of the world and the temptation of the soul. Instead, solitude has the capacity to absorb all manner of pain and to transform all kinds of temptation and tension into hope and joy.

If solitude endows us with a quality of awareness and vigilance, silence educates us in the art of listening and attentiveness. In solitude, the space between ourselves is important; so too is the space between our words in silence. Physical contact and verbal communication are as much associated with intimacy and love as silence is. Solitude provides the space and the capacity to listen to and soak up what another person is saying and conveying. This is because we bring to relationships the same self that we are (or are not) in touch with when we are alone. Silence is a skill whereby we acknowledge that what is going on in someone else's world matters.

Moreover, the fine balance between isolation and intimacy is extremely difficult to sustain without a spiritual director. Through someone else's belief in our self, we begin confidently – that is, by the act of confiding and confessing – to rediscover the solid ground within. Sharing our thoughts and temptations openly with at least one other person enables us to become familiar with the desires and conflicts that drive our behavior. Furthermore, being prepared to listen to and accept the reality of our nature and our self renders us more aware of (and more caring towards) other people. The opportunity to go within in order to learn and grow at one's pace is ultimately the chance also to become aware of the presence of others and be attentive to the burdens of others.

One reason for sharing with others is that most of us are harsher critics of ourselves, striking the most painful blows against ourselves at just the time when we most require tolerance and compassion. And, while obedience goes against the grain of much of our contemporary notions of liberation and independence, when someone is unable to build up from even the smallest patch of solid ground, then terms like 'freedom' and 'will' have little resonance.

Living Tradition: A Contemporary Saint

Orthodox Christians have always travelled great distances to remote monasteries – such as in the secluded peninsula of Sinai, the barren desert of Egypt or the suspended boulders of Meteora – to encounter and consult men and women of intense prayer and attested holiness. Thus, through the centuries, pilgrims have also sought out those hermits and monastics who lived in the solitude and silence of the Cappadocian caves. Until the beginning of this century, Greeks populated this region and preserved the memory of its saints. And today, Ecumenical Patriarch Bartholomew has laboured to negotiate in a systematic and humble manner with local authorities in order to permit occasional services, which are attended by Orthodox Christians from all over the world. One thing is certain: The presence of the early saints is evident and vivid.

In this way, an ancient spiritual tradition survives and thrives as a living tradition. The Orthodox calendar is filled with numerous Cappadocian saints – past and recent, men and women, known and unknown, formally canonized and informally venerated – exceptional witnesses to the sanctifying grace of God. Each of them is unique in their manifestation of God's love, 'one star differing from another star in glory' (1 Cor. 15.41). Each of them bears special importance and influence as genuine examples of holiness, wholeness and healing. Each of them becomes in this life 'an icon of the cherubim', to quote the hymn chanted during the 'great entrance' of the Divine Liturgy. I have met such a person.

As Abba Macarius of Egypt once said: 'I have not yet become a monk myself, but I *have seen monks*'.[13] Like many others, I was privileged to catch a glimpse into the communion of saints in a humble monk, who hailed from

Cappadocia. He was 'filled with light so as to become like a separate link in a golden chain of saints',[14] a precious stone in the extraordinary mosaic of this cradle of Orthodox Spirituality. He was living proof that, in the spiritual tradition of the Orthodox Church, there is no interruption in the event of Pentecost, a heavenly example of human nature – ever frail yet called to burn with divine love, with 'an extraordinary power in a clay vessel' (2 Cor. 4.7).

Elder Paisios was born in 1924 in Farasa, in a cluster of tiny villages of a dry Cappadocian valley and in the shadow of several rock caves.[15] He was baptized by his parish priest, Fr Arsenios (1840–1924), who was recently recognized as a saint in the Orthodox Church (1988). Paisios' family fled as refugees from Asia Minor to Greece where they first settled on the island of Corfu and finally in the northeastern town of Konitsa in Epirus, where Paisios completed his elementary education and military service.

In 1950, Paisios left for Mt Athos where his favorite readings included *The Sayings of the Desert Fathers* and Abba Isaac the Syrian, whose *Mystic Treatises* he kept beneath his pillow at all times. Four years later, he became a monk and in 1962 travelled to Mt Sinai, where he remained for 2 years in a craggy cell opposite the holy mountain of the Burning Bush and the historical St Catherine's Monastery. The local Bedouins adored Paisios, who used to carve wooden crosses and sell them to pilgrims in order to buy food for the natives.

In 1964, he returned to Mt Athos, where he directed the lives of numerous people who sought his advice through visitations and correspondence. In a small bottle with paper and pencil, outside the fence surrounding his cell, people would leave notes with personal problems, names of those seeking intercession, letters requiring counsel and gifts for distribution to the poor. Paisios became a magnet that drew out and transformed human pain and suffering until his own death in 1994.

Paisios saw himself as part of a long spiritual tradition transmitted through the holy man that baptized him. For him, tradition is more than a mere historical lineage; it implies an unbroken sacramental and charismatic heritage traced back to the Apostles and to Christ. Indeed, he did not simply belong to this tradition; he incarnated the deepest convictions of that tradition regarding the personal experience of God: 'I do not care any more if someone tells me that God does not exist!'[16]

Paisios is also one of the few ascetics – of the contemporary present or even the classic past – who underline the sacraments, especially baptism. For him, baptismal grace constitutes the starting point and goal of ascetic discipline. The aim of self-purification is to allow more room for divine grace: *ascesis* looks to *kenosis*. The purpose of ascetic renunciation is 'to count down from ten to zero before sending off our missile into space, like the Americans do!'[17]

However, perhaps the most apparent feature is his positive and edifying counsel. His spirituality resembles that of the desert fathers, with their emphasis on honesty and integrity. Be who you are, is the advice he often gives people who approach him; 'do not pretend'.[18] His was a positive and practical spirituality: 'A single positive thought equals an entire vigil on Mount Athos'.[19] His realism stems from a sense of compassion, which allowed the elder to remain deeply connected with society even while separated in monastic isolation.[20] The aim of containing the passions is gaining a sense of compassion. Then one shares 'God's sympathy towards humanity', 'God's providence for the whole creation' and – as he dares to propose – 'God's joy over the repentance even of the devil'.

Put simply, 'God loves and tolerates everybody. So too should we!'[21] Even the imagery that Paisios adopts is pricelessly simple, reminiscent of the desert fathers: 'God's mercy is like a cork; no matter how hard we press it to the bottom of the sea, it will always come back to the surface'.[22]

Such is the resounding avowal of Orthodox Spirituality. And it is the reverberating echo of the empty Cappadocian caves to this day.

Notes

1 *On the Holy Spirit* 18. See D. Anderson (ed.) (1980), *St. Basil the Great on the Holy Spirit*. Crestwood, NY: St. Vladimir's Press.

2 *On the Holy Images* 11, 12. See A. Louth (ed.) (2003), *Three Treatises on the Divine Images*. Crestwood, NY: St. Vladimir's Press.

3 *On the Holy Spirit* 27.

4 The title of a book by Archimandrite Vasileios, who offers us fresh exploration of the Orthodox spiritual life and teaching through the rite of the liturgy. See *Hymn of Entry: Liturgy and Life in the Orthodox Church*. New York, NY: St. Vladimir's Press, 1984.

5 *Homily I on Order in the Liturgy* 1.

6 See H. U. von Balthasar (2004), *Cosmic Liturgy: The Universe According to Maximus the Confessor*. San Francisco, CA: Ignatius Press, p. 322.

7 Isaac of Nineveh (1986), *Mystic Treatises*, *Homily* 48. Brookline, MA: Holy Transfiguration Monastery, p. 30.

8 F. Dostoevsky (1982), *The Brothers Karamazov*, vol. 1, Harmondsworth, UK: Penguin, pp. 375–6.

9 Originally from an address delivered in Santa Barbara, California, November 1997. See *Cosmic Grace, Humble Prayer: The Ecological Vision of the Green Patriarch Bartholomew*, Grand Rapids, MI: Eerdmans Publishing Company, 2009 [2nd revised edition], pp. 220–1.

10 Based on the words of St John of Damascus, *On the Holy Images* 1, pp. 15–16. See A. Louth (ed.) (2003), *Three Treatises on the Divine Images*, Crestwood, NY: St. Vladimir's Press.

11 See *Gerard Manley Hopkins: Poems and Prose*, London: Penguin Classics, 1985, p. 27.

12 *Science*, 155, March 1967, 1203–7.

13 Macarius 2, in Benedicta Ward (ed.) (1985), *The Sayings of the Desert Fathers*, Kalamazoo, MI: Cistercian Publications, p. 106.

14 Symeon the New Theologian, *Centuries*, 111, p. 3.

15 Elder Paisios is the author of *Saint Arsenios of Cappadocia*. Thessaloniki: Convent of St. John the Theologian, 1975. For Paisios' life, see Christodoulos Angeloglou (1994), *Elder Paisios of the Holy Mountain*, Mt Athos [English trans. 1998].
16 Cf. Christodoulos, *Elder Paisios*, pp. 54–9.
17 Ibid., p. 54.
18 Ibid., p. 26 and 29.
19 Ibid., p. 29.
20 Ibid., pp. 33–4.
21 Ibid., pp. 63, 132 and 133.
22 Op.cit., p. 64.

Bibliography and Further Reading

Bartholomew (2008) (Ecumenical Patriarch), *Encountering the Mystery: Understanding Orthodox Christianity Today*. New York, NY: Doubleday.

Chryssavgis, John (2004), *Light Through Darkness: The Orthodox Tradition*. New York: Orbis and London: SPCK.

Forest, Jim (2008), *Praying With Icons*. Maryknoll, NY: Orbis.

Schmemann, Alexander (1997), *For the Life of the World: Sacraments and Orthodoxy*. Crestwood, NY: St Vladimir's Press.

Archimandrite Sophrony(1999), *Saint Silouan, the Athonite*. Crestwood, NY: St Vladimir's Press.

Ware, Kallistos (1995), *The Orthodox Way*. Crestwood, NY: St Vladimir's Press.

Dominican Spirituality

Richard Woods

Introduction

From its inception in the early thirteenth century, the spirituality of the Order of Preachers (Dominicans) was deeply contemplative and actively apostolic. Originating in the accidental preaching mission of Diego de Azevedo, the Bishop of Ozma (Spain) and his companion, a young canon of the cathedral named Dominic (c. 1172–1221), the Order developed by stages in southern France. There, en route to Denmark in 1203 on a royal mission to procure a bride for the son of the King of Castile, the two Spaniards encountered a Cistercian mission engaged in a faltering effort to stem the tide of heretical activity on the part of radically dualistic but devout Christian dissidents later known as Cathars or (incorrectly) Albigensians. Diego and Dominic did not remain in the Midi but, on the return leg of their second journey to Denmark a year later, they purposely revisited the papal mission. Bishop Diego advised the abbots to relinquish their retinues and fine clothes and travel among the 'Good Christians' in the manner of their own preachers, in evangelical poverty. Daunted by the proposal, the Cistercians claimed that such a plan could succeed only if they had effective leadership, so Diego dismissed all his companions except Dominic, and they began preaching barefoot among the dissidents, begging their bread door-to-door.

Among their meagre achievements was the establishment in 1206 of a refuge for women converts at the village of Prouilhe, which while originally under the Cistercian rule would later become the first house of 'Dominican' nuns. Leaving Dominic in France, in 1207 Diego returned to Spain where he died before he was able to arrange for a successor which would have freed him to return as the head of the preaching band. Left virtually alone, Dominic managed to attract a few followers. As the situation worsened following the assassination of one of the papal legates and the onset of the tragic 'Albigensian crusade', the small band was invited to make their headquarters in Toulouse by the astute Bishop Foulques.

Dominic played no part in the fighting, and in 1215, during a lull in the war, he accompanied Bishop Foulques to Rome where the Fourth Lateran Council was in session. There Dominic appealed to Pope Innocent III to be allowed to establish a preaching order to carry on the mission in France. While sympathetic to the idea, the pope was unable to comply as the Council had just forbade the creation of new orders in the wake of the burgeoning of such groups during the previous century. Innocent instructed Dominic to return to Toulouse and obtain the consent of his preachers to adopt an existing rule and return with their agreement. The preachers chose the Rule of St Augustine and some of the provisions of the Canons of Premontré (the Norbertines), as well as a modified habit. But by the time Dominic returned to Rome, Innocent had died. His successor, Honorius III, nevertheless approved the establishment of the Order on 22 December 1216.

Soon it became clear to Dominic that the scope of the new order's mission would be much greater than the French Midi, and after organizing the new recruits, he shocked the budding preachers by dispersing them in pairs to Paris, Bologna, Oxford and eventually to Spain, Poland and elsewhere, especially to establish houses near the emerging universities where new recruits would be able to study scripture and theology. The headquarters of the new Order was moved to Bologna where, in August 1221, Dominic died, exhausted by his tireless preaching journeys and supportive work of the foundations of friars and nuns. At the time of his death, five provinces of friars and four nunneries were in existence. Within a century, the Order had grown to many thousands and extended its mission from Ireland to Iraq and as far south as Egypt.

The character of the Order of Preachers was determined by its apostolic origins and the personality and spirituality of St Dominic, fusing the contemplative life of the canons regular with the evangelical ardour inspiring the mendicant groups taking root throughout Europe – Franciscans, Carmelites, Augustinian friars, Trinitarians, Mercedarians and Servites among them. But the Order of Preachers was the first and in fact only order established for the specific purpose of preaching, a ministry traditionally reserved to bishops. But in the papal letter of Honorius III to Dominic and the first friars in 1216, the pope described the purpose of Order as 'a life of poverty and regular observance and . . . preaching the Word of God and proclaiming the name of our Lord Jesus Christ throughout the world'. According to the prologue of the earliest Constitutions, the Order 'is known from the beginning to have been instituted especially for preaching and the salvation of souls'.

The Order was also distinctive in identifying its 'work' as study, replacing the manual labour of the monastic tradition with mental work, primarily the study of scripture but eventually, the whole field of the arts and sciences from agronomy to zoology.

Governance and Spirituality

Although not familial in the manner of monastic orders such as the Benedictines and Cistercians, today the Dominican 'family' still comprises a variety of brothers and sisters – the clerical friars and cooperator brothers, the contemplative nuns, the religious sisters and vowed laypersons of both sexes. Each group has its own government, constitutions and procedures. Egalitarian and democratic from the beginning, Dominicans elect their leaders for limited terms and determine policy by vote in local, regional and international assemblies (chapters).

Lacking a special approach or method apart from the general understanding and practice of the spiritual life, it can safely be said that the spirituality of the Order of Preachers is distinguished by indistinction, as one of its great exemplars Meister Eckhart might have said. Especially in its earliest days, its spirituality was far more simple and straightforward than the complex notions and 'exercises' of later Catholic traditions. A contemporary Dominican writer, Simon Tugwell, has observed in this regard that Christian Spirituality 'is not concerned with prayer and contemplation and spiritual exercises, it is concerned with people's ways of viewing things, the ways in which they try to make sense of the practicalities of christian living and to illuminate christian hopes and christian muddles'.[1] So it was certainly for the early Dominicans.

Thus while in the long history of the Order friars and sisters have sometimes adopted and adapted theories and observances of the times, there has never been an 'official' Dominican Spirituality or a set of practices incumbent on its members other than the common life and liturgy, the recitation of the daily choral prayer of the Church, and the celebration of the Eucharist. Even the rule and constitutions of the Order, originally devised in 1221 and revised over the centuries, never obligated observance under penalty of sin, even venial sin. Further, the characteristic 'rule of dispensation' present from the beginning was always liberally applied to free members for the demands of ministry. The evangelical vows typify the life of all Dominicans, although they have always been understood as instrumental to the work of preaching and teaching rather than as ends in themselves.

The Evangelical Life: Radical Witness

Beginning with St Dominic, the Dominicans' strong emphasis on evangelical poverty aligned them with the Franciscans and other mendicant orders of the thirteenth century such as the Carmelites, the Augustinian Friars and the Servites, who shared with dissident groups like the Poor Men of Lyon (Waldensians), Fraticelli and even heretical movements including the 'Cathars' a desire for a life of Gospel simplicity and consequent hostility to the new money economy of the Middle Ages. The commercial revolution that began in the twelfth century had deeply altered the spiritual climate of Europe. The mendicants challenged this directly by appealing to Gospel values of common ownership, social justice – especially compassionate care for the poor, sick and vulnerable – and an aversion towards pomp and luxury of any kind. But unlike the Franciscans, especially the more radical Spirituals, who bitterly opposed them on this, the Dominicans insisted on owning their own houses, lest the preaching of the Gospel be compromised by either penury or the fear of landlords.

In its better moments over the centuries, the Order has remained true to its commitment to evangelical poverty with occasional episodes of greatness, such as the priest-worker movement in France after the Second World War which so annoyed the Vatican that it was squelched. All the French provincials were removed from office and several leading theologians were silenced.

The Dominican commitment to celibacy guided by the virtue of chastity and informed by charity was not, nor is, a protest against married life or a repudiation of sexuality as it clearly was in some of the heretical movements of the Middle Ages. But the eschatological character of vowed celibacy, not only of Dominicans, but of other religious orders, stood in sharp contrast to the exaltation of sexuality, especially the licentiousness of the nobility and wealthy class that typified much of the culture of Europe at the time and was celebrated in the literature of courtly love. Raymond of Capua left an account of Catherine of Siena's entry to the papal court at Avignon which was so flagrantly wanton that she became physically ill from what she perceived as the stench of sin.

As their poverty and chastity were a challenge to the money economy and luxury of the High Middle Ages, radical obedience to God and the Gospel was an affront to the cult of power that also burgeoned then and afterwards. In a headstrong age in which pride and arrogance flourished and often erupted in violence, the subjection of the will to the wisdom of the Gospel embodied in the decisions of the community and its elected leaders, so Thomas Aquinas argued, constituted the perfection of religious life. To this day, Dominicans profess only one vow, that of obedience – properly understood as a radical conversion of the will to God, a commitment that encompasses poverty and chastity and other evangelical counsels. Such fidelity has not, in the Order's best moments, stifled the initiative and courage of friars, nuns, sisters and lay members, the great exemplars being St Catherine of Siena, St Martín de Porres and, in our own era, Joseph-Marie Lagrange, founder of the École Biblique in Jerusalem, and the French theologians M. D. Chenu and Yves Congar.

Intellectual Heritage

The educational enterprise of the Order was a natural development of its spirituality, being founded on the priority of a sound theological, mainly biblical, education for the sake of evangelization, that is, preaching. Within a generation, students were obliged to ground their study of theology in philosophy – originally the arts curriculum (at first forbidden to them), but especially the fundamental works of Aristotle – the logical works, Physics, Metaphysics and Ethics, guided by the commentaries by St Thomas and their later teachers. In addition to the biblical texts and commentaries of the day, more advanced students were also expected to master the theology of St Thomas Aquinas, which by the end of the thirteenth century had become obligatory.

The motto of the Order, *Veritas (Truth)*, consistently guided the development of educational models, even when in later centuries in addition to their own 'houses of study', Dominicans founded universities – among them those of Cologne, Santo Domingo, Mexico City, St Thomas in Manila and the College of St Thomas in Rome (the 'Angelicum'), established in 1222 and elevated to the status of a Pontifical University in 1906. Congregations of Dominican sisters have founded almost 100 colleges and universities in the last two centuries. The intellectual bias was always the 'moderate realism' favoured by St Thomas and his commentators, that is, the assurance that the mind can truly know reality because of the proportionate relation of the knowing mind to the object known. Epistemological realism did not exclude the constructive role of ideas and the imagination, but subordinated that function to the apprehension of reality by the intellect. Although the liberal arts were favoured in the Dominican tradition, the fine arts were not neglected, and the Order not only fostered painting in particular, especially during the Florentine Renaissance, but treasures a panoply of outstanding artists and musicians down to present times.

Over the centuries, the basic pattern of education did not change radically, although handbooks of philosophy (and sometimes theology, especially moral theology) eventually displaced the *ipsissima verba* of Aristotle and St Thomas. The better Houses of Study retained the custom of textual study and commentary, however, especially at higher levels of education. The conservative character of training in the Order favoured exposure to the classics of world literature as well as a cautious approach to scientific innovation (occasionally overly cautious, as the Galileo affair and the very slow acceptance of Darwinian evolution demonstrate).

If there is a dominant theme in the Dominican intellectual tradition, it is perhaps best described as the pursuit of truth by a thorough grounding in the philosophical disciplines of logical method, cognitive discipline and metaphysical realism guided by faith illuminated by understanding. The pillars supporting Dominican education are, in that light, philosophy, theology and the liberal and fine arts.

The Dominican Spiritual Tradition

Fr Simon Tugwell, in his monumental collection of writings by and about the early Dominican friars and nuns observes that,

> The early Dominicans were not particularly concerned, either for themselves or for others, with what has come to be called the 'interior life'. Some of them, certainly, were great men of prayer, but their prayer was simple, devotional, and largely petitionary . . . But there is no hint of any methodical 'mental prayer', such as we find in later centuries, nor is there any sign of any theory of mystical progress attached to these simple prayers. When thirteenth-century Dominicans do comment on the ascent of the soul to God, it is in intellectualist terms that belong more within the domain of speculative theology than in the kind of mystical theology we have since become used to.[2]

Because there is no officially defined spirituality in the Order, identifying its spiritual tradition requires considering its more outstanding proponents, whose influence proved to be lasting and to a large extent, determinative. Of special significance among them, in addition to St Dominic himself, are St Albert the Great (and his 'school'), St Thomas Aquinas, Meister Eckhart and his followers among the 'Friends of God' and St Catherine of Siena with her cohort of disciples.

The Albertine Inheritance

A theology of the spiritual life developed in the school of St Albert the Great (c. 1200–80), among whom it is possible to include both St Thomas Aquinas and Meister Eckhart, although their approaches differed in several important respects. The scope of Albert's interests was astonishing, even in the High Middle Ages, ranging from scriptural studies, commentaries on classics such as the works of Dionysius the Areopagite, the natural sciences (of which he is patron saint) and, of course, theology. Alert to the contributions of great pagan authors as well as Jewish and Muslim scholars and mystics, Albert intended to synthesize these currents into an encompassing *summa*, a goal he was not to accomplish, nor in fact was ever accomplished.

Like other Dominican writers of the period, Albert's treatment of the spiritual life is scattered throughout his manifold works, rather than in a specific volume. Consistent in his teaching (and his life) are the foundational elements of the evangelical counsels and the central importance of the contemplative life expressed in apostolic action.

Many of these insights, refined and developed by the treatment of the spiritual life in the great *summas* of Albert's great disciple, Thomas d'Aquino (c. 1225–74), would continue to inspire and guide generations of friars and sisters to the present. In many respects, it is the received tradition of the Order.

Thomas Aquinas: Spiritual Master

Although justly famed for his huge handbooks, the unfinished *Summa Theologiae* and the *Summa contra Gentes,* as well as his philosophical commentaries and theological treatises, Thomas' major contributions to spirituality are found in his commentaries on the Gospels, especially the Gospel of John. His most incisive theological exposition is contained in a few articles in the *Summa Theologiae*, in which he essentially defends the superiority of a mixed life of action and contemplation to that of either active ministry or the contemplative life taken by themselves (ST, II-II, Question 180). It is a theme that finds expression in a number of other major and minor works as well:

> There are some who have ascended to such a summit of charity that they even put aside divine contemplation, though they delight greatly in it, that they might serve God through the salvation of their neighbours; and this perfection appears in Paul [see Rom. 9.3 and Phil. 1.23]. Such also is the perfection proper to prelates and preachers and whosoever works to bring about the salvation of others. Hence they are symbolized by the angels on the ladder of Jacob, ascending through contemplation, descending, however, through the solicitude they feel for the salvation of their neighbours. (*De caritate*, A. 11, ad 6)

There is nothing particularly original in Thomas' integrative vision of the spiritual life. Characteristically, he insists on the primacy of the mind in regard to both earthly experience and eternal beatitude. But love in both its ordinary and theological senses enjoys enormous importance in Thomas' scheme of things. He affirms, much like his Franciscan counterparts Bonaventure and Duns Scotus, that in our lives as pilgrims and wayfarers, love unites us more closely to God than does knowledge, which remains incapable of attaining to the direct (much less comprehensive) vision of God. In this, Thomas not only builds upon the apophatic element in Christian theology and spirituality in his teaching, but like Bonaventure, the *Cloud* author, and Meister Eckhart, he places divine and human friendship at the very centre of the spiritual life.

The German Masters

Around another if very late student of Albert's, Eckhart of Hochheim (c. 1260–1328), there developed in time a distinctive 'Rhineland' spirituality closely associated with the movement known as 'The Friends of God', which included a number of saintly figures, among them, most notably, the Dominicans Heinrich Süs (or Suso) and Johann Tauler, the secular priest Henry von Nördlingen, several Dominican nuns such as Bl. Margaret Ebner and the eccentric layman and entrepreneur Rulmen Merswin. Although 15 propositions taken out of context from Eckhart's commentaries and sermons were condemned as erroneous by a papal bull in 1329, Eckhart's influence continued to be felt through the Friends of God and works such as *The Book of Holy Poverty* and the *Theologia Deutch*. Modern scholars almost universally concur that not only was Eckhart's doctrine free of heretical content, but he in fact provided a link between the orthodox mystical theology of the ancient Church and the modern age.[3]

If Thomas and Eckhart became the most brilliant exponents of the spirituality of the Dominican Order in the thirteenth and early fourteenth centuries, they were by no means isolated figures. Among other notable students of Albert were John and Gerald Korngin of Sterngassen, Dietrich of Freiburg, Ulrich Englebert of Strassburg, Berthold of Moosburg and Henry of Halle, each of whom passed on the teachings of the 'Cologne school' in distinctive ways. Many, like Eckhart himself, were second-generation disciples, including Eckhart the Younger, John Franko, Henry of Egwint, Giselher of Statheim, Henry de Calstris, Venturino of Bergamo and Dalmatius Monerio.

Sisters Preachers and Lay Dominicans

Women had played an important role in the preaching mission of Diego and Dominic from the beginning. The establishment in 1206 of the convent at Prouilhe was the first 'Dominican' foundation, although its original rule was Cistercian. After receiving approval of the Order from Pope Honorius III in 1216, Dominic soon founded other monasteries for nuns in Italy and Spain. This 'second order' of cloistered Dominican sisters was not formally recognized as part of the Order of Preachers until 1267, but the connection between the friars and the contemplative women's monasteries was a primordial component of the Dominican tradition. From the four monasteries in existence in 1221 (Prouilhe, San Sisto, Madrid and St Stephen of Gormaz in Spain) the number grew to 58 by 1277. By 1358 there were 157. Nuns of other monasteries followed the Order's customs and wore its habit, but were under the bishops' jurisdiction, although the Order often provided for them spiritually.

Similarly, groups of devout laymen and women associated themselves with the Preachers from an early period, receiving formal approval in 1285 under Munio de Zamora, the seventh master of the Order. First known as the Brothers and Sisters of Penance of St Dominic on the model of the Franciscan laity, these men and women members were permitted to wear the distinctive black and white habit of the Order and hold their own chapters. By the thirteenth century, they were styled 'The Third Order' or Dominican Tertiaries, and are now known as the Dominican Laity. The patron and most famous of all was a young woman who was at first declined admission because of her youth, but became in time the greatest of all Dominican women saints, spiritual writers and a doctor of the Church.

Catherine the Greater

Laxity and tepidity took root among many Dominican houses in the later Middle Ages as the first fervour of the founders receded into memory. The lure of wealth and power often proved irresistible. A reform movement countered this tendency, first appearing in Germany towards the end of the thirteenth century. But the great champion of reform in the Order was a woman remarkable for her strength of will, intellect and holiness – Catherine of Siena (1347–80), whose spiritual impact on the Order and the Church remains indelible.

Through her writing, preaching and spiritual guidance, Catherine inspired a generation of reformers, including her own spiritual director and eventual disciple, Bl. Raymond of Capua, who became Master of the Order after Catherine's death. Considered by many to be the 'second founder' of the Order, Catherine did not develop a novel form of spirituality, but recovered the essentials of the tradition and expressed them in a fearless manner, confronting queens, nobles and even the pope when she joined ranks with those who agitated for the return of the Holy See to Rome.

Catherine's letters and her spiritual masterpiece, *The Dialogue*, have become classics of Christian Spirituality. Her influence guided the successes of the Italian reform movement in particular, from Raymond's efforts to those of Bl. John Dominici, St Antoninus of Florence and the great preacher and prophet Girolamo Savonarola. The reform movement effectively culminated in the execution of Savonarola in 1498, but also produced its latest fruit in the life and letters of the mystic nun, St Catherine de' Ricci (1522–90), who so greatly resembled her namesake. Her devotion to the memory of Savonarola, through whose intercession she was cured of serious illness, later became a temporary obstacle to her canonization but also resulted in a reconsideration of the prophetic preacher's own sanctity.

From the Reformation to the Modern Period

If the fourteenth century produced some of the finest mystical writings of Dominican Spirituality, the fifteenth witnessed a return to a more ascetical approach in some of its most illustrious writers and teachers such as St Vincent Ferrer (d. 1419), the apocalyptic preacher of Spain and France. Wary of the metaphysical flights of the Rhineland tradition and hostile towards intellectual approaches to religion in general, as a spiritual writer Vincent nevertheless demonstrates flashes of originality and psychological insight.

Spiritual theology in the Order did not advance significantly after the sixteenth century, but the prophetic spirituality of some of its outstanding members contributed to both theory and practice. The characteristic emphasis on preaching, truth, community, prayer and simplicity of life was especially realized in the lives of the great saints of the New World, Archbishop Bartolomé de las Casas (1484–1566), St Martín de Porres (1579–1639), St Juan Maçias (1585–1645) and St Rose of Lima (1586–1617) – the first canonized saint of the New World, whose unflagging ministry to the poor, whether native peoples or slaves, established the lines of social justice for centuries to come.[4]

In Europe, the Portuguese Dominican John of St Thomas (Jean Poinsot, 1589–1644) was arguably the most brilliant of the Thomistic commentators in the post-Reformation era. Although not as well known for his spiritual writings as his theological works, his small book on the Gifts of the Holy Spirit has exercised a continuing influence on Dominican spiritual writers for centuries.[5]

The eighteenth and nineteenth centuries saw a decline in the Order's numbers, influence and calibre. But the efforts of two remarkable Frenchmen, Henry Lacordaire (1802–61) and Vincent Jandel (d. 1872), defied history and breathed new life into the Order in France and slowly throughout Europe. By the turn of the century, despite waves of anticlericalism in France and Germany, Dominicans were again in the forefront of theological and spiritual life. Among many outstanding figures must be included Bl. Hyacinth Cormier (1832–1916) who, despite serious health problems was received into the Order by Fr Lacordaire. After a distinguished career, he was elected master of the Order in 1904. Cormier penned devotional works, spiritual instructions for novices and biographies of eminent Dominicans. In 1945 the case for his canonization was introduced and Cormier was beatified in 1994.

Other important French spiritual writers were Ambroise Gardeil (1859–1931), whose *Gifts of the Holy Ghost in Dominican Saints* became a standard work on Dominican Spirituality, and A. D. Sertillanges (1863–1948), a prolific author on spirituality and other topics. But solidly, almost obsessively Thomistic, the French theologian, Fr Reginald Garrigou-Lagrange (1877–1964) dominated much Dominican spiritual theology in the mid-twentieth century. Translated into English, his books *Christian Perfection and Contemplation* and *The Three*

Ages of the Spiritual Life wielded enormous influence in the era immediately preceding the Second Vatican Council. Garrigou-Lagrange waged a long and strenuous campaign against the 'two-track' theory that reserved the highest realms of spiritual development to an elite minority of saintly figures while 'ordinary' Christians were called to a life of possibly heroic but nonetheless moral virtue, not the 'higher' awareness of the presence of God and mystical union. It is very likely that his insistence on the unity of the spiritual life, the universal call to the 'perfection' of contemplative union with God, influenced the section on spirituality in the Dogmatic Constitution on the Church (*Lumen Gentium*) of the Second Vatican Council.

Spanish Dominicans similarly contributed major works to the revival of spiritual theology – particularly Victorino Osende (b. 1897), Antonio Royo-Marin (1913–2005), a renowned university professor of Salamanca whose *Theology of Christian Perfection* was successfully translated into English, and Juan Gonzales-Arintero (d. 1928).

Among English Dominicans, several outstanding spiritual writers began publishing in the twentieth century, paramount among them Vincent McNabb (1868–1943) and Bede Jarrett (1881–1934). By mid-century, their students had contributed significantly to Dominican and indeed Christian Spirituality – especially Gerald Vann (1906–63) and Conrad Pepler (1908–93). In more recent times, Fr Simon Tugwell (b. 1943) has made a number of outstanding contributions to the history and practice of spirituality. Fr Timothy Radcliffe (b. 1945), a former Master of the Order, has contributed a number of bestselling works on contemporary religious matters and spirituality.

Although primarily remembered as a systematic theologian, Flemish Fr Edward Schillebeeckx (1914–2009) also contributed significantly to the spiritual heritage of the Order of Preachers. Like that of French Dominican Yves Congar, his phenomenologically driven and sometimes controversial ecclesiology and Christology were a major influence during the deliberations of the Second Vatican Council. His single essay, 'Dominican Spirituality, or The Counter-Thread in the Old Religious Story as the Golden Thread in the Dominican Family-Story', which first appeared in a Dominican journal in South Africa, gradually travelled throughout the world by means of a number of translations and publications in the years that followed.[6] It remains one of the concise and astute summaries of Dominican Spirituality in modern times.

Conclusion

According to William Hinnebusch, the spirituality of the Friars, and by extension all Dominicans, is characteristically,

Theocentric, Christological, sacerdotal . . . monastic, contemplative, and apostolic. It is, in truth, the spirituality of Christ the Preacher and of the Apostles. The primary intention is to elevate the friar to the heights of contemplation, but going beyond this, Dominican contemplation itself is intended to fructify in the apostolate for souls, especially through preaching, teaching, and writing. Contemplation is the generic element, the one the Friars Preachers share with other contemplative Orders, the salvation of souls through preaching is the specific note distinguishing Dominicans from all other Orders.[7]

The traditional emblems of the Order reflect these elements. The single word *Veritas*, 'Truth', often inscribed over the Dominican seal, summarizes the goal and ideal of the Order. The quest for Truth in all its forms – theological, philosophical, scientific, historical and artistic – has always been the star that guided the Dominican spirit.

The motto of the Order found on seals, stationery, documents and inscriptions contains the Latin words *Laudare, Benedicere, Praedicare*: 'to praise, to bless, to preach'. These words indicate the primary mission and therefore the spirituality of the Order as a whole: prayer and worship; evangelical ministry, expressed in sacramental administration, missionary work, teaching, healing and parochial care; and preaching in its many forms, including writing and the expressive arts.

But the third epithet has traditionally illustrated the characteristic spirit of the Order: *Contemplata aliis tradere*, 'to hand on to others what has been contemplated'. Drawn from the teachings of St Thomas Aquinas (*Summa Theologiae* II-II, Q. 188, A. 6), this phrase is meant not to distinguish the mystical, contemplative dimension of Dominican Spirituality from its active expression, but to unite them.

According to Fr Schillebeeckx, however,

A final all-around definition of what is Dominican Spirituality cannot be given! You cannot give final judgement about a story if it is still being told in full strength. We can only look for some main trends in the plot of the story. We cannot do more, because the story is being told through seven centuries with ever new modalities, in which the basic story is repeated in ever new languages and speech, always different in view of constantly changing listeners. The narrative is told and heard in cultural-historical and ecclesiastical surroundings that were never the same.[8]

Notes

1 Tugwell, Simon OP (1985), *Ways of Imperfection*. Springfield, IL: Templegate, pp. 7–8.
2 Tugwell, Simon OP (1982) (trans. and ed.), *Early Dominicans: Selected Writings*. New York: Paulist Press International, 'Introduction', pp. 3–4.
3 For more on the contemporary application of Eckhart see the chapter 'Christian Spirituality and Buddhism' below.
4 The most recent work on Las Casas is the massive study by Gustavo Gutiérrez (1993), *Las Casas: In Search of the Poor of Jesus Christ*, trans. Robert R. Barr. New York: Orbis Books. For an insightful study of the prophetic and mystical achievements of St Martín de Porres, see Alex García-Rivera (1996), *St Martín de Porres: The 'Little Stories' and the Semiotics of Culture*, foreword by Virgil Elizondo, intro. by Robert Schreiter. Maryknoll, NY: Orbis Books.
5 John of St Thomas (1951), *The Gifts of the Holy Spirit*, trans. Dominic Hughes OP. New York, NY: Sheed and Ward.
6 Schillebeeckx, Edward OP (1975), 'Dominican spirituality, or the counter-thread in the old religious story as the golden thread in the Dominican family-story', *Dominican Topics in South Africa*. March, May and August 1975.
7 Hinnebusch, William OP (1965), *Dominican Spirituality: Principles and Practices*. Washington, DC: The Thomist Press, p. 2.
8 Schillebeeckx, 'Dominican spirituality'.

Bibliography and Further Reading

Ashley, Benedict OP (1995), *Spiritual Direction in the Dominican Tradition*. New York, NY: Paulist Press.
Borgman, Erik (2001), *Dominican Spirituality: An Exploration*. London: Continuum.
Hinnebusch, William OP (1965), *Dominican Spirituality: Principles and Practices*. Washington, DC: The Thomist Press.
— (1989), 'Dominicans', *Dictionary of the Middle Ages*. New York, NY: Charles Scribner's Sons, vol. iv, p. 254ff.
Murray, Paul OP (2006), *The New Wine of Dominican Spirituality: A Drink Called Happiness*. New York, NY: Burns and Oates.
Schillebeeckx, Edward OP (1975), 'Dominican spirituality, or the counter-thread in the old religious story as the golden thread in the Dominican family-story', *Dominican Topics in South Africa*. March, May and August, 1975. Also found in *God among Us: The Gospel Proclaimed* (1983). New York, NY: Crossroad, pp. 232–48; and Borgman (2001), pp. 92–110.
Torrell, Jean-Pierre OP (2003), *Saint Thomas Aquinas: Spiritual Master*, trans. Robert Royal, Washington, DC: Catholic University of America Press.
Tugwell, Simon OP (1982) (trans. and ed.), *Early Dominicans: Selected Writings*. New York, NY: Paulist Press International.
— (1986), 'The Dominicans', *The Study of Spirituality*, ed. C. Jones, G. Wainwright and E. Yarnold, SJ. Oxford and New York, NY: Oxford University Press, pp. 296–300.
Woods, Richard OP (1998), *Mysticism and Prophecy: The Dominican Tradition*. London: Darton, Longman and Todd and New York, NY: Orbis Books.
Zagano, Phyllis and McGonigle, Thomas OP (2006), *The Dominican Tradition*. Collegeville, PA: Liturgical Press.

9 Franciscan Spirituality

Michael D. Guinan

Introduction

In seeking to live the common Christian call to life in the Spirit, the Franciscan tradition looks to the medieval Italian saint, Francis of Assisi (1182–1226), as inspiration, guide, model and metaphor. The experiential 'vernacular theology' of Francis's life and writings was later developed more academically, especially by the Franciscan scholars St Bonaventure (1221–74) and Bl. John Duns Scotus (c. 1265–1308).

The guardians of this tradition are found especially in the three Orders founded by St Francis: the first Order (of Friars Minor [i.e. Lesser Brothers]) of men, both lay and cleric; the second Order of cloistered women, the Poor Clares and the third Order which exists in two forms, a Secular Franciscan Order (Third Order) for laymen and women in the world, and a Third Order Regular for religious communities of men or women inspired by Francis. In addition to these, diverse people, throughout the ages, have admired Francis and been inspired by him to be more like Christ in their lives.

St Clare of Assisi (1194–1253), friend and confidant of St Francis and co-founder of the Poor Clares, tended over the centuries to be overshadowed by Francis, but discoveries in the twentieth century of documents related to her life have challenged this picture. Her own spiritual journey was well advanced before she met Francis, and after their meeting, the influences were likely reciprocal, with her witnessing especially to the contemplative side of the tradition. While future study will certainly take her role more into account, throughout most of its history, the Franciscan spiritual tradition has focused primarily on the person of Francis.

God as Father and Trinity

In the writings of Francis, the primary term for God is Father, occurring over 90 times. Obviously, to think of God as Father immediately recalls the Son and the bond of unity between them. Thus, God as Trinity is central. This focus has several consequences. First, we must begin with the inner life of God which is love, the love flowing from Father to Son and back again in the bond of the

Spirit, giving us the Lover, the Beloved and their Love; in this respect relationality is primary. Second, this love of God overflows outside God first of all in creation, and then in redemption. We are all in relationship with God. Bonaventure will call this the *fontalis plenitudo in Patre*, the 'fountain-fullness in the Father'. To understand anything of the Christian mysteries (e.g. creation, incarnation, redemption, sacraments, prayer), we must begin with this bubbling, overflowing love of God. Third, in keeping with the dictum *bonum est diffusivum sui* ('the Good diffuses [overflows] itself'), God is experienced in the first instance as good. In the words of Francis, 'You, Lord, are the Supreme Good, the Eternal Good, from Whom comes all good, without Whom there is no Good'. Francis experienced life as the good gift of the good God – Father, Son and Holy Spirit.

Jesus Christ

The Son, the great King of heaven, 'did not regard equality with God as something to be grasped. Rather, he emptied himself taking the form of a slave . . . and humbled himself becoming obedient even unto death' (Phil. 2.6–8). It was not simply the fact of the Incarnation that impressed Francis, but the poverty and humility manifested in it: 'For you know the generous act of our Lord Jesus Christ, that though he was rich, yet for your sakes he became poor, so that by his poverty, you might become rich' (2 Cor. 8.9). This poverty and humility were focused especially in three events: the crib, the cross and the Eucharist.

The Crib

At Christmas in 1223, in the town of Greccio in Italy's Rieti valley, Francis wanted to preach the good news of the incarnation to those who thought they already understood it. He wanted the event to come alive, to be real, so he staged a nativity scene, a kind of 'living theater', to bring home that, in a true sense, the event is not just 'back then' but is real for us today. The crib scene was meant to help focus the poverty and humility of Jesus in becoming one with us. The Franciscans were inspired by this and would spread the practice through their preaching and ministry.

The Cross

The love of God which overflowed in the Incarnation reached its height (and depth) in the suffering and death of Jesus – he loved us unto the end (Jn 13.1). Francis' great devotion to the passion reached its climax in September of 1224 while he was praying at Mt La Verna in Tuscany. Shortly afterwards, as an early biographer tells us, the stigmata (visible wounds) of Christ's suffering which had been imprinted on Francis' heart, now became manifest in his body. In fact, his is the first known instance of the phenomenon of the stigmata. In a way, he himself became, in his person, the 'living theater'. St Bonaventure would interpret this as a mysticism of seraphic (i.e. burning, from Hebrew, *saraph*, to burn) love. In the later tradition, 'Seraphic' would become almost a synonym for 'Franciscan', (e.g. 'Seraphic Order'). Devotion to the passion, especially as focused in the practice of the Stations (or Way) of the cross would be spread by Franciscan preachers such as St Leonard of Port-Maurice (1676–1751). This would make the expensive pilgrimage to the site of Jesus' death in Jerusalem accessible to those who could not travel there themselves.

The Eucharist

The Incarnation and passion of Christ continue to be re-presented to us in the Eucharist. 'O sublime humility! O humble sublimity! That the Lord of the universe . . . so humbles himself for our salvation He hides Himself under the little form of bread!' (*Letter to all the Friars*). Typical of medieval piety, a strong sense of distance is felt between us and God as well as a stress on the real presence of Christ and on seeing Christ here. We are also told that Francis frequently received the Eucharist, but in the context of the times, it is hard to know exactly what this means; St Clare recommends at least seven times a year. At any rate, the Eucharist itself is a 'living theater' in which to encounter the poverty and humility of the overflowing love of God.

When Francis reflects on who Jesus is, he draws very heavily on images from the Gospel of John. Francis had a special fondness for lambs because they reminded him of the Lamb of God (Jn 1.29, 36). Jesus as the good shepherd (John 10) provides a model for leadership among the friars; and Jesus' washing the feet of his disciples (John 13) exemplifies what it means to be a 'lesser brother/friar minor'. This would in fact become the title of the fraternity, the Order of Friars Minor. And the poverty and humility of Jesus is clearly at the root of the Word becoming flesh in the incarnation (John 1).

Poverty

One prominent aspect of Francis and the Franciscan tradition is the concern with poverty. The basis of Franciscan poverty is thoroughly Christological. The great King of heaven did not 'grasp equality with God' but let go, emptying himself (Phil. 2.6–8); and for our sakes, he became poor (2 Cor. 8.9). Poverty is then a royal virtue. The core of poverty is thus the inner attitude of the Word who became flesh.

More typically Francis speaks of living *'sine proprio'* (with nothing of one's own) and of the dangers of appropriating anything to oneself. Among these, of course, are material possessions of different kinds but other types of 'possessions' are also mentioned, for example, learning, positions of power or authority, preaching and one's own good deeds. All things that are good belong to God, and to appropriate them as one's own is to trespass, as it were, on God's 'property rights'. Whoever appropriates anything to himself or herself in effect fails to attribute every good to God who is all good, and from whom all good flows. Not to acknowledge this is to misappropriate. This view of poverty comes very close to the biblical view of faith in which we recognize that we depend completely on God and that we have nothing of our own: all is gift, all is grace.

Mary

When Francis speaks of the poverty and humility of Jesus, he almost always thinks as well of Mary to whom he had a special devotion. As Queen of heaven, she shares in the 'letting go' of Christ. Francis wrote two prayers in her honour (the 'Salutation of the Blessed Virgin Mary' and an antiphon for his Office of the Passion) and refers to her frequently in his other writings. Three characteristics stand out. First, Mary is always seen in relationship to Christ: her dignity and status derive completely from him. Second, she is seen in relationship to the Trinity – she is chosen by the Father and consecrated by the Son and Holy Spirit. Third, she is seen in relation to the Church. Francis calls her 'virgin made church', and she models what we are all called to be. In his *Letter to all the Faithful*, Francis tells all men and women that they are called to be 'mothers' of Christ, that is, when they carry Him in their hearts and give birth to Him through their holy manner of working. This is the view of Mary in the Gospel of Luke. When someone from the crowd praises His mother because of her physical motherhood, Jesus replies, 'Rather, blessed are those who hear the word of God and keep it [put it into action]' (Lk. 11.27–8).

Creation

Francis is very well-known as a saint of nature, but we have to recognize that this is not really accurate. He was not a saint of nature at all, but rather a saint of creation. 'Creation' here is not a term of art, poetry or, even less, of science; it is a thoroughly religious term. In order to understand everything that exists at its deepest level, it must be seen in relation to another, the Creator. Creation always implies a Creator. All creation, including ourselves, is a gift of the over-flowing goodness of God. This stands in stark contrast to the Albigensian heresy prevalent at the time of Francis, which considered material things to be evil. If everyone and everything derive from the same Creator God, then everything and everyone belong deep down to one family. Thus Francis, with a strong sense of relationality, can speak of Brother Sun and Sister Moon and can preach the Gospel to animals as well as to humans. He thus fulfilled the command of Christ, 'Go into all the world and proclaim the good news to all of creation' (Mk 16.15).

All things not only come from God but also point to God. A rock reminded Francis of Christ, the Rock; light, of Christ the Light; trees, of the tree of the cross. The world is not simply something 'out there', separate from us to be used and abused as we wish, but is rather a mirror that reflects God and leads us back to God. They 'bear the meaning' of the Creator. St Bonaventure especially would develop a theology of all things as footprints (*vestigia*) and/or images of God. Influenced by the medieval Franciscan scholar, John Duns Scotus, the British poet Gerard Manley Hopkins would write in the nineteenth century, 'the world is charged with the grandeur of God'. It is not without reason that in 1979, Pope John Paul II declared Francis the patron of those who foster and work in the area of ecology.

In the light of this, Francis and the tradition have a strong sense of and respect for the unique giftedness of everything and everyone. For Duns Scotus this was so important he coined a special word to describe it; every unique creature has a *haecceitas* (a '*this-ness*'), a positive principle of individuation. Each thing and every person is especially wanted and loved by God. 'Haecceity' can be seen as a personal gift from God. Francis recognized that each of us has also received a personal call from the Spirit of God, and he showed a sensitivity to and respect for this Spirit given to each. He tells his friend Br Leo, who sought advice from him, 'In whatever way it seems best to you to please the Lord God and to follow His footprints and His poverty, do this with the blessing of God and my obedience' (*Francis and Clare* 1986: 47). And 'those friars who, by divine inspiration, desire to go among the Saracens . . . should ask permission' (*Francis and Clare* 1986: 144). This recognition undergirds the great diversity manifested in the tradition as well as its tendency to a certain amount of disorder.

The classic expression of the Franciscan view of creation is the *Canticle of the Creatures* composed by Francis shortly before his death:

> Praised (*laudato*) be you my Lord with all your creatures . . . through (*per*) Sister Moon and the stars . . . through Brother Wind . . . Sister Water . . . Brother Fire Mother Earth. (*Francis and Clare* 1986: 37–8)

The experience of being one family with all things comes through clearly; however, two words especially call for comment.

'Praised' (*laudato*, nine times in the poem). Praise is a prominent form of prayer in the Bible, especially in the psalms: *Hallelu-Yah* (Praise – the Lord

[Yahweh]). In praise we call to others to join us in recognizing the Giver and the gifts we receive, beginning with the simple fact of our own unique existence. Praise is a joyful response to the blessings of life, and Francis' whole life was one of praise. Praise is the characteristic Franciscan form of prayer. Later, Friar Blessed Jacopone da Todi (c. 1230–1306) would become prominent for composing his *Laudi* (Praises).

'Through' (*per*, ten times). This small Italian word can have three meanings: (1) 'for, because of', and this would express an attitude of thanksgiving; (2) 'by', expressing a sense of agency or instrumentality; and (3) 'through', expressing a deeper sense of seeing God's presence in and through creatures. Is Francis praising God because of the gift of creatures? Is he calling on creatures to join him in praising God (as in Ps 148)? Is he seeing and praising God in and through all creatures? Each of these can find support in other writings of Francis as well as in the early sources about him. Each expresses something worthy and true. All are at home in the thought of Francis. We do not have one word in English that captures all of these nuances, so we have to make a choice but it is important to keep all three meanings in mind. Francis was a poet, and poets play with levels of meaning of language.

Francis says of God, 'You are beauty' and St Bonaventure tells us 'in all things beautiful, he "contuited" Beauty itself' (*Francis of Assisi*, II: 596). He experienced God's beauty when he sensed/experienced (contuited) the beauty of creatures. He rejoiced in all the works of the Lord's hands. And Clare tells us, 'Cling to him whose Beauty all the heavenly hosts admire' (*Francis and Clare* 1986: 204). In the Franciscan tradition, the journey of the Christian life is an aesthetical undertaking, a *'via pulchritudinis'*, a way of beauty. The Incarnation itself is primarily a work of beauty, the expression of God's abundant love and generosity, and not an afterthought in view of human sinfulness. Ours is not a journey out of the world to heaven; we journey through the beauty of the world and beyond towards the beauty of heaven in God.[1]

While surely aware of brokenness, suffering and sinfulness, the Franciscan vision is an optimistic one rooted in a vision of the relationship between the divine Artist and the work of art which is all of creation. The experience of beauty is transformative and moves us to restore, where blemished, the beauty of the world, both the natural world and the social world of human life. Beauty will be a pervasive theme in the thought of both Bonaventure and Duns Scotus.

'Make me an Instrument of Your Peace'

These are the opening words of the famous 'Peace Prayer of St Francis'. While the prayer was not written by Francis (it appears for the first time in 1912), it does capture well a very central concern of Francis. He was a saint of peace.

The world of Francis, the early thirteenth century, was one of great transition and much violence, not unlike our own. There were wars and strife between the Holy Roman Emperor and the Pope; between individual Italian city states (e.g. Perugia and Assisi); between the nobles and merchants, the emerging middle class; between the papacy and religious movements pushing for reforms and between the Christian West and Islam (the Crusades). Francis grew up in this world; he fought for Assisi against Perugia, and spent time in prison. Later he was riding off, well armed, to fight with Walter of Brienne against the emperor when he had the dream that marked one of the earliest steps in his conversion process.

In his Testament, Francis wrote, 'The Lord revealed to me a greeting, "May the Lord give you peace"', and we know from the early sources that he indeed used this greeting. He would begin his preaching with it and greet people along the road in the same way. When a brother travelling with him saw the hostility the greeting sometimes aroused (some considered it not appropriately 'religious') and wanted to use another, Francis told him not to worry 'for they do not understand the ways of God'. The same sources also tell how in fact his presence did bring peace to strife-torn cities such as Siena and Arezzo, and his own Assisi where the mayor and the bishop were at odds. He composed another stanza for his Canticle of the Creatures to be sung before them, showing how God is praised (*laudato*) by/through (*per*) those who work for peace.

Like the prophets of the Old Testament and Jesus, Francis did not offer primarily political, economic or social analyses of the problems. He saw them ultimately in religious terms, and he offered solutions in these terms as well. The peacemakers are those 'who grant pardon for love of you' (Canticle); forgiveness is a way to peace. We do not appropriate (hold to ourselves) hurt and wrong done to us, but let go of it. In his *Admonitions* (13–15) and the famous *Dictate on True and Perfect Joy*, Francis tells us that the true peacemakers are those who preserve peace of mind and body for love of our Lord Jesus Christ despite what they suffer in the world.

Historians have noted that two of the biggest causes of the strife and violence in medieval Italy were avarice and offended honour. As noted above, when Francis turned and looked at Jesus in his Incarnation, life, passion, death and resurrection, he was overwhelmed by the poverty and humility of the Son and sought to imitate these in his life. The first words from the risen Christ to his disciples were 'Peace be with you' (Jn 20.9–21) and we read that Jesus reconciled all things 'making peace by the blood of his cross' (Col. 1.20). Poverty and humility were the way to peace with God, so when Francis turned and looked at the violence in his world, he saw poverty and humility also as direct antidotes to the greed and pride at the root of so many problems.

Mission

Francis began his conversion by turning away from his old life, but to what was he turning? He worked with lepers, rebuilt ruined churches and prayed as a hermit. Early in his conversion, he heard the Gospel read which described Jesus sending His disciples out to preach penance and the coming of the kingdom (Mt. 10.9; Lk. 10.4). He responded, 'This is what I wish, this is what I seek, this is what I long to do with all my heart!' This marked a turning point. Francis became a preacher of penance, exhorting others to a *metanoia*, a change of heart and life.

This is the basic mission of the Franciscan tradition; simply put, it is 'to observe the Holy Gospel of Our Lord Jesus Christ'. All preach, all proclaim by the life they live. There is no one or specific Franciscan work. What work one did was entirely secondary and anything was all right that was not against the Gospel and, as Francis put it, 'does not extinguish the Spirit of holy prayer and devotion'. The primary means for living was by work, and the early friars worked; begging was necessary when they did not receive enough from working for their daily necessities. Over time things would shift in the direction of mendicancy.

The primary Franciscan mission, then, is to live the Gospel, but there is 'mission' in a narrower sense, that is, to bring the Gospel to non-Christians. In the world of Francis, this meant the Islamic world, then known as Saracens. He was the first founder of a religious group to mention this kind of mission in his Rule. Those who were moved 'by divine inspiration' (i.e. were led by the Spirit) could request to go, not 'to' the Saracens, but 'among' them. Once approved for this, they were to live the Gospel among them, not engaging in strife and argument, and to proclaim the Gospel explicitly only when they see 'it is God's will'.

By the end of the thirteenth century, the Franciscans could be found at the ends of the known earth, including the Far East, Mongolia and China. When they were gathered in chapter in 1493, word reached them of Columbus' discovery of a 'new world', one which did not know the Gospel, and they responded eagerly. Twenty years later, in 1513, Spanish Franciscans were in what became Florida in the United States. 1523 found them in Mexico, from where they eventually would set sail for the Philippine islands (1578). From 1769 through 1848, initially under the guidance of Friar Bl. Junipero Serra, they founded missions in what is now California.

Contemplation

From the beginning of his conversion, Francis was drawn to prayer, but he and his followers discerned that they should go out, following the example of the Lord, to live and preach the Gospel. But Jesus also took time to go off alone in prayer (e.g. Mk 1.35; Lk. 4.42, 5.16, 6.12; Mt. 14.23; Jn 6.15), and the desire to imitate Christ in this as well was a very strong one in Francis and throughout the movement he led. As he went around on his preaching tours, he would often stop at 'places' (*loci*) to pray and these would often become hermitages or places of retreat. The sources indicate that Francis observed several 'lents' and may have spent as much as 200 days out of the year at such 'places'. Among the best known would be Mt La Verna, Greccio and other sites in the Rieti valley, southeast of Assisi.

Francis wrote a short 'Rule for Hermitages' to guide and inspire his followers. Those who wish (again, led by the Spirit), in small groups (three or four, at most), could retire to a hermitage where two would be 'mothers', who would care for basic needs, and two would be 'sons' to live apart in private cells. After a time, they should exchange roles. The desire to keep this practice alive and meaningful continued throughout the Franciscan movement. Various names have been given to such places (a hermitage, a solitude, a *retiro*, a *sacer recessus* [holy place of withdrawal]). Today throughout the world, there are active movements to embody and adapt this practice for all, regardless of their living situations.

The balance between activity and mission in the world, on the one hand, and withdrawal for prayer and contemplation, on the other, has been a tension in the movement from the beginning, appearing clearly in Francis himself. At one time, desiring to make contemplation his main activity, Francis asked his friends Sylvester and St Clare for advice. They both independently advised him to continue to preach in the world as well. But it is especially St Clare and her followers, the Poor Clares, who will embody and represent the need and challenge for contemplation to be a regular and recurring part of any life that seeks to follow the Gospel of Christ.

Conclusion

The Christian faith and its spiritual traditions are marked by diversity and a number of tensions (e.g. God is both One and Three; Jesus is both human and divine). These need to be held together, and different traditions do this in various ways. Where a tradition begins and what it stresses will make a difference and will give it a certain style or tone. As indicated here the Franciscan spiritual tradition looks to the example and the model of Francis and Clare of Assisi in following the footsteps of Jesus Christ and holding these tensions in fruitful union.

Note

1 For more on this see Chapter 30 on 'Art and Spirituality'.

Bibliography and Further Reading

St Bonaventure (2002), *Journey of the Soul into God – Itinerarium Mentis in Deum*, trans. and intro. Zachary Hayes OFM and Philotheus Boehner OFM (Works of St Bonaventure, Volume II), St Bonaventure, NY: Franciscan Institute Publications.

Delio, Ilia OSF (2003), *A Franciscan View of Creation: Learning to Live in a Sacramental World*. St Bonaventure, NY: Franciscan Institute Publications.

Francis and Clare: The Complete Works (1986), trans. Regis J. Armstrong OFM and Ignatius C. Brady OFM, New York, NY: Paulist Press.

Francis of Assisi: Early Documents (1999–2001), trans. and ed. Regis J. Armstrong OFM. 3 vols, New York, NY: New City Press.

Lynch, Cyprian OFM (ed.) (1989), *A Poor Man's Legacy: An Anthology of Franciscan Poverty*. St Bonaventure, NY: Franciscan Institute Publications.

Moorman, John R. H. (1963), *Saint Francis of Assisi*. London: SPCK.

Osborne, Kenan OFM (2003), *The Franciscan Intellectual Tradition: Tracing Its Origins*. St Bonaventure, NY: Franciscan Institute Publications.

Short, William J. OFM (1999), *Poverty and Joy: The Franciscan Tradition* (Traditions of Christian Spirituality Series). Maryknoll, NY: Orbis Books.

10 Carmelite Spirituality

Peter Tyler

The School of Carmel

The Carmelite order which would eventually include such illustrious members as Ss Teresa of Avila, John of the Cross, Simon Stock, Thérèse of Lisieux, Elizabeth of the Trinity and Edith Stein traces its origins to the Jewish 'School of the Prophets' traditionally established by Elijah on the sides of Mt Carmel near Haifa in present-day Israel.[1] Varied etymologies are suggested for the origins of the word including that from the words *krm* and *l* suggesting 'a vineyard', others include 'a scrubby area'. Today it remains a green verdant place that dominates the Mediterranean landscape for miles around. As well as its Jewish and Christian associations, for the Muslims it is associated with *Khidr* – 'The Green One' or 'Verdant One', another name given to Elijah in this tradition. Thus the cave of Elijah, situated adjacent to the present day Carmelite Priory of 'Stella Maris' and currently a synagogue, has during its 2,500 year existence been a church, a mosque, a synagogue and possibly a Roman shrine (See: Florencio del Niño Jesús 1924 and Giordano 1995[2]).

Carmel is frequently mentioned in the Jewish scriptures, perhaps most famously in the Song of Songs 7.5: 'Your head crowns you like Carmel and your flowing locks are like purple'. It is the place where Elijah performs some of the most important acts of his ministry, in particular the fight with the prophets of Baal (1 Kings 18. 20–40), the prophecy from the cloud in the sea and his final taking up in the fiery chariot watched by Elisha (2 Kings 2).This latter is said to have inspired the original habits of the Carmelite order which were streaked to represent the cinders from the chariot scorching their robes.

Thus, the mystical mountain maintained and maintains a pull and a power for Christian, Jewish and Muslim people alike and throughout the history of the Carmelite order, the metaphors and tropes of Elijah and his mountain continue to recur: the ascent of the mountain, the chariot, the raven, the fire, the cloud from the sea, the desert and the vineyard.

Historically the origins of the order are cloudy. The eleventh and twelfth centuries had seen the first significant medieval encounter between Islam and Christianity known as 'The Crusades' begun with the First Crusade preached by Pope Urban II in 1095 at Clermont-Ferrand in France and continuing throughout the twelfth century. By the early thirteenth century we begin to hear reports of groups of former Crusaders settling on the 'Holy Mountain' near the Wadi 'ain es-Siah associated with Elijah. Thus we find Jacques de Vitry, Bishop of nearby Acre, writing around 1216: 'Others after the example and in imitation of the holy solitary Elijah, the Prophet, lived as hermits in the beehives of small cells on Mount Carmel . . . near the spring which is called the Spring of Elijah' (Smet 1988, 1.3). It was this disparate group, of whom we know so little, who approached Albert of Vercelli, Patriarch of Jerusalem, for a Rule sometime between 1206 and 1214. This Rule, the original form of which is not known[3] was finally promulgated by Pope Innocent IV in his 1247 Bull *Quem honorem Conditoris*.[4] After 1214 the fortunes of the young order underwent another twist as increasing Muslim incursions into the Christian lands around Acre had made it necessary for the group of hermits to leave the Holy Land in 1238. A General Chapter of the Order in Aylesford, Kent in 1247 eventually produced *Quem honorem Conditoris*. Thus this final version of the Rule holds all the contradictions and tensions that the fledgling order had experienced up to this point. In it we find echoes of the free-range hermits of the Holy Land, the small group who wanted to live as a community on the Sacred Mountain and the final manifestation of the order as a European mendicant order akin to the well-established Franciscans and Dominicans. It is these tensions and contradictions that make the *Rule* such a fascinating and potentially controversial document. As Kees Waaijman puts it,

> The Rule of Carmel embodies three religious concepts: the eremitic way of life, the cenobitic form of life and life as a mendicant brother. The combination of these three concepts is not the product of careful thought but of life lived within a single century: from hermit to cenobite, from cenobite to mendicant. The tensions between these three types of religious life have internally led to conflicts, down to this day. But they have also forced the Carmelites to go below the surface, to a deeper level, to look for the mystical space of contemplation, a level from the perspective of which all forms and concepts are relative. (1999: 9)

The simplicity and openness of the *Rule* contains a *nostalgie* for the fresh vistas and solitariness of the Holy Mountain of Carmel and it is to this *nostalgie* that later reformers such as Teresa of Avila and John of the Cross would respond in their sixteenth century 're-formation' of the Order. The 'mitigations' of 1247 included stipulations that brought the order closer to the mendicant life as then envisaged in Europe. Thus, foundations no longer needed to be made in desert places, meals were to be taken in common, the canonical office was recited and abstinence was mitigated. In the words of Joachim Smet: 'The Carmelite Rule of 1247 brought solitude to the town when life in the desert was no longer feasible . . . and all reforms in Carmel have always been to their contemplative origins' (1997: 47). For McGreal 'the essence of the Rule (of 1247) is the desire to live a life of allegiance to Jesus Christ, serving him faithfully with a pure heart and a clear conscience' (1999: 26). This service of Christ, through prayer and service to one's neighbour, is at the heart of all subsequent Carmelite Spirituality. The life is lived through seeing the face of Christ in the people around us and in service of the world. Thus, the early Carmelites were part of the struggle to regain the Holy Land from Muslim control, but they saw that struggle not in armed terms but in the terms of a peaceful and God-centred prayerful ushering in of the Kingdom. Thus, solitude, silence, prayer and reconciliation are central to this task. Chapter 7 of the Rule, which is taken by many Carmelites to be the heart of the Rule, states 'Let each remain in his cell or near it, meditating night and day on the Word of the Lord and keeping vigil in prayer, unless he is occupied with other lawful activities' (Waaijman 1999: 31). In this respect, the Carmelite Rule embodies some of the key elements of the earlier 'Desert Spirituality' which Sr Benedicta Ward has already analysed above.[5] Where Carmelite Spirituality differs from this earlier Desert Spirituality is in its added emphasis on finding silence and solitude in the midst of the world and active engagement in, for example, preaching and works of mercy: 'The following of Christ, the great project of the Rule, is achieved by becoming a community of disciples who are everything to Christ' (McGreal 1999: 30). A vision of community inspired by that described in Acts, Chapters 2 and 4, was the original vision of the early Carmelites.

This new form of life, the prototype of all later orders in the church, was ratified at the Second Council of Lyon of 1274, with the Rules of life of the three other great mendicant orders of the Western Church: the Franciscans, the Augustinians and the Dominicans. From hereon, the wildness of the original denizens of Mt Carmel would be tamed as they became plugged into mainstream religious life in medieval Western Europe. Vincent de Beauvais gives 1238 as the traditional date for the move of the order from the Holy Land to Europe; however, this is probably just an approximation. What we do know is that by the middle of the thirteenth century communities with the name 'Carmelite', and a connection to the Crusader states of the Middle East, were appearing in Cyprus, Messina in Sicily, Aylesford and Hulne in England and Marseilles in France. The origin of the Carmelites in England was largely typical of how the order spread throughout Europe. The original invitation to come to Aylesford in Kent was given by Sir Richard Grey of Codnor in 1242 who had earlier gone on Crusade with Sir Richard of Cornwall, having landed in Acre in the Holy Land in October 1240. There he would no doubt have met the order, been impressed by their presence and later been happy to offer them sanctuary on his own lands when they needed it. Similar foundations were quickly followed in Kent (Lossenham) and Norfolk (Bradmer).

As has been said, in this transition from the semi-eremetical life of Palestine to the cold Northern European lifestyle many changes had to be adapted in the mitigation of the order of 1247 and by 1291 the Carmelites had had to abandon their beloved Mt Carmel altogether. It would be 500 years before they were allowed to return to their spiritual home.

In the meantime, the order spread with some success throughout Western Europe, so that by the end of the thirteenth century in England, for example, the order had 30 houses under four 'distinctions': London, Norwich, Oxford and York, as well as new houses in Scotland and Ireland. Around this time (1281 at a General Chapter in London) the order began to assert its origins among the 'school of prophets' of Elijah and Elisha around the 'fountain of Elijah' at Carmel. Marian devotion was also enshrined at the heart of the order and in particular to Our Lady of Mt Carmel.[6] John Baconthorpe ('doctor resolutus', d. 1348) was instrumental in reinterpreting the story from 1 Kings 18.44 about the small cloud that arises from the Mediterranean Sea which will eventually float over the land and form a downpour to refresh the land. He interpreted the cloud as representing the Virgin Mary – the pure essence of water condensed from the saline of humanity – from whom eventually would come the saving cloudburst of Christ, refreshing and bringing the Water of Life to humanity. At this time the order also took to itself the special titles accorded to Mary such as 'Stella Maris' and 'Rosa Mystica'.[7] The replacement of the original sizzled, striped mantle of the order in 1287 with a white one resembling the more conventional habits of the Franciscans and Dominicans and Pope John XXII's Bull of 1326 'Super Cathedram', which extended to the order all the rights and exemptions as existed for these older established orders, meant that by the middle of fourteenth century the order was firmly established at the heart of Western medieval theocracy.

Crises and Growth

Thus the order was well-established to withstand the great crises of the traumatic European fourteenth and fifteenth centuries: the Great Plague, the Schism and the Hundred Years War. In Britain, for example, the order was intimately connected with the promulgation of the 'new mysticism' of such great mystics as Walter Hilton and Richard Rolle. Thus, Thomas Fishlake undertook the first translation of Walter Hilton's 'Ladder of Perfection' into Latin and Richard Misyn (d. 1462), one time Prior at Lincoln, translated Richard Rolle into English. Robert Southfield, a member of the community at Norwich, was a renowned spiritual director who was visited by Margery Kempe on her peregrinations. Yet the order was also establishing a reputation as producing some of the most formidable and sharp theological minds of the age. Recent work by Kevin Alban, for example (see Alban 2010), has established the deep significance of writers such as Thomas Netter of Waldon (d. 1430) in shaping the study and curriculum of scholastic theology right up the end of the medieval period. However, as well as his penetrating theological work, Netter, as Prior Provincial, also promoted and defended the development of 'lay spirituality', especially among women.[8] In retrospect, Netter's promotion of lay female spirituality seems prescient of the future path the order would take as it moved into the renaissance and reformation periods. In this respect, one of the most significant moments for the future development of the order can be seen to be the authorization by John Soreth (Prior from 1451–71) of the reception of women into the order. Beginning in Florence with the foundation of the convent of Our Lady of Angels in 1452 the female wing rapidly established itself in France, Belgium, Italy and Spain. And it would be in Spain that the next significant moment in the history of the order would happen in the sixteenth century.

Reform from Within: Teresa of Avila and John of the Cross

As stated above, the Carmelite Order contained a *nostalgie* for its home at Mt Carmel from its very inception and it was a female Carmelite, St Teresa of Avila (1515–82), who would intuitively embody this desire to return to the roots of Carmel. She took the name for her reform movement, *Descalzo* or 'Discalced', from the association of being shoeless,[9] a spiritual reform that predated her and included such famous 'shoeless' Franciscans as her great mentor, St Peter of Alcantara, who was to do so much to shape subsequent Spanish sixteenth-century spirituality. Teresa's reform was essentially a desire to return to the original eremitical and cenobitic element of the Carmelite life at the expense of the mendicant element (although this would remain). Thus, two of the greatest enemies that Teresa of Avila's male co-worker St John of the Cross (1542–91) would make in the emerging reform, Fray Francisco Crisóstomo and Padre Diego Evangelista, were both rebuked by John for spending too much time preaching outside of their communities and not enough in recollection. In this respect, their charism seems closer to that of the medieval mendicant Carmelites rather than the more eremetical Teresa and John.

As well as representing a new form of female Carmelite Spirituality, Teresa is the first of a illustrious line of female Carmelite saints whose intellectual contribution to the church would be outstanding.[10] As well as her reformation of the order Teresa is perhaps best known today for her extraordinary writings – a tradition of exceptional spiritual writing which later would be taken up by Thérèse of Lisieux and Edith Stein.

In 1561 the Inquisitor of Toledo, Francisco de Soto y Salazar, suggested that Teresa present a description of her experiences as Foundress of the Discalced Carmelite reform and her methods of prayer. The consequence was her writing of the *Book of Her Life (Libro de la Vida)*, the first draft being completed in 1562 and the final draft in 1565.[11] In this text, one of the great classics of early Spanish literature, Teresa revealed her gifts as a noted writer in the vernacular, stylist and mystical theologian. As I have argued elsewhere (Tyler 2011a), although Teresa, as a woman, was not allowed to study theology formally at university (unlike her esteemed co-worker, St John of the Cross) she absorbed and reinterpreted the medieval tradition of mystical theology (*theologia mystica*) that she had been able to read as a young woman in the writings of, among others, the great Franciscan masters Francisco de Osuna and Bernardino de Laredo. These works, freely available to a laywoman in early sixteenth-century Spain, had recently been proscribed in the 1559 Spanish Index of Valdés. Although intended as a means of controlling lay spirituality (perhaps the opposite of the gentle support that the English Carmelites had been offering to laywomen only a hundred years before), the effect of the Index was to galvanize writers such as Teresa into producing some of the greatest spiritual classics of the Western Church. Space does not permit a fuller exposition of the techniques and approaches to the spiritual life developed by Teresa in her subsequent *Camino de Perfección (Way of Perfection)*, *Meditaciones del amor de Dios (Meditations on the Love of God)*, *Libro de Las Fundaciones (Book of Foundations)* and *Las Moradas (The Interior Castle)*. Suffice it to say that we have in these few precious books the writings of one of the great masters of prayer on the nature of the human quest for the Divine and the Divine response in love and mercy (See Tyler 2011a).

As mentioned, while Teresa was developing her Discalced reform of the order, she met her outstanding co-worker, St John of the Cross, or as he was known at the time, Juan de Santo Matía[12] in Medina del Campo in 1567.[13] At this time, Teresa was 52, more than twice John's age and fresh from founding her first convent in Avila and preparing her second foundation at Medina.[14] Like Teresa, John was finding it difficult to pursue the life of greater asceticism closer to the eremetical life of the first Carmelite fathers in the order as then constituted in Spain. Although John felt he wanted to leave the order and join the stricter (and more eremetical) Carthusians, Teresa persuaded John to remain in the Carmelite order and work with her to reform it from within. Calling him 'my novice' she persuaded him to begin the first male house of the reform at Duruelo near Avila with four others. On 28 November 1568, the Carmelite Father Provincial heard the four friars renounce the Mitigated Rule of the Carmelites and embrace the Primitive Rule of Our Lady of Mt Carmel. John also now took the name for which he has become universally known – San Juan de la Cruz, Saint John of the Cross.

Duruelo, where the first friars[15] announced 'the Primitive Rule' in 1568, directly embodied the desert spirit of the first Carmelite hermits. It was 'an unknown, out-of-the-way place. Rather than a town, it amounted to an insignificant group of farmhouses' (Ruiz 2000: 96). Even today it is still a remote place and virtually nothing remains of the original foundation. Although primitive and poor in the extreme the little hermitage of Duruelo gave John and the first companions exactly what they were looking for. Julián of Avila, a frequent visitor, wrote,

> This little house, and the other friars who began to take the habit, so stirred one's devotion that I, along with a very religious priest, named Gonzalo de Aranda, felt devoutly moved to go there on a pilgrimage by foot; and we stayed there I don't know how many days, for it seemed we were in paradise. (ibid.: 106)

The primitive community at Duruelo would always stay close to John's heart even if, as we learn from accounts of his death bed, he vowed never to speak of it. His co-founder, Teresa, was as usual less reticent in her descriptions:

> The choir was in the garret. The centre part was sufficiently lofty to enable them to say the Hours, but they had to stoop a great deal to get in far enough to hear Mass. In the two corners nearest the church they had two small hermitages (full of hay – for the place was very cold), in which there was only room for them to lie prostrate or be seated, for the roof was almost on their heads . . . I knew that from the end of Matins until Prime they did not retire to their cells but remained there in prayer – for their prayer was so deep that it sometimes happened to them to go to Prime with a considerable quantity of snow on their habits and not to feel it. (Teresa of Avila *Fundaciones*: 14)

Following Teresa's pattern as described in the *Book of the Foundations* John would spread the reform by embracing already exisiting communities. As we have seen already in the history of Carmel, this would often be about embracing existing groups of devout laypeople who already practiced deep contemplative prayer; in the case of sixteenth-century Spain, these women were known as *beatas*, literally 'blessed ones'.[16] In this respect Teresa and John can be seen as responding to the ancient call to Carmel and its itinerant group of devout, usually lay, souls that formed the nucleus of that early community – a theme that recurs throughout the history of the order.

In 1574 Teresa's work came under inquisitorial suspicion – due, among other things, to the vindictive malice of the Princess of Eboli, and her manuscript of 'The Book of the Life' disappeared into the Inquisition's hands until after her death in 1582. This was only the beginning of many and various troubles for John and Teresa which ended up with them both being confined and ordered not to found any new convents. In the case of Teresa she was confined to the Carmel of Toledo, John himself was spared this luxury, being arrested in Avila on the night of 2 December 1577 by a group of Carmelite friars and conveyed by night, blindfolded, to the Mitigated Priory in Toledo there to be held prisoner. In June 1616, almost 40 years after the event, Juan de Santa María, John's second jailer in Toledo gave this account of John's imprisonment in Toledo:

> During the time I was in charge, which was the latter part of his imprisonment, they brought him to the refectory three or four times, with all friars present, to receive the discipline, which they gave him with a certain severity. He never spoke, but rather bore it with patience and love. When this was over, they sent him back at once to his prison. (Tyler 2010)

A lesser man may well have cracked under such physical, psychological and spiritual strain. But yet, confined, as he said later 'in the belly of that whale', John was able to find God in the deepest darkness of this dark night and so begin his remarkable career as a poet and theologian. His great poems, including *The Dark Night of the Soul*, *The Living Flame of Love* and *The Spiritual Canticle*, along with their surviving accompanying commentaries, present the truths of the life of faith in a remarkably perceptive fashion. As with Teresa, the paradox is that inquisitorial and institutional attempts to suppress their spirituality led to an ecstatic embrace of God's love resulting in some of the greatest spiritual writings in the history of Christianity. In this Teresa and John remain true sons and daughters of Carmel and able to inspire countless souls to the present day.

Carmel in the Modern World

One such soul was the twentieth-century Jewish philosopher, Edith Stein (1891–1942), later to be known as Sr Teresa Benedicta of the Cross.[17] Born of a devout Jewish family in Breslau, Germany, Edith developed an early love and skill in philosophy which was to remain with her throughout her life. The greatest influence on her philosophical development was the work of Edmund Husserl and the newly emerging phenomenological school. From her Jewish faith, Edith turned to atheism, although always with a lively interest in the 'God question'. Later in this volume Stephen Bullivant will quote the dialogue between the Orthodox bishop, Tikhon, and the enigmatic Stavrogin in Dostoevsky's 1872 novel *The Demons*. In this dialogue Tikhon informs the unbelieving Stavrogin that: 'A complete atheist stands on the next-to-last upper step to the most complete faith'. This quote could have been directly applied to the young Edith. In all her atheistic questing she sensed the importance of the divine perspective for all phenomenological research. The key moment of her conversion occurred in 1921 when she stayed at the house of some friends, the Conrad-Martiuses, at their home near Bergzabern. Wanting some reading for the evening she looked through the bookshelves of her hosts and found Teresa of Avila's 'Book of the Life' referred to above. She was not able to sleep that night and was completely gripped by the narrative that Teresa presented. Afterwards she would say of Teresa's book: 'This is the truth'; finally she had found what she had been looking for (See Herbstrith 1992: 65). As she would write later 'It is just the people who at first passionately embrace the world who penetrate farthest into the depths of the soul. Once God's powerful hand has freed them from its allurements, they are taken into their innermost selves' (From 'Die Seelenburg' in *Welt und Person: Beitrag zum christlichen Wahrheitsstreben*, Stein 4: 66).

Once Edith had found 'the treasure hidden in the field' she went away, sold everything she had and bought the field. She was baptized a Christian in 1922 and began an extended study of the Church Fathers and scripture, especially the works of St Thomas Aquinas. The next 10 years were ones of teaching and work to reconcile Christian and atheist philosophy, in particular the phenomenology of her 'master' Husserl and the high scholasticism of Thomas Aquinas. Perhaps the most remarkable fruit of this time is the delightful *Festschrift* she wrote for Husserl's seventieth birthday, 'What is Philosophy?', where a tired Husserl slumps down on his sofa after a long day's lecturing only to be surprised by the shade of St Thomas Aquinas who then proceeds to question the master on the nature of phenomenology and God (reprinted as *Knowledge and Faith*, Edith Stein, Collected Works, 8).

Husserl would end his days a Christian having experienced a deathbed conversion in 1938. On hearing the news, Edith, just about to take her solemn vows in the Cologne Carmel,[18] wrote to another sister: 'As regards my dear Master, I have no worries about him. To me, it has always seemed strange that God could restrict his mercy to the boundaries of the visible Church. God is truth, and whoever seeks the truth is seeking God, whether he knows it or not' (Stein, Letter 259, quoted in Herbstrith 1992: 139).

From the original fathers on the Jewish mountain of Israel, to the *converso* Teresa of Avila and John of the Cross, and now in these words Edith summarizes the Carmelite charism of openness to all cultures. For her, and for all true Carmelites, God's saving action does not stop at the doors of the church but extends to all humanity in all its suffering and confusion. For Edith, this would become a terrible reality as the Nazi persecution of the Jews gathered pace and the net slowly closed in on her and her family. Despite her conversion to Christianity she was still a target for Nazi persecution and after the horrendous events of *Kristallnacht* on 8 November 1938 she was forced to leave Germany to seek shelter with the Carmelite community at Echt, Holland. Despite the persecution throughout all this time Edith was able to continue her philosophico-theological writings on the interface of phenomenology and theology. We are fortunate today that most of them have been or are being translated in the splendid series of her writings published by the Institute for Carmelite Studies in Washington (see bibliography below). What they reveal, and scholars are still working hard on interpreting them,[19] is a woman who grasped the essence of Carmelite Spirituality in all its intellectual depth and existential consequence. Since her student days Edith had been fascinated by the 'nature of empathy', and in fact had written her doctoral thesis on the subject (published as *On the Problem of Empathy* in The Collected Works, 3). Commenting on this interest, Roman Ingarden writes that 'What interested her most was the question of defining the possibility of mutual communication between human beings, in other words, the possibility of establishing community. This was more than a theoretical concern for her; belonging to a community was a personal necessity, something that vitally affected her identity' (Ingarden 1979: 472 in Herbstrith 1992: 146). Once again we have that other great Carmelite theme – the need to find God in community. Perhaps, as Edith realized, our hope as alienated, atomized, late capitalist individuals lies in the return to community as the manifestation of our essential natures as *homo empathicus*.

The other great theme that emerges from these late writings of Edith is the need for *radical Christian life*. It is not enough, says Edith, to be '"a good Catholic" who "does his duty", "reads the right newspaper", and "votes correctly" – and then does just as he pleases'.[20] At a time of general Christian indifference to the fate of the Jews in Germany (with some notable and noble exceptions), her critique of complacent bourgeois 'Christendom'[21] is as striking as it is relevant to us in the West today who see a tired old bourgeois church brought to its knees by complacency and indifference. Such indifference, suggests Edith, will lead to disaster. Rather, we should strive for *radical Gospel living*, 'in the presence of God, with the simplicity of a child and the humility of a publican'. This call for radical Christian life, especially in the mystery of following Christ on the path to Calvary, would come to her suddenly when the SS officers arrived at Echt on the afternoon of 2 August, 1942 demanding that she leave with her sister, Rosa, who had become an extern sister at the convent. In the shock and surprise, the whole neighbourhood came out to protest this indecent act. In the crowd and confusion Rosa became alarmed and upset. In her distress Edith took her hand gently and said 'Come, Rosa. We're going for our people'.[22] We have fragmentary accounts of what happened to Edith next including reports from Westerbork, the Nazi holding camp in Holland for all deported Jews (where the other great Jewish mystic, Etty Hillesum, would also be held) and from guards and functionaries as her train moved slowly East to the killing fields of Auschwitz. One account, from the Dutch official Mr Wielek at Westerbork, will suffice to give a sense of Edith's last days on earth:

The one sister who impressed me immediately, whose warm, glowing smile has never been erased from my memory, despite the disgusting incidents I was forced to witness, is the one whom I think the Vatican may one day canonize. From the moment I met her in the camp at Westerbork . . . I knew: here is someone truly great. For a couple of days she lived in that hellhole, walking, talking and praying . . . like a saint. And she really was one. That is the only fitting way to describe this middle-aged woman who struck everyone as so young, who was so whole and honest and genuine. (in Herbstrith 1992: 186)

Edith went to her death at Auschwitz, we assume it was on 9 August 1942, the day on which she is now celebrated as St Teresa Benedicta of the Cross since 1998. I have ended with this account of Edith's life, thought and terrible death, as a condensation of all that has created Carmelite Spirituality and sustained it through its 1,000 years of existence. From the mountains of Palestine to the Gates of Auschwitz the Carmelite calling can be seen as one that places the individual into the deepest and most intimate relationship with God as a call to radical personal transformation. From this transformation arises the need to seek Christ in all His beloved children, regardless of race, creed or religion. As we have seen, Carmelite Spirituality transcends the boundaries of any small creed or sect to present a universal call to holiness in union with Our Lord and Saviour through His Blessed Cross and Resurrection. In its unique tensions and potentialities, Carmelite Spirituality is wonderfully adapted to promote the development and transformation of the individual into a son or daughter of Jesus Christ.

Notes

1 Sadly space will not permit a full exposition of all the great Carmelite saints. For more on the other saints not discussed in this chapter please refer to the bibliography at the end of this chapter.
2 P. Florencio's book written before the troubles in the Holy Land in the middle of the twentieth century gives some fascinating details about the mutual respect between the 'dervish and sufi' communities of the Holy Mountain and the Carmelite Order.
3 Bernard Oller in the late fourteenth Century wrote that 'good faith and prescription were sufficient for them' (Smet 1988, 1.18). A manuscript that comes closest to the form of the original is that preserved in the collection of Carmelite writings edited by the Catalan provincial, Philip Ribot (d.1391). Although many scholars dismiss the reliability of Ribot, Waaijman, whose account of the *Rule* I draw heavily on here, is happy that his manuscript gives us a close perspective on the original rule (Waaijman 1999: 18 ff).
4 Just to complicate scholarship, the original text of this Bull is also lost. A copy of the original is however still in the Vatican (See Waaijman 1999: 19).
5 See also Tyler (2011b).
6 Found in the so-called *Rubrica Prima* at the beginning of the new Constitutions of the Order.

7   But on this, see also Margaret Barker's concluding comments in her opening chapter on Temple Spirituality.

8   His most famous spiritual daughter was Emma Stapleton whose anchorage hole still remains on the premises of a local printing firm in Norwich which now lies over the site of the medieval priory of Norwich. See Alban 2010: 49.

9   The possession of shoes was associated with wealth, akin to the English phrase for well-off people – 'well heeled'. A number of commentators (e.g. Crisógono) refer to the un-Discalced Carmelites as 'Calced'. Conversations with un-Discalced Carmelites suggest that this term is not considered appropriate. Thus, throughout this chapter when I refer to the un-Discalced Carmelites I shall call them the Carmelites of the Ancient Observance or simply Carmelites. Teresa herself refers to these friars as 'of the cloth' (*del Paño*) or 'of the Observance', see, for example, *El Libro de Las Fundaciones*, chapter 13.

10 Teresa of Avila was declared 'Doctor of the Church' by Pope Paul VI in 1970 and Thérèse of Lisieux was given the same title by Blessed John Paul II in 1997. Edith Stein was declared Co-Patroness of Europe in 1999, again by Blessed John Paul II.

11 For more on the process and technique of her writing see Tyler 2011a.

12 Also declared 'Doctor of the Church', this time by Pope Pius XI in 1926.

13 John may well have been introduced via his mother. See Tyler 2010.

14 See Teresa of Ávila, *Libro de las Fundaciones*, chapter 3.

15 As well as John, the group consisted of F. Antonio de Heredia, F. José de Cristo, who subsequently either died or left the reform and another 'infirm father' of whom we know nothing.

16 These devout women, often widows, formed a spiritual network in pre-reformation Spain. In many ways their spirituality was akin to that of their Northern European counterparts, the Beguines. Teresa was close to many *beatas* and in fact the Carmelite Convent she joined, the *Encarnación* in Avila, was originally founded as a *beatorio* by Doña Elvira González de Medina, one time concubine of a Canon of Avila Cathedral, Don Nuño González del Aguila. Originally her house housed a community of some 14 women living under the Carmelite Rule established in 1479 only to be given the deeds to the Jewish cemetery of Avila in 1495 after the expulsion of the Jews from Spain. The house was officially opened as a Carmelite convent in 1515, the year of Teresa's birth (See Tyler 2010).

17 Canonized under this name by Blessed John Paul II in 1998.

18 She entered Carmel in 1933 having considered vocations with the Dominicans and Benedictines.

19 See, for example, Alasdair McIntyre's recent *Edith Stein: A Philosophical Prologue, 1913 – 1922*. London: Sheed and Ward, 2007.

20 From 'Weihnachtsgeheimnis' quoted in Herbstrith 1992: 154.

21 As Kierkegaard called it in his critique a 100 years before, another significant influence on the young Edith.

22 From the *Kölner Selig- und Heiligsprechungsprozess der Dienerin Gottes Sr. Teresia Benedicta a Cruce – Edith Stein* (Cologne 1962: 92) in Herbstrith 1992: 180.

Bibliography and Further Reading

Primary Sources (English Translations)

The Collected Works of St Teresa of Avila (1980–7), Trans K. Kavanaugh and O. Rodriguez. 3 Vols. Vol. 1: 2nd edn; Vols 2 and 3; 1st edn. Washington: Institute of Carmelite Studies (Kavanaugh and Rodriguez CW).

The Collected Works of St John of the Cross (1979), trans. K. Kavanaugh and O. Rodriguez. Washington, DC: Institute of Carmelite Studies.

Edith Stein, Collected Works (1986 to present), ed. L. Gelber and M. Linssen. Washington, DC: ICS.

Secondary Sources

Alban, K. (2010) *The Teaching and Impact of the 'Doctrinale' of Thomas Netter of Walden (c.1374 – 1430).* Turnhout, Belgium: Brepols.

Del Niño Jesús, P. Florencio (1924), *El Monte Carmelo: Tradiciones e Historia de La Santa Montaña, de la Virgen del Carmen y De La Orden Carmelitana y la Luz do Los Monumentos y Documentos.* Madrid: Mensajero de Santa Teresa.

Giordano, S. (1995), *Carmel in the Holy Land: From Its Beginnings to the Present Day,* Arenzano: Il Messaggero di Gesu Bambino.

Herbstrith, W. (1992), *Edith Stein: The Untold Story of the Philosopher and Mystic who Lost her Life in the Death Camps of Auschwitz,* trans. B. Bonowitz, San Francisco, CA: Ignatius.

Ingarden, R. (1979), 'Über die philosophischen Forschungen Edith Steins', in *Freiburger Zeitschrift für Philosophie und Theologie,* February 1979.

McGreal, W. (1999), *At the Fountain of Elijah: The Carmelite Tradition.* London: DLT.

Mosley, J. (2004), *Edith Stein: Woman of Prayer,* London: Gracewing.

Ruiz, F. (ed.) (2000), *God Speaks in the Night,* Washington, DC: ICS.

Smet, J. (1988), *The Carmelites: A History of The Brothers of Our Lady of Mount Carmel* (3 Vols), IL: Carmelite Spiritual Center.

— (1997), 'The Carmelite Rule after 750 Years', in *Carmelus* 44 (1).

Tyler, P. M. (2010), *St John of the Cross: Outstanding Christian Thinker.* London: Continuum.

— (2011a), *The Return to the Mystical: Ludwig Wittgenstein, Teresa of Avila and the Christian Mystical Tradition.* London: Continuum.

— (2011b), 'The Roots of Desert Spirituality', in *The Pastoral Review,* September–October 2011.

Waaijman, K. (1999), *The Mystical Space of Carmel: A Commentary on the Carmelite Rule.* Leuven: Peeters.

11 Reform Spirituality: The Lutheran Tradition

Jonathan Linman

Introduction

The Lutheran spiritual tradition began in Germany as a reform movement within the Catholic Church in the sixteenth century, a time of particular religious fervour. What became known as Lutheranism, something of a misnomer because its founder, Martin Luther, did not desire that his name be used for a distinct church, was among many attempts to introduce reform in the church of that time. Like so many reform movements throughout Christian history, Lutheranism sought to call the church back to a faithful understanding of Christianity and to practices consistent with that right teaching.

As a reform movement, Lutheranism perhaps has much in common with the various religious orders within the Roman Catholic Church, such as the Augustinian tradition of which Martin Luther was a friar, movements which also had their beginnings as calls to steer Christian understanding and practice in more faithful directions. Luther's calls for reform, however, were not accommodated by the church authorities of his day, an unfortunate circumstance of history that divided the church. Thus, the Lutheran reform resulted in a church in the West that was not under the authority of the pope, the first among many that emerged as the Protestant tradition. While many churches of the Lutheran tradition include the word *evangelical* in their names, the word does not connote the kind of ethos common in North American Protestantism. Rather, *evangelical* as a term employed by Lutherans is best understood in terms of its Greek root *evangelion*, that is, having a focus on good news, the Gospel.

Chief among Martin Luther's concerns was the practise of selling indulgences whereby donations to the church were said to have reduced time in purgatory for souls of believers, or in the language of a marketing slogan of the day, 'As soon as the coin in the coffer rings, the soul from purgatory springs'. Luther enumerated what we saw as abuses in the teaching and practice of the sixteenth-century church in the 95 Theses which he nailed to the door of the Castle Church in Wittenberg, Germany, as an invitation, and perhaps provocation, to academic debate. The date of this event, 31 October 1517, commonly marks the beginning of Lutheranism. The concurrent invention of the printing press allowed Luther's ideas to be disseminated widely, calling significant attention to the movement of reform and providing extra energy for it to take hold.

The Lutheran reforms spread throughout Germany, Scandinavia and Eastern Europe in the sixteenth century, resulting in ethnic and national churches, the heritage of which continues to influence the Lutheran tradition to this day. In this blending of ethnicity and national culture with Christianity, the Lutheran tradition arguably has commonalities with the various ethnic Eastern Orthodox Churches, Greek, Russian and the like, which intertwine spirituality with ethnicity.

Major trends have marked the Lutheran spiritual tradition in its 500-year history. The sixteenth century saw the clarification of the Lutheran understanding of Christianity, especially its codification in various confessions or summary teaching statements, principally the 'Augsburg Confession' and other writings contained in the *Book of Concord*, statements of faith which persist as sources of authority in current-day Lutheran practice. Seventeenth-century Lutheranism is noteworthy as a period of Lutheran Scholasticism or Orthodoxy, an era that emphasized the intellectual apprehension of the faith. In reaction to the headiness of this scholastic period, eighteenth- and nineteenth-century Lutheranism was marked by religious revival and emphasis on emotional spiritual experience, trends known broadly as the Pietist Movement. The eighteenth and nineteenth centuries also saw the spread of Lutheranism beyond Northern and Eastern Europe to North America via immigration from European countries and to other countries in Asia, Africa, Latin America and elsewhere through sending missionaries, thus making Lutheranism a truly international phenomenon. The twentieth century and its upheaval in two World Wars and the Great Depression eventually resulted in greater international Lutheran cooperation expressed in the formation of the Lutheran World Federation in 1947. Twentieth-century Lutheranism was also noteworthy for various national and international ecumenical agreements that have resulted in some rapprochement with other Christian traditions and churches. There are some 70 million Lutherans in the world today.

Martin Luther

Like many spiritual traditions and religious orders, Lutheranism is influenced and characterized by the charisms (that is, spiritual gifts), concerns and peculiarities of its founder, Martin Luther (1483–1546). An astute reader of religious practice may note characteristics of Martin Luther being lived out in current adherents of the Lutheran tradition and in contemporary Lutheran Churches.

131

Luther's father desired that he study law. However, a dramatic experience in a thunderstorm, namely a near miss with a lightning strike, resulted in his commitment to become a monk. Luther joined the Augustinian Order, was ordained a priest and became a particularly scrupulous friar, struggling through religious practices to find peace of mind for what he perceived to be his many sins and shortcomings.

Luther was also a professor, specializing in the study of the Old Testament, so there is a sense in which Lutheranism as a theological movement had its birth in the university. As a student of the scriptures, Luther turned his attention to the New Testament, particularly the writings of the apostle Paul. Engaging Paul's thought, Luther had the spiritual and theological awakening that would transform his life and come to be the key insight and emphasis of Lutheranism, namely, the rediscovery in the Epistle to the Romans that sinners are justified, or made right with God, through God's grace effective by faith, that is, trust in God's mercy. In short, spiritual practices, or works, cannot achieve or even influence the outcome of our salvation. Rather, it is God who saves through Christ in the power of the Holy Spirit. Spiritual practices according to Lutherans, then, are best viewed as thankful responses to God's grace.

As part of the upheaval of the Reformation, Luther left the Augustinian Order. Later he married a former nun, Katharina von Bora, and had six children. Family life, in addition to the church community, became for Luther, and then by extension for Lutheranism, a focal point for spiritual life. Like so many major historical figures, Luther was a complex man, for example, sometimes given to vitriolic diatribe as seen in his condemnation of Jewish people in some writings that were used centuries later by National Socialists in Germany to further their justification of the slaughter of Jews in the Holocaust.

Luther lived his vocation variously as husband and father, priest, church leader and reformer, debater and polemicist, biblical scholar and, quite significantly, translator of the scriptures into German, the translations of which are still used in Germany today. Luther was a pastoral or practical theologian, that is to say, he engaged in his theological scholarship and writings in the service of the vitality and faithfulness of life in the church. Above all, Martin Luther is arguably best understood as a theologian of deep faith and spirituality who employed this personal engagement with God in his life and calling in the world as he lived out the many facets of his vocation.

Contemporary Luther scholarship based in Finland reveals a mystical dimension to the thought of the reformer unnoticed in recent centuries. Finnish interpretation of Luther, while not accepted by all Lutherans, highlights aspects of his writings which suggest that faith unites the believer to Christ, making persons of faith partakers of the divine nature, a 'little Christ' for the world, and thus offering a more positive assessment of the human condition than is common in most Lutheran theological understanding. Faith in this sense does not only justify the sinner, but also makes the Christian a participant in the things of God, much in the same way that a husband and wife share, as it were, one flesh in marriage. In this way, Luther's thought has resonance with the bridal mysticism common in medieval Christian Spirituality, and currently is an important point of dialogue between Lutheran and Orthodox Churches.

Key Ideas of the Lutheran Spiritual Tradition

First and foremost among the theological affirmations of Lutheranism that give coherence to this spiritual tradition is justification by faith, as suggested previously. This insight places primacy on God's initiative and not human effort in spiritual matters. Related is a rather pessimistic assessment at worst, and realistic assessment at best, of the possibility of human spiritual progress. In keeping with Pauline insights found in the scriptures, Lutheranism is sceptical of innate human capacities for spiritual engagement, broken and compromised as they are by human sin, our misplaced trust in forces other than God. In short, human will is captive to sin. Thus we need help from outside of ourselves, namely from Jesus Christ, the very Word of God incarnate, who reveals the fullness of divine nature, that is, a God who is merciful and full of loving compassion, and who in Jesus' death by crucifixion gives full expression to this saving love. Lutheranism is, then, a christocentric spiritual tradition, oriented to the work of Jesus, emphasizing especially Jesus' Passion, giving prominence to the cross, and his sacrificial death overcome and vindicated by new life in the resurrection of Jesus.

A chief challenge and also opportunity for the Lutheran spiritual tradition, then, has to do with the place of human activity in spiritual practices and other works. Or as some have quipped about the Lutheran dilemma which revolves around the proper place of human activity, particularly that human effort does not save us: 'what do we do now that we do not have to do anything?' In brief, we are freed by Christ *for* spiritual activity, *for* good works which benefit the world. Or to quote the paradox that Martin Luther offers in his treatise, 'The Freedom of a Christian', arguably the most succinct and complete articulation of Luther's theology in a single work: 'The Christian is a perfectly free lord of all, subject to none; a Christian is a perfectly dutiful servant of all, subject to all' (Luther, Martin, *Works* 1957–86). That is to say, while works are not necessary for salvation, human activity necessarily flows from the foundational reality of our experience and apprehension of God's grace as a way of giving thanks to God, particularly as we engage in God's mission in the world. Moreover, since we are freed from the necessity of works for salvation, we are still more fully free to give ourselves away in service to others, a key component of a Lutheran approach to social ethics in which we can be fully *for* others in their dignity and uniqueness as God's children, and not as means to ends, namely, that of our achieving a right relationship with God.

Continuing to emphasize the primacy of God's initiative in the spirituality associated with Lutheranism, it is important to acknowledge that even faith is not the result of human effort. To quote the apostle Paul, to whom Luther's theology is most fully indebted, 'No one can say, "Jesus is Lord", except by the Holy Spirit' (1 Cor. 12.3). Central then to Lutheran Spirituality is the role of the Holy Spirit in the life of Christians and Christian community. Lutheran pneumatology, that is, the doctrine of the Holy Spirit, emphasizes the power of God that comes *extra nos*, from outside of ourselves, especially since innate human capacities for spiritual transcendence are inhibited by the forces of sin. Moreover, the Holy Spirit speaks through means, namely the means of grace, the proclaimed Word of God and the sacraments, principally for Lutherans, baptism and the Eucharist. It is the Holy Spirit active through these means that creates faith and empowers Christians to engage in practices and works.

Thus, communal worship, the context for the Spirit's activity of speaking through Word and sacraments, is central to the Lutheran spiritual tradition. Likewise, the holy scriptures, the texts which contain the Revelation of God's Word, hold primary place in Lutheran Spirituality and are the authoritative source for theological methodology and the norm for carrying out life in the church. In short, the Holy Spirit's activity is carried for Lutherans on the pages of scripture and in sacramental practice.

Lutheranism embraces a spirituality that is not shy about imperfection, noting that the Christian life is one of paradoxical tension, that we are simultaneously saints and sinners, that we thus need God's Word addressed to us both as Law and Gospel, that while Christ's saving work is once and for all, humanity will know the fullness of the world's salvation only with consummation of God's reign in the last days when Christ promises to come again. All that we now know and experience in Christian life in community is a foretaste of the feast to come.

Christian Practices in the Lutheran Spiritual Tradition

Spiritual reform movements tend to attempt to get back to basics, peeling away accretions of practice that cloud core teachings. So it is that sixteenth-century Lutheranism represented a simplified version of Christian Spirituality compared with its medieval antecedents. Such basic activities as Bible reading and study, corporate worship, confession of and absolution for sins, mutual conversation and consolation among brothers and sisters in the faith, family devotions, singing hymns and spiritual songs are pillars of Lutheran spiritual practices. The Lutheran Spirituality of the sixteenth century importantly brought spiritual practice out of monasteries, the domain of the professed religious and into people's homes and the lives of ordinary Christians, and all of this in the language of the common person. One of Luther's major liturgical reforms was to render the liturgy and the Bible in the German vernacular and not in ecclesiastical Latin.

Because Lutheranism affirms that the Holy Spirit speaks through means such as Word and sacraments, central to Lutheran practice are the sacraments of baptism and the Eucharist. Baptism, a ritual washing with water in the name of the Trinitarian God, Father, Son and Holy Spirit, is a once-and-for-all entry point into the Christian life, commonly undertaken with infants in the Lutheran tradition. While baptism happens once in the life of the Christian, it is remembered and affirmed and given thanks for repeatedly in Christian practice, particularly in liturgy. Lutheran Spirituality is rooted in and focuses a great deal on the Christian life as a living out of the baptismal covenant. Lutherans also centre their practice on the regular celebration of the Eucharist, the liturgical ritual meal of bread and wine that with God's Word in the power of the Holy Spirit conveys to communicants in Lutheran understanding the real presence of Jesus Christ, whose last supper this meal also commemorates. Whether or not Lutheran Churches celebrate Holy Communion at each Sunday liturgy, this sacrament is held in balance with the proclaimed Word of God, and is viewed by Lutherans as the visible Word of God which communicants eat and drink for their forgiveness of sins and their participation in all the blessings that Christ imparts through his real presence.

Also, as a scripturally oriented tradition, Lutheranism gives prominence of place to preaching, the proclamation of God's Word in communal worship. For public ministers of the Gospel, preaching has a central focus in the practice ministry. For those who hear, listening to sermons is central to Lutheran spiritual practice, as the aural experience of the proclamation of God's Word is indispensable to Christian experience, since 'faith comes from what is heard' (Rom. 10.17).

Central to Luther's home-oriented spirituality is his 'Small Catechism', a simple primer on the Christian faith for use in family settings that articulates basic understandings of the Ten Commandments, Apostles' Creed, Lord's Prayer, Baptism, Confession and Absolution and the Lord's Supper. Throughout the centuries, and still today, Lutherans have studied, memorized and explored in discussion the basic teachings found in the 'Small Catechism' offered in question and answer format. In terms of specific prayer practices, Luther wrote a treatise to his barber, 'A Simple Way to Pray', in which he outlines his own devotional practices rooted in the themes of the Small Catechism, practices which dwell with and elaborate on the commandments, the articles of the creed and the petitions of the Lord's Prayer.

Luther was also a hymn text writer, a composer of melodies, as well as one who adapted popular music for use in the church and in devotional life. From Luther's day on, the singing of hymns and performance of music have been central to Lutheran spiritual practice. For Luther and for Lutherans, putting God's Word to music is almost sacramental, an effective and powerful means through which to proclaim the living voice of the Gospel. The centuries of Lutheran practice have seen such prominent composers as Johann Sebastian Bach, Johann Pachelbel and George Frederick Handel among others.

As a reform movement within the church, Lutheranism has been a comparatively conservative movement in that it has not abandoned the inherited traditions of previous centuries of churchly life. So it is that Lutheran worship practice has retained the Mass, the structure and texts of the rites of the Western church, along with other practices and organizational principles common in the Catholic Church throughout the centuries. In this way Lutheranism stands in contrast with other expressions of the Protestant tradition, such as the radical reformation Anabaptist tradition and other iconoclastic traditions.

However, because of the schism of the sixteenth century and the different ways that Lutheranism spread through Europe, Lutheran Churches have been organized in various ways in the five centuries of the existence of this tradition, ranging from structures that emphasize the autonomy of the local congregation to national churches that deviated little in structure from Roman Catholic forms, all of this depending on the country in which Lutheranism was spreading. Because no Roman Catholic bishops in Germany left the church to follow Luther and the movement for reform, for example, what emerged as Lutheran Churches in Germany were organized in an *ad hoc* fashion, variously structured depending on which region in Germany one was located. In contrast, the Church in Sweden became Lutheran with the proclamation of king in consultation with parliament, thus retaining significant continuity with the 500 previous years of Christian history in Sweden. The Church of Sweden, for example, has retained episcopal orders, with bishops, priests and deacons serving in public ministries. Most Lutherans affirm that God has ordained the office of ministry, particularly to Word and sacraments. Operationally, most Lutheran Churches include ministries of oversight, often using the term bishop; ministry to Word and sacraments (presbyters) and forms of diaconal ministries, that is, ministers of Word and service. The organizational structures of Lutheran Churches throughout the world tend now to resemble the churches of the countries which sent them missionaries.

Lutheran Engagement with the World

The Lutheran tradition has had an ambivalent relationship to social and political affairs in the world, sometimes fraught with conflict and violence and sometimes promoting peace, justice and reconciliation. On the negative side, the appropriation of, or as the case may be, misappropriation of Luther's so-called two kingdoms teaching has been the source of difficulty in Lutheran relationship to world affairs. In brief, Luther identified two realms, that of God and that of the world, which were distinct from each other, though each had its source in God's providence. The presence of this teaching in the Lutheran tradition has contributed to Quietism, a reluctance and passivity on the part of many Lutheran adherents, for example, to confront injustice and evil in the world, as was the case in Nazi Germany in the mid-twentieth century. Lutheran complicity in, and too often compliance with, the initiatives of Hitler and the Third Reich permitted and advanced the ravages of war and genocide.

On the positive side, Lutherans see the church and society in paradoxical tension in the context of which Christians are called upon to engage the world to bear witness to Christ and promote God's reign of peace and justice. This creative engagement is supported by Luther's focus on vocation, that each person is called by God for particular work in the world and that all expressions of vocation, secular and sacred, can give glory to God and allow us to live out our God-given callings.

According to Luther, Christians undertake their callings amid three God-given estates, that of family, church and the temporal realm in society. This focus on vocation has prompted much missionary work throughout the world in the five centuries of the existence of the Lutheran tradition. Moreover and quite significantly, Lutheran Churches are known internationally for social ministries which respond compassionately and generously to human need. Moreover, nations in Western and Northern Europe where Lutheranism has been influential are also known for their emphasis on the state in providing for the common good and commonwealth.

A sampling of noteworthy historical figures steeped in the Lutheran tradition include: Philip Melanchthon, contemporary of Luther and a significant figure in the Lutheran reform movement, particularly in giving expression to Lutheran theological ideas; Lucas Cranach the Elder, sixteenth-century artist, whose paintings express themes of Lutheran Spirituality; Henry Melchior Muhlenberg, eighteenth-century patriarch of the Lutheran tradition in North America who had a significant hand in planting the Lutheran Church independent from European national churches in the early decades of United States history; Søren Kierkegaard, nineteenth-century Danish philosopher, who gave poignant expression to themes of Lutheran theology and spirituality in his writings, despite his stinging critiques of the national Lutheran Church in Denmark; Albert Schweitzer, theologian, musician, philosopher, physician and medical missionary and recipient of the Nobel Peace Prize for his philosophy of 'reverence for life'; Dietrich Bonhoeffer, twentieth-century

German theologian and martyr, who resisted the Third Reich in his teaching, writing and preaching, and was implicated in a plot to attempt to take Hitler's life; and Dag Hammarskjöld, first Secretary General of the United Nations, and a Swede, though not known for his churchly adherence, nonetheless revealed his deep spirituality in his journal, posthumously published as *Markings*.

Bibliography and Further Reading

Bonhoeffer, Dietrich (1995), *The Cost of Discipleship*, trans. R. H. Fuller, New York, NY: Simon and Schuster.

Gritsch, Eric W. (2010), *A History of Lutheranism*. Minneapolis, MN: Fortress Press.

Hammarskjöld, Dag (1983) (ed.), *Markings*, trans. W. H. Auden and L. Fitzgerald Sjoberg, New York, NY: Ballantine.

Hendrix, Scott H. (2009), *Luther*. Nashville, TN: Abingdon Press.

Krey, Philip D. W. and Krey, Peter D. S. (2007), *Luther's Spirituality*, Classics of Western Spirituality, New York, NY: Paulist Press.

Luther, Martin (1957–86), *Works*. Various translators. 55 Vols, St Louis, MO and Minneapolis, MN: Concordia Publishing House, Fortress Press.

12 Reform Spirituality: Calvin

Judith Rossall

Introduction

As with most historical figures the work of John Calvin is best understood when it is read with some understanding of his historical context. Recent scholarship has emphasized that Calvin lived in an age of anxiety, both spiritual and worldly. Although the height of the Black Death had occurred two centuries earlier, there were still regular outbreaks of plague along with the new and catastrophic threat of syphilis. Poor harvests and famine were a regular experience. In addition Europe perceived itself to be threatened by Islamic aggression and the expansion of the Ottoman Empire. It was typical of the age that all of these misfortunes were interpreted as being signs of God's judgement on human sin. It is clear that Calvin believed himself to be living at a time of spiritual, moral and religious crisis and considered the task of calling people back to the true service of God to be vital. 'How many are the distresses with which Europe has been afflicted for the last 30 or 40 years! How many are the chastisements by which she has been called to repentance! And yet it does not seem that these have done any good' (*Commentary on Isaiah* 9.10). This widespread concern with the fear of God's judgement goes some way to explain why, to modern ears, Calvin has a strong emphasis both on sin and on the fear of God.

Calvin, perhaps more than other Christian writers, has been read through the eyes of his later interpreters and it is important that an effort is made to read him for himself, particularly by those to whom 'Calvinism' and 'belief in predestination' are synonymous.

Biographical Sketch

John Calvin became an exile from his native France because of his sympathy with the Reformation movement. Having published the first edition of the *Institutes* in 1536, he was approached by Guillaume Farel while staying in Geneva and persuaded to remain to help to organize the Reformation in the city. Internal opposition and a disagreement with the city council led to Farel and Calvin's exile from Geneva in 1538 and he settled in Strasbourg. Returning to Geneva, without Farel, in 1541 Calvin was in a stronger position although he was constantly challenged by the city council until 1555 and did not become a citizen until 1559. He wielded great personal and moral authority as a religious leader. Geneva became a centre for Protestant exiles and in 1559 the Genevan Academy was established. These factors along with Calvin's extensive writings, including several editions of the *Institutes* and his commentaries on biblical books, made Calvin a leading figure of the Reformation and ensured his continuing influence as a theologian.

Spirituality and the Non-believer

Calvin assumed that all people have some innate awareness of both the existence and the majesty of God and could therefore, in this sense only, be said to experience a form of spirituality. He describes this awareness as both a 'sense of deity' and 'a conviction that there is a God' (*Institutes* 1.3.1). However, far from being welcome, this sense of the deity has negative connotations for Calvin: it both removes any excuse for not believing in God and leads those who experience it to a 'slavish, forced fear' of God's judgement and a dread and hatred of His power which in turn leads to idolatry; it also leads to a religion which is forced and insincere rather than to true worship (*Institutes* 1.4.4). It is quite possible for one who has not met Christ to express truths about God but he could never be united to God in true faith. Sin, according to Calvin, has ruptured the divine human relationship with two results: both that God hates the sin but also people hate and fear God. In Calvin's theology Christ is necessary in order to know God truly because only Christ shows the loving, benevolent God, gives peace to the conscience and gives the confidence necessary to approach God (*Institutes* 2.6.4).

Christian Spirituality

If those who have not met Christ find in their experience of God only fear and hatred then the Christian according to Calvin finds her/himself instead in a delicate balance between the love of God and the fear of God.

The word spirituality was foreign to Calvin, he spoke instead of *pietas* which English translators render as both 'piety' and 'godliness'. The one definition which he gave of *pietas* was brief: 'I call piety that reverence joined with love of God which the knowledge of his benefits induces' (*Institutes* 1.2.1). This piety is an inner disposition which profoundly shapes outer action. In *pietas* both the fear and the love of God have a positive role to play. Thus,

Calvin confidently affirmed that the fear of God is necessary to ensure true faith and obedience to God:

> Then, when the apostle teaches us that we should 'work out our own salvation in fear and trembling' [Phil. 2.12], he demands only that we become accustomed to honour the Lord's power, while greatly abasing ourselves. For nothing so moves us to repose our assurance and certainty of mind in the Lord as distrust of ourselves, and the anxiety occasioned by the awareness of our ruin. In this sense we must understand what is said by the prophet: 'I, through the abundance of thy goodness, will enter thy temple; I will worship. . . . in fear' [Psalm 5.7]. Here he fitly joins the boldness of faith that rests upon God's mercy with the reverent fear that we must experience whenever we come into the presence of God's majesty, and by its splendour understand how great is our own filthiness. (*Institutes* 3.2.23)

Important as the fear of the Lord was to Calvin's understanding of *pietas* he never forgot that the recognition of God's love and benevolence was even more important. The person who focuses too much on God's judgement and the dread of God's power is in danger of collapsing with terror; the mark of the true knowledge of God is rather that God is seen as being attractive and benevolent. The proper view of God invites people to seek after God (*Commentary on the Psalms* 145.8).

A Spiritual Theology

Calvin's single most important work is the *Institutes of the Christian Religion* which is now recognized as one of the foremost works of Protestant theology. The *Institutes* includes a preface addressed to King Francis I of France which explained Calvin's basic aim in publishing the work. He described his purpose as being to shape those who felt some interest in religion to what he called 'true godliness' (*ad veram pietatum*). As this comment makes clear, for Calvin theology itself was an exercise in spirituality. In this concern he again showed that he was responding to his own historical context and in particular he was opposing the mediaeval division between mystical or affective theology and speculative theology. Calvin set out to write a spiritual theology, that is a theology which draws upon but more importantly nourishes the piety of the believer. *Pietas* and the building up of *pietas* is intimately related to what the believer knows, how she knows it and how that knowledge affects and shapes her way of life; for example, the believer needs to understand the nature of Christ's saving activity in order to find a firm basis for salvation (*Institutes* 2.15.1). This means that the subject of Calvin's spirituality has to be addressed by means of understanding his theology; to attempt to focus solely on Christian experience and practices while ignoring his emphasis on the importance of true knowledge of God is to misunderstand Calvin's vision of the Christian life.

The first two books of the *Institutes* are dedicated to the issue of the knowledge of God and Calvin constantly insisted that a true knowledge of God is one which touches the believer at a deeper level than the merely rational. The true knowledge of God gives life and calls forth from the believer a new way of living; this has far deeper implications than simply the arousal of emotions or the creation of a contemplative inner state, rather the true knowledge of God binds the believer to God not simply by rights or duty but by his own love and desire for God. It is quite literally life-giving.

The following quotation demonstrates some of the different aspects of this knowledge of God which Calvin explores:

> For it is a doctrine not of the tongue but of life. It is not apprehended by the understanding and memory alone, as other disciplines are, but it is received only when it possesses the whole soul, and find a seat and resting place in the inmost affection of the heart . . . We have given the first place to the doctrine in which our religion is contained, since our salvation begins with it. But it must enter our heart and pass into our daily living, and so transform us into itself that it may not be unfruitful for us . . . We detest these trifling Sophists who are content to roll the gospel on the tips of their tongues when its efficacy ought to penetrate the inmost affections of the heart, take its seat in the soul, and affect the whole man a hundred times more deeply than the cold exhortations of the philosophers. (*Institutes* 3.6.4)

The knowledge of God is not simply apprehended rationally; it possesses a Christian, entering deeply into the entire personality. Thus, while doctrine is vital to spirituality it must lead to *transformation* and what is known of God must be worked out in daily living.

Calvin's emphasis on the life-giving nature of the knowledge of God can be seen more clearly from his characterization of what he saw as the opposite of true knowledge of God, that is, speculation. Speculation is invariably a pejorative word for Calvin, referred to that knowledge of God which is intrinsically useless, at best it is dismissed as 'bare speculation' at worst it is carnal or wicked and harmful. The most pejorative adjective which Calvin could apply to such knowledge was the Latin term *frigidus*. This word can mean not only cold but also lifeless and lacking in energy and it would seem that this was the understanding which was most on Calvin's mind when he used it: knowledge which was *frigidus* implied a knowledge which failed to impart life and energy.

The useful and life-giving knowledge of God has a specific content. God is known truly when the Christian sees himself as dealing with God in every aspect of his life (*Institutes* 3.7.2, 1.17.2, 3.3.6, 3.3.16 and 3.20.29). In addition, God is known as the 'fountain of every good'. Knowing that God has provided all good things the believer learns to both seek all things from him and to respond with gratitude for God's gifts (*Institutes* 1.2.1). Gratitude for God's goodness is a particular emphasis in Calvin's spirituality.

Calvin's constant realization that the knowledge of God could be false and speculative leads him to emphasize the importance of Scripture which functions to focus the vague human experience of God and to show clearly God's true nature. Calvin's favourite metaphor for Scripture was that of a pair of spectacles; he commented that someone with poor vision who was shown a beautiful volume might be able to recognize that there is writing in front of her/him but she/he would be unable to actually read that writing without spectacles. Scripture works in the same way, it gathers together what is otherwise a confused knowledge of God, it disperses human 'dullness' and it allows people to see God properly (*Institutes* 1.6.1). It is worth noting that the reading of Scripture therefore is not an end in itself for Calvin, rather, the Christian looks through Scripture as a means of seeing the world, and God's activity within the world, more truly.

The Real Presence of Christ

The centre of the Christian life according to Calvin is what he called the union with Christ. He explored this most fully in the third book of the *Institutes* where he described how the Holy Spirit binds the Christian to Christ in such a way that Christ's life flows through him. The importance of this concept to Calvin can be seen in his assertion that all that Christ has done for the salvation of the human race is of no value without this union (*Institutes* 3.1.1). One of his favourite analogies to explain the union was taken from St Paul. He argued that the union with Christ is like the grafting of trees, at stake is not simple conformity to Jesus's example but rather the transference of power between Christ and the Christian; it is from this union that the Christian draws the nourishment needed for the growth of his spiritual life (*Commentary on the Epistle to the Romans* 6.5). This union is created and maintained by the Holy Spirit who binds the believer to Christ and communicates all of Christ's benefits to him. Calvin's wide-ranging description of the activity of the Spirit in the Christian life included that the Spirit makes the believer fruitful and righteous, that the Spirit restores and nourishes the believer and that the Spirit gives the believer a new way of living so that he no longer lives from himself but rather is ruled by the Spirit's actions and prompting (*Institutes* 3.1.3).

It is also the principle of union with Christ which explains why Calvin avoided separating justification from sanctification and either making the Christian life consist in justification alone or treating them as being related chronologically, with justification given at the point of conversion and sanctification coming later. For Calvin, the believer's regeneration by faith is the fruit of the union with Christ and since both newness of life and free reconciliation are the result of being incorporated into Christ, they are indissolubly bound together.

> Christ justifies no one whom he does not at the same time sanctify
> . . . Although we may distinguish them, Christ contains both of them
> inseparably in himself. Do you wish, then, to attain righteousness in Christ?
> You must first possess Christ; but you cannot possess him without being
> made partaker in his sanctification, because he cannot be divided into
> pieces. Since, therefore, it is solely by expending himself that the Lord gives
> us these benefits to enjoy, he bestows both of them at the same time, the one
> never without the other. Thus it is clear how true it is that we are justified
> not without works yet not through works, since in our sharing in Christ,
> which justifies us, sanctification is just as much included as righteousness.
> (*Institutes* 3.16.1)

The union with Christ had a profound influence on how the believer is to interpret her own experience; according to Calvin the Christian life is experienced as a sharing in Christ's death and resurrection and the Christian both partakes in Jesus death by mortification (i.e. putting off her old life and denying herself in order to serve God) and participates in Christ's resurrection by vivification, that is, being invigorated by the Spirit and leading to holiness of life (*Institutes* 3.3.8).

The Church

Calvin's spirituality was profoundly corporate; he affirmed with St Cyprian that the church must be Mother to those to whom God is Father. God, he argued, has given to the church gifts which are vital for a Christian to be built up in *pietas*: these are first the treasure of effectual preaching of the Gospel and secondly the sacraments which he described as 'useful helps in fostering and confirming our faith' (*Institutes* 4.1.1).

Although he encouraged all Christians to have a Bible at home in their own language, Calvin believed that hearing expository preaching was much more important for building up faith than the individual reading of Scripture. Preaching for Calvin was not simply a way of conveying knowledge; rather it evoked an encounter with God to the extent that it would be possible to speak of 'the real presence of Christ' in the preached word. Since God has instituted preaching, is present in preaching and requires that that presence be recognized, to refuse to listen to preaching is to reject God's own spiritual food and to deservedly perish of hunger and famine (*Institutes* 4.1.5). What is more, it is pride and fastidiousness which encourages people to prefer private reading and meditation over attending public preaching and Calvin assumed that such a preference was bound to lead to error and delusion. God's deliberate choice to employ preachers rather than speaking to individuals without any human aid has an important role: it demonstrates God's willingness to descend to a human level, provides an excellent training in humility and binds the church together in unity (*Institutes* 4.3.1 & 5).

Added to the preached word is the gift of the sacraments which Calvin valued extremely highly and regarded as external and visible signs by which God represents what he has promised in the Gospel in order to confirm and fortify the faith of the believer. However this language of signs should not be taken to mean that Calvin regarded the Eucharist as only symbolic. Once again his understanding of the work of the Holy Spirit is vital to his understanding of spirituality. Through the Spirit the Christian who receives the bread and wine also truly partakes of Christ's life-giving body and blood.

Calvin also emphasized the value of prayer which he regarded as the 'chief exercise of faith' (*Institutes* 3.20.1). Refuting the idea that prayer is unnecessary because God already knows all that the believer needs, Calvin set out six ways in which the exercise of prayer is vital to the building up of *pietas*. Prayer helps to fire the heart with desire for God, the need to set all desires before God keeps the believer from desires of which she should be ashamed. Prayer also prepares the believer to receive all from God with gratitude and leads to an ardent meditation on God's kindness. It increases the believer's delight in those things which come through prayer and it confirms the experience of God's loving providence (*Institutes* 3.20.3). Calvin held to a careful balance between private and corporate prayer – valuing highly the mutual encouragement of praying together.

Conclusion

While much of the above may appear to be quite theoretical, Calvin had no doubt that true spirituality was worked out in action and that the word of God had not truly taken root in the human heart unless every part of life was dedicated to God's service. Like the other reformers he emphasized that the vocation to serve God should be worked out in human society and in the struggles of ordinary everyday human life. Calvin's spirituality is profoundly active. He emphasized what he called the 'third use of the law' which he considered to be the law's principal function. The third use of the law is to instruct the

Christian day-by-day so that she understands the exact nature of God's will; therefore the Christian should search out and meditate frequently upon the law in order to be strengthened, to be aroused to obedience and to be drawn back from sin (*Institutes* 2.7.12). In this meditation she will pay attention not only to the words of the law but also to the issue of why God gave a particular commandment, thus while the first commandment teaches us that God alone is to be worshipped the fifth commandment teaches us to honour not only our parents but all of those on whom God has bestowed excellence (*Institutes* 2.8.8). The law teaches the Christian not simply that they have a duty to God but also that they have a duty to other men and women, the believer owes reverent obedience and gratefulness to those who have been placed over her, she is to be concerned always for the good of others, she is to live modestly and in purity, and she should desire only honest and lawful gain. She must practice the truth and banish from her heart all desire which is contrary to love (*Institutes* 2.8.35/50). In this way every sphere of life is seen as a way of being engaged with Christ and far from being a matter only of inner attitude, true *pietas* is worked out in daily service and vocation.

Calvin further underlined the sense of the importance of working out one's *pietas* by his emphasis on stewardship. The Christian should always remember that one day he will need to render account for the use of all that he has been given and that he will render this account to the God who has greatly commended abstinence, sobriety, frugality and moderation (*Institutes* 3.10.5). What is more God has assigned to each person their calling and the outward demonstration of *pietas* must be governed by the sense that God has given the Christian her place and her task in life, and that, no matter how obscure, sordid or base that task may seem, it is a precious thing to obey God's calling within it (*Institutes* 3.10.6).

Bibliography and Further Reading

Bouwsma, W. (1989), 'The Spirituality of John Calvin', in J. Raitt (ed.), *Christian Spirituality: High Middle Ages and Reformation*, New York, NY: Crossroad.

Calvin, John (1960), *Institutes of the Christian Religion*, trans. Ford Lewis Battles, 2 vols, Philadelphia, PA: Westminster Press.

Hageman, H. G. (1986), 'Reformed Spirituality', in F. Senn (ed.), *Protestant Spiritual Traditions*. New York, NY: Paulist Press.

McKee, E. A. (2001), *John Calvin: Writings on Pastoral Piety*. New York, NY: Paulist Press.

Selderhuis, H. (ed.) (2009), *The Calvin Handbook*. Grand Rapids, MI: William B. Eerdmans.

13 Ignatian Spirituality

Gerard W. Hughes

From Daydreams to Earthed Spirituality

The source of Ignatian Spirituality is Ignatius of Loyola, Basque aristocrat, born at Loyola, (1491–1556), author of *The Spiritual Exercises* and founder of the the Society of Jesus, its members later known as 'Jesuits'.[1] The basic manual of his spirituality is in his *Spiritual Exercises*, a very characteristic Ignatian title. The value of the book comes not from academic study, but from doing the recommended exercises. In this chapter, I shall offer a method of daily prayer, which summarizes core characteristics of his spirituality. If done occasionally, it may have little or no effect on our lives: if done regularly, it begins to change the way we see things. This is the most revolutionary activity in which any of us can engage. It is the only thing we can change, and it changes everything around us.

At one stage in my Jesuit life I began to dislike the *Spiritual Exercises* in the way they were presented to us and realized I could not remain a Jesuit unless I faced this problem. The problem turned out to be a blessing, for it introduced me to a new understanding of the *Spiritual Exercises*, of the attractiveness of God, of the giftedness of life. I am still on that journey into 'God in All Things', the phrase used by the early Jesuits to describe Ignatius' spirituality. In this respect Ignatius' spirituality is very 'earthed' – a discovery of the extraordinary in the ordinary, of God in all things.

Educated in the Spanish court, he emerged in his mid-twenties, 'a man given to worldly vanities' as he later described himself, 'being filled with a great and vain desire for fame'.[2] He had a strong streak of Don Quixote in him. 'Great desire' was an early characteristic: Desire is a central feature of his spirituality, a word which appears in every 'Exercise' in his book.

In his late twenties, he was seriously wounded in both knees in the battle of Pamplona. His 'conversion' came about through reflection on his own daydreams during his 5-month convalescence. 'Reflection' means looking at experience and allowing it to teach us. Ignatius looked at his daydreams and at their after-effects, a characteristic which runs through his *Spiritual Exercises*, where he calls this reflective process, 'a repetition'. At first, his daydreams were all centred on the great deeds of valour he would perform once his knees had mended, and the great lady, 'No mere Duchess',[3] as he later described her, whose love he would win. He could lose himself in these day-dreams for hours at a time. In his *Spiritual Exercises*, use of the imagination will play an important role. Eventually he grew bored and asked for novels. Loyola's library had none. He was given two books: a life of Christ, written by a monk, Ludolf of Saxony, and 'Lives of the Saints'. In his boredom, he began on these, then began dreaming of a future Saint Iñigo, who would outdo all other saints in his prayer, mortifications and saintly behaviour! He was particularly fascinated by a ferociously austere Desert Father called Humphrey.

When he reflected on his experience, what he observed was a qualita-tive difference in the after-effects of the two sets of daydreams; both were enjoyable at the time, but the after-effects were different. The first set, about the great deeds and winning the great lady, left him bored, empty and sad, while outdoing all the saints left him hopeful, happy and strengthened, so he decided to become a saint! A modest start to his saintly career might be a pilgrimage to Jerusalem, to visit the Holy Places and convert the Muslims, who occupied the country. He could then return to Europe and see what he might do there! He later described this experience as his first lesson in discernment, which led him on his limping way to the Holy Land and to the conversion of the Muslims. En route for Barcelona, he stopped at Montserrat, a Benedictine monastery, where he stayed for a few days, pre-paring to make his general confession. From there he stopped at nearby Manresa where he lived in a cave by the river Cardoner. There he under-went a series of inner experiences of darkness and light. There too, he, a 'raw' convert, a spiritually and academically uneducated layman, began writing his *Spiritual Exercises*.

Other characteristics of his spirituality which emerge from his early life include his use of imagination and his emphasis on the importance of feel-ings and of felt experience in our search for God. Ignatius also depicts a most attractive characteristic of God. God takes him as he is, full of vanity and without much sign of humility, which he was later to describe as being the most radical of all the virtues. Later, in his advice to givers of the *Spiritual Exercises*, he emphasizes the need to accept people where they are and to adapt the Exercises to the capacity, energy, ability and willingness of the pil-grim. This advice mirrors Ignatius' own experience of God in his life, a God who draws, attracts, not a God who drives. When this advice is heeded, trans-formation happens in the pilgrim; when it is ignored, rigidity is reinforced in the pilgrim.

At the end of each section of this chapter, I shall suggest an Exercise, based on Ignatius' spirituality. Here is the first part of the first Exercise, called vari-ously 'Review of the Day' or 'Examen':

For about 15 minutes daily, preferably towards the end of the day, before you are too exhausted, be still and as relaxed as possible. This is a method of reflecting on the day, 'gawking at it', learning from it, as distinct from analysing it.

Focus your attention on whatever you have enjoyed, appreciated, found life-giving during the day . . . Recall, reflect on and relish those moments. Avoid, like the plague, any moralising, self-approval or disapproval. The events are God's gift to you, given to you not because of your virtue, your good deeds, your merits, but simply because you are, and they are signs of God's longing to share in your life. Now speak to God from your heart, and thank God as simply and as honestly as you can. Afterwards, notice your felt reaction to this exercise.

Done once, this exercise will have little or no effect on us: done regularly it will begin to change the way we see reality. This is the beginning of transformation in us and beyond us.

God's Daily Question 'Did you Enjoy My Creation?'

'Spirituality' is about our growing in awareness of the reality of the Spirit, who is God, in our lives. In St Augustine's words, this Spirit 'is closer to me that I am'![4]

Where can we find this Spirit? The only place where any of us can find the Spirit is within our own experience. Many of us have been conditioned to believe that we have little, or nothing to learn from our own experience. That is why we can so easily lose our freedom, which we profess to love, preferring the deadly icebergs of 'security'. If we are religious believers, we can turn our religion into a security system, so secure that we need no longer worry or care about anyone else's security, or even about our own humanity! Scripture calls this attitude 'idolatry'.

By 'gawking' at our own experience in the 'Review of the Day', we can slowly begin to distinguish what is creative in our lives from what is destructive. 'Doing God's will' means pursuing what is creative and avoiding what is destructive. The universal, cosmic struggle between good and evil occurs within each of us in our own experience. That is why reflecting on it is so important, not only for ourselves, but for every other human being. We are all far more closely interconnected and interdependent than we realize.

In the first part of the 'Review of the Day', we focus our attention on and relish those moments that we enjoyed, appreciated. What about those moments we did not enjoy and from which we are still suffering? Do not worry, we shall be looking at these shortly.

'The Review of the Day' is not just a memory exercise: it is a life-giving one. Getting in touch with memories is not like consulting our personal archives. Memories are more like a personal power house on which we can draw. Reflecting on positive memories can release energies, like an inner spring of peace, joy, delight, hope, gratitude welling up within us. Allow this to happen. That is why we must avoid any moralizing, self-approval or disapproval at this point, otherwise we choke the inner spring. Reflecting on the source of our gratitude, we can become more aware of our essential relatedness to everything else in existence. 'In God we live and move and exist' (Acts 17.28).

The early Christian Church thought of creation itself as a sacrament, that is, a sign and an effective sign of the reality of God in everything. God's gifts, which we have been recalling in the 'Review of the Day', are signs of God's wanting to share God's very life with us. They are God's invitation to us to let God be the God of love, the God of compassion, the God of truth to us and through us. These are astonishing truths, too great for us to assimilate: they may even reduce us to silence, a silence charged, like the world, with the presence of God.

There is a prayer at the beginning of the Eucharist which begins. 'It is our duty and it leads to our salvation', solemn words, from which we might expect 'that we should avoid sin at all times' to follow. But that is not what follows: the prayer continues, 'that we should thank you always and everywhere'! These few words are revolutionary! If we really believed them and put them into practice, they would transform us, and God's transformation of an individual is always for the good of all. We are all called to share in the priesthood of Christ, whose life is for others.

Ignatius has a short and very compact introduction to his *Spiritual Exercises*. It was later called 'The First Principle and Foundation' and it begins with a formal and traditional statement, 'We are created to praise, reverence and serve God' (*Spiritual Exercises*: 4). For years I was bored with the phrase through over familiarity. Years later, its meaning struck me. If our thanks is genuine, it must spring from a genuine appreciation of the gift and the giver. Therefore the opening sentence of Ignatius' First Principle could read 'It is our duty and it leads to our salvation that we should appreciate, value, cherish and wonder at God's creation'. I read of a Jewish writer who claimed that at the final Judgement, God will ask us only one question, 'Did you enjoy my creation?' How will God respond if I reply, 'Certainly not: I have been far too busy examining my conscience!'

I once gave an individual retreat to a man who was of a lugubrious disposition. One evening when I visited him, he was smiling happily. I almost asked 'What's wrong?' Fortunately, I asked, 'How has today been for you?' 'Wonderful' he said, beaming. 'What was it that you found so wonderful?' I asked. 'It was having a cup of coffee this morning. I suddenly realised that God was enjoying it in me!'

For many years I have had the opportunity to meet and work with people who are actively engaged in some kind of justice and peace work. The characteristic, I discovered, which distinguishes the effective and peaceful worker from the angry and aggressive one lies in their ability to love, enjoy and appreciate life. The more they can do so, the more sensitive they become to the negative and destructive forces around them and within them. Their struggle against violence and oppression springs from their appreciation and love of creation.

In training people for justice and peace work, the most basic attitude required is a growing love and appreciation of life. The 'Review of the Day' done regularly, sustains and deepens this basic attitude.

Before ending this thanksgiving part of the Review of the day, have a conversation in your heart with God. What response do you want to make for the gifts of the day, these tokens of God's desire to share life with you? Throughout the *Spiritual Exercises*, Ignatius recommends these responses from the heart. Whatever form they take, let them be simple, spontaneous and heartfelt.

God's Will, Our Will. What is the Connection?

In general, how are we to find God in what we experience, not merely as negative moments, but as negative states of being? Pursuing this question can lead us into surprising places. Zeno, a fourth century BCE Greek philosopher, asked it. He was founder of the Stoic School in Athens. The Stoics believed that happiness could only be attained by ignoring our desires and submitting to whatever fate might bring. Desire is then considered the source of all our unhappiness. Traces of Stoicism keep reappearing in human thought, particularly among the fundamentalists of any religion. In Christian circles, desire has not infrequently been presented as a dangerous tendency, something to be resisted. 'God's Will' appears to be the only legitimate desire for the conscientious Christian. The impression conveyed by this pernicious teaching is that if I desire anything, it must be wrong and contrary to God's will! To love such a God demands a very perverse nature!

Imagine a Christian wedding in which the bride and groom have been encouraged to express their marriage vows in their own words. See the scene in your imagination – Ignatius would approve of this! The Wedding March is being played as the bride proceeds down the aisle, accompanied by her father, till she joins her beloved before the altar. The presiding minister welcomes them both, then invites the groom to declare his marriage vows. He begins, 'I love you very much, my dear, but do realise that from this moment onwards you must not expect me to have any interest in what you may desire. Your future happiness in this marriage depends entirely on your readiness to do my will. If you do so, our marriage will be a happy one: if you fail to do so, our marriage will be a misery and after death, you will enter eternal damnation'. Having declared his love so movingly, the presiding minister turns to the bride and asks, 'Will you take this man to be your husband till death?'

Progress on our inner journey has often been compared to mountain climbing. Pursuing the mountain metaphor, it is as though we are roped to God, our lead climber. What corresponds to the rope in human experience? Human desire is the rope attaching us to God.

What is it that we long for? When we ask ourselves this question we soon become aware of our many and very varied desires. We also begin to see that almost all of them conflict, one with another. I want to be healthy, fit and slim; I also love eating chocolate and hate taking exercise. I long to be transparently honest: I also want to be popular and well thought of. I am forced to prioritize my desires. Unless I do so, my desires will tear me apart and will tear others apart, too, because of my inner unresolved conflicts.

What, basically, do I most desire? This is the most valuable question we can ask ourselves. We then discover that this search appears to be endless: we start discovering the many different levels of desire there are in us. We also begin to realize that desire is not something we create: it arises in us. As we pursue the various desires, we become increasingly frustrated. Having pursued my desire to eat, drink and be merry, I end up with severe stomach and weight problems. Having pursued my desire to become the wealthiest person in record time, I find myself doing long-term imprisonment for trying to take shortcuts on my way to a personal fortune. In view of these difficulties, I may take to religion, only to discover that God is uncomfortably demanding. The American thinker, David Henry Thoreau (1818–62) commented on this process when he said that the majority of people live lives of quiet desperation.

There is a wonderful truth, a pearl of great price lying hid in this desperate saying. St Augustine spotted it towards the end of his life – he died in 430 CE – and wrote 'Thou hast created us for thyself, and our heart cannot be quieted till it may find repose in thee' (*Confessions* 1.1.).

God is always transcendent, greater than anything we can think or imagine. God is 'a beckoning word' as I once heard bishop David Konstant say. God beckons us beyond ourselves into God's own life. The transcendence of God, which we are called to share, is already working in us in our experience of desire, which no created thing, or person, or group, or system can ever satisfy, thank God!

God's will is our good, our freedom, our delight in our at-one-ness in God, with all creation and within ourselves. St Paul described this in his letter to the Ephesians, 'God's power working in us, can do infinitely more than we can ask or imagine' (Eph. 3.20).

The final prayer which Ignatius presents at the end of his *Spiritual Exercises* is: 'Take, Lord, and receive all my liberty, my memory, my understanding and my entire will, all that I have and possess. You gave it all to me; to you I return it. All is yours, dispose of it entirely according to your will. Give me only the love of you together with your grace, for that is enough for me'.

What is my deepest desire? One way of starting on this question is to imagine you have died and someone writes your obituary notice. Write your own obituary, not the one you are afraid you might receive, but the one which, in your wildest dreams, not letting reality limit you in the slightest, you would love to have. This will not provide you with a neat answer to your question, but it will provide you with lots of interesting and valuable self-awareness discoveries.

I will now offer a method, derived from Ignatius' *Spiritual Exercises*, of using these reflections on the nature of desire in the second section of the 'Review of the Day'.

Discovering the Wisdom of our Moods and Feelings

So far, in describing 'The Review of the Day', we have focussed our attention on those events for which we are grateful, seeing the events as signs of God's love, tokens of God's desire to be at one with us, for at-one-ment. In this section, to increase our sense of gratitude and wonder, we continue to focus our attention on our experience, but in a different way. We begin by asking God for enlightenment, so that we can become more aware of God in all things, including those things we dislike intensely, our hurts, our times of inner darkness, of failure, fragility and desperation. Our petition is not that they should all be taken away and replaced with comforting assurances: our petition is for enlightenment, that we may understand more clearly what is happening, recognize God inviting us to change, to move out of the prison in which we have consented to live so that we may delight in the freedom of life God is continuously offering us. This part of the prayer increases our gratitude and brings about transformation in a way that moralizing can never effect.

Let me illustrate this through an imaginary role play.

I have prayed for enlightenment. On what do I now focus my attention? I look at, without attempting any analysis, approval or disapproval, my moods and feelings during the day. This is a kind of contemplative prayer, a 'gawking' prayer, letting the moods and feelings communicate with me rather than my telling my moods and feelings what they mean. This contemplative attitude lies at the heart of Ignatian Spirituality, which is to become 'a contemplative in action'. It is not a peculiarly Jesuit thing; it is a gift offered to all human beings. In the fifth century BCE Socrates stated that an unreflective life is no life at all.

Focus only on predominant moods and feelings experienced during the day. On this particular morning, my predominant feeling was enjoyment, but in the afternoon, I began to feel irritated, a mood which worsened during the working day, continued, then settled into a black, depressing mood, which discoloured everything, including my Review of the Day.

Now I look more closely. As far as I can tell, what occasioned this change of mood? I was happy in the morning because the people I was working with agreed with my suggestions and one of my colleagues congratulated me on the efficiency of my plan. In the afternoon, I offered further suggestions. This did not meet with my colleagues' approval and one of them criticized me. This brought about the change of mood: the more I thought about what had happened, the more unsettled I became.

Why do I advise against moralizing? Briefly, because moralizing can lead us to miss the enlightenment we need.

There is a kind of moralizing which can appear to be very sensible and right, but it keeps us at a superficial level of consciousness and masks the painful truth which is, in fact, offering us healing. In reaction to what I have experienced so far through looking at my moods and feelings, I may then slip into prayer, including a little superficial moralizing, perhaps something like this:

> Thank you, God, for the excellent morning, which I enjoyed. I ask forgiveness for this afternoon, for becoming irritated, angry, self pitying and miserable.

Having prayed in this way, I may feel a faint glow of self-satisfaction: I did not, in fact, do any physical damage to my uncooperative and critical colleagues. Being irritable is not the ideal attitude for a Christian, but it is a very minor failing, so I can close my prayer for the evening with, 'Thank you, God, for saving me from more serious sin' before falling asleep!

In contrast to this moralizing is the 'gawking' method, looking at our moods and feelings and what has occasioned them without labelling my reactions right or wrong, true or false, trivial or serious. Instead of moralizing, 'gawking' is followed by the all important, but most frequently ignored question, 'What was the desire underlying these moods and feelings?' The point of this question is that our moods and feelings arise from our desires. When our desires are satisfied, we are happy: when our desires are frustrated, we grind inside and also tend to blame others. This method unmasks my moralizing, but it can also reveal a much more uncomfortable truth. This truth, if we can face it, can begin to reveal to us what our heart really longs for. It is out of this realization that transformation can begin.

In the example I have given, I was happy in the morning because my colleagues agreed with my suggestions and one of them complimented me on my efficiency. The error does not lie in my felt reactions. As human beings we need recognition and grow through it.

My changes in mood began when my colleagues no longer accepted my suggestions, a change accelerated when I was criticized by one of them. Then comes the shattering revelation – the underlying desire, indicated by my feelings and moods of that particular day, that my felt reactions on this particular day are revealing a basic desire that all creation should praise, revere and serve me. This is a desire, which is the exact opposite of what I perceive it to be, of what it should be, and what, in the depths of myself, I want it to be! God's enlightenment shows up my sinfulness: I have ignored my own deepest longing – to let God be the God of love, of compassion, of forgiveness and freedom to me and through me, by replacing God with my own ego, wanting all creation to praise, revere and serve me!

The value of this 'Review of the Day' is that its regular practice builds up deeper and more permanent awareness in us that we really are cherished by God, yoked with God at all times and in all circumstances. This is the peace which the risen Jesus brought to his followers in the evening of the first Easter Sunday (Jn 20.19 ff). The disciples are gathered in an upper room, terrified for their own lives, in despair at the loss of Jesus, in whom all their hopes for the future rested. It is in their terror and hopelessness that Jesus appears and greets them with 'Shalom', the Hebrew word for peace. A peace which nothing can shatter, a peace which he hands on by showing them his wounded hands and side, a peace won, not by domination, but by vulnerability.

Conclusion: Does Ignatian Spirituality have Anything to Say to a Post-Christian, Postmodern World?

What I have written so far on Ignatian Spirituality is based on my own experience of making, of giving and of training others to give the *Spiritual Exercises*. Academic study of the *Spiritual Exercises* is very valuable, especially for those who give the *Exercises* to others, but it is through doing the *Spiritual Exercises* that transformation occurs. That is why I have given so much space to 'The Review of the Day'. It is a daily Exercise, which includes essential elements of Ignatian Spirituality. The subject matter is our personal experience of each day. That is the only place where any of us can meet God. The exercise is simple and takes about 15 minutes!

All effective human change begins in individuals and starts with a change in perception. Beginning to see all creation as sacramental, as a freely given gift of a loving, compassionate God, beckoning us all to become at one, a God nearer to us than we are to ourselves, this slow dawning in our consciousness transforms everything in us and around us.

155

Jerome Nadal, a Jesuit contemporary of Ignatius and one of the first Generals of the Society of Jesus once claimed that the *Spiritual Exercises* were suitable for Catholics, Protestants and Pagans. 'Pagans', in those days, was a generic term classifying all who were not Christian. Interfaith communication was still centuries ahead! I first read this phrase in 1975: it has stayed with me ever since. In all the work I have done as a Jesuit since 1975, I have remembered and been guided by Nadal's words and have been amazed and delighted to discover their truth in my own very limited experience.

I went through 18 years of Jesuit training, which included two 8-day retreats annually besides a 30-day retreat as a novice and another 30-day retreat at the end of my training, without realizing that Ignatius wrote his *Spiritual Exercises* on the assumption that they should be given individually. That ignorance was shared by all my contemporaries. Our experience of the *Spiritual Exercises* was through 'preached retreats', consisting of four to five talks daily, followed by private prayer. The common practice of the 'preached retreat' only began in the seventeenth century. The reason normally given for this astounding memory lapse of several centuries is that the individually given retreat was too labour-intensive. I question that assumption. The practice of the individually given retreat was only reintroduced in the twentieth century, after the Second Vatican Council, 1963–5, when all Religious Orders and Congregations were encouraged to reflect on their origins. This recovery of the individually given retreat has had a profound effect, not only on Jesuit life, but also on many other Christian denominations, among those involved in interfaith work and also among some who profess no religion!

At present, in the 'Developed World', the Christian Church is undergoing the greatest crisis in its history. The post-Christian, postmodern cultures question the validity of all religions. Christians are abandoning churchgoing in such numbers that if the exodus continues at the same rate as in the last 10 years, there will be very few churches still open by the end of the twenty-first century in most developed countries. On the other hand, while churchgoing is dwindling, interest in spirituality, a word rarely used 50 years ago outside church circles, appears in government statements and in all kinds of secular organizations.

I am grateful to have lived through this age of rapid change. I do not see our religious crises as threats, but as invitations to radical change. Vast numbers of men and women, compassionate, intelligent and searching, complain that they cannot find the spiritual support they need for life in the churches, as they experience them.

I am grateful for the lessons I have learned through giving retreats individually to many Catholics who consider themselves to be on the fringe, or beyond the fringe, of the Roman Catholic Church, to people of many different Christian denominations, of different faiths or of no professed religious affiliation. Briefly, what I have learnt is that God is at work in every human being without exception and does not appear to be so worried about religious affiliation or status as his clergy. Strangely, the effect of this has not been to alienate me from my Catholic roots, but to appreciate them more in their essentials, and to appreciate the spirituality of other denominations, of other faiths and of people who profess no faith. God is always greater. Salvation comes to us through the poor, the voiceless, the estranged, the disregarded. That is where the harvest is greatest, it is also where the labourers are fewest.

The present interest and popularity of spirituality today is to be welcomed, encouraged, fostered and nurtured. But genuine spirituality is not a commodity, the preserve of a particular nation or religious organization. It is about the Spirit, 'giver of breath and bread, world's strand, sway of the sea, Lord of the living and dead' (Gerard Manley Hopkins, *The Wreck of the Deutschland*). When we speak of Spiritualities, we normally mean ways and means, methods and practices which enable us to become more aware of the reality in which we all live, from which we came, to which we all return, for which we long, whether consciously or unconsciously. Recently, I read with amazement, this extraordinary prayer from Tukaram, an Indian Peasant mystic of the seventeenth century (1608–49). It speaks so clearly of the essential element in all true religion.

Take, Lord, unto Thyself.
My sense of self; and let it vanish utterly:
Take, Lord, my life,
Live Thou Thy life through me.
I live no longer, Lord,
But in me now
Thou livest:
Aye, between Thee and me, my God,
There is no longer room for 'I' and 'mine'.[5]

And I end with a remarkable quote from a leading atheistic humanist of the twentieth century, mathematician and philosopher, Bertrand Russell, on the nature of desire, as he experienced it in his life:

The centre of me is always and eternally a terrible pain – a curious wild pain – a searching for something beyond what the world contains, something transfigured and infinite – the beatific vision – God. I do not find it, I do not think it is to be found – but the love of it is my life – it's like passionate love for a ghost. At times it fills me with rage, at times with wild despair, it is the source of gentleness and cruelty and work, it fills every passion that I have – it is the actual spring of life within me.[6]

I hope he and Jerome Nadal, in the love and laughter of God, enjoy their conversations!

Notes

1 Quotations from the *Spiritual Exercises* are taken from Michael Ivens SJ (1998), *Understanding the Spiritual Exercises – Commentary and Text*. Herefordshire, UK: Gracewing

2 Details of Ignatius' early life are to be found in: William J. Young (1980), *St Ignatius' Own Story*, Chicago, IL: Loyola University Press and William Yeomans (1985). *Iñigo: Original Testament*, London, UK: Inigo Enterprises.

3 See previous footnote. Quotations from the *Spiritual Exercises* are taken from Ivens, *Understanding the Spiritual Exercises*.

4 See Chapter 5 by Martin Laird.

5 From (1991), *Says Tuka: Selected Poetry of Tukaram*, trans. Dilip Chitre, London: Penguin Classics.

6 From a letter dated 23 October 1916 to his lover Colette when Russell was 44. (2001), *The Selected Letters of Bertrand Russell: The Public Years, 1914–1970*, ed. Nicholas Griffin, assisted by Alison Roberts Miculan, London: Routledge.

Bibliography and Further Reading

English, John (1982), *Spiritual Freedom*. Guelph, ON: Loyola House.

Fleming, David (1996), *The Spiritual Exercises of St Ignatius: A Literal Translation and Contemporary Reading*. St Louis, MO: The Institute of Jesuit Sources.

Ganss, George E. (ed.) (1991), *Ignatius of Loyola: The Spiritual Exercises and Selected Works*. New York, NY: Paulist Press.

Hughes, Gerard W. (1985), *God of Surprises*. London: Darton, Longman and Todd.

— (2003), *God in All Things*. London: Hodder and Stoughton.

Lonsdale, David (1990), *Eyes to See, Ears to Hear: An Introduction to Ignatian Spirituality*. London, UK: Darton, Longman and Todd.

Ravier, Andre (1987), *Ignatius of Loyola and the Founding of the Society of Jesus*. San Francisco, CA: Ignatian Press.

Sobrino, John (1978), 'The Christ of the Ignatian Exercises' appendix in *Christology at the Crossroads*. London, UK: SCM Press.

14 Anglican Spirituality

Gordon Mursell

Introduction

As its name implies, Anglican spirituality is rooted in, though by no means confined to, England: the term *ecclesia Anglicana* seems first to have been used to describe the medieval church in England, which was of course a part of the wider Catholic Church under the leadership of the popes. The first to speak of the 'English people' (the *gens Anglorum*) appears to have been Bede, the seventh-century English monk whose *Ecclesiastical History of the English People* seeks to set the life and work of the English church within the context of God's purposes, which for Bede were always both local and transcendental. For all the insularity of his life, almost all of which was spent in a Northumbrian monastery, Bede's outlook was catholic and universal, in at least three fundamental ways: he saw the English church as coterminous with the English people; he saw prayer as inseparable both from the practice of the Christian life and from the theology that inspired it; and he saw the English Christian community, not only as a part of the universal church, but in turn as belonging within the whole company of the saints, from the dawn of creation to the final consummation of history. All three of these principles, central to patristic theology but given distinctive local expression by Bede, influenced the English church and its spiritual life.

From the beginning, then, Anglican spirituality is rooted in the specificity of just one people's history and spiritual journey, yet a specificity which was always a part of a wider picture, part of the whole people of God. Anglicanism has never claimed to be the only, or even the truest or most authentic, part of the Christian church. Rather it is that strand in the rich texture of global Christianity that began in one community, the English people, and which claimed to be, from the beginning, the church for the whole of that community, not simply for the Christians within it. It has also, from the beginning, seen itself as part of something much larger. It was the later history of England, and above all its exploration and colonization of other parts of the globe, which led to Anglicanism becoming a worldwide faith, and to the exporting of much of what had come to constitute English Anglican spirituality to many vastly different contexts. The churches in those contexts rapidly adapted what they received, some even abandoning the use of 'Anglican' in preference for 'Episcopal';[1] and by various means Anglicanism came to flourish in some

159

countries which had never been part of the British sphere of influence.[2] But then Bede in his turn adapted what he received: Christian truth, by its very nature, has to be incarnated in specific cultures and eras. As time passes since the sun set on the British Empire, it may be possible to revalue Anglicanism's English birth and upbringing as an example of incarnational particularity rather than of colonial privilege. What is not possible, however, is to discuss Anglican spirituality without acknowledging both its English character and its more recent global dimension, a dimension which (albeit from his very different perspective) Bede would certainly have celebrated.

Common Prayer

Bede's view of the church as both the church of the whole people in one particular place, and also as part of a much wider communion, both global and eternal, provides the appropriate starting point for any understanding of Anglican spirituality. The most famous, and to some extent the defining, characteristic of that spirituality is arguably the *Book of Common Prayer*, the first version of which was produced by Thomas Cranmer, archbishop of Canterbury, in 1549. As its title suggests, this was from its inception conceived as something more than a manual of prayer for clergy or individual Christians; and, notwithstanding its indebtedness to medieval precedents, Cranmer seems to have envisaged from the start that this Book would both encourage all Christians to come together daily in their local churches for Morning and Evening Prayer, and that common (not private) prayer would always be primary in the Church of England.[3] And, since subsequently almost every province of the Anglican Communion has produced its own Prayer Book, modelled originally on that of Cranmer, we may see in its distinctive features some defining characteristics of Anglican spirituality as a whole, and especially of the vision which Bede bequeathed to his spiritual descendants.

Even a cursory perusal of the *Book of Common Prayer* underlines Cranmer's intention, derived ultimately from Bede, that the English church existed to serve the whole people of God. The Litany (first produced in English by Cranmer in 1544) illustrates this well: the moral and spiritual well-being of the entire nation is its concern; and, although to modern ears the prayers for monarch and state might appear unhealthily sycophantic, they reflect this pervasive concern for the whole people, and the consequent refusal to separate the holy from the everyday, the ecclesiastical from the political.[4] And the Calendar, listing the feasts and other holy days to be observed throughout the year, includes both the feasts of the universal Church and a number of local celebrations (such as Bede, on 27th May, and St Crispin, on 25th October, the patron saint of English shoemakers). In his explanatory article *Of Ceremonies*, Cranmer wrote about the principles that underlay his new Prayer Book:

And in these our doings we condemn no other nations, nor prescribe any thing but to our own people only; for we think it convenient that every country should use such ceremonies as they shall think best to the setting forth of God's honour and glory, and to the reducing of the people to a most perfect and godly living, without error or superstition.[5]

Later versions of the Prayer Book, produced by different provinces of the worldwide Anglican communion, reflect these core principles. Thus the 1979 Book of Common Prayer of the Episcopal Church of the USA (TEC) includes a wide selection of prayers, following the pattern and spirit of the 1662 book, including prayers 'for those who suffer for the sake of conscience', for schools and colleges, for the good use of leisure, for prisons, for those who live alone, for the conservation of natural resources, and thanksgiving 'for the diversity of races and cultures' and many more. The calendar is both local and global in perspective. In its worship, the Episcopal Church of Sudan (ECS) (one of the largest Anglican churches, with over 5 million members) customarily takes the bones of Cranmer's Morning Prayer and enfleshes them with vernacular music, dance, extemporary prayer and African biblical interpretation.[6] The church in the Sudan has incarnated the Christian gospel in the context of local culture, just as Bede did: 'crosses are fashioned from the razed sacred posts and trees that once stood at the heart of sacrificial shrines. Sacred spears, long the symbols of Nilotic religion, have evolved into finely carved crosses to serve as "swords of the Spirit" against unseen powers.'[7] In New Zealand, the canticle *Benedicite, omnia opera Domini*, or Song of Creation, included by Cranmer in Morning Prayer, is rendered in a striking local context, drawing in distinctive features of New Zealand's ecology.[8]

Practical Divinity

Underlying the spirituality of common prayer in the Anglican tradition, then, is a concern very close to St Paul's theology of life in the Spirit: all of life held together, and seen in the perspective of, our relationship with God through Jesus Christ. We might say that Anglican spirituality reflects a desire not only to serve the whole people of God, but the whole person within the people of God. There is something both profoundly simple and profoundly challenging about the words included in the exhortation to confession in the Prayer Book's eucharistic liturgy:

Ye that do truly and earnestly repent you of your sins, and are in love and charity with your neighbours, and intend to lead a new life, following the commandments of God, and walking from henceforth in his holy ways; draw near with faith . . .

Few comparable orders of service from other Christian traditions so succinctly and sharply insist on the fundamental inseparability of worship and prayer from morality and justice. This is what came, in the Anglican tradition, to be called 'practical Divinity'; and it is supremely articulated in the work of one of the finest and most influential Anglican minds, that of Richard Hooker (1553/4–1600), who in 1585 became Master of the Temple in London. Like Bede's, Hooker's understanding of the church was inseparable from the English nation in which it was set; in Book VIII of his masterwork, the *Laws of Ecclesiastical Polity*, he took as his model for the relationship of church to nation the ancient covenant relationship between Israel and God:

> In a word, our estate is according to the pattern of God's own ancient elect people, which people was not part of them the commonwealth, and part of them the Church of God, but the selfsame people whole and entire were both under one chief Governor, on whose supreme authority they did all depend.[9]

It follows that, for Hooker, as for Cranmer, public prayer takes precedence over private inasmuch as 'a whole society of such condition exceedeth the worth of any one'.[10] Furthermore, the devotion of others inspires us when our own flags.[11] This latter point is beautifully made by another major figure in the formative years of Anglican spirituality, Lancelot Andrewes (1556–1626), bishop successively of Chichester and Winchester, who wrote in a sermon:

> Albeit we pray but faintly and have not that supply of fervency that is required in prayer, yet we have comfort that ever when we most faint in prayer there are of God's saints that pray for us with all instancy, by which it comes to pass that being all but one body their prayers tend to our good as well as their own, for the faithful howsoever they be many and dispersed into diverse corners of the world yet they are but one body; and as they are the members of one body, so they pray not privately for themselves but for the whole body of the Church; so that the weakness of one member is supplied by the fervent and earnest prayer of the other.[12]

Hooker's theology of the spiritual life is central to the development of Anglican spirituality. He writes vividly about the nature of true prayer as holding together a clear awareness of our own unworthiness with a sense of Christ's mercy:

> The knowledge of our own unworthiness is not without belief in the merits of Christ. With that true fear which the one causeth there is

coupled true boldness, and encouragement drawn from the other. The very silence which our unworthiness putteth us unto, doth itself make request for us, and that in the confidence of his grace. Looking upward we are stricken dumb, looking upward we speak and prevail. O happy mixture, wherein things contrary do so qualify and correct the one the danger of the other's excess, that neither boldness can make us presume as long as we are kept under with the sense of our own wretchedness; nor, while we trust in the mercy of God through Christ Jesus, fear be able to tyrannize over us![13]

Prayer and Social Justice – 'O happy mixture!'

'O happy mixture!' – the phrase might encapsulate one of the core features of Anglican spirituality: a refusal to separate human sinfulness from divine mercy, the individual from the community, the church from the wider nation, the everyday from the eternal, the local from the universal. Not the least impressive aspect of Hooker's theology is his emphasis on the last of these, which serves to moderate at least somewhat the English church's tendency to nationalism. Hooker defends the use of the Litany in the Prayer Book not only on account of its venerable history, but also because

What dangers at any time are imminent, what evils hang over our heads, God doth know and not we. We find by daily experience that those calamities may be nearest at hand, readiest to break in suddenly upon us, which we in regard of times or circumstances may imagine to be furthest off. Or if they do not indeed approach, yet such miseries as being present all men are apt to bewail with tears, the wise by their prayers should rather prevent. Finally, if we for ourselves had a privilege of immunity, doth not true Christian charity require that whatsoever any part of the world, yea any one of all our brethren elsewhere doth either suffer or fear, the same we account as our own burden?[14]

As Anglicanism expanded into a global communion, this instinctive recognition of our need for one another within the body of Christ found wider expression. John S. Pobee has written that in Africa, where European individualism was an unwelcome intruder, Christianity's most significant growth really began once the colonial era was at an end:[15]

The prototypical community is the family which consists of the living, the dead (the living dead, the ancestors) and those yet-to-be-born . . . As an African I am dissatisfied with only my salvation. I am happier if it embraces my ancestors and descendants.[16]

But the tensions that comprise Hooker's 'happy mixture' are not always so easily held together. The spirituality of the Prayer Book did nothing to discourage European Christians from supporting, and profiting from, slavery, even though it was eventually evangelical Anglicans, Africans as well as Europeans, who led the movement to abolish it.[17] One of the finest spiritual writers in twentieth-century English Anglicanism, Alan Ecclestone, has noted that neither the old Prayer Book collects nor most of the new ones 'have set prayer for the Kingdom's coming at the heart of devotional life'.[18] And John Stott, perhaps the greatest Anglican evangelical of the twentieth century, has memorably said that:

> Good Samaritans will always be needed to succour those who are assaulted and robbed; yet it would be even better to rid the Jerusalem-Jericho road of brigands.[19]

In this context it is important to emphasize the role of women in nurturing a less conformist, more passionate and subversive spirituality within the Anglican tradition. In the eighteenth century Hannah More (1745–1833) and Sarah Trimmer (1741–1810) were deeply engaged, not only in promoting religious education among women and children and in opposing social injustice at every level, but also in encouraging a pattern of spiritual life which would promote good relationships within each family and household, and attack the exploitation of the poor. The work of the Mothers' Union (MU) (founded by Mary Sumner in 1876) has enabled this kind of spirituality to spread throughout the Anglican world.[20] MU members are committed to make prayer, worship and Bible study central to daily life: Esla Crawford, from the MU of Trinidad and Tobago, articulates in a very different context the heart of both Bede's and Hooker's vision of what spiritual life was about:

> Our prayer lives . . . must be intensified. We have to develop disciplined spiritual lives *because as Christian women we have a responsibility for the spiritual condition of our nation.*[21]

Worship and Beauty of Holiness

Among the greatest of all Anglican writers on the spiritual life was the Anglo-Catholic laywoman Evelyn Underhill (1875–1941), who believed that true worship should invariably lead both to a greater awareness of the needs of the world around us ('The eyes of worship have a wide-angle lens'), and to a spirit of exploration ('The spirit of worship is the very spirit of exploration').[22] And there was something even more important still:

We talk and write easily and freely about spiritual values and the spiritual life; but we remain fundamentally utilitarian, even pragmatic, at heart. We want spiritual things to work; and the standard we apply is our miserable little notion of how they ought to work. We always want to know whether they are helpful. Our philosophy and religion are orientated, not towards the awful vision of that principle before which Isaiah saw the seraphim veil their eyes; but merely towards the visible life of man and its needs. We may speak respectfully of Mary, and even study her psychology; but we feel that the really important thing is to encourage Martha to go on getting the lunch.[23]

This emphasis on adoration, on worship being offered without calculation of outcomes or expectation of returns, is another crucial strand in Anglican spirituality. It finds expression in both Evangelical revivalism and hymnody and solemn Anglo-Catholic Liturgy, all of which profoundly influenced global Anglicanism; but it goes back further than them. There is space to quote just one exemplar: Thomas Traherne (1637–74), whose own life – as parish priest, theologian, political activist and contemplative – encapsulates so much of the quintessence of Anglican spirituality, and who wrote:

GOD never shewd Himself more a GOD, then when He appeared Man. Never gained more Glory then when He lost all Glory. Was never more Sensible of our Sad Estate, then when He was bereaved of all Sence. O let thy Goodness shine in me! I will lov all O Lord by thy Grace Assisting as Thou doest: And in Death it self, will I find Life, and in Conquest Victory.[24]

An emphasis on the beauty of holiness – but on an incarnate, not disembodied holiness – is also found in the Prayer Book. The fact that Cranmer's Book, in the adapted version produced in 1662, was written in English of exceptional beauty, both elevating and yet accessible, both poetic in tone and yet rooted in the concerns of contemporary laypeople, has immeasurably enhanced its influence, as have two other factors. One was the inclusion, in the 1662 Book, of Miles Coverdale's wonderfully evocative translation of the Psalms;[25] the other was the appearance, in 1611, of the King James Version of the Bible. The result was that, at the heart of Anglican spirituality as it developed its own character following the break with Rome, was a whole-hearted commitment to the needs (both spiritual and physical) of lay Christians, not simply (or even primarily) of the clergy – a desire both to give voice to their aspirations, and to address their primary concerns. Whatever its defects, the Prayer Book is emphatically not narrowly churchy or clerical in tone or range.

Furthermore, there is in Anglican spirituality a palpable concern to make the Word flesh in such a way as to reveal its beauty: to make God attractive.

A sense of the importance of taking great care over liturgical content and performance is no narrow aestheticism, nor an unconscious consequence of privilege or leisure, but a recognition of the power of the Word to transcend, as well as to give expression to, the raw reality of everyday life. One of the greatest figures in Anglican spirituality is George Herbert (1593–1633), who like Traherne was both parish priest and theologian, poet and contemplative with a profound concern with social and political as well as spiritual issues. In his *A Priest to the Temple* (1652) he wrote:

> Besides his example, he [the priest] having often instructed his people how to carry themselves in divine service, exacts of them all possible reverence . . . causing them . . . to do all in a straight, and steady posture, as attending to what is done in the church, and every one . . . answering aloud both Amen, and all other answers . . .; which answers also are to be done not in a huddling, or slubbering fashion, gaping, or scratching the head, or spitting even in the midst of their answer, but gently and pausably, thinking what they say.[26]

The Holy Place: 'Thinking what they Say'

'Thinking what they say' – this expression, like Hooker's 'happy mixture', might be taken as emblematic of Anglican spirituality, expressing as it does Anglicanism's assent to the ancient Christian principle that *lex orandi, lex credendi*: the way we pray forms, and gives expression to, what we believe. Spirituality and theology, the eternal and the everyday, are not to be separated. From the evocative beauty of choral Evensong in English cathedrals to the care taken by a lay reader or catechist to make common prayer in the remotest village church an act of life-changing holiness, this concern has remained characteristic of Anglican spirituality and worship. It reflects a search for beauty, but a beauty rooted in the everyday. One of the greatest Anglican leaders of the twentieth century, Michael Ramsey, wrote that

> The prayer with beautiful buildings and lovely music must be a prayer which also speaks from the places where men and women work, or lack work, and are sad and hungry, suffer and die. To be near to the love of God is to be near, as Jesus showed, to the darkness of the world. That is the 'place of prayer.'[27]

There is a recognizably Anglican spirituality of the holy place or building, which also goes back to Bede. He describes Benedict Biscop's visit to Rome, returning with a wealth of books, orders for chants and many holy pictures of the saints to adorn the church of St Peter he had built:

Thus all who entered the church, even those who could not read, were able, whichever way they looked, to contemplate the dear face of Christ and His saints, even if only in a picture, to put themselves more firmly in mind of the Lord's Incarnation and, as they saw the decisive moment of the Last Judgement before their very eyes, be brought to examine their conscience with all due severity.[28]

This recognition of the imaginative potential of the holy place was never entirely lost in the English spiritual tradition, though it was challenged at the Reformation. Where the late medieval church sought to express God's *presence*, its Protestant equivalent sought to express God's *truth*: reverence for the sacrament was replaced in Puritan and Lutheran buildings with reverence for the pulpit. Cranmer sought to combine both. As we have seen, the people were encouraged to come to church twice each day to pray with their priest; and it is in the church that the clergy are to teach the faith. In the official homilies issued in 1547 for use in Anglican churches, it is made clear that the church building is still a holy place, a place where Christ is to be found:

If we lack Jesus Christ, that is to say, the saviour of our souls and bodies, we shall not find him in the market-place, or in the guildhall, much less in the ale-house or tavern, amongst good fellows, (as they call them,) so soon as we shall find him in the temple, the Lord's house, amongst the teachers and preachers of his word, where indeed he is to be found.[29]

In Anglican spirituality, the presence of Christ is real but not confined: Christ is not restricted to the church; but he is present there, for as long as his teaching governs and animates the lives of his people.[30] And it is just this synthesis of scripture and daily life, of prayer and morality, which the Prayer Book was designed to uphold.

The Religious Life

A final example of this synthesis must be mentioned: the recovery, within Anglicanism, of the religious life. Apart from the short-lived experiment at Little Gidding in the seventeenth century, this recovery was the fruit of the nineteenth-century Tractarian (or Oxford) Movement, beginning with the establishment of the Park Village sisterhood in 1845. The movement spread rapidly, both in England and across the Anglican world, although it contracted severely in the second half of the twentieth century.[31] Among its most significant figures is Ini Kopuria (c. 1900–45), who founded the Melanesian Brotherhood in 1925 as a form of the religious life adapted to the context of the Pacific region. This was a profound commitment to poverty of spirit and rejection of private ownership, a concern to incarnate the Gospel in the communal, anti-individual context of the Pacific islands, a practical commitment to conflict resolution, a willingness to permit people to commit themselves for five years after which they could leave and get married, and a joyful spirituality rooted in local dance, music, drama and the celebration of nature.[32]

Conclusion

In his commentary on the prayer of Hannah in the First Book of Samuel, Bede invited his readers to reject a narrowly individualist or religious view of prayer:

> For if prayer is understood as being only what we commonly refer to by the word, then neither will Hannah appear to have prayed with these words, nor will any of the just be praying without ceasing, as the apostle commanded. But if all the actions of the just person, who lives according to [the will of] God, are regarded as prayers, because the just person does what is just without ceasing; then by this means the just person will pray without ceasing, nor will he ever cease from prayer unless he ceases to be just.[33]

There is nothing in these words that might not have been said by any of his great patristic forebears. Yet in them Bede encapsulates that integrated view of prayer and Christian life which became in time the heart of Anglican spirituality. If Anglicanism can be criticized for a lack of dogmatic precision and a well-meaning but woolly comprehensiveness, then it is worth stressing that it has been precisely this refusal to separate head from heart, prayer from action, holiness from justice which has allowed it to rediscover itself in many cultural guises and to continue to inspire and nurture Christians across the world.

Notes

1 Such as the Anglican churches in Brazil, Scotland and the United States. On this subject, see especially Ward, *Global Anglicanism*.

2 There are today thriving (though relatively small) Anglican churches in Japan, Korea, Haiti, Brazil and the Congo, for example, and larger ones in Rwanda and Burundi (evangelized from Uganda) and in Namibia.

3 On this, see especially Diarmaid MacCulloch (1996), *Thomas Cranmer*. Yale University Press, esp. p. 224.

4 For the tendency of Anglicanism to veer towards conformism, see for example, the 'Form of Prayer with Thanksgiving, to be used yearly upon the Fifth Day of *November*, for the happy Deliverance of King *JAMES* I and the Three Estates of *England*, from the most traiterous and bloody intended Massacre by Gunpowder; and also for the happy Arrival of his Majesty King *William* on this Day, for the Deliverance of our

Church and Nation', which was included in the 1662 Book of Common Prayer and remained there until in 1859 an Act of Parliament repealed its observance. Yet part of a concern for the whole people of God is precisely this engagement with political realities, even if the way it finds expression is unacceptable to twenty-first-century minds.

5 From *Of Ceremonies*, placed at the end of the 1549 Book but transferred to the beginning in 1552. The Articles of Religion, which are not a part of the Prayer Book but are invariably printed as an appendix to it, includes an explicit acknowledgement that 'every particular or national Church hath authority to ordain, change, and abolish, ceremonies or rites of the Church ordained only by man's authority, so that all things be done to edifying' (Article 34).

6 See Marc Nikkel, 'Death has Come to Reveal the Faith: Spirituality in the Episcopal Church of the Sudan amidst Civil Conflict' in *Anglicanism: A Global Communion*, p. 74.

7 Ibid. art.cit., p. 76 and Ward, *Global Anglicanism*, p. 210.

8 The 'Benedicite Aotearoa' can be found in *A New Zealand Prayer Book*, p. 457, and is available online at www.liturgy.co.nz.

9 Hooker, *Of the Laws of Ecclesiastical Polity* in *The Works of Mr Richard Hooker*, 3 vols, ed. J. Keble (1841), Oxford University Press, VIII:1:7, vol. 2, pp. 493–4.

10 *Of the Laws* . . . V:23:1, vol. 1, p. 512.

11 Ibid.

12 Sermon 4 on Prayer, in *Ninety-six Sermons by* . . . *Lancelot Andrewes*, ed. J. P. Wilson (1841–3), Library of Anglo-Catholic Theology. Oxford: Parker, vol. 5, p. 339.

13 *Of the Laws* . . . V:47:4, vol. 1, p. 580.

14 *Of the Laws* . . . V:41:4 vol. 1, p. 559.

15 See Philip Jenkins (2002), *The Next Christendom: The Coming of Global Christianity*. Oxford University Press, p. 56; Kevin Ward, *Global Anglicanism*, p. 3.

16 John S. Pobee, 'An African Anglican's View of Salvation', in *Anglicanism: A Global Communion*, p. 81. For this pervasively corporate emphasis on African Christian spirituality, see also John S. Mbiti (1971), *New Testament Eschatology in an African Background*. London: SPCK, esp. chap. VI.

17 Among the vast literature on this subject, see Olaudah Equiano's profoundly spiritual autobiography *The Interesting Narrative*, ed. Vincent Carretta (1995). Harmondsworth: Penguin Classics.

18 *The Night Sky of the Lord* (1980). London: Darton, Longman and Todd, p. 149.

19 *The Cross of Christ* (1986, repr. 1999). Leicester: Inter-Varsity Press, in The Essential John Stott, p. 271

20 The MU is the largest women's group in many churches (such as the Anglican Church of Kenya) and has played a crucial role in rebuilding Rwandan society following the 1994 genocide. See the articles by Esther Mombo, Martha Nkoane, Krupaveni Prakasha Rao and Julie Lipp-Nathaniel and Emma Wild in *Anglicanism: A Global Communion*.

21 Quoted in *Anglicanism: A Global Communion*, p. 381; italics added.

22 'Education and the Spirit of Worship', 1937, repr. in L. Menzies (ed.), *Collected Papers of Evelyn Underhill*; London: Longmans, Green, 1946, pp. 198–9. See also her classic study *Worship* London: Nisbet & Co., 2nd edn, 1937.

23 'The Philosophy of Contemplation', in *The Essentials of Mysticism and Other Essays*. Oxford: Oneworld, 1995, p. 98.

24 From *Centuries of Meditations* I:90, quoted in Denise Inge (ed.) (2008), *Happiness and Holiness: Thomas Traherne and His Writings*. London: Canterbury Press, pp. 303–4. See also Mary Grey's chapter below.

25 For the complex history of this, see the article by E. C. Ratcliff in *Liturgy and Worship: A Companion to the Prayer Books of the Anglican Communion*, ed. W. K. Lowther Clarke. London: SPCK, 1964, pp. 287–92.

26 *A Priest to the Temple*, chap. VI ('The Parson Praying'). The work was originally entitled *The Country Parson*; in *The Works of George Herbert*, ed. F. E. Hutchinson. Oxford: Clarendon, 1941, pp. 223–90.

27 Michael Ramsey (1982), *Be Still and Know*. London: Collins, pp. 13–14.

28 Bede (1969), *Ecclesiastical History of the English People* 6, ed. and trans. Colgrave and Mynors. Oxford University Press, pp. 190–1. For an introduction to Bede, see Benedicta Ward, *the Venerable Bede*. London: Geoffrey Chapman, 1990.

29 From the homily *Of the Right Use of the Church or Temple of God*, in *Certain Homilies Appointed to be Read in Churches in the Time of the Late Queen Elizabeth*. Oxford University Press, 1840, p. 149.

30 'It is very characteristic of Anglican sacramental theology . . . to emphasize the presence of God as action rather than object in the sacrament' (Rowell, Stevenson and Williams, General Introduction to *Love's Redeeming Work*, p. xxii).

31 See Mumm, *Stolen Daughters*, the excellent article by Petà Dunstan in Stebbing, *Anglican Religious Life*, and Una Kroll, 'A Vision for the Religious Orders in the Anglican Communion in the Next Century', in *Anglicanism: A Global Communion* pp. 372–7. For the history of Anglican religious life, see Peter Anson, *The Call of the Cloister: Religious Communities and Kindred Bodies in the Anglican Communion*. London: SPCK, 1956.

32 See the article by Brother Richard ('Transforming Missionaries: The Melanesian Brotherhood'), in Stebbing 2003; Ward, *Global Anglicanism* pp. 293–4; Richard A. Carter, 'Where God Still Walks in the Garden: Religious Orders and the Development of the Anglican Church in the South Pacific', in *Anglicanism: A Global Communion*, pp. 45–51.

33 *In I partem Samuhelis* (On the First Book of Samuel) 1, ed. D. Hurst, in *Corpus Christianorum: Series Latina* vol. 119. Turnhout: Brepols, 1969, pp. 21–2.

Bibliography and Further Reading

Kaye, Bruce (2008), *An Introduction to World Anglicanism*. Cambridge: Cambridge University Press.

Mumm, Susan (1999) *Stolen Daughters, Virgin Mothers: Anglican Sisterhoods in Victorian Britain*. London: Leicester University Press.

Mursell, Gordon (2001), *English Spirituality.*, 2 vols London: SPCK.

Rowell, Geoffrey; Stevenson, Kenneth and Williams, Rowan (eds) (2001), *Love's Redeeming Work: The Anglican Quest for Holiness*. Oxford: Oxford University Press.

Stebbing, Nicolas, CR (ed.) (2003), *Anglican Religious Life – A Well Kept Secret?* Dublin: Dominican Publications.

Ward, Kevin (2006), *A History of Global Anglicanism*. Cambridge: Cambridge University Press.

Wingate, Andrew; Ward, Kevin; Pemberton, Carrie and Sitshebo, Wilson (eds) (1998), *Anglicanism: A Global Communion*. London: Mowbray.

15 The French School

David D. Thayer

Introduction

The French School of Spirituality – its very name betrays a problem.[1] Most of the great spiritual traditions of the Roman Catholic Church can be traced back to a single, primary individual whose mystical insight captured a glimpse of the train of God's glory and was able to embody it intellectually, affectively and institutionally. Their names are all familiar: Benedictine, Franciscan, Dominican, Theresan, Ignatian, to name a few. While Pierre Cardinal de Bérulle (1575–1629) may rightly be called the chief architect of the French School, the insights of the other major initial figures of what is now commonly called the French School of Spirituality, Charles de Condren (1568–1641), Jean-Jacques Olier (1608–57), and Jean Eudes (1601–80) do not simply develop the thoughts of the Cardinal. They all have significant mystical insights that arise from their profound lives of prayer and their reflection upon their experience of God. To this extent, the notion of a particular school of mystical theology called the 'French School' has the same fluidity that a movement like existentialism has in the field of philosophy.

The issue becomes more complex as one explores the problem further. While one could easily name a number of other great French spiritual writers of the seventeenth century who are also members of the French School of Spirituality, including Gaston de Renty (1611–49), Jean-Baptiste de La Salle (1651–1719) and Louis-Marie Grignion de Montfort (1673–1716), whether one would include a figure like Vincent de Paul (1581–1660) within the movement is open to question.[2] Add to this the number of congregations of apostolic life founded in the latter half of the nineteenth century that can rightfully trace their inspiration back to the spiritual theology of the four great founders of the French School and the issue becomes all the more complicated. Does this resurgence of the themes of the French School constitute a new movement that should be called something else, or are they part of a larger living tradition?

Perhaps there is no single bright star which dominates the French School because of the type of men and women they were, because they understood with Jean-Jacques Olier that their role:

Ought to be a bit like the star which appeared to the Magi in order to lead them to our Lord: once it had shown them the way, it immediately was eclipsed[3] and disappeared. We must do the same: we must be as stars leading people to our Lord, but we must serve only to show them the way. As soon as we have accomplished this and have helped them experience our Savior, we must disappear, we must withdraw without even wanting them to cast a backward glance at our departure.[4]

Emulating the hidden life of Jesus upon which they so often meditated, the primary members of the French School of Spirituality sought to reform the church in France in light of the Council of Trent not by being a pillar of fire that led it forward, but by concentrating on the hearth of its daily life. Guided by the Spirit, they breathed the dark coals of a church dissipated by, at best, a mediocre fervour, including a clergy marked more by political ambition than care for souls, into fiery renewal: in parish and foreign missions, in the reformation and education of the diocesan priesthood, in service to the poor, until the greatest age of France's political ascendancy was matched by a spiritual flowering as omnipresent as the *fleur-de-lis* of the Sun King.

The tradition of the French School has remained, not only in the Church of France, but throughout the world. At times its light has faded, only to be renewed in the voices of such as François Libermann (1802–52), Frederick William Faber (1814–63), Thérèse of Lisieux (1873–97)[5] and Madeleine Delbrêl (1904–64).

When one explores all the writings of the four primary figures of the founding of the French School, however, certain words begin to sing a certain melody: mysteries and states, *anéantissement*,[6] apostolic spirit. They provide a *leitmotif* of concerns and themes that can be clustered within the framework of Father Olier's prayer method,[7] divided into three movements or moments – *Adoration*: to have Jesus before our eyes, *Communion*: to have Jesus in our hearts, and *Co-operation*: to have Jesus in our hands – that enable one to have a beginning appreciation of this spiritual movement.

Adoration: Jesus before my Eyes

All of the founders of the French School insisted that adoration was the primary pulse note of prayer. The beginning, centre and goal of their mystical journey was a vision of the grandeur of God which resulted in the virtue of religion, that virtue that renders to God what is due Him – everything. In the words of Cardinal de Bérulle,

> Mystical theology attempts to draw us to God, to unite us with God, to lose ourselves in God. It does the first through the grandeur of God, the second through the Divine unity, the third through His plenitude. The grandeur of God separates us from ourselves and every created thing. It draws us into

God. His unity receives us and unites us in himself. His plenitude loses us, empties us and drowns us in the immense ocean of His perfections, as when we see the sea lose and swallow a drop of water.[8]

The goal of the spiritual life, then, is to be lost in God, to live in a manner that God is all in all. Again, Cardinal de Bérulle prays,

> Holy Trinity, divine and adorable! May I diminish myself and raise myself in You to give You what I ought, to know Your grandeurs, to receive Your influences, to abandon myself to Your will, to enter into Your ways, to carry the effects of Your eternal mercies . . .
>
> Finding myself in You as the effect is found in its cause and in its principle, I adore who You are in relationship to me and in relationship to every created being. I adore Your power that produces all things, Your immensity that contains everything, your bounty that embraces all things, Your knowledge that anticipates everything, Your providence that provides for all things. I adore You as the beginning and search for You as the end of my being and every being. I adore You and look upon You as my way. I rest in You as does the subsistence of every creature who proceeds from You as its origin, that holds You at its center, that reposes in You as its subsistence and loses itself in You as in an abyss.[9]

This insistence upon the grandeur of God flows out in the writings of the French School into an understanding of humanity as *anéanti*, a pure relation which has no being except in and through God. Our lives flow from, find their continuance and meaning through, and seek their fulfilment in the relations that constitute the one being of the Trinity. We are relations which echo in shadow the light and life-giving being of the Triune God. Constantly being created by God, we are continually called to communion in the Divine Mystery.

Given the reality of sin, however, such communion with God is not possible except through a second divine action. In Christ, the Trinity incarnates the second person, the Son to be 'one like us in all things but sin' (Heb. 4.15). In Christ, through Christ and with Christ, we become a new creation, able to live fully for God as his adopted sons and daughters:

> Saint Paul calls us 'the creatures of Jesus Christ.' This is a great word that teaches us the secret of our condition . . . It teaches us that we are created in Jesus Christ and that, just as the living God is the principle of our existence in nature, God mortal and dying is the principle of our existence in grace, 'created in Christ Jesus.' It teaches us that, as we have two emanations from God and two different beings, we also have two entrances into two

very different worlds for very diverse ends. In the first creation we enter into this world which we see; in the second creation we enter into a world where we adore, that is to say, we enter, we live, we act in Jesus: 'Creatures of Jesus Christ.' Just as he is our principle, he is our universe as well, he is our world and we live in him.[10]

Thus, the Trinitarianism that lies at the heart of the French School is always filtered through an incarnational Christocentrism. It is through imitation of the mysteries of Christ and through participation in His states that we begin to live within the deepest reality of our Faith, the Trinity. In the incarnation, God reveals a perfect adorer, the God-Man Jesus Christ, in whom we are able to offer 'a perfect sacrifice of adoration to the Father' (Heb. 5.7–10).

Entrance into the life of Jesus, living the spirit of Jesus, then is the focal activity of prayer, life and ministry from the perspective of the French School. We are to be and to do as He is and has done:

> The first and last purpose of this Institute will be to live supremely for God in Christ Jesus our Savior, so that the inner life of his Son penetrates the depths of our hearts in a way that permits each one of us to repeat with confidence what St Paul claims: 'It is no longer I who live, it is Christ who lives in me' (Gal. 2. 20). This will be the unique hope and single thought, the only action embodied in everyone: to live the life of Christ interiorly and to manifest that life incarnately in every action.[11]

The Christian enters into the life of Jesus through contemplation that always leads to action. We keep the mysteries of the life of Christ, those events revealed in the Scriptures and tradition, before our eyes so that we might enter into the states they image. In classic Neoplatonic fashion, the French School considers the events of history, the mysteries of Christ, as impermanent icons of eternal states, those lasting relational realities that express the being and action of the Trinity. We contemplate the birth of Jesus in Bethlehem to enter into his state of incarnation, that moment of *anéantissement* in which the Divine Word empties itself, enfleshes itself in silence, so that we might see the perfect servitude of Christ preparing itself for the ultimate act of obedience, 'death, even death on a cross' (Phil. 2.8), in order that we might experience the fullness of God's glory in eternal life.

Entering into the states of Jesus, living his spirit, entails a hermeneutic that teaches us how to understand the passage and events of our own lives. Our personal histories are aftertones of the life of Jesus. Our lives make sense insofar as they recapitulate the inner truths of the life of Jesus. Our lives have been chosen by God to reveal the plentitude of His compassion through our participation in the Lord's mysteries and states in a variety of ways:

God has diverse manners for directing souls in the Church. We need rather to attach ourselves to the one God wants for us without desiring another. There are different ways, but all lead to the same end, God. Our fidelity consists in walking the one God has shown us, but walking it with the greatest stride possible for us, in the manner which enables us to arrive most quickly to him, and to possess him perfectly.

This is one of the principal rules those who guide souls ought to follow: keep them from turning away from their proper route and from taking another way than that where God has called them to come to him. Even if God wants to give himself to everyone and to be the possession of everyone, it is nevertheless in a variety of ways, and by different means for each one.[12]

Communion: Jesus in My Heart

The many paths of the Christian life lead us into the heart of the Christian mystery:

> You see what we mean by the Christian life: it is a continuation and fulfillment of the life of Jesus. All our actions must be a continuation of the actions of Jesus. We are to be, as it were, Jesus on earth, so as to continue his life and his works, to do and to suffer all that we do and suffer in a holy, divine manner, in the spirit of Jesus. That means, with the holy and divine dispositions and intentions with which Jesus carried out his actions and his sufferings.[13]

While the French School insists upon protecting the liberty of each Christian, those diverse lives are all oriented towards one end, the continual expression of the life of Jesus here and now. In this sense, the state of the Incarnation continues to embody itself in the life of the Church, Christ's mystical body.

Through the graces given in baptism, the Christian begins to live the life chosen for him or her for the sake of the Church. Thus, the mystical body of Christ expressing itself in its source and summit, the liturgy, becomes a major source for daily meditation on the part of the founders of the French School.[14] These went further in their meditation upon the liturgical life of the Church, creating their own feasts to highlight particular aspects of the life of Jesus and the life of Mary to assist the faithful given into their charge to come closer to the mysteries of the life of Jesus and dwell within His states. Jean Eudes' Liturgy of the Sacred Heart, currently embodied in the Roman Liturgy, is a primary example of this:

> Insofar as we commune with the Holy Spirit, we commune with the actions of Jesus Christ as well, and in Him, and in His Church, we receive the effects of the Holy Spirit only for the sake of building up the body of Christ.

It is there we find the abundance of the feast of the Lamb and the diversity of foods He presents to us in Himself and in His members. He calls us to all, and sets the same things before us. It is up to us to choose, according to the instinct of the interior spirit within us, some meat that is pleasing to Him, all for the fulfillment of the saints.[15]

This perspective of living in the spirit of Jesus for the sake of building up the mystical body inspired another major concern of the founders of the French School. They understood that the Church would be reformed only if her clergy were reformed. Thus, they set about establishing seminaries for the sanctification of the clergy.

This concern for the priesthood, however, did not entail a separation of the ordained priesthood from the priesthood of the faithful. Most of the writings of the founders were addressed to all Christians. They did not think that a priest had a special spirituality. Indeed, whatever differences they called for were differences in intensity. The priest was called to be an icon through which others might learn the path to holiness:

From this [apostolic spirit] their [the priests'] great care to establish themselves in Jesus Christ and to study His interior life ought to arise, so that they may live in accordance with it to the glory of God. They must study these sentiments, virtues, and practices deeply so that they may conform themselves entirely to them and live a life of Jesus Christ, saying with Saint Paul: 'I live, but not myself, it is Christ who lives in me' [Rom. 15.3]. This was an exhortation for all Christian people, not simply for priests. What causes this obligation to live in this Spirit to be great for priests is that they are obliged to be infinitely more perfect than the people, so that the people may always taste the wisdom of God through them and instruct themselves in the Christian life, conforming themselves on account of them to the Divine Life of Jesus Christ.[16]

The ordained ministry is consecrated to service of the baptismal ministry:

The heart of the priest ought to be as large as the heart of the Church. He is obligated to pray for the whole Church, not only assiduously, praying more diligently than anyone particular in the Church, but also with more affection, more ardently, more purely, more humbly and more confidently that all the Church in its particulars.[17]

A vicar of the one Pastor, Jesus Christ, each priest needs to do as He did, offer Himself in adoration to the Father for the salvation of all. Doing so, they call all Christians to the same vocation and virtue of religion.

Co-operation: Jesus in My Hands

Living the Spirit of Jesus is thus the vision and the heart of the French School of Spirituality. Enlivened by the Holy Spirit, all Christians are called to live as Jesus does, participate in His life for the glory of God alone. But how did they go about cultivating this Spirit within themselves? What devotions and spiritual disciplines held a special place in their lives so that they might learn to co-operate more fully with the actions of the Holy Spirit? While there are many, a double trinity briefly mentioned will suffice here.

Devotion to the Eucharist

Pride of place in the devotional life of the French School is given to devotion to the Eucharist. As was typical of their day, they emphasized the Eucharist as sacrifice, an act of perfect adoration in which the God-Man offered Himself to God and ourselves in Him:

> The Son of God is not content with being offered up to his Father in just one place; His wish is to be offered up in several. Although it is one and the same sacrifice, not only the sacrifice itself but its extent also renders homage to God. Now, the soul that receives communion is really an altar containing Jesus Christ and offering Him to God continually, not only by intention or thought as we can offer Him without physically receiving communion, but really and in truth itself. Jesus Christ finds more delight and God more glory in being thus offered up in all souls than on all the altars throughout the world.[18]

It is through this sacrament that each one of us enters most deeply into union with God. When we eat this bread and drink this cup, it acts like no other food. It does not become us, we become it. In the Eucharist,

> Our Lord Himself pervades the entire soul, and since the word communion connotes a common union between the soul and Jesus Christ and between Jesus Christ and the soul, the entire soul is possessed by Jesus Christ, the entire soul is transformed into Jesus Christ.[19]

In the Eucharist we are spiritually transubstantiated, come to live no longer for ourselves but in, through, and with Christ to the glory of the Father in the power of the Holy Spirit.

The Cross

Closely related to devotion to the Eucharist, the French School proclaimed a special reverence for the Cross. They took to heart the command of Jesus, 'If anyone wishes to come after me, that one must deny oneself and take up his or her cross daily and follow me' (Lk. 9.23). While they were certainly in favour of ascetical practices, their devotion to the Cross entailed not the choosing of crosses for oneself, but embracing the crosses that arose from one's state in life. In fact, Father Olier warns against choosing particular acts of mortification as potential sources of pride and self-love.[20]

Instead, devotion to the one cross of Jesus entails embracing the crosses that arise from our 'state of life'[21] – that existential condition that defines who we are and what we do. Unlike the crosses we choose, and to which we grow accustomed, which we can put down at will, the crosses of our state of life are realities, sufferings, humiliations, to which we never grow accustomed, which we can never abandon and still claim to be who we are. These crosses present themselves to us, 'as if we were stung again and again by bees: the last often sickens us as much as the first, and each sting is neither less nor more painful than any of the others!'[22] We make sense out of these crosses only by joining them to the one saving cross of the Lord Jesus. There our sufferings are transformed, find meaning, become salvific. The crosses that arise from our state of life teach us in a radically way the meaning of *anéantissement*, our radical dependance upon God, God who double-crosses the meaning of perceived reality by taking the most vile instrument of torture in the Roman world and placing the victory of life eternal within it.

Devotion to the Word of God

Not only did Pope Urban VII call Cardinal de Bérulle 'the apostle of the Incarnate Word',[23] the Bible was the principal Prayer Book of the founders of the French School. Their writings are inspired and infused with the Scriptures, especially the texts of St John and St Paul. The early Sulpicians, the community of apostolic life founded by Jean-Jacques Olier, gathered each evening to reflect upon the Word of God in what were called 'Conférences de l'Écriture' wherein one of the members of the group commented either on the scripture of the day or on a section from a continual reading of the Scriptures.[24] These conferences enabled the confrères to share in common prayer what they had meditated upon individually earlier in the day.

Further, this constant meditation upon the Scriptures had an apostolic thrust. Again and again we find the founders of the French School insisting upon the sacramentality of the Word, raising it even to the level of Eucharist:

God has two treasures for which he made the Church his depository: the first is his body and precious blood; the second is the word or his scripture, his divine testament, which is the deposit of his secrets and his divine will . . .

[We] should treat it with even more care as one must have more faith to respect it and to give it the reverence it merits, following St Augustine's remarks when he says that he wants us to give the same respect to the least syllables of Scripture that we give to the particles of the Blessed Sacrament, because they are like envelopes, curtains and sacraments which contain the Holy Spirit, as they are the ordinary instrument through which He acts in the Church.[25]

They also insisted that preaching was one of the most fecund acts a priest could do:

Preaching is giving God's children the bread of life, and of eternal life, to enrich, strengthen and perfect in them the divine life they received from the heavenly Father in their new birth in Baptism: You have the words of eternal life. (Jn 6.69)

Preaching has its origins in the bosom of God himself, from which emanated the divine Word of Christ, the first preacher. From this source flowed all the truths He preached Himself on earth and wants to see preached even now.

The end and purpose of this heavenly office is to give birth to Jesus Christ and form Him in human hearts as well as to cause Him to live and reign there.[26]

Devotion to Mary

In a letter to a recently ordained priest, Father Olier articulates four reasons for cultivating a strong devotion to the Mother of God. First, after the Father, Mary was the one Jesus loved most. Second, Mary lives only for and through her son. Third, in accordance with the Fathers of the Church, Mary's character provides a strong attractive force for drawing people to God. As such, she is also a model of the kind of Christian life we need to lead. Finally, Mary's motherhood provides a pattern for engendering the life of Christ in others.[27]

Thoroughly Christocentric, all devotion to Mary deepens devotion to Christ enabling us to live His spirit more fully:

When we speak of you, Mary, we speak of Jesus. When we speak of your grandeurs, we speak of the grandeurs of Jesus. When we speak of your dispositions, we speak of those in which He had to be conceived, because it is for Him that you received this grace and admirable purity. You are the throne where He desired to dwell, and your purity is the purity in which He desired to be conceived. You are to Him, through Him, and for Him. And as the divine Persons have no subsistence in the Trinity except in their mutual relations, you also, O holy Virgin, O person divine and human altogether, divine in grace and human in nature, you have no subsistence in the being of grace except through your relation to Jesus. You lived only through His grace before He lived in you by nature. You only breathe through His spirit, and your graces and grandeurs are His. It is He who obtained them for you, He who conferred them on you, preparing a tabernacle in you for Himself.[28]

Thus, all Marian devotion must lead us to Christ, when it does not it is to be avoided as superstition. She is the perfect disciple, the one who disappears so deeply into her Son that Jean Eudes claims that they have but one heart.

Spiritual Direction

All of the founders of the French School were also noted for their abilities as spiritual directors. The letters of Charles de Condren, Jean-Jacques Olier and Jean Eudes all bear witness to this facility and interest. Indeed, Pierre Cardinal de Bérulle once exclaimed, 'to govern a soul is to govern a world.'[29] They understood this ministry as fully Trinitarian:

Directors ought to be:

- fully strong in the power of the Father to assist souls,
- fully wise in union with the Word to guide them,
- and completely full of love that the Holy Spirit might dwell in them so that they might support their directees in their faults and love them in the midst of their imperfections.[30]

A ministry of compassion and conversion, a ministry of discerning the presence of the Spirit of Jesus alive in those who came to them for direction, a ministry of chiseling[31] away whatever prevented that inner light and life from shining to the full, spiritual direction lay not only at the heart of what the founders of the French School did, but also at the heart of how they defined themselves as Christians.

Ésprit Apostolique

They saw themselves inflamed by the same Spirit that settled upon the Apostles, called forth in the same way to proclaim the good news of salvation to the ends of the earth. Father Olier certainly considered this apostolic spirit a central motivating force beneath his understanding of reform:

> The Seminary of Saint-Sulpice will be considered by all who enter it as an Apostolic College where all are assembled under the protection of the holy apostles, to study their maxims, to invoke their spirit, to imitate their habits, and to live in conformity with the Gospel they proclaimed.[32]

This apostolic spirit impels the current successors of the French School to lives of apostolic service grounded in a contemplative spirit through the varieties of charisms particular to their communities throughout the world today.

Conclusion

So is it a school of spirituality or not? It has a constant emphasis, living the Spirit of Jesus. It understands its mission in a particular way, resting in the heart of the life of the Church, moving from mysticism to mission. It teaches its own forms of meditative prayer, as witnessed in the writings of Jean Eudes, Jean Baptiste de La Salle and Jean-Jacques Olier, to name a few. Its pedagogy is institutionalized, especially in its seminaries and its schools. It emphasizes the writings of St Paul and St John. It is rooted in an intense spiritual experience, not of one, but of many. All these are marks that it is, indeed, a living spiritual tradition.

What makes it different from other schools is that there is not a single founder. Instead, it is a spiritual tradition that arises from the profound spiritual collaboration of a great number of men and women, for all of the first male founders of the French School – with the exception of Charles de Condren – were profoundly influenced by the spiritual accompaniment of women: Cardinal de Bérulle and Madame Acarie (Marie de L'Incarnation), Jean-Jacques Olier and Agnes de Langeac, St Jean Eudes and Marie des Vallées. It is that spirit of collaboration that perhaps makes the school most unique, revealing the French School finally as a model of what the ordinary lives of Christians finally entail – the joining of all in the harmony of the one body of Christ to the glory of the Father, a life hidden in ordinariness, made extraordinary in the heroic effort to make Christ's presence, Christ's Spirit, the very breath and depth of all that is.

Notes

1 See Yves Krumenacker (1998), *L'école française de spiritualité*. Paris: Les éditions du Cerf, for a detailed discussion of the issue.
2 Raymond Deville (2008), *L'École française de spiritualité*. Paris: Desclée de Brouwer includes a chapter on Vincent de Paul in the augmented edition that was not in the

original published text. His theological anthropology differs enough from that of the major figures of the French School to suggest that he is a cousin rather than a direct member. See Robert P. Maloney (2008), 'Vincent de Paul and Jean-Jacques Olier – Unlikely Friends', in *Bulletin de Saint Sulpice*, 34. Paris: Society of Saint-Sulpice, pp. 208–23.

3 The French here *s'est éclipsé* allows for both a passive voice and a reflexive translation that is impossible in English. For Olier, both seem appropriate to denote an action to which the star willingly submits.

4 Jean-Jacques Olier (1991), *Le directeur spirituel selon Jean-Jacques Olier*. Textes transcrits et introduits par Gilles Chaillot, pss. Paris: Compagnie de Saint-Sulpice, p. 66. All translations are my own unless otherwise noted. The text can also be found in Pitaud, Bernard and Chaillot, Gilles, *Jean-Jacques Olier Directeur Spirituel*. Paris: Les éditions du Cerf, pp. 87–8.

5 Thérèse of Lisieux may be considered a member of the French School of Spirituality because of the importance of Christocentrism in her thought and her understanding of herself as 'an Offering like the holocaustal victim to merciful Love'. See Krumenacker, p. 606. From their very beginnings the Carmels of France have been highly influenced by the theology of Bérulle. See Stéphane-Marie Morgan (1995), *Pierre de Bérulle et les Carmélites de France*. Paris: Éditions du Cerf.

6 The term *anéantissement* is finally impossible to translate. As understood by the French School, depending on context, it can mean the absolute contingency of human existence in creation resulting in an absolute dependency upon God, the self-destruction of sin and the re-clothing of the Christian in Christ in redemption. See David D. Thayer (1996), '*Néants capables de Dieu: Anéantissement*, Freedom and Individuation in the Anthropology of the French School', in *Bulletin de Saint-Sulpice*, 22. Paris: Society of Saint-Sulpice, pp. 94–107.

7 See Jean Jacques Olier (1953), *Chatéchisme Chrétien pour la vie intérieure. Leçon VIII*. Paris: Le Rameau, pp. 71–4 and *Introduction á la vie et aux vertus Chrétiennes*, pp. 22–6.

8 Pierre Cardinal de Bérulle (1995), *Oeuvres, de Piété*, 12. *Oeuvres complètes*, texte établi et annoté par Michel Dupuy, vol. 3. Paris: Les éditions du Cerf, p. 57.

9 Ibid., 192, vol. 4 (1996), p. 65.

10 Bérulle, *Oeuvres de Piété*, vol. 4, pp. 176, 4, 30–1.

11 Jean-Jacques Olier (1954), 'Pietas Seminarii Sancti Sulpitii', in *Introduction à la vie et au vertus Chrétienne. Pietas Seminarii*, texte revu et annoté par François Amiot. Paris: Le Rameau, pp. 162–3.

12 Olier, *Le directeur spirituel*, pp. 45–6.

13 Saint Jean Eudes, *Life and Kingdom of Jesus*, 2.2. Quoted in Raymond Deville (1994), *The French School of Spirituality: An Introduction and Reader*, trans. Agnes Cunningham, SSCM. Pittsburgh: Duquense University Press, p. 141.

14 For example, volume 3 of the *Oeuvres Complètes* of Pierre de Bérulle is completely dedicated to conferences he gave to highlight the liturgical year. Bérulle, *Oeuvres Complètes*, vol. 3. See also John Baptist de La Salle (1994), *Meditations*, trans. Richard Arnandez, FSC, and Augustine Loes, FSC. Ed. Augustine Loes, FSC, and Francis Huether, FSC. Landover, MD: Christian Brothers Conference.

15 Olier, *Catéchisme Chrétien*, p. 83.

16 Jean-Jacques Olier (1984), *Divers écrits II*, 98 in *Traité des Saints Ordres (1676) comparé aux écrits authentiques de Jean-Jacques Olier (†1657)*, edition critique avec introduction et notes par Gilles Chaillot, Paul Cochois et Irénée Noye. Paris: Procure de la Compagnie de Saint-Sulpice, p. 262.

17 Olier, *Mémoires VII*, 30, in *Traité des Saints Ordres*, p. 300.

18 Charles de Condren, (1989), *Letters*, 67 (Auvray ed.), in *Lectionary Proper to the Congregation of Jesus and Mary*, trans. from the original French by Louis Levesque, CJM. Charlesbourg, pp. 216–17.
19 Olier, *Mémoires*, II, p. 53. Unpublished manuscript.
20 Jean-Jacques Olier (1992), 'La Perfection Chrétienne Passe par la Croix', in *La Sainteté Chrétienne*, texte choisis par Gilles Chaillot. Paris: Les Éditions du Cerf, p. 37.
21 Ibid., pp. 35–8.
22 Ibid., p. 36.
23 William M. Thompson (ed.) (1989), *Bérulle and the French School: Selected Writings*, intro. by William M. Thompson, trans. Lowell M. Glendon, SS, preface by Susan A. Muto. New York: Paulist Press, p. 16.
24 Gilles Chaillot, pss. (1996), 'L'Expérience Biblique de J.-J. Olier, Le Témoignage des Mémoires', *Bulletin de Saint-Sulpice* 22, p. 30.
25 Olier, *Mémoires*, V, pp. 87–79, passim.
26 Eudes, *The Apostolic Preacher*, ch. 2, *Oeuvres complètes* 4, 12–16, in *Lectionary*, p. 131. I have modified the translation slightly for purposes of inclusive language.
27 Jean-Jacques Olier (1885), Lettre CCCCXVI, *Lettres de M. Olier*, nouvelle edition, tome second. Paris: Librairie Victor Lecoffre, pp. 570–2.
28 Bérulle, *Oeuvres de Piété*, 140, vol. 3, p. 384.
29 Deville, *French School*, p. 151.
30 Olier, *Le Directeur Spirituel*, p. 158.
31 Ibid., p. 64.
32 Jean-Jacques Olier, *Divers Écrits*, ms. 1, p. 281.

Bibliography and Further Reading

de La Salle, John Baptist (1994), *Meditations*, trans. Richard Arnandez, FSC, and Augustine Loes, FSC. Ed. Augustine Loes, FSC, and Francis Huether, FSC. Landover, MD: Christian Brothers Conference.

Deville, Raymond (1994), *The French School of Spirituality: An Introduction and Reader*, trans. Agnes Cunningham, SSCM. Pittsburgh: Duquense University Press.

Eudes, St John (2011), *The Sacred Heart of Jesus*. Fitzwilliam, NH: Loreto Publications.

Thompson, Edward Healy (2010), *The Life of Jean-Jacques Olier, Founder of the Seminary of St Sulpice*. Memphis, TN: General Books LLC.

Thompson, William M. (ed.) (1989), *Bérulle and the French School: Selected Writings*, intro. by William M. Thompson, trans. Lowell M. Glendon SS, preface by Susan A. Muto. New York: Paulist Press.

Part III
Spirituality in Action

16 Spirituality and Politics

Michael Kirwan

Introduction

For many, perhaps even for most, contemporary Christians, the title of this chapter implies a puzzle or dilemma: how to connect or relate two essentially distinct and contrasting realms or spheres of human life and activity. There is still, for many of us, an instinctive sense that 'spirituality' pertains to an individual's authentic interior relationship with God (or however we choose to name the transcendent), while 'politics', the sphere of collective existence and cooperation, will always be at one remove from such authenticity (indeed, for many, the notion of 'religion', especially in its institutional form, is similarly removed). Society and the political are essentially secondary to the Christian's 'core' concerns and activities. The implied tension may even cause some of us to think of an incompatibility between the two spheres, requiring a clearly marked border or *cordon sanitaire* in need of rigorous policing.

Such a conviction is implicit, it seems, in the insistence of Jesus that we should 'give unto Caesar . . .' But this very astute retort of Jesus, in response to opponents trying to entrap him, did not (and could not) mean that he held religious faith to be a private matter, to be kept in strict quarantine from social and political life. Charles Davis puts it thus:

> The Christian religion has always been thoroughly political, with social and political action the major vehicle of the distinctively Christian religious experience. Briefly, Christians find God in their neighbour rather than in their consciousness or in the cosmos. (Davis 1993: 58)

This, surely, is the biggest single challenge facing Christians, in the West at least: how to make sense of and to affirm Davis' insight – especially when so many of us, secretly or openly, wonder if it is really true. One person who disagrees with Davis is the Jewish political theorist, Hannah Arendt, who maintained that Christianity and politics were incompatible. 'Love is a stranger to politics', she maintains – meaning that I should be ready to recognize the rights and needs of my fellow citizens, and act justly towards them, regardless of whether I 'love' them or not. Too much of contemporary politics is founded on tribalism, nepotism, factionalism etc., and on mobilization of sentiments such as pity or compassion, rather than of the genuine indifference towards the other which is demanded by justice and true citizenship. Arendt offers a perplexing syllogism: love and politics are strangers, Christianity is a religion of love, therefore . . .

Arendt is interesting for many reasons, one of which is that her doctoral thesis was on the concept of love in St Augustine of Hippo. Augustine is, as we shall see, one of the key players, when we try to break through the police cordon and articulate what a 'spiritual politics' or 'political spirituality' might look like.

Accordingly, I wish to argue that two imperatives define this enterprise. First, such a spirituality implies and requires *a conversion from false to true worship*: a discernment and renunciation of political institutions and regimes which idolatrously masquerade as divine. The second imperative is related to it: an acknowledgement of *the immense fragility of the modern subject*. The first issue, idolatry, is 'of the ages', while the second – the paradoxical vulnerability of the contemporary 'Enlightenment' subject – alleges a distinctively modern problematic. We will therefore explore these two imperatives by consideration of one ancient and one modern thinker: Augustine, and the German political theologian Johann Baptist Metz (b. 1928).

St Augustine and the Two Cities

We begin with the powerful and moving anecdote in Augustine's *Confessions*, concerning his friend Alypius. This young man is dragged along to a gladiatorial show by the 'friendly violence' of his fellow law students, even though he loathes and opposes these cruel spectacles. He protests to his colleagues that he will resist by keeping his eyes tightly shut, thus demonstrating his self mastery and his superiority to their decadence. Unfortunately, he does not close his ears! On hearing the clamour as one of the gladiators goes down, Alypius opens his eyes out of curiosity:

> For directly he saw that blood, he therewith imbibed a sort of savageness, nor did he turn away, but fixed his eye, drinking in madness unconsciously, and was delighted with the guilty contest, and drunken with the bloody pastime. (*Confessions*, Bk 6, ch. 8)

Augustine tells us that the young man is no longer the same person who entered the stadium, but is now 'one of the throng', and a true companion of those who brought him there. Alypius even becomes more fanatical about the games than his companions, and in his turn seduces others to participate. Only many years later is he able to free himself of this addiction, by placing his trust, not in his own powers of self-mastery, but in God.

In the *City of God* (Bk XIV, ch. 28) Augustine defines true and false politics precisely in the same terms, as a polarity between love of and reliance on God, and on oneself, respectively:

> The two cities, therefore, were created by two loves: the earthly city by love of oneself, even to the point of contempt for God; the heavenly city by the love of God, even to the point of contempt for oneself. The first glories in itself, the second in the Lord . . . The first, in its princes, loves its own strength; the second says to its God, 'I will love you, Lord my strength.'

Taken together, these passages affirm Augustine's concurrence with the slogan of the 1960s, that 'the personal is the political'. The health of our political arrangements depends, quite simply, on what we love: on where our heart is. To be bound to the 'earthly city' is to be dominated by our appetites, above all by our lust for domination over others. Only when this is turned around, and our desires are redirected towards God, can there be any hope of genuine peace.

We shall return to the struggle of Alypius. Here, we need simply note how contemporary he is: so in control of himself, so 'above the fray', and yet fatally vulnerable to the persuasions of his friends, yielding to a temptation which turns out to be highly addictive and pornographic. Alypius presents a classic example of the immense *fragility of the subject*; yet the German political theologian Johann Baptist Metz argues that this vulnerability is especially acute in our present age. The modern Enlightenment individual, according to Metz, is flattered and assured on all sides of his or her emancipated autonomy and power, and yet at the same time deprived of the vital communal and traditional resources he or she needs for identity, resistance and survival. Without such resources, the danger of a lapse into political idolatry is increased, much as a computer without a firewall is vulnerable to attack by viruses.

Hence the other imperative: a political spirituality implies and requires *a conversion from false to true worship*: a renunciation of political institutions, regimes or leaders arrogating divine status to themselves. Such imposters are given unflattering names in the Book of Revelation, where the imperial power is referred to as 'the Beast', 'the Whore', 'Babylon' etc. For all that there are strains within early Christianity of an alignment with government (Paul's injunction in Romans 13 to 'obey the secular powers'), the major key is one of resistance and opposition. The persecution of Christians arose precisely because of their refusal to comply with even the minimal requirements of state religion, namely, the offering of a token act of worship to the Emperor.

Once the Roman Empire had become Christian, the situation is less clear-cut, and the tendency to blur the workings of divine providence and human leaders becomes evident in 'Eusebian' imperial histories. It is one of the significant achievements of Augustine's *City of God* that we are shown how, even in a Christian polity, the need to be prepared to 'refuse to bless the state'.[1]

In the *Confessions* and in the *City of God* Augustine depicts the spiritual quest as a painful pilgrimage from falsehood to truth: specifically, a detachment from whatever presents itself, falsely, as God. This discernment is more than intellectual apprehension: it implies a total and often painful recasting and realignment of a person's entire religious identity. Idols must be identified, and then rejected: only with this decoupling can true worship and a true relationship with God ensue. Augustine offers a magisterial diagnosis of what all this means on a political level, when he describes how three things – true love of God, the true worship of God (sacrifice), and true, lasting social peace – are interrelated. Even though the two cities are 'mixed together from the beginning to the end', they are distinguishable by their practices of worship (Bk XVIII, ch. 54):

> One of them, the earthly city, has made for itself the false gods that it wanted from any source whatsoever – even from human beings – and it serves them with sacrifices. The other city, the heavenly city journeying on earth, does not make false gods, but is itself made by the true God, whose true sacrifice is that very city.

Love of the 'earthly city' and its values is therefore a form of idolatry, which can at best achieve a tenuous social stability through the coercion of others – 'peace-keeping', rather than peace – but can never provide the foundation for a genuine conviviality.

This theme is not new, even with Augustine. Old Testament theology insists on the disastrous political consequences of idolatry for the people of Israel. As to its relevance in the modern period, German political theologians such as Karl Barth and Johann Baptist Metz would readily concur. Metz was an adolescent first-hand witness of a catastrophic political idolatry, namely the messianism of National Socialism.

Metz and the Modern Christian

Here the convergence of Augustine and Metz is apparent. We introduced the theme of the fragile self by means of Augustine on the hapless Alypius. A literary critic, Erich Auerbach, is emphatic about the significance of this episode:

> [Alypius] trusts in his closed eyes and his determined will. But his proud individualistic self reliance is overwhelmed in no time. And it is not merely

a random Alypius whose pride, nay, whose inmost being, is thus crushed; it is the entire rational individualistic culture of classical antiquity: Plato and Aristotle, the Stoa and Epicurus. A burning lust has swept them away, in one powerful assault ['Nor was he now the same he came in, but was one of the throng into which he came']. The individual, the man of noble self reliance, the man who chooses for himself, despiser of excesses, has become one of the mass. (Auerbach 2003 [1953], 69)

Johann Baptist Metz's political theology alleges a similar collapse to have befallen the modern subject. Two traumatic events, or what he called 'interruptions', shattered his adolescent world, namely the slaughter of young comrades in combat, and later the chilling realization of what had taken place in the death camps. For Metz, Christianity's capitulation, and the descent of so many Christians into blood lust and mass identity, demanded a drastic self-examination and conversion, not least with regard to the Church's historical complicity in anti-Semitism. Only then will it be possible to 'face the Jews after Auschwitz'.

The fault lines run through modernity itself, however, and through the Enlightenment ideals of freedom and autonomy. Metz argues that the accommodation of religion by the modern enlightened world, such that religious commitment is tolerated as a set of private beliefs, but forbidden from public debate or decision, has disastrously domesticated Christianity, and blunted its radical edge. The Christian faith has become distorted, 'middle-class' (*bürgerlich*), and as such is unable to discern the challenge and to offer resistance. This debilitation is exacerbated by a pervasive utilitarian ideology which seeks to insulate us from suffering and pain: the 'freedom' of the *bürgerlicher* subject is broadly understood as the freedom to minimize any kind of negativity in his or her life, and to maximize happiness and fulfilment. Put simply, there is no room in such a worldview for the Cross.

A related point is that Christians, like other moderns (whether capitalist or communist) are too easily drawn into ideologies of progress, which posit humanity moving into an optimistic future; one which will transcend the suffering of the past and present. Time has no significance other than as a passageway to this utopian future: 'evolutionary' time is 'empty'. The idea that ritual time or seasons might contain privileged possibilities for spiritual and ethical transformation – such as Jews and Christians have recognized in feast days and holy seasons, and in institutions such as Sabbath and Jubilee – has become alien to us. These seasons are precious occasions for regathering our strength, for enabling resistance. They are 'eschatological', insofar as they preserve the memory of God's 'interruptions' into history, and anticipate the fulfilment of history as precisely one further such interruption. Totalitarian capitalism, on the other hand, because it is itself a religion (as Walter Benjamin famously recognized in his tract *Capitalism as Religion*), has no interest in such events, and precisely undermines such pockets of resistance in its obsessive intolerance of any time which is not spent at its own altars.[2]

Metz even notes in recent decades a 'growing weariness with being a subject', and wonders if we actually really want to be subjects after all. The attractiveness of a 'new immaturity' pervades the postmodern *Zeitgeist*, while the Enlightenment, which was supposed to liberate the individual subject, has paradoxically left him or her exposed and vulnerable in the face of dehumanizing forces, by isolating the individual from vital sources of identity, strength and resistance: specifically the community, and its resources of tradition, solidarity and memory. Any act of intended emancipation merely lops off the very branch on which the subject is perched. Metz argues from this that the current crisis of Christianity is nothing to do with the credibility or adequacy of the Gospel message – this message remains as powerful and radical as ever – but of the particular vulnerability of the *bearers* of the message, both the community called Church and the individual Christian, insofar as these have been co-opted, made *bürgerlich*.

It is for this reason that Metz's relationship with the Jesuit theologian Karl Rahner is significant.[3] Metz was a pupil and then a colleague of Rahner, remaining always appreciative of and indebted to his teacher. Nevertheless, he felt constrained to move beyond Rahner in certain important respects. Rahner's 'transcendental existentialist' approach to theology posited an openness to God in all human beings, insofar as they are actively reaching beyond themselves in intellectual apprehension and in love. Each person is the 'event of God's mysterious self-revelation', whether they are aware of it or not. Even if we consciously deny or resist the idea of a transcendental dimension in our lives, we are all, inescapably, 'theologians'.

Rahner offers a broadly optimistic affirmation of the mystical as an everyday dimension of our lives, and of the pervasive action of grace throughout the whole of humanity, not just among Catholic Christians. His 'theological-anthropological' articulation of the problem of grace represents a marvellous breakthrough, and his significance for post Vatican II Christianity can scarcely be exaggerated. For Metz, however – in the light of the 'interruptions' of his own youth – this achievement is flawed, for the reason we have given above: on account of its distorted understanding of the human subject. Rahner is still working with an 'Enlightenment' version of the subject – individualized, ahistorical – which, for all its celebrated autonomy, is fragile and incapable of bearing the weight of religious experience laid upon it, or of resisting the evil forces which seek to undermine and negate that responsibility. The human subject may indeed be first and foremost a 'hearer of the Word', a graced recipient of God's self-revelation; but Metz sees this subject as a kind of faulty radio set, incapable of receiving the divine transmission in anything other than a weak and distorted form.

The Role of Prayer

Crucial to Metz's argument is his conviction that the Nazi catastrophe was not a Middle European aberration, which happened to occur over 12 years in the middle of the twentieth century. On the contrary, it demonstrated the fault lines that run the length and breadth of modern civilization and its social and political arrangements. In this he is not alone. Metz follows in the tradition of the Frankfurt School theorists who wrote of the 'dialectic' (i.e. paradox) of Enlightenment, whereby modern attempts to assert or achieve emancipation seem to lead only to new forms of enslavement or barbarism.

A short essay in *Love's Strategy* (Metz 1999: 157–66), entitled 'The Courage to Pray', explores many of the important themes. Metz begins the essay by speaking of the 'historical solidarity' of prayer. We are part of a great tradition as old as humankind, which includes not just the great and powerful, but all the unknown millions who have ever suffered and grieved. 'Those who pray are part of a great historical company': to refuse to pray ourselves, because we are too enlightened, sophisticated or embarrassed, is to refuse this solidarity with the dead, to patronize them for their naiveté or superstition. We would be persisting in the illusion that the people of the present age are more advanced than our predecessors. And prayer is possible, even after Auschwitz, because people prayed in Auschwitz.

To pray is in fact to say 'yes' to God, even as we experience contradiction and negativity. It is precisely these experiences that must be included, whether prayer is induced by fear (in the prayer of Jesus in Gethsemane), or by guilt, it brings us to a place of honesty and responsibility. Metz recognizes that too many of our petitionary prayers are evasive in their bland concern: 'Lord, help give food to the countries of the third world, etc'. Even so, it is impossible, if we are praying truly and responsibly, to turn our back on those who suffer.

Metz, surprisingly, points out that meditation 'reminds us of ourselves' – though this is less surprising when we remember what was said above, about the fragile and endangered subject. This subject is inclined to forget itself, in the face of an anonymous evolutionary modernity which mercilessly insists that 'our days are like grass' (Ps. 103). In prayer, on the other hand, the subject is reminded that it is called by name (Isa. 49.1): 'In saying "Yes" to God we are reminded of ourselves. Prayer is the oldest form of the human battle for subjectivity and identity against all odds' (Metz 1999: 164). There is an interesting link for Metz with the difficulties – the unanswered questions and longings – of childhood, adapting a dictum from Ernst Bloch, the great theorist of utopia:

'Prayer is at times the daydream of that home whose light shines in our childhood, yet a home where none of us has ever been' (165).

Once we have seen how prayer is a means of recovery and preservation of the fragile self, then it is possible to see prayer is also an act of opposition and resistance, directed against the reductive debasement of human life to needs and consumerism, and against a culture which exhorts us to insensitivity and apathy towards the pain of others. This culture is resigned to not expecting anything new or different, which has nothing to hope for or anticipate:

> The radio announcer gives a brief, matter of fact report about some shattering catastrophe, and the music begins again. It is as though the music were an acoustic metaphor for the course of time, halted by nothing, submerging everything mercilessly and endlessly. Or can we see it differently? (Metz 1999: 166)

Critique

It is true that in choosing Augustine and Metz as the principal guides for constructing a political spirituality, we find ourselves drawing on two thinkers who are often regarded as 'pessimistic' in their overall orientation. The charge is different in each case, and will be considered briefly here.

Augustine needs handling with care, since he is not, strictly, articulating a fully rounded political vision in the *City of God*. As the title implies, his overriding interest is in establishing the priority and superiority of the Heavenly City; many aspects of its terrestrial counterpart are not theorized. As we have seen, Hannah Arendt has argued on her reading of love in Augustine that Christianity and politics are in fact incompatible. More measured judgements, from Rowan Williams, R. A. Markus, John Milbank and others, consider that Augustine relegates the Earthly City because it is not political enough: only the City of God shows us what a perfect *polis* is like, in which peace is originary, and not the mere absence of conflict that comes about from keeping disorder in check. The *City of God* calls us to redefine our understanding of 'the political', rather than escape from politics.

It is interesting, therefore, to note that Arendt makes use of an Augustinian concept which is vital to her understanding of politics. She cites Augustine's definition of humanity (*City of God*, XII, 20) in terms of *initium*, or beginning: the capacity to begin and take initiative. 'With the creation of man the principle of beginning came into the world itself' (Arendt 1958: 177); because we are 'natal', it is possible for the actions of each individual to be startlingly new and unique, and not just a recoil against the thought of death. Arendt is distancing herself from philosophy's longstanding preoccupation with death – mortality – which can paralyse, enervate, or worse, if the preoccupation becomes an obsession.

Arendt is close to Metz in regarding as 'totalitarian' those social forces which threaten to prevent or undermine the individual's potential for empathy, and for independent thought and action. Her report of the trial of the Nazi war criminal Adolf Eichmann caused scandal, because she refused to join in with everyone else in describing Eichmann as a sadistic monster. What struck her about the man in the dock was his ordinariness: he was the kind of anonymous, 'thoughtless' functionary who is all too evidently produced by modern bureaucracies; this is the force of her notorious phrase, the 'banality of evil'.

Johann Baptist Metz writes similarly of the constraints upon the individual subject, forbidden by our culture to 'suffer the sufferings of others'. Are these commentators wise, however, in their use of the adjective 'totalitarian'? Surely this trivializes the experiences of those who have really suffered under totalitarian political oppression? And what about the many examples of progress and transformative hope which have emerged in the postwar era, and which Metz seems to ignore? A number of critics do indeed argue that Metz is too negative, that his political theology allows for a denunciation of false messiahs, but leaves little room for a constructive vision of how God's kingdom should be allowed into being. Put bluntly, is Metz an alarmist, whose horrific wartime experience has jaundiced and limited his view of human capacity for political action as an expression of Gospel freedom?

The suitability of Johann Baptist Metz as an inspiration for a contemporary political spirituality hangs on how we answer these questions. Perhaps it is necessary at this point to step back for a wider view. A key commentator, J. Matthew Ashley, situates Metz, together with his Jesuit mentor, Karl Rahner, in terms of the different weeks of the Ignatian *Spiritual Exercises* (Ashley 1998; see also introduction to Metz 1998 and Gerard Hughes' chapter above). The *Exercises* comprise four phases or 'weeks', with 'Week Three' given over to contemplation of the Passion of Christ, and (in a liberationist or political key) that of the 'crucified peoples' whose suffering Christ embraces on the Cross. According to Ashley, this moment of the Exercises is transformational for Metz, while for Rahner, the hermeneutical key is the 'Fourth Week'. The Resurrection meditations of Week Four include a neo-Platonic 'Contemplation for Attaining Love', in which the all-pervasive action of God is gratefully celebrated. Metz does not deny the hope and confidence of Resurrection faith, but wishes to ensure that the still present cries of the suffering are not drowned out. This, for Ashley, is the basis of a deep mystical-political convergence of Rahner and Metz, despite their differences. In the dynamic of the *Exercises*, both Weeks Three and Four are required.

I find much in Metz that still resonates, not least when I introduce his ideas to undergraduates. I point out to them the wonders of 'rolling news' stations, supplying us with live reports on the latest disaster – an earthquake, or a campus massacre – even as the football results or stock exchange prices scroll across the bottom of the screen. It is striking how students intuit what Metz is getting at, just as they relate to so many other thinkers – Blaise Pascal, Søren Kierkegaard, Simone Weil, René Girard – who question whether the personal autonomy which our culture urges them to nurture and celebrate is less extensive and more problematic than they are led to believe. They are in a better position than the rest of us to understand Metz when he alleges in postmodern culture a 'new immaturity', a shying away from the daunting responsibility of becoming adult subjects in and of history. For Metz, both the contemporary disengagement with politics in general, and the resurgence of a 'caretaker' mentality in the Church, are manifestations of this regression.

Conclusion

Here we may add an interesting if unlikely voice to the mix, that of Slavoj Žižek, the Slovenian Marxist philosopher. Žižek has little time for institutional Christianity, yet argues for the importance of the Christian legacy, given the paucity of the 'nauseating' alternatives on offer. We are faced with an unappetizing choice between the various forms of crass fundamentalism, and postmodern, self-massaging froth: 'Against today's onslaught of New Age paganism, it thus seems both theoretically productive and politically salient to stick to Judaeo-Christian logic' (Žižek 2000: 107). Žižek has argued at length that it is atheists like himself who are the 'true' Christians, insofar as they are closer in spirit to the repeated 'unplugging' or 'uncoupling' which, for him, is the heart of the message of Jesus (who tells us to 'hate father and mother') and Paul, the apostle to the Gentiles.[4] Christianity requires 'a readiness to disengage ourselves from the inertia that constrains us to identify with the particular order we were born into' (129), whether that be family, tribe, nation and so on.

This action of 'decoupling', for Žižek an essential prelude to the task of Christian love, is to be found in Augustine and Metz also. I have chosen to explore the theme of 'political spirituality' through these writers, because these exemplify the two interrelated imperatives which I consider of crucial interest: the refusal of idolatry (Žižek's decoupling), and the need to bolster the debilitated human subject. I am conscious of a paradox, since neither Augustine nor Metz is noted for a positive appraisal of 'the political' in its everyday sense. To use the traditional categories, their contribution may be described as 'purgative', rather than illuminative or unitive.

With this in mind, there are plenty of reasons why they are appropriate guides. Augustine's self-description of the individual soul painfully shifting its centre of gravity from itself to God, mirrors the dialectic of the two cities (the two loves). Though no detailed account of the Earthly City is forthcoming in

Augustine, neither is there a complete abdication of responsibility. We have seen how, even though she is sceptical about the adequacy of the Augustinian political heritage, Hannah Arendt nevertheless borrows from him the notion of 'natality', an acknowledgement of the wondrous uniqueness of each person's capacity for new action. She is surely correct in helping us to retrieve this perspective. Augustine's *caveat* remains, however: that when that capacity for action is rooted in the self-confident individual (such as Alypius, or indeed Augustine himself for much of his life journey) rather than God, things go seriously awry.

Johann Baptist Metz confirms this diagnosis, which is exacerbated under the distorting and self-defeating ideology of Enlightenment emancipation. He is an important commentator for several reasons, not least his closeness to Karl Rahner's project of theological anthropology. Rahner's conception of 'humanity as the event of God's self revelation', with its understanding of God's accessibility to every human being, and its assertion of 'everyday' mysticism, is perhaps the most powerful paradigm of the spiritual life in the post-Vatican II period. Metz's alternative account, indebted to Rahner yet in real tension with it, therefore demands attention.

Ashley seeks to reconcile the differences between their 'mystical political' approaches through the scheme of Weeks Three and Four of the Ignatian *Exercises*, though there must be a question as to whether this is a little too neat. If Metz is correct, the human subject under modern conditions is too weak to be the vehicle of God's self-revelation, and the primary task of theology and spirituality is to shelter and strengthen it. In this enterprise, of replacing *bürgerliche* with 'messianic' Christianity, important resources are recovered: memory (*anamnesis*), solidarity, narrative and a re-engagement with apocalyptic expectation.

The term *anamnesis*, of course, carries explicit eucharistic connotations; for Metz it is in the eucharistic commemoration that we preserve the interruptive, dangerous memory of Jesus Christ. As with prayer, so the Eucharist is a place where we can recover lost strength, shore up identity for resistance and counter the emptiness of 'evolutionary' time with messianic hope.[5] We may note the same with Augustine, for whom as we have seen, there is a complicity between three polarities of love, worship and social existence. Love, or desire, which is wrongly aligned (self-love) expresses itself in idolatry and forms of violent sacrifice; the only politics which can emerge from this is an *ersatz* peace which comes from violent self-assertion and the coercion of others. This is the vortex into which Alypius falls, when his self-mastery is overcome by peer pressure and blood lust. On the other hand, love which is directed towards God involves authentic self-sacrifice and a participation in a genuine, because original, peaceful conviviality.

In each case, the middle term, the link between love (of God, of self) and politics (true and false) is liturgical. This is why Augustine's vision of authentic sacrifice in Book X of the *City of God* is so important. Eucharistic sacrifice is not a ritual intended to overcome alienation or expiate sin: the 'work of sacrifice' itself constitutes an already existing fellowship with God, rather than a means towards it. It arises from a sense of identity and union already achieved: at the altar we are exhorted to 'be what you see, and receive what you are':

> So then, the true sacrifices are acts of compassion, whether towards ourselves or towards our neighbours, when they are directed towards God; and acts of compassion are intended to free us from misery and thus to bring us to happiness . . . Thus the Apostle first exhorts us to offer our bodies as a living sacrifice, holy, acceptable to God, as the reasonable homage we owe him, and not to be 'con-formed' to this age, but to be 're-formed' in newness of mind to prove what is the will of God – namely what is good, what is acceptable to God, what is perfect because we ourselves are that whole sacrifice.
>
> *City of God*, Book X: 6.

> We ourselves – his city – are the best and most radiant sacrifice
>
> Book XIX: 23.

Notes

1 Eusebius is the 'court historian' whose *Ecclesiastical History*, written in 323/4, celebrates the hand of divine Providence at work in the conversion and subsequent reign of Constantine. For an account of Augustine's 'refusal to bless' the Emperor, see Markus 1988 and 1989.
2 As Metz reminds us, the earliest Christian prayer is also the most up to date: 'Come, Lord Jesus!' (Rev. 22.20). I have made the point with students by offering a prize for the most absurd 'Advent calendar' on sale during the festive season, which is usually adorned with photos of pop stars, football players etc. The co-option of this most sacred season of expectation is, in a way, even more sinister than the commercialization of Christmas itself.
3 Two essays in the collection *A Passion for God* (Metz 1998) set out Metz's critical appreciation of his mentor, Karl Rahner.
4 See also chapter by Stephen Bullivant below.
5 For a dialogue between Metz's political theology and the liturgical theology of Alexander Schmemann, see Morrill 2000.

Bibliography and Further Reading

Arendt, Hannah (1958), *The Human Condition*. Chicago: University of Chicago Press.
— (1963), *Eichmann in Jerusalem: A Report on the Banality of Evil*. London: Faber and Faber.

Ashley, J. Matthew (1998), *Interruptions: Mysticism, Politics and Theology. The Work of J.B. Metz*. Notre Dame: University of Notre Dame Press, in particular, 'A Map of Metz's Theological Journey', pp. 52–8.

— (1998), 'Introduction: Reading Metz', in Johann Baptist Metz and Matthew Ashley *A Passion for God: The Mystical Political Dimension of Christianity*. New York: Paulist Press, pp. 7–21.

— (2004), 'Johann Baptist Metz', in Scott and Cavanaugh (eds), 2004, pp. 241–55.

Auerbach, Erich (2003) [1953], *Mimesis. The Representation of Reality in Western Literature*. Princeton, NJ: Princeton University Press.

Cavanaugh, William T. (2006), 'From One City to Two: Christian Reimagining of Political Space', *Political Theology* 7/3 (July 2006), 299–321.

Davis, Charles (1993), *Religion and the Making of Society: Essays in Social Theology*. Cambridge: Cambridge University Press.

Elstain, Jean Bethke (1995), *Augustine and the Limits of Politics*. Indiana: University of Notre Dame Press.

— (2004), 'Augustine', in Scott and Cavanaugh (eds), pp. 35–47.

Markus, Robert A. (1988) [1970], *Saeculum: History and Society in the Theology of St Augustine*. Cambridge: Cambridge University Press.

— (1989), 'Refusing to Bless the State: Prophetic Church and Secular State', *New Blackfriars*, 70, 372–9.

Martinez, Gaspar (2001), *Confronting the Mystery of God: Political, Liberation and Public Theologies*. New York: Continuum, ch. 2, 'J.B. Metz: Political Theology', pp. 22–88.

— (2005), 'Political and Liberation Theologies', in *Cambridge Companion to Karl Rahner*, ed. D. Marmion and M. E. Hines. Cambridge: Cambridge University Press, pp. 249–63.

Metz, Johann Baptist (1980), *Faith in History and Society: Towards a Practical Fundamental Theology*. London: Burns & Oates.

— (1984), 'Facing the Jews: Christian Theology after Auschwitz', *Concilium*, 175, 26–33.

— (1998), *A Passion for God: The Mystical-Political Dimension of Christianity*, trans. and ed. J. Matthew Ashley. New York: Paulist Press.

— (1999), *Love's Strategy: The Political Theology of Johann Baptist Metz*. Ed. with an introduction by John K. Downey. Harrisburg, PA: Trinity Press International.

Morrill, Bruce T. (2000), *Anamnesis as Dangerous Memory: Political and Liturgical Theology in Dialogue*. Collegeville, MN: Liturgical Press.

O'Daly, Gerard P. (1999), *Augustine's City of God: A Reader's Guide*. Oxford: Clarendon Press.

Ormerod, Neil (1990), 'Johann Baptist Metz: Political Theology', in *Introducing Contemporary Theologies*. Australia: E.J. Dwyer, pp. 117–27.

Price, Richard (1996), *Augustine*. London: Fontana Press.

Scott, Peter and Cavanaugh, W. T. (eds) (2004), *Blackwell Companion to Political Theology*. Oxford: Blackwell.

Williams, Rowan (1987), 'Politics and the Soul; A Reading of the City of God', *Milltown Studies*, 19/20, 55–72.

Žižek, Slavoj (2000), *The Fragile Absolute: Or Why the Christian Legacy is Worth Fighting For*. London: Verso.

17 Christian Spiritual Direction

Peter Tyler

Introduction and Terminology

Reflecting on the history of spiritual direction in the Orthodox tradition, Bishop Kallistos Ware writes:

> There are in a sense two forms of apostolic succession within the life of the Church. First there is the visible succession of the hierarchy, the unbroken series of bishops in different cities, to which Saint Irenaeus appealed at the end of the Second Century. Alongside this, largely hidden, existing on a 'charismatic' rather than an official level, there is secondly the apostolic succession of the spiritual fathers and mothers in each generation of the Church – the succession of saints, stretching from the apostolic age to our own day, which Saint Symeon the New Theologian termed 'the golden chain'. (Hausherr 1990: vii)

Both types of succession, he argues, are essential for the true functioning of the Mystical Body of Christ ('the Church'). Mark Cartledge notes in the following chapter the importance of this 'charismatic' element in church history. This chapter will explore the other element mentioned by Bishop Kallistos: the apostolic succession of spiritual fathers and mothers, what we tend to call nowadays, the apostolic line of 'spiritual direction'.

Before talking about the role of the 'spiritual director' it is worth pointing out that I use the labels 'spiritual director' and 'spiritual direction' here largely out of convenience. Ware, as we have seen, prefers the Orthodox designation Spiritual Father/Mother/Elder (*pneumatikos pater/mater*) while we will find other contemporary authors referring to the spiritual accompanier, guide or even *Anam Cara* (literally 'Soul Friend', see Leech 2001). On one level the terminology is unimportant, an essentialist would argue that we are talking about the same phenomenon with different names. Yet, on another, the shift of designation and terminology betrays underlying shifts in attitude and practice to this aspect of Christian spiritual life. In this chapter I will trace some of the main themes and practices in the development of Christian spiritual direction before ending with the situation as increasingly practised in Christian communities today in a post-Freudian, 'psychologized' world.

The Spiritual Mother or Father: *Pneumatikos Mater/Pater*

St Paul, Clement and Origen can be seen as precursors of the *pneumatikos pater* or *mater*. 'So far as possible' says St Antony, the first and greatest of the so-called Desert Fathers and Mothers of the post-apostolic age:[1] 'the monk should in full trust ask the elders how many steps to take and how many drops of water to drink in his cell, in case he is in error about it' (*Sayings of the Desert Fathers*: Antony: 38).[2] The Spiritual Elder is not a rabbi who explains or applies the Torah, nor a specialist in legal advice, a mufti or imam, nor a canonist who resolves a canonical problem but rather a spiritual parent, a *mother or father* (see Hausherr 1990: 9). This 'spiritual father or mother' as understood by the early church fathers and mothers is *pneumatikos* in the Pauline sense of having their life directed to and centred around Christ in the manifestation of his Mystical Body in the Church (not in the sense of 'spiritual' as opposed to 'material' see McIntosh 1994). Accordingly, all the early descriptions of the spiritual father or mother do not so much emphasize what the elder *does* as who they *are*.

Despite the importance of solitude in the desert tradition from which this practice arose, the desert elders realized the importance of having a guide or at least someone to whom a seeker can open up their consciences and thoughts. Indeed, John Cassian in the *Conferences* sees this disclosure of thoughts as the most important element of the monk's life. 'Not only all our actions', he writes 'but even all our thoughts should be offered to the inspection of the elders' (*Conferences* 2.10.1). Traditionally this process happened through two means, the disclosure of temptations and desires to another more experienced seeker, and the process of 'seeking a word' from a spiritual elder. Cassian is at pains to stress, however, that this discernment of spirits is not necessarily a gift of grey hairs and many years. The elderly are as much prone to deception as the young (*Conferences* 2.8.1). He gives numerous examples of this. For example, the elder Heron who was revered by many disciples yet finally took his own life jumping down a well for a devil 'disguised as an angel of light' had tricked him into thinking God's angels would protect him as he jumped in the well and the miracle would bring many more to the faith. As Cassian states:

> Just as all young men are not similarly fervent in spirit and instructed in discipline and the best habits, so neither in fact can all the elders be found to be similarly perfect and upright. For the riches of elders are not to be measured by their grey hairs but by the hard work of their youth and the deserts of their past labours. (*Conferences* 2.13.1)

Once having carefully selected a guide Cassian counsels suspicion of motives. True discernment of spirits requires a hermeneutic of suspicion regarding the very nature of ourselves. The old are as susceptible as the young, if not more so. Within this tradition, then, *everything* we experience must be explored with another, nothing should be left out of our account of ourselves to our fellow Christians:

> Everything that is thought of is offered to the inspection of the elders, so that, not trusting one's own judgement, one may submit in every respect to their understanding and may know how to judge what is good and bad according to what they have handed down. (Abba Moses in Cassian's *Conferences* 2.10.1)

This suspicion of motives goes alongside a deep humility in following the advice of the one to whom the seekers disclose their story. Just as clients seeking therapy today must trust the skill of the therapist and open themselves up to their judgement so we find the same relationship in the desert tradition. For 'as soon as a wicked thought is revealed it loses its power' (*Conferences* 2.10.1). As Freud and the early psychologists were to rediscover at the beginning of the twentieth century, the act of telling a secret or desire can often kill its power over us. Spiritual direction in the desert tradition realized that the *act of speaking* holds its own power over the passions of the soul. In this way spiritual direction becomes a choreography between what is said and what is unsaid.

Part of the practice of this humility in the disclosure to the elder is to free ourselves from the tyranny of desire. We must be careful then to 'reject with unwavering strictness of mind those things which cater to our power and which have the appearance of a kind of goodness' (*Conferences* 9.6.4). Cassian is here referring to a world of subtle self-delusion, made stronger by the apparent cloak of respectability that all those involved in altruistic or religious works wrap around themselves. Evagrius calls it the 'spirit of vainglory' and his pen portrait of its poison is psychologically subtle and still relevant today:

> The spirit of vainglory is most subtle and it readily grows up in the souls of those who practice virtue. It leads them to desire to make their struggles known publicly, to hunt after the praise of men. This in turn leads to their illusory healing of women, or to their hearing fancied sounds as the cries of demons . . . It has men knocking at the door, seeking audiences with them. If the monk does not willingly yield to their request, he is bound and led away. When in this way he is carried aloft by vain hope, the demon vanishes and the monk is left to be tempted by the demon of pride or of sadness. (*Praktikos*: 13)

For the early desert fathers and mothers, then, the spiritual guide must be an astute counsellor and psychologist. However over and above it all the fathers counsel compassion towards those who struggle. Spiritual guides must never get too full of themselves and feel they are morally superior. The weakness of the passions can strike anyone at anytime. Cassian gives the telling story of the young man troubled with lust who goes to see the elder who scorns him and tells him he is not worthy of the life of a monk. As he leaves, dejected, to return to the fleshpots of a local town he meets another wiser elder, Abba Apollos. Unlike the first father, Apollos shows compassion and discloses that he himself has to struggle with this demon on a regular basis. As he prays for the young man the demons assail the first old man with the temptations. This old man now 'runs around hither and thither as if he were crazed and drunk' (*Conferences* 2.13.7) finally setting off on the same route to the local fleshpots. In his 'obscene excitement' Abba Apollos confronts him, asking innocently where the former upright father is now heading. Realizing that he has been deceiving himself and others the old man falls abashed at Apollos' feet. Apollos' final words to the would-be spiritual director are magnificent:

> The Lord let you be wounded by this so that at least in your old age you might learn to be compassionate toward others' infirmities and might be taught by your own example and experience to be considerate with respect to the frailty of the young . . . Learn to be compassionate to those who struggle and never frighten with bleak despair those who are in trouble or unsettle them with harsh words. Instead encourage them mildly and gently. (*Conferences* 2.8.9)

This gentle and compassionate tradition lives on today in the Orthodox lineage as deeply accomplished spiritual fathers and mothers continue to appear in that tradition.[3]

Discernment and the Ignatian Tradition

Mention has already been made of the importance of *diakresis* in the Greek apostolic tradition. As the desert tradition flowed into the Western European medieval tradition this would become *discernio* in the Latin tradition which finds its way into English with the term 'discernment' or, in the language of the author of the *Cloud of Unknowing*, 'discretion in stirrings'.[4]

For Origen the *pneuma* is present through practical action (*praxis*), above all in *diakresis, discernio* or the discernment of spirits. As we have seen, the monk without *discernio* (*Conference* 2), says Cassian, is like a person wandering in a desert at night, they may fall down a precipice themselves and take others with them. Paul mentions the discernment of spirits in 1 Cor. 12 as does

St John in his First Letter: 'Do not believe every spirit, but test the spirits to see whether they are from God, for many false prophets have come into the world' (1 Jn 4.1). In Athanasius' 'Life of Antony' it primarily describes the discernment of demonic activity. However, as we have seen, for Cassian it is a wider gift that can help the distinction between general trends of virtue or vice. For Cassian it is a 'discernment of passions'. It is not an attribute of 'grey hairs' or 'many years' but rather a gift or charism that can be imparted to anyone (see *Conference* 2.8). In the present re-emergence of the sacred in world affairs this *discernio* is probably the most important gift the Christian tradition can bring to the feast of contemporary spiritual seeking.

The art of spiritual discernment is particularly associated with St Ignatius of Loyola (1491–1556) in the Western Christian tradition who in the Appendix to his 'Spiritual Exercises' gave his 'Guidelines for the Discernment of Spirits' memorably condensing over a thousand years of Christian teaching on the theme. Ignatius divides his Rules for Discernment into two categories, those for beginners (simply put, to discern the good from the bad) and those for seekers with more experience (simply put, to discern the difference between the good and the better). These simple rules of thumb from the *Rules* are equally valid in pastoral care, spiritual direction and even psychotherapy/counselling.

Ignatius bases his rules for discernment on the 'disposition of the soul'. Is the disposition of the soul directed towards that which is life-giving, up-building and creative or is it directed towards that which is life-denying, destructive and ultimately futile? The 'rules' which follow help the individual to assess if a particular course of action or way of life leads to a building up of the self or to greater disintegration and fragmentation.

Some may be pursuing a way of life that they find exciting and fun but ultimately it is becoming destructive. Ignatius cautions us to look at the *effects* of any action or decision and this is the basis of such discernment. Similarly, Teresa of Avila (1980, see also Tyler 1997: 90) in the 'sixth mansion' of her *Interior Castle* stresses that we should not so much pay attention to the spiritual experiences that we have as the *after-effects* that they have upon us. Are they bringing us a greater sense of peace and fulfilment or are they leading to more unhappiness and dissatisfaction?

In these periods of dissatisfaction there is often a desire to go back on decisions made when all was going well, the sun was shining and the birds were singing. Now, as the rain pours down and the skies are gloomy (metaphorically speaking) we go back on the decision made 'in consolation'. Ignatius cautions against this and gives one of his 'rules' as follows:

(318) When we find ourselves weighed down by a certain desolation, we should not try to change a previous decision or come to a new decision

. . . At a time of desolation, we hold fast to the decision which guided us during the time before the desolation came on us. (Ignatius of Loyola 1980: 118)

However:

Although we should not try to make new decisions at a time of desolation, we should not just sit back and do nothing. We are meant to fight off whatever is making us less than we should be . . . The important attitude to nourish at a time of desolation is patience.

Likewise, when all is going well, when we experience a certain spiritual peace and 'can see the bottom of the well' we should use this time wisely to make plans as a bulwark against possible future times of 'desolation':

(323) When we are enjoying a consolation period, we should use foresight and savour the strength of such a period against the time when we may no longer find ourselves in consolation. (Ignatius of Loyola 1980: 119)

Such 'periods of consolation' should be distinguished from the technical working out of plans that follow them:

(336) When the consolation experience in our life comes directly from God, there can be no deception in it . . . A spiritual person should be careful to distinguish between the actual moment of this consolation-in-God-himself from the afterglow which may be exhilarating and joyful for some period of time . . . it is often in this second period of time that we begin to reason out plans of action or to make resolutions which cannot be attributed so directly to God as the initial experience which is nonconceptual in nature.

Ignatius spoke and wrote in the language of late medieval theology, his psychic world is populated with angels, demons, good spirits and bad spirits. At first sight this may seem to put him beyond use to contemporary seekers.[5] Yet, it is possible to distil the psychological wisdom and good common-sense advice that he gives from his work, a wisdom drawn not only from long personal experience of directing individuals but distilled from over a thousand years of Christian thought and reflection on this area. As Fr Hughes makes clear in his earlier chapter on Ignatian Spirituality, Ignatius is essentially counselling us to ponder on the different outcomes of our desires and observe *the effects on our feelings* (what Fr Hughes rather poetically terms 'gawking' at our feelings). Often, I would argue, we have this intuitive awareness but we have been taught not to trust this basic human intuition. Such 'exercises' in discernment that St Ignatius presents us can continue to help us embrace the spiritual wisdom that each of us holds within us.[6]

Spiritual Direction According to St John of the Cross

Another great sixteenth-century Spanish writer who throws light on the practice of spiritual direction as developed in the Latin West is St John of the Cross (1542–91).[7]

As a student, John was educated at the newly established Jesuit college of Medina del Campo and so would have been familiar with the ethos and training of Ignatius' *Spiritual Exercises*. Like Ignatius he cherishes 'discernment' or, as he terms it, *discreción*, in the spiritual director and realizes that this special commodity is at the heart of spiritual direction (see *Ascent of Mount Carmel* 2.18). Unlike Ignatius, however, central to John's conception of the right mode of practice of the spiritual director is an ability to perceive the need not to become attached to spiritual 'goods' on behalf of either the director or the directee.

The clearest exposition of John's understanding of spiritual direction is to be found in Book Three of *The Living Flame of Love*. Here we find from John's basic spiritual anthropology that we need to 'excavate the caverns of the heart' to allow God's Holy Spirit to act in us. This process, often painful, is the basis of the Christian journey and the 'wound' on which everything else is predicated. It is the sublime wounding of the Spirit which touches us at the deepest centre or *fondo del alma*. While this is happening we should remember that 'If a person is seeking God, his Beloved is seeking him much more' (*Living Flame* 3.28). The basic human spiritual condition that John proposes is a dynamic one where we are running out to find God and God is running in to find us (see *The Spiritual Canticle* 1).

Therefore in all talk of spiritual direction we must constantly remember that 'God is the principal agent in this matter' (*Living Flame* 3.29) who acts 'as a blind man's guide' to lead us to the 'place we know not' (*Ascent of Mount Carmel* 1.13.11). John always remembers that ultimately we cannot *know God in God's self*, in this life at least, therefore there will always have to be a trust and letting go as we are led by God to that 'place we know not':

> God transcends the intellect and is incomprehensible and inaccessible to it. Hence while the intellect is understanding, it is not approaching God but withdrawing from him. It must withdraw from itself and from its knowledge so as to journey to God in faith, by believing and not understanding. In this way it reaches perfection, because it is joined to God by faith and not by any other means, and it reaches God more by not understanding than by understanding . . . thus it advances by darkening itself, for faith is darkness to the intellect. (*Living Flame* 3.48)

Our Christian response to this ongoing love of God is, as far as possible, not to put any blocks in the way of this outpouring love. So, as well as avoiding obstacles put in the way by ourselves we should avoid, counsels John, obstacles put in the way by the Bad Spirit and by other people such as spiritual directors.

This then, is a crucial point that spiritual directors must observe according to John, they must not put anything in the way (including themselves) between the soul and God. The chief agent, says John, in spiritual direction is the Holy Spirit and all guides must never forget this (*Living Flame* 3.46).

John, as is common in the tradition to which he is heir, sees the spiritual directees as 'putting on' the nature of their guide from constant meetings with them so he attaches great importance to the quality and characteristics of the guide. The guide should be 'learned and discreet' (LF 3.30) as well as having experience. Knowledge and *discreción* (i.e. *diakresis*) are both important. However, he suggests, without 'experience of pure spirit' the guide will be useless. This immediately raises the bar regarding the suitability of a director and it is no surprise that he adds that the directees will rarely find 'a guide accomplished as to all their needs' (LF 3.30).

At the heart of John's writing on direction is the notion that at different times in the spiritual life different laws and rules apply. We come into difficulty when we adopt a 'one size fits all' approach to spiritual direction. This, John stresses, is spiritual death – to the director as well as the directee. In *The Living Flame* 3.59 he reminds us that 'God leads each one along different paths so that hardly one spirit will be found like another in even half its method of procedure' which really should be written up in large letters on a board before anyone who practises the art of spiritual direction. In spiritual guidance, he suggests, a certain slovenliness and apathy creeps in, a sort of sense that 'it has worked in the past so why shouldn't it work now'. John is always cognizant of the fact that spiritual direction is a 'mindless activity' and in the words of Meister Eckhart 'God's in, I'm out' (see Smith 2004). As the soul itself does not know what is happening, how, asks John, can the director possibly know? (LF 3.41):

> Since (God) is the supernatural artificer, he will construct supernaturally in each soul the edifice he desires, if you, director, will prepare it by striving to annihilate it in its natural operations and affections, which have neither the ability nor strength to build the supernatural edifice. The natural operations and affections at this time impede rather than help. It is your duty to prepare the soul, and God's office, as the Wise Man says, is to direct its path, that is, toward supernatural goods, through modes and ways understandable to neither you nor the soul. (LF 3.47)

The ultimate aim of the director, then, for John is to lead the soul to greater 'solitude, tranquility, and freedom of spirit' (LF 3.46). This latter quality, 'freedom of spirit' is very much at the heart of John's whole theology and teaching on the life of the spirit:

> When the soul frees itself of all things and attains to emptiness and dispossession concerning them, which is equivalent to what it can do of itself, it is impossible that God fail to do his part by communicating himself to it, at least silently and secretly. It is more impossible than it would be for the sun not to shine on clear and uncluttered ground. As the sun rises in the morning and shines on your house so that its light may enter if you open the shutters, so God, who in watching over Israel does not doze or, still less, sleep, will enter the soul that is empty, and fill it with divine goods. (LF 3.46)

So then, John advises, if we would be a spiritual director the first and last qualification is to 'know thyself'. If we are more proficient at guiding people at the more meditative stages then we should stick to that. Dangers arise when we go beyond our competencies and think that we know about spiritual things of which we have little knowledge and experience (LF 3.58). Within it all we should ask ourselves 'are we holding on to spiritual directees?' 'are we feeding off them?' If this is the case we should always be quick in finding someone else for them to work with for such a holding onto a souls is tantamount to depriving them of its spiritual freedom, which for John is the most heinous crime a spiritual director can commit (see LF 3.59).

Spiritual Direction and Psychological Models – Similarities

I began this chapter by making reference to spiritual direction as it is practised by Christians today. The models I have explored already: that of the Desert/ Orthodox Spiritual Elder and the Ignatian/Juanist Discerner of Spirits, both have their adherents and contemporary practitioners.[8] To conclude I would like to summarize my views as to the nature of Christian spiritual direction and how it differs, if at all, from psychological and therapeutic practices in our post-Freudian/post Jungian world.

When we consider spiritual direction as it is practised in the West today it is important to recognize that despite its independent origins it has often adopted the forms, practices and methods of the psychological 'talking cures' created after Freud. As well as numerous differences between the two approaches, there are of course many similarities.[9] Spiritual direction, counselling and psychotherapy are all concerned in creating a helping relationship which has at its heart the facilitation of growth and transformation of the client/directee/pilgrim. It would seem odd to embark on any of these relationships, with all their time and money commitments, without expecting some sort of transformative process to occur. In all these interactions one person is putting certain knowledge and skills at the service of another, this is largely through one-to-one meetings although group discernment/direction/therapy may also be used. Words and conversation are of fundamental importance to the process. Yet, as we saw above, there is a choreography between words and silence. The Austrian philosopher Ludwig Wittgenstein, a contemporary of Freud, wrote that 'what can be said, cannot be shown and what cannot be said can be shown' (*Tractatus Logico-Philosophicus*). He suggested that the meaning of language and human communication derived from the choreography of what is spoken and what is unspoken. In both spiritual direction and counselling/therapy we pay as much attention to what is *not* said as to what is said.

Both forms of work are client-led in that the therapist/counsellor/director interprets or comments upon material that the client brings to the relationship. The involvement is voluntary and not coerced and there must be a sense of trust between the two to create a 'safe space' in which material can be explored in a gentle and generous fashion. The relationship is not value free and there will be an unequal power relation in the interaction which needs to be acknowledged for a healthy and fruitful relationship to develop. Certain boundaries have to be observed and common norms of good practice are assumed. As we saw in the case of St John of the Cross, to a certain extent the therapist/counsellor/director should have already travelled some of the road upon which the other person is embarking, or should at least have some experience of the areas under discussion. Success in all cases depends upon the ability of the therapist/counsellor/director to reflect experientially upon material as well as having intellectual knowledge of the subjects raised. As the medievals said, the *affectus* is as important as the *intellectus*.

Accordingly, then, we can see many similarities between the different healing relationships. However, it would I think be misleading to suggest there were no differences between the two approaches. It is to these I turn next.

Unique Practices: Spiritual Direction

As we have seen there is a 'golden thread' of spiritual direction that stretches from apostolic times to the present day. In Christian terms it takes place within a *faith context* and this cannot be overstressed enough. It *assumes a shared faith context* between the two people involved. It also takes place against the background of the larger 'Mystical Body of Christ', the Church. It is a charism given to certain people and the ministry itself is not intended for all people at all times. It may be appropriate for certain people at certain times in their lives, especially times of increased or rapid spiritual change such as middle age or old age. The revelation of God in the life, ministry, death and resurrection of Jesus Christ is essential to understanding spiritual direction in the Christian context and it employs knowledge of that life through use of scripture, reference to liturgy and so on. Spiritual direction in the Christian tradition has an important *catechetical* role as well as a thera-peutic role – it can often have a defined teaching component. As we saw in John of the Cross' writings, traditionally three persons are involved in the Christian relationship of spiritual direction – the director, the directee and the Holy Spirit. Of the three relationships involved, that between the Holy Spirit and the directee is considered the most important. This holds the key dynamic of the relationship and drives a lot of what happens in the meet-ings (i.e. the meetings reflect upon the material that has arisen in that rela-tionship). We could say that the Holy Spirit is the true Director in Christian spiritual direction. Central to this process, as we have seen, is *diakresis* or discernment.

In summary then, spiritual direction in the traditional Christian sense assumes the following:

- That the process takes place within the context of a shared and mutual faith relationship.
- Importance is given to the faith relationship between the directee and the 'higher power' of the Holy Spirit. This is seen as the source of all that happens in the process.
- The direction takes place within the theological context of the life, min-istry, teachings, death and resurrection of Jesus Christ,
- And within the context of the community of His believers – the Church.
- It relies on specific processes and techniques, especially the discernment of spirits.
- It is a 'charism', a 'golden thread' or gift of the Spirit that extends from apostolic times to our own times.
- It is an activity that relies upon and presupposes engagement in prayer and contemplation from all participants, it holds *contemplatio* at its cen-tre (see Tyler 2007).

Finally, we can add that spiritual direction within the Christian tradition is not seen as something that necessarily only benefits the people participating directly in it. As part of a wider community or ecclesial context the activ-ity may allow discernment on what 'the Spirit is saying to the churches' and allow the whole church to discern 'the signs of the times'. All who engage in Christian spiritual direction do so not only for themselves but for the whole ecclesial community. It therefore has an important *prophetic* dimension (see Brueggemann 2001).

Conclusions – Spirit and Psyche, Similarities, Differences and Synergies

As will be apparent by now, the basic argument of my chapter has been that spiritual direction and psychotherapy are two approaches, methodologies or entrances into the worlds of human *psyche* and *spiritus*. I have argued that there is much in common between the two processes. Both are helping 'cures' that aim to give space to the individuals to explore their own journey largely through the choreography of the *logos* in 'saying and showing'. Yet I have emphasized that there are crucial divergences as well between the two approaches. Christian spiritual direction presupposes a whole hinterland of faith development, prayer and the *ecclesia* that is not necessary for psychotherapy. The psychological therapies, on the other hand, explore the minutiae of interpersonal interaction to such a precise extent that its analysis is brought to a refined science. The codification and systemization of transference, countertransference, developmental issues and individuation give us a highly refined tool to engage in interpersonal discourse as never before. Yet, I would argue, to subsume *spiritus* into a province of *psyche* or see all of *psyche* as a manifestation of *spiritus* is a grave mistake. The past decades have seen a growing trend to equate the action of the Holy Spirit with good mental health. However, it would be wise for the Christian spiritual director to remember, as St John of the Cross counsels us, that the spirit/*pneuma* 'blows where it will' (Jn 3.8). A salutary reminder to the spiritual director (or counsellor or psychotherapist for that matter) to remember that the action of God's Holy Spirit can never be restricted to any one particular consulting room with a particular registered person at a particular time slot on a particular weekday. The spirit blows where it will and the true *pneumatikos pater/ mater* must sniff the spirit where it blows, this *may* be in the spiritual direction consulting room, but it may equally turn out to be on the train, in the park, at the post office or in the pub.

In summary, as we see in church circles a tendency to adapt the rigours and professionalizations of therapy/counselling to the ancient practices of spiritual direction I would counsel a little caution. As a working model I would prefer to see spiritual direction as a form of *befriending* which by its nature will sometimes have to transcend or transgress the firm boundaries of therapy/ counselling.

Just as Christians need to be cautious in adopting too easily the tropes and forms of psychology, so I would argue that psychologists must be cautious about how they tread on the sacred ground of the spiritual. As argued, psychologists may want to see 'spirituality' as a province of 'good mental health' but, I suggest here, this may sometimes not be the case. The Living

Spirit of the Lord will, by definition, always resist such tendencies, leading its followers 'where it will'.

Notes

1 See earlier chapter by Sr Benedicta Ward.
2 In Ward 1984.
3 For more on this see the chapter by John Chryssavgis on 'Orthodox Spirituality' in this volume. Clear examples of this tradition in the Orthodox lineage are St. Seraphim of Sarov (1759–1833) and Staretz Silouan of Athos (1866–1938), see Archimandrite Sophrony 1999, *Saint Silouan, the Athonite*. Crestwood, NY: St. Vladimir's Press.
4 See *The Epistle in Discretion in Stirrings* published in *The Pursuit of Wisdom: And Other Works by the Author of The Cloud of Unknowing* (1988), translator, James Walsh, Paulist Press.
5 For more on this see the chapter by Fr. Gerard W. Hughes above.
6 In this respect the whole of Fr Hughes' chapter acts as a gateway to this process of 'education of desire'.
7 For more on John's life and background see chapter on 'Carmelite Spirituality' above.
8 Again, for more on these two schools as presently practised see the chapters by Hughes and Chryssavgis above.
9 I am indebted to the work of David Lonsdale in this section, see in particular his *Dance to the Music of the Spirit* (1992). London: Darton, Longman and Todd.

Bibliography and Further Reading

Brueggemann, W. (2001), *The Prophetic Imagination*. Minneapolis: Fortress.

Cassian, J. (1997), *The Conferences*. trans. B. Ramsey, New York: Newman.

Evagrius Ponticus (1981), *The Praktikos and Chapters on Prayer*. trans. J. Bamberger, Kalamazoo, MI: Cistercian Publications.

Hausherr, I. (1990), *Spiritual Direction in the Early Christian East*. Kalamazoo, MI: Cistercian Publications.

Ignatius Loyola (1980), *The Spiritual Exercises of St Ignatius: A Literal Translation and a Contemporary Reading*. ed. D. Fleming. Saint Louis: The Institute of Jesuit Sources.

John of the Cross (1979), *The Collected Works of St John of the Cross*. trans. K. Kavanaugh and O. Rodriguez, Washington: Institute of Carmelite Studies.

Leech, K. (2001), *Soul Friend: Spiritual Direction in the Modern World*. Harrisburg, PA: Morehouse.

Lonsdale, D. (1992), *Dance to the Music of the Spirit*. London: Darton, Longman and Todd.

McIntosh, M. (1994), *Mystical Theology*. Oxford: Blackwell.

Smith, C. (2004), *The Way of Paradox: Spiritual Life as Taught by Meister Eckhart*. London: Darton, Longman and Todd.

Teresa of Avila (1980), *The Interior Castle* in *The Collected Works of St Teresa of Avila*. trans. Kavanaugh and Rodriguez. Washington: Institute of Carmelite Studies.

Tyler, P. M. (1997), *The Way of Ecstasy: Praying with St Teresa of Avila*. Norwich: SCM/Canterbury Press.

— (2007), 'Divine Unknowing: Lessons from the Christian Mystical Tradition for Healthcare Today', in *Spirituality and Health International* 8: (2).

— (2010), *St John of the Cross: Outstanding Christian Thinker.* London: Continuum.

— (2011), *The Return to the Mystical: Ludwig Wittgenstein, Teresa of Avila and the Christian Mystical Tradition.* London: Continuum.

— (2011a), 'The Roots of Desert Spirituality', in *The Pastoral Review,* September/ October 2011.

Ward. B. (ed.) (1984), *The Sayings of the Desert Fathers: The Alphabetical Collection.* Kalamazoo, MI: Cistercian Publications.

Wittgenstein, L. (2001), *Tractatus Logico-Philosophicus.* London: Routledge.

18 Charismatic Spirituality

Mark J. Cartledge

Introduction

All forms of Christian spirituality give an account of the workings of the persons of the Trinity and it is the relationship between the Holy Spirit and the human spirit that gives rise to the notion of spirituality. However, the ways in which the Holy Spirit is located theologically within the different traditions varies enormously. There are some forms of spirituality that are so ordered that spontaneous workings of the Spirit would be regarded as quite improper and indeed impossible. Charismatic spirituality, on the contrary, regards the work of the Spirit to be free and spontaneous as well as, to some extent, patterned and predictable. It is this openness to the workings of the Spirit in ways that might be regarded as 'enthusiastic' as well as mundane that marks out the Charismatic spiritual tradition. It is also a spirituality that can be seen within a variety of other spiritual traditions. It has its roots in the Charismatic movements throughout the history of the church, but especially the Pentecostal movement of the twentieth century. Since the 1960s this particular form of spirituality has travelled widely and has been incorporated within mainstream Protestant and Roman Catholic denominations. New churches have also emerged seeking to build different forms of church structures around a charismatically orientated spirituality.

It is estimated that Pentecostal and Charismatic spirituality is embraced by around 500 million people worldwide. Of course these numbers would include the many and various expressions of Pentecostal and Charismatic Christianity. It has been suggested that these expressions can be classified in terms of three 'waves' of the Spirit. The first wave is the classical Pentecostal denominations, the second wave is the mainline Renewalists and the Third Wave is the new independent churches, including the indigenous churches of Africa and Asia as well as the Vineyard denomination. The Third Wave is also now referred to as 'Charismatic' or 'Neo-Charismatic' Christianity.[1] There is diversity between these groups in terms of theology and values, and in how they organize their church life. However, common features would unite them and this enables them to be categorized as 'Charismatic'. Essential to these features is the emphasis on an *encounter with the Holy Spirit*. This encounter is free, spontaneous, dynamic, transformative and should be an ongoing experiential reality within the purposes of God. It could be argued that every kind of Christian Spirituality is an expression of a process of searching for God, who once encountered effects change within the life of the searcher, who is then transformed or renewed in order to continue the journey. The search-encounter-transformation sequence is, of course, continuous and demands constant engagement within both corporate and private spiritual devotions.

A spirituality defined in this way contains stories through which humans view reality. Narrative is the most characteristic expression of one's spirituality. In addition, symbols express aspects of the narrative. These can be artefacts such as buildings, or they can be events such as festivals. Symbols tend to function as boundary markers. They are actions and visible objects that express the spirituality at the deepest level. Finally, spirituality contains praxis, that is, a 'way-of-being-in-the-world'.[2] The real shape of a person's spirituality can be seen in the actions they perform, especially from behaviour that is habitual. Thus, spirituality literally gives a location from which to view and inhabit the world, enabling purposeful action. Therefore narrative, symbols and praxis interpret the spirituality at every point and the search-encounter-transformation process can be considered in these terms.

The narrative is provided by the overall shape of Scripture itself, although enlivened by the Spirit as the church continues to live in the biblical story. In this respect, the narrative structure is similar to those found in other expressions of Christianity, but the difference lies in pneumatology and participation. There is an expectation and experience, which suggests that the God of the Bible is at work in a similar kind of way today.[3] 'The point of Pentecostal spirituality . . . [is] to experience life as part of a biblical drama of participation in God's history.'[4] This obedient participation is a *via salutis*, a journey of salvation. Historically, this has derived from the locus of Pentecostal and Charismatic experience, namely a second crisis spiritual experience subsequent to conversion called 'baptism in the Spirit', often associated with the sign of *glossolalia* (speaking in other tongues). Later Charismatics relativized this experience by speaking of more frequent 'encounters' with the Holy Spirit as part of the ongoing life of the believer. Therefore, Charismatics expect God to reveal his glory in worship, to answer prayer, to perform miracles, to speak directly by means of dreams, visions and prophecy.

The symbolic world of Charismatics is also shaped by this overarching Christian narrative. Until the late twentieth century, Pentecostals have been the poor relations in the church. This is still the case in most parts of the non-Western world. As such, they could not afford to build enormous edifices that symbolized God's power. Instead, they had a 'baptism in the Spirit' and spoke in strange tongues, otherwise known as *glossolalia*.[5] Speaking in tongues is a key symbol for Charismatics because it is the 'cathedral of the poor'.[6] You can speak in tongues anywhere. It does not locate you. Indeed, it becomes a kind of universal language, which is not tied to privilege, power and status. It demonstrates the power of God in the weakness of humanity. It enables a person to identify with a particular group and yet to retain individuality. There are other embodied symbols, often embedded in rituals, such as falling over under the power of the Holy Spirit, or crying or laughing in worship. Indeed, these symbols give expression to one of the deepest domains of personal knowledge: the human emotions.

The praxis of Charismatics can be seen in an enthusiasm for prayer with others. It is the primary theological activity of Pentecostals and Charismatics. It appeals to the intuitive and extrovert: prayer is something to be encountered with others, as well as the Spirit. The primary way of being in the world is therefore socially expressed prayer. Life is so imbued with the presence of God that prayer becomes a habit. This is a habit formed 'in the Spirit' and received 'through the Spirit'. Praying in tongues is as natural to many Charismatic Christians as any other kinds of prayer. In the various ecclesial traditions, the evidence of prayer ministry teams displays this concern for prayer that is expectant of transformation.[7] So, people express care for one another by praying for each other in an extrovert manner. The expectation is that God answers prayer in the lives of believers and the world in which we all live. The Kingdom of God has broken into this present age with the coming of Christ and the foretaste of this kingdom is opened up by the end-time Spirit.

Key Themes

There are four key themes that characterize Charismatic spirituality, namely: praise and worship, inspired speech, holiness and empowered witness in the kingdom of God. In many respects the kingdom of God is a dominant category and could be said to encapsulate the others. This category contains the subjects of signs and wonders, healing and miracles, as well as eschatology, witness and baptism in the Spirit. Praise and worship is crucial to Charismatic spirituality and is driven by various contemporary approaches to music and hymnody. Inspired speech includes such activities as speaking in tongues, prophecy, prayer, testimony and preaching. Holiness represents the nature of the encounter with the Spirit of God, namely that God's Spirit is Holy.

Worship

The musical style of Charismatic worship is very obviously contemporary. Even the older hymns are given a contemporary feel with the addition of different melodies and a drummer's backbeat. Visitors to Charismatic churches may be surprised to encounter the sheer energy with which worshippers start their services. It may sound more like a rock concert than a church service. However, it is usually the case that energetic praise songs give way to more reflective songs that draw the worshipper into a quieter mode of singing. The experience of singing worship songs in a Charismatic setting will look considerably different to traditional worship for a number of reasons. Typically, during the first part of a service (in the search phase of the spirituality), the congregation will be expected to sing a number of songs that have been linked together as a kind of medley. The words for the songs will be displayed either through the (now outdated) overhead projector screen or through the screen displaying words projected from a PowerPoint computer presentation. There are usually no books (or they are an option) and the expectation is that people are free to engage in worship with enthusiasm unconstrained by a book in their hands. This means that people are able to use their arms and hands to raise them to heaven. They are also enabled to clap, dance, jump and sway should they wish to do so in time to the rhythm of the music. Generally people are free to stand or to sit as they sing, but in practice the congregation would tend to do similar things at the same time. Songs are memorized and internalized in a much greater way than a book-holding culture would expect and this is an important feature to understand.

There is full participation from those who have embraced the spirituality. In the singing of hymns there is an energetic engagement with praise. When there are readings from the Bible many participants will follow the text from their own copies that they have brought to church. During the sermon there is often an interactive style of preaching that does not allow the hearer 'to go to sleep' – they may be asked a question and a reply will be expected! In some churches the congregation can interrupt the preacher with shouts of 'Hallelujah' and 'Praise God'. During the praise phase and when there is a pause, or when the leaders so designate, there may be opportunity for a contribution from the congregation.

Prayer ministry is an important dimension of Charismatic spirituality and in recent years has been given enormous attention. This usually occurs towards the end of the church service when people are invited to come forward and receive prayer for matters that concern them. In some contexts words of knowledge are read out to encourage people to come forward and receive prayer. These words of knowledge can be, for example, medical conditions, or personal circumstances or needs. Prayer more generally is a characteristic that permeates the worship service. In the preparation for worship many members will have spent time in prayer, waiting upon God and asking him to reveal something that they might share with the rest of the congregation. At the beginning of worship the leader will pray for the worship time together in an extemporary fashion. He or she may invite others to pray at certain times, either in an audible way so that others can hear and agree, or as part of a prayer shout as the congregation simultaneously prays out aloud together. On some occasions the congregation will be invited to pray together in groups, perhaps in an intercessory way. This may be in response to something that the preacher has said or in response to a prophetic word that has been received by the congregation. Indeed, as I have already noted, prayer is at the heart of Charismatic spirituality but in a social and corporate sense. People would be expected to speak out aloud and to pray as the Spirit inspires them in spontaneous ways.

Inspired Speech

There are a number of categories that are used to describe and define inspired speech within Charismatic spirituality.

Speaking in Tongues is the form of inspired speech most associated with Pentecostal and Charismatic spirituality since the Azusa Street Revival of 1906. In classical Pentecostalism, speaking in tongues, or *glossolalia*, is most often understood as the definitive sign or evidence that someone has received a post-conversion blessing of empowerment for ministry, known as baptism in the Spirit. Its subsequent use by the same person in the context of prayer and worship is regarded as its second function, namely as a gift of the Spirit enabling communication with God. Most people who speak in tongues regularly can do so at will and without any heightened sense of emotion (what Hollenweger calls 'cool' tongues). However, for first-time speakers there is often both an overwhelming sense of God's presence and an inescapable urge to articulate the speech that is beginning to be formed in one's mind (Hollenweger's 'hot' tongues).[8] It can be used in the context of praise, as people shout out their praise to God and declare his wonders. It can also be sung and accompanied by music, in which case it has an aesthetic quality similar to other forms of Christian expression such as plainsong or chant. It can also be used in prayer as people intercede for others or for themselves. In these respects it can mirror the Charismatic spirituality process of search through praise (offering a sense of beauty and awe), encounter in adoration (offering a sense of intimacy and empowerment) and transformation through intercession (edification of one's faith).[9]

When there is a distinctly audible tongues speech, that is, a speech act heard by everyone in the assembly, and one that has attracted everyone's attention, there may be a subsequent message or 'interpretation' in the common language of the worshippers. This is understood as corresponding to the type of tongues speech reported by Paul in 1 Cor. 12.10; 14.27–8. In this scenario there will be the expectation that someone else, if not the speaker, has an 'interpretation' of the meaning to be conveyed through intelligible speech. This message, once articulated, is understood to correspond to prophecy, although there is some debate regarding its direction (i.e. whether the prayer is directed to God or is a message from God).

Prophecy is understood as a gift of the Spirit used within the Christian life for the edification of the congregation and/or the individual concerned. Again it is understood to be a spontaneous speech act inspired by the Spirit that is specific to the occasion on which it is received. The prophetic message is expected to fulfil the Pauline criteria of 1 Cor. 14.3, namely: edification, encouragement and consolation. The language of the prophecies can, in many places, sound like echoes of the Old Testament canonical prophets, with messages beginning in the first person singular. The use of King James English can give prophetic messages a highly ritualized feel and is in many respects at odds with the culture of Charismatic worship, which is extremely contemporary. Many Charismatics, however, believe that prophecy is a mixture of the human and the divine and as such needs to be discerned and tested for authenticity.[10] The classical biblical categories of foretelling (prediction) and forthtelling (proclamation) are still used to describe the contemporary phenomenon, although generally predictive prophecies are few in number. Usually, contemporary prophecy found within a worship setting will generally be short messages with a single idea.

The *word of wisdom* and the *word of knowledge* are also categories that are used in relation to prophetic speech and arguably are closely related. The *word of wisdom* was often understood by classical Pentecostals as referring to information revealed concerning the future. Although this understanding would not be necessarily dismissed it is not the current one within the tradition. The most popular appreciation of this category is that it refers to an inspired application of a piece of knowledge or information. It is the wisely spoken application of knowledge, the wisdom of which is based upon some form of inspiration. The *word of knowledge* has often been regarded as a companion gift to the *word of wisdom*, being a divinely given fragment of information or knowledge. It is thus interpreted as a revelation of information concerning a person, thing or event, but with a purpose. The purpose of this knowledge makes its application very specific. It is not for general usage but for particular individuals at specific times and places. This fact or insight could not have been known with the natural mind, hence it has a supernatural quality. It is often used within the Third Wave Charismatic stream as a way of attending to God in the context of prayer ministry or evangelism.

The *discernment of spirits* was understood by classical Pentecostals to refer to insight into the spirit world, especially in relation to demons. The gift is associated with insight into the dispositions of people, the origins of sickness and 'supernatural manifestations'. The use of spiritual sight is regarded as important and, again, it has been associated with prayer ministry and spiritual counselling. Douglas McBain suggests that the category be understood as the ability to 'separate spiritual manifestations at their point of origins'.[11] Thus the idea of sifting, separating and distinguishing is advanced. He also suggests that the gift is a mixture of the human and the divine and provides a check on all other claims to inspired speech in that it can offer insights into the motives and meanings of an event or situation.

Testimonies are an important component of Charismatic spirituality and give expression to the alignment of individual and social story-telling with the Christian story of the Gospel.[12] That is why, traditionally, Pentecostals have turned to the narrative of Luke-Acts as the main source for their theology. It enables them to situate their own story, following their own Pentecost, within the biblical narrative. This means that there is a great emphasis upon continuity with the biblical story. Thus the Spirit who acted in such dramatic fashion in the Bible is the same Spirit who acts today. This means that life in the Spirit is a journey with God and a 'way' of salvation. Therefore, when individuals tell a story of what God has done in their lives they do so by referencing themselves and their church community to the overarching Gospel story.

The Sanctified Life

Towards the middle and end of the nineteenth century the Methodists worked with other smaller holiness groups through camp meetings to promote the teaching of holiness and in the United States 'The National Holiness Association' was born and published material to promote its message of a post-conversion experience of holiness often referred to as a 'clean heart'.[13] Methodist preachers promoted the message both home and abroad. For a time it was extremely successful, reaching its peak in the 1880s. However, the interdenominational character of the National Holiness Association caused problems for those wishing to promote Methodist church polity. Individuals and groups began to break away from Methodism and establish themselves as Holiness 'bands'. One of the important aspects of the Wesleyan and Holiness tradition is the use of 'holiness codes' to define identity. For example, at one General Assembly of a Holiness church, the Church of God (Tennessee), which was to become Pentecostal in due course, decided that 'Coca Cola, chewing gum, rings, bracelets, and earbobs were sinful', thus prohibiting members to use such things. Other churches condemned the use of neckties or the attendance at fairs, or political parties and work unions.[14] As these churches became Pentecostal churches (after the Azusa Street Revival) the same kinds of codes were in force, for example, prohibiting mixed bathing, going to the cinema or theatre and the use of face make-up.

The American Pentecostal movement, associated with the Bible school of Charles Parham at Topeka, Kansas in 1901 and with William J. Seymour and the Azusa Street Revival from 1906, has its roots in the Holiness movement of the period. Both of these men were holiness preachers. However, the emphasis at the meetings was not simply an experience of sanctification, but also on a third experience of empowerment, known as 'baptism in the Spirit', and evidenced by the phenomenon of speaking in tongues. The early Pentecostals believed in a three-stage process (conversion, sanctification and baptism in the Spirit). This was accepted by early Pentecostal groups until 1908, when W. H. Durham reduced the stages to two and abandoned sanctification as a distinct stage by incorporating it within the conversion stage.

The Roman Catholic Charismatic Renewal, at its height in the 1970s, produced many important books and articles. One of the earliest accounts of the influence of Pentecostal and Charismatic spirituality within Roman Catholicism is by Edward D. O'Connor.[15] In discussing the effects of the baptism in the Spirit he notes that there is no instant sanctity. The baptism in the Spirit may have removed moral bonds and secured psychological healing but for most people life in the Spirit is part of the process of growing in Christ and is gradual. It places them further along the road to sanctity that would have previously been possible but still they have not arrived. There are no cases of 'instant sanctity', even if the charisms are powerful aids towards sanctity. Thus a progressive growing into holiness is envisaged, with powerful jumps forward and support along the way.

Another Roman Catholic writer, Heribert Mühlen, has also reflected on this area in relation to gifts of the Spirit.[16] In addition to prophecy, tongues and healing, he advocates what he calls socio-critical charisms and it is these that have ethical and therefore holiness dimensions, although the language of 'holiness' is missing. Instead the language of 'purification' is used to describe how the Spirit takes abilities and sets them apart to be used for the kingdom of God. Thus St Paul uses the gift of administration to make a collection for the poor, so that there is an equilibrium between rich and poor. This has wider implications for the social involvement of Christians, since it is an expression of *charisma*, that is, it is graced (2 Cor. 8.1). Charismatics, like Jesus, should be willing to become poor so that others might become rich (2 Cor. 8.9). Therefore, the implications of this are that the social and charismatic experience of God in worship should flow out into social and political commitment. To be inspired by the Spirit will mean action on behalf of others (Jas 2.15–17). Mühlen gives the following warning to those who do not see the social and ethical implications of life in the Spirit: 'Baptism of the Spirit takes hold of your powers, including your emotions; but if such an experience estranges you from society, if you think that you are now really able to lead a purely private bourgeois life, it would be better if you had never come into contact with the Charismatic renewal. Either you strip your faith of its private character for the sake of society or you remain even in regard to God in a private, segregated existence and – in what you call "experience of God" – you are perhaps enjoying only your own feelings'.[17]

Empowered Kingdom Witness

Charismatic spirituality believes that the church is also anointed by the Spirit to continue the ministry of Jesus until he returns at the end of time. In particular, the anointing upon the church bestows power, power to witness to the kingdom of God here and now. This power comes via the same anointing that Jesus displayed in signs and wonders. God's reign in the ministry of Jesus is witnessed by means of both a proclamation of the arrival of the kingdom and by a demonstration of its arrival through signs. The New Testament material is interpreted as providing examples and a rationale for expecting similar experiences through the ministry of the church today. David Pytches, for example, begins his book in the Third Wave strand of tradition with a chapter on signs and wonders.[18] He maintains that the great commission of Mt. 28.18–20 includes the imperative: 'obey everything I have commanded you', and that the 'everything' referred to here includes a ministry of signs and wonders. In the Gospels the disciples participate in the healing ministry of Jesus and this is a model for the church as evidenced in Acts and should be throughout history. Harvey Cox, in his celebrated book on Pentecostalism, calls this feature *primal piety*, the integration of the mystical experiences of healing, dancing and laughing in the Spirit.[19] This feature of Charismatic spirituality breaks the barrier erected between the cognitive and the emotional sides of life, between rationality and symbol or sign, uniting individuals and communities in ways that are holistic. The early Pentecostals of Azusa Street broke down a key racial barrier between Black and White as both embraced the signs of the kingdom and thus became one in witnessing to the unity that is available in Christ.

It is certainly true that the theme of 'signs and wonders' as a feature of empowered kingdom witness has become more at home in non-Western rather than Western societies. Charismatic writers argue that in societies privileging scientific rationalist thinking the 'spirit world' has been submerged or marginalized. Therefore the piety associated with 'primal' societies, to use Cox's category, becomes suspicious. Other naturalistic explanations must be found to account for these apparently strange phenomena. However, in non-Western societies where the worldview entertains the possibility of the spirit-world being much more obviously expressed within the public domain, this spirituality flourishes.[20] The challenge for the Charismatic tradition is to show how it can be integrated within Western contexts as well as non-Western ones, where the worldview is less accommodating. Hollenweger suggests that one way this might be accomplished is by beginning with a theology of creation, which is also alive with the Spirit of God, and by integrating natural and supernatural categories.[21]

As noted above, the kingdom of God is a central category for understanding the other features of Charismatic spirituality. Most importantly it is the anointing experienced by the king, Jesus Christ, being bestowed upon the church and continued through history. The kingdom has been inaugurated through the life, ministry, death, resurrection and ascension of the king and will one day be consummated upon his return. In the meantime the church lives between the times and knows the comfort and power of the Spirit to be with her on the journey until the end of all things. However, evil and suffering continue to mark the world in which we live, including the church.[22]

This tension between the inaugurated reign of God, bringing the 'first fruits' of the harvest, and the consummation of the reign, when the harvest will be fully gathered in, marks the nature of the Christian life. Charismatic spirituality appreciates this tension, although at times the 'now' is stressed at the expense of the 'not yet'. Nevertheless, there is sufficient understanding of this tension within the tradition to see it as a significant feature. This means that while Charismatic Christians pray for God to demonstrate his power through the lives of his church, there is also the recognition that not all one's prayers are answered and that pain and suffering persist in this world. The inauguration of the kingdom did not result in the manifestation of humanity with resurrection bodies!

Conclusion

Charismatic spirituality refers to a strand of Christianity that stresses the role of the Holy Spirit, and in particular 'encounters' with the Spirit in a variety of ways. I have suggested that this spirituality is given shape by considering it in terms of a process and a framework. The process is a cyclical one of searching for God, encountering him and being transformed by him for his purposes and glory. The agent of this process is God's Spirit. The spirituality can also be understood as a framework of narrative, symbols and praxis as each gives expression to a coherent worldview in which the Spirit of God is understood, symbolized and engaged. In this context there are key themes stressed by the tradition, namely: worship, inspired speech, the sanctified life and empowered kingdom witness. All of these themes are interpreted by the Christian community for the sake of its identity and life.

A number of metaphors can be used to attempt to understand the ways in which this tradition has been active throughout the history of the church, and indeed how it is played out today. The first is the metaphor of 'plug n play', taken from the use of electrical instruments or devices. In this sense, the tradition can plug into and be played alongside other traditions. This is probably a more suitable metaphor for describing some of the Charismatic renewal movements where it is expressed within the structures of another tradition rather than creating its own structures. However, this metaphor can appear mechanical or automatic and the notion of 'plugging in' can have its limitations. The second metaphor is the 'infusion' of different flavours in the culinary process. Here the flavour of the Charismatic tradition influences and permeates other traditions. It is in the mix, being distinct and yet cannot be separated from other traditions. In a sense the Charismatic tradition's relation to Evangelicalism in contemporary Christianity is perhaps a good example of this. Often there is an infusion of one in and with the other. Third, there is the metaphor of a stream or river that flows through the landscape and brings life and vitality to the land. In this topographical metaphor there is one main source of life, namely the Spirit of God. Charismatic spirituality would see itself as a witness to this source of spiritual life as a challenge to exclusively formal expressions of Christianity.

Notes

1 S. M. Burgess and E. M. Van der Mass (eds) (2002), *The New International Dictionary of Pentecostal and Charismatic Movements – Revised and Expanded Edition*. Grand Rapids: Zondervan, p. xx.
2 N. T. Wright (1993), *The New Testament and the People of God*, 2nd edn. London: SPCK, p. 124.
3 J. D. Johns (1995), 'Pentecostalism and the Postmodern Worldview', *Journal of Pentecostal Theology*, 7, 73–96.
4 S. J. Land (1993), *Pentecostal Spirituality: A Passion for the Kingdom*. Sheffield: Sheffield Academic Press, pp. 74–5.
5 M. J. Cartledge (2002), *Charismatic Glossolalia: An Empirical-Theological Study*. Aldershot: Ashgate.
6 W. J. Hollenweger (1988), *Geist und Materie*. Muenchen: Chr. Kaiser Verlag, pp. 314–15.
7 J. Leech (2002), *Developing Prayer Ministry: A New Introduction for Churches*. Cambridge: Grove Books Ltd.
8 W. J. Hollenweger (1972), *The Pentecostals: The Charismatic Movement in the Churches*. London: SCM Press, p. 344.
9 M. J. Cartledge (2005), *The Gift of Speaking in Tongues: The Holy Spirit, the Human Spirit and the Gift of Holy Speech*. Cambridge: Grove Books, pp. 15–17.
10 Perhaps one of the most significant influences in this regard has been the book by W. Grudem (1988), *The Gift of Prophecy*. Eastborne: Kingsway.
11 D. McBain (1981), *Eyes that See*. Basingstoke: Marshall Pickering, p. 5.
12 M. J. Cartledge (2002), *Testimony: Its Importance, Place and Potential*. Cambridge: Grove Books Ltd.
13 V. Synan (1997), *The Holiness-Pentecostal Tradition: Charismatic Movements in the Twentieth Century*, 2nd edn. Grand Rapids: Eerdmans, pp. 26–7.
14 Synan, *The Holiness-Pentecostal Tradition*, p. 81.

15 E. D. O'Connor (1971), *The Pentecostal Movement in the Catholic Church*. Notre Dame: Ave Maria Press, pp. 171–2.
16 H. Mühlen (1978), *A Charismatic Theology: Initiation in the Spirit*. London: Burns & Oates, pp. 157–60.
17 Mühlen, *A Charismatic Theology*, p. 160.
18 D. Pytches (1985), *Come Holy Spirit: Learning How to Minister in the Power of the Holy Spirit*. London: Hodder & Stoughton, pp. 11–16.
19 H. Cox (1996), *Fire from Heaven: The Rise of Pentecostal Spirituality and the Reshaping of Religion in the Twenty-First Century*. London: Cassell.
20 See also chapters below on Christianity and Indigenous Spiritualities.
21 W. J. Hollenweger (1997), *Pentecostalism: Origins and Development Worldwide*. Peabody, MA: Hendrickson, pp. 243–5.
22 W. W. Menzies (2004), 'Reflections on Suffering: A Pentecostal Perspective', in W. Ma and R. P. Menzies (eds), *The Spirit and Spirituality: Essays in Honour of Russell P. Spittler*. London: T&T Clark, pp. 141–9.

Bibliography and Further Reading

Bonnington, M. (2007), *Patterns in Charismatic Spirituality*. Cambridge: Grove Renewal Booklets.

Boone, R. J. (1996), 'Community and Worship: The Key Components of Pentecostal Christian Formation', *Journal of Pentecostal Theology*, 8, 129–42.

Cartledge, M. J. (2006), *Encountering the Spirit: The Charismatic Tradition*. London: Darton, Longman and Todd.

— (2010), *Testimony in the Spirit: Rescripting Ordinary Pentecostal Theology*. Farnham: Ashgate.

Cox, H. (1996), *Fire from Heaven: The Rise of Pentecostal Spirituality and the Reshaping of Religion in the Twenty-first Century*. London: Cassell.

Goldingay, J. (1996), 'Charismatic Spirituality: Some Theological Reflections', *Theology*, 789, 178–87.

Part IV
Christian Spirituality in Dialogue with Other Faiths

19 Christian Spirituality and Hinduism

Martin Ganeri

Introduction: What is Hinduism?

There are estimated to be between 800 million and a billion Hindus living in the world today, or around 15 per cent of the world's total population. The vast majority of Hindus live in India and the other countries of South Asia, especially Nepal, where, as in India, they form the majority, but Hindus are also to be found all around the world as sizeable minorities. Hindus thereby form the third largest religious grouping in the world after Christianity and Islam.

Both the terms 'Hindu' and 'Hinduism' can be misleading. The term, 'Hindu', has long been used to refer very generally to those inhabitants of India (*al-Hind* in Arabic), who were not easily identifiable as Muslims or members of another religious tradition. The term 'Hinduism' itself was coined in the nineteenth century by Europeans to refer to the religious culture of the Hindus. Because any '-ism' suggests a single system with a definable set of beliefs and practices, it has often been assumed that there is a single religion that all Hindus ascribe to or at least that there is some system within Hinduism that might be taken to represent the 'essence' of Hinduism and might serve as a parallel for the kind of religion represented by Christianity or Islam. In reality, there is no single system of this sort to be found in Hinduism. There is no single founder, or commonly accepted sacred book or creed. As the German Indologist, Heinrich von Stietenchron has put it, Hinduism is best understood to denote a 'civilisation that contains a plurality of distinct religions'.[1] 'Hinduism' thus simply refers to everything that is present in Hindu culture, including its religions.

In what follows no attempt is made to describe or engage with Hinduism as a whole. Most emphatically, no claim is being made to define Hinduism or set out the 'essence' of Hinduism. Instead, two important features of Hinduism are picked out, which are very significant for a very large number of Hindus and which continue to be very important for Christian approaches to Hindus and Hinduism. As the Indologist Hardy has put it, 'the religious history of

India is marked by the conflict and the interaction of two major trends: to conceive of the Absolute either in terms of a (mystical) state of being or as a personal God.'[2] To represent the first trend we shall consider the traditions of Vedānta and Yoga, both of which have appealed to Christians seeking to engage with Hindu Spirituality. To represent the second we shall consider some aspects and traditions within Hindu theism and the devotional spiritualities that have emerged in it. Over the centuries both trends have given rise to highly sophisticated and intellectually rigorous traditions of theology and philosophy (*darśana*), which explain and support the spiritual paths they promote.

Vedānta

Vedānta means the 'end of the Veda', referring to both the final section of the Vedic revelation, the sacred texts known otherwise as the *Upaniṣads*, and the traditions of theology that are based on them, the Vedāntic schools. Following the *Upaniṣads*, the Vedāntic traditions commonly call ultimate reality, *Brahman*, but they differ as to whether they take a monist or a theistic view of how *Brahman* relates to the world, that is to say, whether they conceive of *Brahman* as the sole impersonal spiritual reality with which the finite self is identical, or whether they conceive of *Brahman* as a personal divine Lord with whom the finite self is in communion. The *Upaniṣads* teach that there is a close relationship between *Brahman* and the finite self, saying for instance, 'this self is *Brahman*,' (*ayam ātmā brahma*), or 'you are that' (*tattvamasi*), 'I am *Brahman*', (*aham brahmāsmi*). The Vedānta schools differ on how precisely to interpret these and other texts. The monist tradition is known as Advaita (Non-dualism) and its most important teacher is Śaṃkara (788–820 AD/CE). The theist traditions are many, but among them two of the most important are Viśiṣṭādvaita (Non-dualism of the Differentiated), whose great teacher is Rāmānuja (1017–137 AD/CE) and Dvaita (Dualism), whose great teacher is Madhva (c. 1238–317 AD/CE).

For monists, liberation from the world consists in the blissful realization of identity with *Brahman*. The later tradition of Advaita Vedānta that developed after Śaṃkara and which has become accepted as the standard form of Advaita asserts that *Brahman* is ultimately the only reality there is, being spiritual and pure blissful consciousness, and that the conscious core or self within each of us is identical with Brahman. The central teaching of Advaita has often been summed up as '*Brahman* is real, the world is false, the self is *Brahman* not other.' For theists liberation consists in the realization of a communion of knowledge and love with God. In Viśiṣṭādvaita Vedānta, for instance, Brahman is identified with the personal divine Lord of theism. The permanent reality and distinction of God, spiritual finite selves and material things are affirmed. In the teaching of the great teacher of this tradition, Rāmānuja, the central conception of this relationship is that the entities of the world form the body of *Brahman*. Liberation consists in the blissful realization of this relationship and of the direct knowledge or vision of *Brahman*. This comes about through *bhakti* (devotion), which Rāmānuja depicts in Vedāntic terms as a form of devotional meditation on the Vedāntic texts, a steady calling to mind of God that leads into vision of God. This process and the attainment of the final goal are, however, dependent on the God's own choice for the devotee and the gift of his grace (*anugraha*).

Yoga

The term 'yoga' comes from a verbal root (*yuj*) meaning 'to yoke together' or 'to unite'. Yoga refers to a wide range of ethical, physical and meditational disciplines, which serve to control human behaviour, the body and the consciousness. Yoga is used as a general term in many different traditions for such disciplines, but also more specifically for the Yoga traditions, where there is systematic exposition of yoga as a discipline and path to liberation from the confines of material embodiment.

One of the most important systematic traditions of yoga is the *Rāja Yoga* found in Patañjali's *Yogasūtra* (around third century AD/CE). Here yoga is said to be an 'eight-limbed' (*aṣṭāṅga*) process, whose aim is 'the suppression of the fluctuations of the consciousness (*citta*)' (*Yogasūtra* 2). Yoga accepts a dualist view of reality, in which there are two separate principles: a plurality of non-material conscious selves (*puruṣa*) and matter itself in its different forms (*prakṛti*). The self mistakenly thinks that it has a connection with matter and thus becomes bound up with bodily rebirths and experiences the suffering that this entails. The consciousness fluctuates because it has lost control of itself, influenced by the sense impressions and memories generated in the embodied state. One much favoured simile for yoga is that of a horse-drawn chariot. The fluctuating consciousness is like a man in a chariot when the horses are out of control, whereas yoga is like learning to control the horses. Yoga enables the consciousness to be controlled and to become 'one-pointed' (*ekāgra*), restraining human behaviour and the body.

The 'eight limbs' of *Rāja Yoga* are: restraint, observance, posture, breath-control, sense-withdrawal, concentration, meditation and absorbed concentration. By 'restraint' is meant general ethical practices of refraining from injuring other beings, lying, stealing, unchaste behaviour and greed. By 'observance' is meant the promotion of purity, contentment, austerity, study of sacred texts and devotion to the Lord. The stages of ethical, physical and mental control lead onto each other and allow the practitioner to control his or her consciousness. In the final stage of absorbed concentration (*samādhi*), the practitioner becomes no longer conscious of his or her body and environment. This leads eventually to final liberation (*mokṣa*), which in yoga is thought of as a state of 'isolation' (*kaivalya*). Liberation is, thus, a freedom from any involvement with matter, the self becoming isolated in blissful absorption in its own consciousness.

Hindu Theism

Within Hinduism as a whole there is a vast number and huge variety of theistic cults and gods and goddesses. Theistic religion is the primary religious expression of the majority of Hindus. These theist religious traditions (*sampradāya*) have also developed sophisticated systems of theology and demanding paths of ethical and spiritual practice, centred around the particular deity worshipped in them. While the many different local and regional cults and traditions have diverse historical origins, they are often depicted as all being forms of three great pan-Indian theistic traditions: Vaiṣṇavism centred on the god Viṣṇu; Śaivism centred on the god Śiva; and Śākta religion centred on the Goddess often simply known as Śakti.

The different theistic traditions in various ways draw on the many sources of Hinduism, such as the Vedic, Tantric, Purāṇic and more local traditions. The South Indian Śrī Vaiṣṇava tradition, for example, is centred on Viṣṇu in the form of Nārāyaṇa together with his consort or Śakti, Śrī. This tradition bases its theology and practice on the theistic Vedānta of Rāmānuja, the Viṣṇu Purāṇa, the Tantric Pāñcarātra texts, as well as the devotional hymns of the Tamil saints, the Āḻvārs. Within this tradition Viṣṇu is depicted as having five forms or modes of manifestation: his supreme form; his creative manifestations; his descents in human or animal form (the *avatāras*); his descents into consecrated images (*arcāvatāra*) and as the inner controller immanent in all things. Śrī Vaiṣṇava practice affirms variously the Vedāntic path of meditation on Upaniṣadic texts, yogic discipline similar to that found in the *Yoga Sūtras*, the performance of the ritual and social *dharma* we have considered, and the devotional worship of the deity, focused especially on the images found in the South Indian temples of the tradition. Another South Indian tradition, Śaiva Siddhānta, is centred on Śiva, as the one who, along with his Śakti, has the five-fold action of producing, maintaining and destroying the world, and of concealing and revealing himself. Within this tradition reality is divided into a characteristically Śaiva scheme reflecting the depiction of Śiva as 'Lord of beasts' (*Paśupati*). Accordingly, there is said to be: *pati* (the Lord, Śiva); *paśu* (the 'beast', the finite conscious self); and *pāśa* (the 'bond', the material substrate, which binds the selves through impurity, karma and the obscuring power of the Lord). Through ritual action and the grace of Śiva, the *paśu* becomes freed of pāsa and comes to be like Śiva. Śaiva Siddhānta has its own

Tantric Āgama texts as well as the devotional hymns of the Tamil Śaiva poet-mystics, the Nāyanmārs.

Bhakti

Hindu theistic religion is also called *bhakti* religion. *Bhakti* means 'attachment' or 'devotion' and this encompasses all the different ways in which the deities are worshipped and human beings are attached to them, be it in the performance of rituals, recitation of sacred texts, singing of devotional hymns or meditating on the deity. Theist traditions often distinguish between lower and higher forms of *bhakti*. Lower *bhakti* is shown to deities for protection and success in this life. A higher *bhakti* is when men and women cultivate intense devotional relationships of love and service for the deities, patterned on human relationships, such as that of parent and child, servant and master or two lovers. Such devotion is focused on the deity as himself or herself the supreme object to be obtained, rather than the lesser motivation of protection or mundane goods. This is a source of delight in this life, as well as the means to get release from rebirth and realize blissful communion with the deity. Such release (*mokṣa*) is experienced as the fullest manifestation and eternal enjoyment of the relationship cultivated in this life. A central emphasis in different Hindu theistic traditions is the human need for divine grace (*anugraha*) and God's willingness to give it to those who wish it either for success in this life or liberation from the world.

Conception of Deity

It is true that many Hindus treat the deities as distinct and localized forms of divine presence. However, within the sacred texts and practice of the developed theistic traditions there is the assertion that there is only one God and they relate the vast number of gods and goddesses to that God in some way, as manifestations of it or as inferior beings. We have already seen that in Vedānta the concept of *Brahman* is that there is one ultimate reality, which is the source, or the reality, of everything else. Within the sacred literature of Hindu theism there is also found the concept of *Bhagavān* (the Lord) or *Bhagavatī* (the female form) and which asserts that there is one God or Goddess who is the creator, sustainer and destroyer of all the world, who is concerned for the welfare of human beings and who reaches out to them out of love for them. The members of the different theistic traditions, be they Vaiṣṇava, Śaiva or Śākta, simply identify the deity they worship as *Bhagavān/Bhagavatī* with all that entails in terms of attitudes towards other religious traditions. In theistic forms of Vedānta, moreover, the two concepts of *Brahman* and *Bhagavān* are naturally identified. Thus, it is perhaps fair to say that Hinduism as a whole contains many different monotheist religions within it, as well as some polytheistic elements.

Christian Spirituality and Hinduism

Theological and spiritual engagement with Vedānta has, in fact, proved very significant in Christian engagement with Hinduism, especially in the modern period. Because of the particular importance of Thomism (the theology based on the thought of Thomas Aquinas) for Catholic theologians, there has been a particular emphasis among Catholic Christians on exploring what relationship Thomism might have with Vedānta both in the general assessment of how Christianity and Hinduism relate as religious traditions, as well as within a particular interest in how Vedāntic ideas might help develop an Indian Christian Thomist theology. Thus, in the modern period, a considerable number of theologians working in India, such as Fr Pierre Johanns S. J. (1885–1955), de Smet (1916–98) and Grant (1922–2000) all studied the Vedānta and sought to relate it to the Thomist account.

Likewise, there has been an interest in a deep experiential encounter with Vedāntic spirituality in a monastic context, bearing fruit in the development of Christian Ashrams, modelled on Hindu religious communities. Thus, the French Benedictine monk, Fr Henri Le Saux (otherwise known as Swami Abhishiktananda, 1910–73), founder of the best known Christian Ashram, Shantivanam, immersed himself totally into the lifestyle of a Hindu saṃnyāsin and into Vedāntic spirituality as he found it in the *Upaniṣads* and in the teaching of the contemporary Hindu guru, Ramana Mahārshi (1879–1950).

Much of the encounter with Vedānta in this period has been an engagement with the particular tradition of Advaita Vedānta, for the historical reason that at the end of the nineteenth century and into the first half of the twentieth century, Advaita Vedānta was given huge prestige by Western and modern Hindu scholars, so that it seemed that this was *the* Hindu tradition that Christians should engage with, often to the relative neglect of other traditions, Vedāntic or otherwise. In its standard form outlined above, Advaita is, however, clearly incompatible with the articles of Christian faith. Christianity is theistic and Trinitarian, whereas the Brahman in Advaita Vedānta is not the personal Lord of theism, nor is there any real parallel for the Trinitarian distinction within Brahman. Christianity holds to the reality and goodness of a created world, whereas Advaita takes the world to be the product of ignorance and the arena of rebirth and suffering. Christianity maintains that the human being is an integral composite of body and soul, created in the image of God and an entity distinct from God, whereas Advaita maintains a dualist understanding of the human person, in which the spiritual core, the self, is identical with Brahman. Christianity is concerned with the redemption of the world, whereas in Advaita the goal is the transcendence of the world.

Some theologians engaging with *Advaita*, such as de Smet and Grant, however, have suggested that Thomism and Advaita are in fact compatible.[3] Śaṃkara, the greatest teacher of Advaita, they argue, has a theist and a realist account very different from the later form Advaita takes and they read Śaṃkara's account in terms of the Thomist account of God and creation. For de Smet the difference between Śaṃkara and Aquinas is one of expression, not of content. Śaṃkara affirms contingency by a more negative approach, whereby the reality of the finite pales into insignificance when set against that of absolute being, whereas Aquinas has a more positive approach, using the language of participation. De Smet and Grant have also come to talk of the Advaitic account as a complementary expression that might enrich the Thomist account and Christian experience. Grant argues that non-dual language and experience, as well as the Vedāntic emphasis on the immanence of Brahman, challenge tendencies in western theological discourse towards a dualism between God and the world, in which God is depicted as outside and remote from the world.

This attempt to argue for an alternative reading of Advaita remains problematic, since it has won little wider acceptance, despite the painstaking efforts of de Smet and Grant to argue that this is the meaning of Śaṃkara's own account. Nonetheless, we could say that it is at the least a possible Christian re-reading of Śaṃkara's Advaita in the light of Thomas Aquinas and very much in the tradition of what Aquinas himself did with non-Christian accounts. Likewise, spiritual or contemplative encounter with Advaita has often worked well as a form of a Christian transformation of the Advaitic experience. This is the case with the early work of Henri Le Saux. In his earlier encounter with Advaitic spirituality, Le Saux sought to find ways in which Advaita might be transformed by and fulfilled in Christian Trinitarian faith. Contemplating the Vedāntic description of Brahman as 'being, consciousness and bliss' (*sat-cit-ānanda*), he found there a Vedāntic understanding of Brahman that could be transformed into a Trinitarian concept, of Father (*sat*), Son (*cit*) and Spirit (*ānanda*). In this he picked up a longstanding Christian Trinitarian reading of this Vedāntic formula that still remains popular in India.

Unfortunately, later in life, Le Saux failed to maintain the balance needed in such an encounter. Instead, he allowed his Christian faith in the Trinity to be sublimated by the Advaitic experience of the unity of all in Brahman. For Le Saux Christian faith about the Incarnation of Christ had to be transformed into Advaitic categories, so that Christ is no longer the unique union of God and man, but an exemplar of the relationship that all human beings have with Brahman. His final assimilation to the Advaitic perspective is evident in the letters written in his last year of 1973.[4]

Apart from Advaita, there are the many theistic traditions of Vedānta with which Christianity might seem to have more immediate common ground. Such forms of Vedanta, such as that developed by Rāmānuja, are monotheistic and realist and so already lack some of the marked incompatibility that Advaita has with the Christian account of God and creation. Theistic Vedānta, moreover, serves as the intellectual system supporting many of the devotional (*bhakti*) traditions in Hinduism, which would also seem to have much in common with Christian theism.

Theistic Vedānta would, in fact, seem to have much that is compatible with the classical Christian account of God and creation, although also manifestly different in certain respects. The concept of God found in theistic Vedānta is in many ways fundamentally similar to Aquinas' account of God considered in the unity of the divine essence. Both traditions affirm that God is one, omniscient, omnipotent, wholly perfect and immutable, intimately present in all things. Theistic Vedānta can also be said to teach a creational relationship between God and the world, insofar as it maintains both that the world depends on Brahman at all times for its existence and that God governs the world in general and exercises a particular moral rule over human affairs, without undermining the freedom of human beings. On the other hand, theistic Vedānta also affirms the eternity of the world. The world as we experience it is produced from a more subtle state at each beginning of a new cycle of time, rather than created *ex nihilo* in the sense of created in or with time. Like Advaita, much of theistic Vedānta uses language and imagery that affirm a unity between God and the world in a way unfamiliar to Christian imagery, as in Rāmānuja's depiction of the world as the body of God. However, it is a mistake to think that theistic Vedānta is pantheistic as a result, since the language and images are interpreted in such a way as to affirm the transcendence of God, as well as the world's difference from God.

At the same time, when it comes to the understanding of human nature and hence human destiny, theistic Vedānta remains the product of a very different tradition from the Christian account. As with other Hindu traditions it affirms a fundamentally dualist anthropology that contrasts with the Christian understanding of the human person as a body and soul composite.

Yoga

Many Christians have been on courses in Yoga and found it to be of considerable value as a method of control over the body and mind, whether for therapeutic purposes or better concentration. However, it is important to bear in mind that Hindu traditions of yoga and meditation are also embedded in spiritual paths with goals somewhat different from those found in Christianity. There is a need for a certain caution, then, in taking up these forms of practice.

A considered official guide on these matters from within the Catholic tradition is to be found in *Some Aspects of Christian Meditation,* a document issued by the Congregation for the Doctrine of the Faith in 1989. The document notes the interest many Christians have in Eastern methods, be they derived from Hindu or Buddhist traditions. As the document asserts, however, the value of engagement with such traditions is determined by the degree to which it accords with authentic Christian Spirituality, which is determined by the principles and goals of Christian faith. Christian Spirituality is Trinitarian and incarnational in character and aims at a personal encounter with God and a communion of knowledge and love with God's triune life. Thus, while the Church rejects nothing that is true and holy in Eastern traditions, 'one can take from them what is useful so long as the Christian concept of prayer, its logic and requirements, are never obscured'.[5]

In terms of the systematic yoga of the *Yoga Sūtra*s the difference in goals and the means to them is quite marked. The dualist metaphysics of Yoga and the goal of separation from any materiality contrasts with the Christian view of creation, human nature and the goal of bodily resurrection. Although, in Yoga the concept of a Lord is affirmed, this is simply an object for meditation. The goal is not union with the Lord, nor is the Lord the creator of the world. Moreover, the path of Yoga remains something the practitioner has to achieve for him- or herself, in contrast to the fundamental Christocentric and grace-dependent path of Christian soteriology.

Bhakti

Hindu theism abounds in a rich mythology, which includes many vivid accounts of the exploits of the gods and goddesses depicted within them. Christians have often found the events and the imagery contained in these myths to be surprising and even shocking. A particularly difficult case for Christians has been the rich and very important body of erotic mythology, which comes to play a central part in the formation of Hindu devotional attitudes towards the divine. A good example of this is the account of the male deity, Kṛṣṇa, who descents as a human being to live with the cowherding people of the North Indian region of Vraja. Here he grows up and as a young man engages in various love games with the cowherd women (*gopīs*), even though many of them are already married and hence such a relationship flaunts the established *dharma*. Enchanted by the sound of his flute and driven by intense desire for him, they abandon homes and husbands to dance with their divine lover in the autumnal moonlight. The pain of separation, and the bliss of erotic union, especially the love affair between Kṛṣṇa and his favourite cowherd woman, Rādhā, has been retold time and again in the devotional literature, often in quite graphic detail.

Here, however, it is important to have an informed understanding of what myths and imagery do within Hinduism. For Hindus, these serve as vehicles

237

for expressing the nature of the divine and to promote human relationships with the divine. They serve to explore and evoke devotional and ethical attitudes. It is, then, these truths and models for behaviour that Hindus derive from the myths and imagery that need to be considered in any Christian approach to Hindu mythology. In the mythology of Kṛṣṇa, for example, the erotic exploits of the deity with the cowherd women of Vraja serve as a vehicle for promoting intense devotion to God, both with the blissful delight of mystical union with God and the unbearable pain of separation from God. The mythology itself is not understood to encourage sexual licence between human beings. The problematic nature of such mythology is acknowledged and addressed in the devotional literature and their commentaries. In the case of Kṛṣṇa and the women of Vraja, one explanation is that Kṛṣṇa remains untouched by such acts and engages in them only in order to arouse devotion in human beings (*Bhāgavata Purāṇa* X. 33).

The imagery and modes of Hindu *bhakti* find their counterpart in the rich devotional traditions of medieval Christian Spirituality. As we have seen, Hindu devotional theism emphasizes and explores the cultivation of a range of devotional relationships found expressed in its mythology and which mirror the different relationships human beings have with each other, such as that of master and servant, parent and child, as well as that of two lovers. Christian Spirituality has likewise explored and cultivated these relationships in developing the devout and mystical life. We might call to mind here the long tradition of Christian commentary on the *Song of Songs*, such as that by Bernard of Clairvaux, and the 'bridal mysticism' of the medieval period, or the exploration of the motherhood of God in the writings of Julian of Norwich.

Christianity would, then, find some common ground in those traditions of Hindu theism that are centred on *bhakti*, when this cultivates a loving relationship with God, and when the need for divine grace is emphasized. It is with Hindu *bhakti* traditions that Christianity finds a common experience of divine love as being at the heart of the human encounter with God and as the dynamic within a God-centred life. Reflecting his own deep knowledge of the South Indian devotional tradition of Śaiva Siddhānta and affirming his sense of the common ground between this tradition and Christianity, the Indian theologian Dhavamony, for instance, describes the Hindu *bhakti* religions as India's 'Religions of Love'. He sees this as the proper meeting point of Christianity and Hinduism. As he puts it:

> Of all Hindu religious experience, *bhakti* experience comes close to Christian experience, for in this experience we come across the necessity of repentance and of a purified heart before God's grace can become effective, the need of realizing fellowship with God in union with Him, and the profound sense of dependence on Him alone and of loyal service and surrender to Him.[6]

Other Indian Christians have also engaged with the literary forms, concepts and sentiments found in Hindu devotional theism in order to develop forms of Indian Christian hymns and poets, directed towards the Trinity, Christ and the Blessed Virgin Mary.

This chapter is an abridged version of Ganeri, M (2011), 'Catholicism and Hinduism' in G. D'Costa (ed.), The Catholic Church and the World Religions: A Theological and Phenomenological Account, London and New York: T&T Clark: 2011, pp. 106–40.

Notes

1 H. Von Stietenchron (2001), 'Hinduism: On the Proper Use of a Deceptive Term', in G.-D. Sontheimer and H. Kulke (eds), *Hinduism Reconsidered*. Delhi: Manohar Books, p. 33.
2 F. Hardy (1983), *Viraha Bhakti: The Early History of Krisna Devotion in South India.* Oxford: Oxford University Press, p. 13.
3 For de Smet see B. J. Malkovsky (ed.) (2000), *New Perspectives on Advaita Vedanta; Essays in Commemoration of Professor Richard de Smet S.J.*, Leiden: Brill, and for Grant see S. Grant (2002), *Towards an Alternative Theology: Confessions of a Non-dual Christian.* Indiana: University of Notre Dame.
4 See J. Stuart (1995), *Swami Abhishiktananda: His Life Told Through His Letters.* New Delhi: ISPCK.
5 F. Gioia (ed.) (1994), 'Some Aspects of Christian Meditation', in *Interreligious Dialogue: The Official Teaching of the Catholic Church (1963–1995).* Boston: Pauline Books, p. 600.
6 M. Dhavamony (2002), *Hindu-Christian Dialogue: Theological Soundings and Perspective.* Amsterdam and New York: Rodolpi, p. 47.

Bibliography and Further Reading

Introductions to Hinduism

Flood, G. (1996), *An Introduction to Hinduism.* Cambridge: Cambridge University Press.
Klostermaier, K. K. (1994), *A Survey of Hinduism*, 2nd edn. Albany: State University of New York.
Lipner, J. J. (2010), *Hindus: Their Religious Beliefs and Practices*, 2nd edn. London: Routledge.

Christian Approaches to Hinduism and Hindu-Christian Dialogue

Coward, H. (1990), *Christian-Hindu Dialogue: Perspectives and Encounters.* New York: Orbis.
Dhavamony, M. (2002), *Hindu-Christian Dialogue: Theological Soundings and Perspectives.* Amsterdam and New York: Rodopi.
Ganeri, M. (2011), 'Catholicism and Hinduism', in G. D'Costa (ed.), *The Catholic Church and the World Religions: A Theological and Phenomenological Account.* London and New York: T&T Clark.

20 Christian Spirituality and Buddhism

Brian J. Pierce

Introduction

Christianity and Buddhism might be compared to two magnificent, beautifully coloured fish swimming in the same ocean. They are not the same species of fish; in fact, they are quite different. Both, however, swim gracefully and freely in the cool, deep waters, and though both call the great ocean their 'home', they describe their experience of the ocean in vastly different ways.

The Buddhist fish glides freely through the ocean, calling it *Tatha*, or 'Suchness'. One of the ten names of the Buddha, she says, is *Tathagata*, literally the one 'who has arrived from suchness, remains in suchness, and will return to suchness. . . . It is the substance or ground of being, just like water is the substance of waves' (Nhat Hanh 1995: 41–2). When asked to say more about how she relates to the ocean, she responds by saying that they are not two separate entities, but one – united in the emptiness of non-duality, known as *sunyata*. 'The ocean and I inter-are', she explains, which means that 'the barriers between [us] are dissolved, and peace, love and understanding are possible' (Nhat Hanh 1995: 11). She goes on to describe *sunyata* as 'Absolute Emptiness, transcending all forms of mutual relationship, of subject and object, birth and death, God and the world, something and nothing, yes and no . . . there is no time, no space, no becoming, *no-thing-ness*; it is what makes all these things possible . . . it is a void of inexhaustible contents' (Suzuki 1957: 30–3).

The fish called *Christianity* also experiences the ocean in a transcendent way, though she defines its seemingly limitless expanse not as emptiness, but as an *all-ness*, an infinite, loving fullness, something akin to a divine Mother who is the source of life.[1] 'The ocean, whom I call *God*', she says, 'is the one in whom I live and move and have my being, the one who fills all in all' (Acts 17.28; Eph. 1.23). She tells the story of swimming through the cool waters one day, and hearing God whisper these words to her: 'Just as the fish is in the sea and the sea in the fish, so am I in the soul and the soul in me, the Sea of Peace' (St Catherine of Siena 1980: 211). She realized that day that God is, 'an essence that embraces all essence', and that 'when all images are detached . . . and the soul sees nothing but the one alone, then the naked essence of the soul finds the naked, formless essence of the divine unity' (Eckhart 1979: I, 160; 96, 331). 'If this is true', she adds, 'then it must mean that God and I are one'.

So what really *is* the ocean that is home to both of these fish? Is it an essential emptiness of *inter-being* or is it a fullness that *fills all in all*? Is it *Tatha* or *sunyata* or God? Both fish admit, once they open up and speak honestly and from the heart, that they experience life and existence as a kind of *empty fullness* – a union with the Ground of all being. They swim in *that*, though both admit that trying to describe just what *'that'* is, can be somewhat difficult.

Empty Fullness

The language of paradox, though difficult to grasp, might be all we have as we seek a path of dialogue between Christian Spirituality and Buddhism. When a Jew or Christian, for example, reads the story of creation in chapter one of the Book of Genesis, he or she cannot help but be confronted with the paradoxical image of a dark void from which flow the many manifestations of God's creation: 'In the beginning when God created the heavens and the earth, the earth was a *formless void* and darkness covered the face of the deep, while a wind from God swept over the face of the waters' (Gen. 1.1–2). It is a dark, deep emptiness that *fills all in all*, or as we heard above, a 'naked, formless essence of divine unity'.

In the Genesis story the *formless void*, which swirls with divine energy (symbolized by the wind that sweeps over the water), sounds very much like Suzuki's 'void of inexhaustible contents'. And this void is – paradoxically – the Source of all of creation. The story goes on to say that God speaks a Word from deep within this emptiness, and suddenly light and water, land and vegetation, flying birds and human beings come into existence. Fr Bede Griffiths, a Christian monk who lived much of his life in India, comments, 'This divine energy has intelligence, and the intelligence is manifest in consciousness . . . There is a conscious power behind the universe, organizing the universe' (Griffiths 1985).

So we might conclude by saying that within this empty abyss we discover a consciousness – a Word of God – and this Word echoes in the deepest centre of all of creation and in each human being. Fr Cyprian Smith says it this way:

In us, as in God, there is a nameless abyss . . . [God's] Word is first uttered within the Trinity, as God the Son, in the eternal silence of heaven. But it is also uttered 'outside,' bringing the created universe into being . . . Whether we know it or not, we are vibrating with [that same Word] now, at this very moment. If we did not do so, we would immediately cease to exist. (Smith 1987: 58–60)

The Mahayana Buddhist tradition teaches that emptiness – *sunyata* – is the ground, or background, of all that exists. Bede Griffiths, reflecting on the teachings of Japanese Buddhist Master, D. T. Suzuki, points out that, '*Sunyata* is not static, but dynamic . . . In the void there is a constant urge to differentiate [manifest] itself . . . Creation is the differentiation of the void' (Griffiths 1985). It is intriguing to note that, for both the Judeo-Christian and Buddhist worldviews, the Ground of all being is a *dynamic* emptiness, a void vibrating with energy, a formless essence which organizes matter intelligently. In Hebrew, the word for the *wind* that sweeps over the watery chaos is *ruah*, which also translates as *breath* or *spirit*. Many Christians associate that *wind* with the Holy Spirit that appears later in the Pentecost story in the Acts of the Apostles (2.1–41).

How, then, do we understand this dynamic emptiness? The Christian tradition has for many centuries employed the phrase *creatio ex nihilo* in its attempt to explain that God does not use pre-existent matter to create; God creates *ex nihilo* – from *nothing*. One contemporary author invites us to go beyond this term as a mere philosophical doctrine, and to see it as an invitation to discover, 'the nothingness that is at the heart of our being, that becomes the fulcrum for experiencing the infinite life of God pulsing through this being, through the universe, from moment to moment' (Habito 2004: 23). In other words, we are invited to sink into this emptiness, this divine womb, and discover that God is not a *thing*. In fact, it is precisely because God is *no-thing* that we are able to go beyond *things* – into the essence of the world of matter – and experience the infinite Ground of all being, the fullness that fills all in all.

Here and Now

We can only *sink* into the *all-ness* of God in the here and now, and this sinking helps us to discover that God simply *is*. The medieval theologian, Thomas Aquinas, distinguished between the verb *esse*, God's *being* and the noun *ens*, which corresponds with things, *beings*. As one theologian, commenting on Aquinas, says, 'God is not a static reality on a shelf (*ens*). God is active everywhere in the sense that wherever anything exists, God's is the present, active force of its existence' (Philibert 1995: 42).[2] In other words, God is not *this* or *that*. God is not some-*thing*. God is *is-ness*. God is a verb. Says Meister Eckhart, 'If a [person] should seek to indicate something by saying "it is," that would be silly . . . When everything is removed . . . so that nothing at all remains but a simple "is" – that is the proper characteristic of God's name' (Eckhart 1979: I, 227). Is this not the same answer that Moses received when he posed his big question to God in the desert? ' "When I go to the Israelites and say to them, "The God of your ancestors has sent me to you," if they ask me, "What is his name?" what am I to tell them?" God replied, "I am who am" ' (Exod. 3.13–14).

If God simply *is*, then to live a spiritual life is to awaken to God's life flow-ing through us and around us in this very moment. It is to realize in our own lives the very *is-ness* of God. This is the meaning of the Buddhist doctrine of *Tatha*, suchness, 'reality as it is' (Nhat Hanh 1995: 142). Meister Eckhart challenges us with this radical invitation: 'You should wholly sink away from your *you-ness* and dissolve into God's *His-ness*, and your "yours" and God's "His" should become so completely one "Mine" that with God you understand His unbecome *Is-ness* and His nameless Nothingness' (Eckhart 1979: II, 333).

Are we prepared to awaken to this annihilating reality of mystical union? To not set off on this journey into unitive consciousness is to risk spending our entire lives wandering about in spiritual ignorance. The Buddha called ignorance the root of all suffering. We suffer because we are ignorant of our union with God, the Divine Ground; we live immersed in God's love and do not know it.

There is an ancient Japanese Buddhist chant called 'The Song of Zazen', composed by Master Hakuin (1685–1768), which serves as a wake-up call to us. Says Hakuin, 'Not realizing that Truth is so close, beings seek it far away ... It is like one who, while being in the midst of water, cries out for thirst. It is like the child of a rich household who gets lost in a poor village' (Habito 2004: 51).[3]

For me personally, the wake-up call came through my contact with Thây Thich Nhat Hanh, whose life and teachings helped me to rediscover the inti-mate nearness of God in the present moment. With pristine simplicity, Thây says, 'Life is available only in the present moment. If you are distracted, if your mind is not there with your body, then you miss your appointment with life ... Mindfulness is the capacity ... to live deeply every moment of your daily life' (Nhat Hanh 1999: 84). It seems so simple, and yet we spin our wheels dur-ing so much of our lives re-living the past or worrying about the future. God is *here and now*, eternally present to us and in us at all times – in every breath we breathe. All we have to do is open our eyes and be mindful of this presence. As Jesus says in the Gospel of Matthew,

> I tell you, do not worry about your life, what you will eat or what you will drink, or about your body, what you will wear. Is not life more than food, and the body more than clothing? Look at the birds of the air; they neither sow nor reap nor gather into barns, and yet your heavenly Father feeds them. Are you not of more value than they? ... Strive first for the reign of God and God's righteousness, and all these things will be given to you as well. Do not worry about tomorrow, for tomorrow will bring worries of its own. Today's trouble is enough for today. (Mt. 6.25–6, 33–4)

Jesus is not inviting us to live in a bubble, as if we could live in a world free from problems. In fact he is quite realistic: 'Tomorrow will bring worries of its own.' He is simply inviting us to be grounded, to discover the freedom of the present moment. We do not have to live tomorrow's problems today! One day at a time – that is enough. We see God, listen to God and touch God here and now, which is to say that everyday life is the principal context for our spiritual practice. Again Eckhart says, 'There is no becoming: it is one Now . . . a becoming without becoming, newness without renewal, and this becoming is God's being' (Eckhart 1979: II, 319).

Unfortunately, Christians frequently speak of a God who is faraway, *up* in heaven, a Savior who will one day come back for us. God may be in heaven, but the question is: Where is heaven? Jesus spoke quite clearly after his resurrection, 'I am with you always; yes, to the end of time' (Mt. 28.20). Are we not invited to discover that the risen Christ lives here and now in our midst? Thanks to our dialogue with the spiritual traditions of the East, we are rediscovering our own 'pearl of great price'. Our Eastern brothers and sisters have thrown some cool, fresh water in our faces to wake us up to the wisdom of our own tradition! I was surprisingly shocked when I visited a Buddhist monastery several years ago and saw a sign hanging in a tree that read, '*The Kingdom of God is now or never.*' I certainly was not expecting to see a sign referring to the Kingdom of God in a Buddhist monastery, much less something so powerful and truthful as that one. That day a bell sounded deep in my heart, waking me up and allowing me to remember a truth that I had known indirectly all my life. I smiled, and heard my heart say, 'Yes. I am home.'

Practice of the Presence of God

Brother Lawrence of the Resurrection was a Carmelite friar who died in France in 1691 after many years of humble service in the kitchen of his monastery. He was known for his simple holiness, the fruit of a continual, prayerful awareness of the presence of God. He wrote in a letter to one of his spiritual friends,

> I cannot understand how religious people can live contented lives without the practice of the presence of God. For myself I withdraw as much as I can to the deepest recesses of my soul . . . It is not necessary to always be in church to be with God; we can make a private chapel of our heart where we can retire from time to time to commune with Him, peacefully, humbly, lovingly . . . I keep myself in his presence by simple attentiveness and a loving gaze upon God, which I call the actual presence of God, or to put it more clearly, an habitual, silent and secret conversation of the soul with God. (Lawrence 1977: 61–8)

We do not have to sit on a meditation cushion or kneel for hours in a church in order to be in the presence of God. Both of these exercises can help us stay awake spiritually, but God is present in all the stuff of daily life: eating an orange, contemplating the smile of a child, studying for an exam or driving to work in busy, frustrating traffic. When we hold the hand of a loved one who is dying, we can experience God's presence flowing through us like a river of life and love. God's *is-ness* always *is* – as close and real as the air we breathe.

Grounded in Love

While Buddhism refers to the Ground of being from which we come and in which we live as *Tatha*, and the Judeo-Christian tradition calls that Ground *God*, both traditions teach the importance of flowing outwardly from this Ground or Source into the practice of loving kindness and compassion. The Christian Scriptures say very succinctly that 'God is love' (1 Jn 4.8). In other words, *Love* is the Source from which we come and in which we dwell. Jesus says, 'Abide in my love' (Jn 15.9). What does it mean for us to dwell *in* God, who is love? This is not something we earn because of good behaviour; it is a gift; we only have to receive it and live it. 'Divine love is not taken into us . . . Divine love takes us into itself; we are one with it' (Eckhart 1979: I, 50).

We respond to God's love by loving (cf. 1 Jn 4.19). A baby who is loved unconditionally learns the art of loving through her experience. Pope Benedict XVI says that, 'Since it is God who has loved us first (cf. 1 Jn 4.10), love is no longer just a "*commandment*", but the response to the gift of love' (Benedict XVI 2005: *Intro.*). Jesus, who knew that he was deeply loved by God, his Abba, spoke to his followers, saying, 'As the Father has loved me, so I have loved you. Abide in my love' (Jn 15.9). The spiritual path is an invitation to become one with love.

Jesus could be imaged as a river of love, flowing forth from the eternal abyss of the heart of God into a world touched by suffering, sin and violence. He flows towards the world, towards the *other*, towards the neighbour: 'God so *loved* the world that God gave his only Son, so that everyone who believes in him . . . might have eternal life' (Jn 3.16). Every disciple of Jesus is called to participate in this same outward (Trinitarian) journey of love, as a response to the call, 'Come and follow me.' We become one with the river of love that flows out from its source in God, sharing life-giving water with a thirsty world.

Yes, the world is thirsty; it experiences suffering and pain. The First Noble Truth of Buddhism is about suffering (*dukkha*).

Everyone knows that if you run away from suffering, you have no chance to find out what path you should take in order to get out of the suffering. So our practice is to embrace suffering and look deeply into its nature . . .

[By doing this we learn] to stop, to cut the source of nutrition for suffering, and then healing will take place . . . Siddhartha [Buddha] and Jesus both realized that life is filled with suffering. The Buddha became aware at an early age that suffering is pervasive. Jesus must have had the same kind of insight, because they both made every effort to offer a way out. (Nhat Hanh 1999: 124–5; 1995: 48)

Every truly *spiritual* path leads the practitioner beyond his or her own self-centred needs, into a communion of love with the neighbour, especially with the poor and suffering. 'Blessed are you who are poor,' said Jesus, 'for the reign of God is yours. Blessed are you who are now hungry, for you will be satisfied' (Lk. 6.20–1). God's love is always close to the poor. In a prayer traditionally attributed to St Francis of Assisi, we read: 'Make me a channel of your peace, where there is hatred, let me bring your love. Where there is injury, your pardon Lord . . .' Love and compassion are the only *true* responses to suffering.

The call to love can at times demand that we embrace our own and others' suffering, as well. This is why the crucifixion of Jesus is so central to Christianity. It is not a fascination with suffering, but an icon of love. Shortly before his death, Jesus said, 'I am the good shepherd. The good shepherd lays down his life for the sheep. . . . No one takes it from me, but I lay it down of my own accord' (Jn 10.11, 18). Thich Nhat Hanh, referring to Jesus' commitment to love, says with profound insight, 'There was a person who was born nearly two thousand years ago. He was aware that suffering was going on in him and in his society, and he did not hide himself from the suffering' (Nhat Hanh 1999: 37).

In all the ancient spiritual traditions one finds this essential truth: Suffering is overcome through love and compassion. The Buddha said, 'Conquer anger by love. Conquer evil by good . . . Hatreds never cease through hatred in this world; through love alone they cease. This is an essential law' (Siddhartha, the Buddha *The Dhammapada*, I. v.5). It is clear that in both the Christian and Buddhist traditions, there is a deep commitment to the practice of non-violent, self-giving love. In the writings of the sixteenth-century Spanish mystic, St John of the Cross, we find this gentle invitation: 'Where there is no love, sow love, and you will reap love' (*Letter to Madre María de la Encarnación*).

The 14th Dalai Lama, the spiritual leader of Tibetan Buddhism, reflects in the following interview on his own discovery of the common ground of love and compassion which is shared by Christians and Buddhists:

Finding common ground among faiths can help us bridge needless divides at a time when unified action is more crucial than ever. As a species, we must embrace the oneness of humanity . . . An early eye opener for me was my meeting with the Trappist monk Thomas Merton in India shortly before his untimely death in 1968. Merton told me he could be perfectly faithful to Christianity, yet learn in depth from other religions like Buddhism. The same is true for me as an ardent Buddhist learning from the world's other great religions.

A main point in my discussion with Merton was how central compassion was to the message of both Christianity and Buddhism. In my readings of the New Testament, I find myself inspired by Jesus' acts of compassion . . . His healing and his teaching are all motivated by the desire to relieve suffering . . . The focus on compassion that Merton and I observed in our two religions strikes me as a strong unifying thread among all the major faiths. And these days we need to highlight what unifies us. (14th Dalai Lama 2010)

Perhaps it is the practice of loving compassion towards one's enemy that most deeply unites the great spiritual traditions. Again from the Dalai Lama:

Genuine compassion . . . can be extended even to one's enemies . . . [The] recognition that another person wishes to harm and hurt you cannot undermine genuine compassion – a compassion based on the clear recognition of that person as someone who is suffering, someone who has the natural and instinctual desire to seek happiness and overcome suffering, just as oneself. (14th Dalai Lama 1996: 68–9)

Jesus, in the Sermon on the Mount, also invites us to the practice of loving non-violence: 'You have heard that it was said, "You shall love your neighbor and hate your enemy." But I say to you, love your enemies, and pray for those who persecute you, that you may be children of your heavenly Father, who makes the sun rise on the bad and the good, and causes rain to fall on the just and the unjust' (Mt. 5.43–5). It was in his own attempt to be faithful to the teachings of Jesus that Martin Luther King, Jr, a Baptist minister from Georgia, in the southern United States, travelled to India to steep himself in the philosophy of active non-violence championed by Mahatma Gandhi. Bringing together these two great traditions, Dr King was able to give a new expression to the Gospel call to love one's enemy. In this way he was able to open up a path of healing in the midst of the violence of racial hatred and discrimination in the United States. King said:

To our bitterest opponents we say: We shall match your capacity to inflict suffering by our capacity to endure suffering. We shall meet your physical force with soul force. Do to us what you will, we shall continue to love you . . . Throw us in jail, and we shall still love you. Send your hooded perpetrators of violence into our community at the midnight hour and beat us and leave us half-dead and we shall still love you. But be ye assured that we will wear you down by our capacity to suffer. One day we shall win freedom, but not only for ourselves. We shall so appeal to your heart and conscience that we shall win you in the process, and our victory will be a double victory. (King 1957)

We live and move and have our being in the great abyss of a love that knows no limits; it is a love that crosses boundaries and speaks many languages. We do not own this love or the truth that is its Ground; we are simply their servants. And to the extent that we embody these gifts we discover a pathway to a deep, inner freedom, which allows us to live fully – today and every day – our appointment with life.

Notes

1 Ruben Habito, a Christian theologian and teacher of Zen, points out that the root of the Sanskrit word *sunyata*, which means essential emptiness, is *sunya*, meaning zero. 'If zero is the mother of all numbers', says Habito, 'then maybe *sunyata* could be defined as the infinite "zero-ness" which is the mother of all that is'. Cited from Ruben Habito (2004: 29).
2 See also Thomas Aquinas, *Summa Theologiae* II, 1.3.4.c.
3 Master Hakuin Zenji, cited in Habito (2004: 51). The translation of Hakuin's song has been slightly revised, based on a version which Habito and his students use at the Maria Kannon Zen Center in Dallas, Texas.

Bibliography and Further Reading

Benedict XVI (2005), Encyclical *Deus Caritas Est*. Rome: Vatican Library.
Buddha, Siddhartha. *The Dhammapada*. trans. Eknath Easwaran, 2007, Berkeley, CA: The Nilgiri Press.
Dalai Lama (1996), *The Good Heart: A Buddhist Perspective on the Teachings of Jesus*. Boston: Wisdom Publications.
— (2010), 'Many Faiths, One Truth', *The International Herald Tribune* (24 May 2010).
Eckhart, Meister (1979), *Meister Eckhart, Sermons and Treatises*. 3 vols, ed. Maurice O' C. Walshe. Shaftesbury: Element Books.
Griffiths, Bede OSB (May 1985), 'Eastern mysticism and Christian faith', audio talk given in Australia.
Habito, Ruben (2004), *Living Zen, Loving God*. Somerville, MA: Wisdom Publications.
King, Martin Luther, Jr (1957), sermon, 'Loving your enemies', preached on 17 November 1957 at Dexter Avenue Baptist Church, Montgomery Alabama.
Lawrence of the Resurrection, Brother (1977), *The Practice of the Presence of God*. trans. John J. Delaney, New York: Doubleday.

Nhat Hanh, Thich (1995), *Living Buddha, Living Christ.* New York: Riverhead Books.

— (1999), *Jesus and Buddha as Brothers.* New York: Riverhead Books.

Philibert, Paul OP (1995), *Seeing and Believing: Images of Christian Faith,* in Frank Kacmarcik, OblSB and Paul Philibert OP, *Seeing and Believing: Images of Christian Faith.* Collegeville, MN: The Liturgical Press.

Smith, Cyprian OSB (1987), *The Way of Paradox: Spiritual Life as Taught by Meister Eckhart.* New York: Paulist Press.

St Catherine of Siena (1980), *The Dialogue.* trans. Suzanne Noffke OP, New York: Paulist Press.

Suzuki, D. T. (1957), *Mysticism, Christian and Buddhist.* New York: Harper and Row.

21 Christian Spirituality and Judaism

John T. Pawlikowski

Introduction

Any discussion of the Jewish foundations of Christian Spirituality is essentially a post-Vatican II reality both for Catholic Christians and those in the Protestant world who have also benefited from documents on Christian-Jewish relations which move in the same vein as *Nostra Aetate*, the Second Vatican Council's declaration on the Church's relationship to non-Christian religions, whose special focus was Church's relationship with Judaism (Sherman 2011). Prior to the mid-60s Christian scholarship had little respect for post-biblical Judaism. Judaism as a religion was viewed as obsolete after the Christ Event. What positive features it had included were now taken up by Christianity leaving Judaism an empty shell. This outlook was essentially prominent in the biblical scholarship of the first part of the twentieth century and the attitudes of biblical scholars carried into systematic theology and spirituality.

A clear-cut example of the dominant outlook in Christian biblical scholarship emerges in the writings of prominent exegete Martin Noth. Noth's volume *History of Israel* became a standard reference for students and professors alike. In this volume Noth described Israel as a strictly 'religious community' which died a slow, agonizing death in the first century AD/CE. For Noth, Jewish history reached its culmination in the arrival of Jesus. His words are concise to the point in this regard:

> Jesus himself no longer formed part of the history of Israel. In him the history of Israel had come, rather, to its real end. What did belong to the history of Israel was the process of his rejection and condemnation by the Jerusalem religious community. Hereafter the history of Israel moved quickly to its end. (Noth 1966)

If Christian theology and spirituality did turn to the Old Testament it was generally to show the supposed enhanced teaching on a particular subject in the New Testament or to argue that elements of the New Testament were foreshadowed in the Old Testament. The prevailing view was that the Old Testament could be properly understood only through the lens of the New Testament. If there was an exception to this pattern, it was the regard for the biblical prophets among Christians. But in many cases they were looked to mainly as people predicting the coming of Christ. By and large there was little appreciation among Christians of the internal spirituality of the Hebrew Scriptures and hence these texts were not seen as useful in the development of an authentic Christian Spirituality.

Some may legitimately ask about the use of the Psalms which constitute the heart and soul of the Divine Office, the most important prayer of the church for several Christian denominations, particularly Catholicism and the Anglican tradition. There is no question that the extensive use of the Psalms does represent a somewhat positive use of Jewish prayer in Christian prayer. But I say 'somewhat' because there was a widespread belief that the authentic meaning of the Psalms could be perceived only through Christ. In this vein I recall attending sung vespers of Advent at Holy Name Catholic Cathedral in Chicago some years ago. The vesper service was organized by the Liturgy Training Publications office of the Archdiocese of Chicago. This office had demonstrated a sensitivity for Judaism in the light of *Nostra Aetate*. Yet even in this service a reader proclaimed that the Psalms can be properly interpreted through Jesus Christ. There is not much to be gained by Christians from the Psalms' respective inner spirituality.

There are positive signs within the church in terms of incorporating the Hebrew Scriptures more fully into the dynamics of Christian Spirituality. But we have a long way to go to the time when the texts of the Hebrew Scriptures would become a central focus of preaching and retreats (Holmgren/Schalmaan 1995). One particularly glaring omission comes in the Easter season. This is the time each year when the church brings before us the spirituality of the early Christian communities. As the church narrates this story which ought to be formative for Christian Spirituality there is no use of the Hebrew Scriptures in the Sunday readings in the Catholic Church.[1] This omission clearly conveys the message that the Hebrew Scriptures do not stand at the heart of Christianity.

The Parting of the Ways

One reason why we are finally seeing some change in attitude towards the role of the Hebrew Scriptures in the formulation of Christian spiritual identity has to do with what is termed as 'the parting of the ways' scholarship. This scholarship of the last decades has transformed our understanding of Christian origins in relation to Judaism. We now know that a sense of Christian-Jewish bonding persisted in many places for several centuries beyond the death of

Christ. This 'parting of the ways' scholarship has also uncovered a far more positive picture of the outlook of Jesus and Paul towards the Judaism of their time.

One of the first biblical scholars to contribute to this 'parting of ways' discussion was Robin Scroggs. Scroggs posited four basic points about the new understanding of the initial Jewish-Christian relationship. These were: (1) The movement begun by Jesus and continued after his death in Palestine can best be described as a reform movement within Judaism. There is little evidence during this period that Christians had a separate identity from Jews. (2) The Pauline missionary movement, as Paul understood it, was a Jewish mission which focused on the Gentiles, a proper object of God's call to his people. (3) Prior to the end of the Jewish war with the Romans in 70 AD/CE, there is no reality as Christianity. Followers of Jesus did not have a self-understanding of themselves as a religion over against Judaism. A distinctive Christian identity only began to emerge after the Jewish-Roman war. (4) The later portions of the New Testament all show signs of a movement towards separation, but they also generally retain some contact with their Jewish matrix (Scroggs 1986).

A growing number of biblical scholars have added to the new picture of the early Jewish-Christian relationship presented initially by Scroggs. The late Anthony Saldarini, for example, underlined the continuing presence of the 'followers of the way' within the wide tent of Judaism in the first centuries of the Common Era in several essays. Saldarini especially underscored the ongoing nexus between Christian communities and their Jewish neighbors in Eastern Christianity whose theological outlook is most often ignored in presentations about the early church within Western Christian theology (Saldarini 1996 and 1999).

The initial scholarship on the 'parting of the ways' by Scroggs and Saldarini was eventually reaffirmed by John Meier in the third volume of his comprehensive study of the New Testament understanding of Jesus. Meier argues that from a careful examination of New Testament evidence Jesus must be seen as presenting himself to the Jewish community of his time as an eschatological prophet and miracle worker in the likeness of Elijah. He was not interested in creating a separatist sect or a holy remnant along the lines of the Qumran sect. But he did envision the development of a special religious community within Israel. The idea that this community 'within Israel would slowly undergo a process of separation from Israel as it pursued a mission to the Gentiles in this present world – the long-term result being that his community would become predominantly Gentile itself finds no place in Jesus' message or practice' (Meier 2001). And a scholar within the 'parting of the ways' movement, David Frankfurter, has insisted that within the various 'clusters' of groups that included Jews and Christian Jews there existed a mutual influence persisting through Late Antiquity. There is evidence for a degree of overlap that, all things considered, threatens every construction of an historically distinct 'Christianity' before at least the mid-second century (Frankfurter 2003).

Jesus' Jewish Context

One of the most important aspects of the 'parting of the ways' scholarship has been the rooting of Jesus and his ministry very much within the context of the Jewish community of his time. This represents a total reversal of the outlook of earlier scholars such as Martin Noth whom we quoted at the beginning of this chapter. This process actually began in Catholicism at the Second Vatican Council. One of the three principal points of the conciliar declaration *Nostra Aetate* is the affirmation that Jesus drew heavily and positively from aspects of Jewish religious practice in first century Palestine. Determining what segment of Judaism offered the most to Jesus in terms of his own teaching is not an easy task. First century CE Judaism was experiencing a creative period with many new groups coming on the scene. The best answer is what the 1985 Vatican *Notes on Teaching and Preaching about Judaism* argued: Jesus was closer to the Pharisaic movement than any other part of the Jewish community at the time, despite his strong criticism at times of part of that movement.

The link to Pharisaism is especially important for one dimension of Christian Spirituality: the liturgical. To the extent that liturgical spirituality assumes primacy in a particular Christian domination as is the case in Roman Catholicism the changes introduced by the Pharisaic movement, particularly its emphasis on the meal setting for basic ritual, take on central importance. If we wish to understand eucharistic spirituality today, especially in light of the liturgical reforms of the Second Vatican Council, the emergence of that spirituality out of Jesus' involvement in Pharisaic ritual becomes crucial. It helps to resolve the controversial issue of whether the Eucharist should be interpreted and structured more as a meal rather than a sacrifice (Pawlikowski 1989; Meier 2001).

What the 'parting of the ways' scholarship, including its strong emphasis on Jesus' fundamental Jewishness which has now become commonplace, implies for Christian Spirituality is the recognition that any such spirituality must in principle see the Jewish tradition past and present as a fundamental building block. The late Pope John Paul II emphasized that when Christianity examines its soul there we find Judaism at its centre. So the development of an authentic Christian Spirituality in our time has to involve permanent links to Judaism as it was practiced in the time of Jesus and as it is conceived today. Judaism, as Pope John Paul II underlined, has a relationship with Christianity unlike any other religious tradition. Without denying differences between Judaism and Christianity in terms of theology and spiritual orientation, Judaism remains to a degree 'an is-in-house' resource for the church.

Contemporary scholarship has made it quite clear that Jesus, rather than opposing Judaism as was the commonplace view in the church for centuries, actually significantly depended in a positive sense on important parts of the Jewish tradition. The prophet Isaiah, for example, was deeply influential on Jesus' personal spirituality and public preaching. This reality certainly challenges Christians today to follow suit even if in somewhat different ways. The strong emphasis by contemporary scholars on Jesus' positive appropriation of the Jewish tradition forces a major transformation both in theology and spirituality. The Jewish tradition must now stand front and centre in any formulation of both by present-day Christians.

Genesis and Ecology

Another area where there is the new sense of a deeply rooted linkage to Judaism within the church is with regard to the ecological. The sacredness of land has always been a much stronger theme in Jewish Spirituality than has generally been true for Christianity. Understanding the Jewish tradition with respect to ecology can help rescue key biblical texts from Genesis which some in the ecological movement have branded as hostile. I speak especially of early leaders of the ecological movement such as Professor Lynn White of UCLA and those groups that deliberately selected a pagan religious symbol (the inverted 'e') as the symbol of the ecological movement.

Traditional Jewish commentary is particularly important in 'rescuing' the Genesis creation texts from the kind of misinterpretation that Lynn White and the early leaders in the ecological movement correctly denounced. Now that the two most recent Popes (but Benedict XVI in particular), have joined the Ecumenical Patriarch Bartholomew in identifying ecological concern as a core element in contemporary Christian Spirituality it becomes especially imperative to clarify the actual meaning of the Genesis texts over against the one-sided interpretation given to them in the initial period of the ecological movement, an interpretation that still persists in certain quarters today. These biblical texts need to undergird a creationist spirituality and a study of how they have been understood in Jewish tradition will prove immensely helpful in restoring their positive sense.

Jeremy Cohen, in a thorough study of how Gen. 1.28 was read and exegeted in both Jewish and Christian commentaries over the centuries points out that the post-Reformation negative perspective on this passage and the other creation texts found in Genesis proceeded from a:

> Flawed methodology. Scholars simply assumed that their own understanding of the verse matched that of the author, that this understanding characterized Jewish and Christian readers of the Bible

throughout the intervening centuries . . . Hence it was perfectly permissible to link the verse directly to social and scientific tendencies of our own day and age. (Cohen 1989)

My late colleague at Catholic Theological Union, Hayim Perelmuter, reminded us of a central statement in Deut. 20.9–20 which he argued had to be included in any discussion of the authentic meaning of the Genesis creation narratives. That statement reads as follows:

When in your war against a city you have to besiege it a long time in order to capture it, you must not destroy the trees wielding the axe against them. You may eat them but you must not cut them down. Any crusading ecologist would enthusiastically seize upon this verse. (Perelmuter 1994)

The rabbinic tradition made the above text from Deuteronomy a central part of its biblical vision and spirituality. They extended the prohibition of cutting trees to all wanton acts of destruction (B. Kiddushin 32a), whether in times of war or periods of peace. In this context Jewish ethicist Robert Gordis has emphasized that any destruction of food or vessels is a clear violation of the *bal tashit* ('you may not destroy'), a central principle in the rabbinic tradition (Gordis 1986).

This principle is rooted in the clear recognition that what we often mistakenly regard as 'our property' in the last analysis really belongs to God. The rabbinic tradition is consistent in emphasizing that the Bible, while showing great respect for the human person, should not be seen as person-centred in any exclusive way. The human community in the Hebrew Scriptures is never presented as a colossus who is free to do whatever it wills with the rest of creation. There is absolutely no mandate for exploitation of creation by the human community in any part of the Bible including the Genesis texts critiqued by Lynn White and the early ecologists. The 'image of God' in men and women does not transform us into God-like beings. Rather it confers upon all humanity a fundamental obligation to hallow and preserve the creation that surrounds it. Ecological preservation thus falls within the important ethical category of *miztvah*, a divine command to humans. Perelmuter refers to ecological preservation as a 'supreme miztvah' for Judaism for both religious communities.

Other examples can be found in rabbinic commentaries of the Hebrew Scriptures which help contextualize the creation narratives in Genesis in terms of human responsibility. One such discussion concerns animal sacrifice as part of divine worship. We hear in Lev. 22.28 that 'no animal from the herd or from the flock shall be slaughtered with its young.' While a committed vegetarian might object to any killing of animals for food, the commentary by Nachmanides on this text from Leviticus surfaces an overall principle that both vegetarians and non-vegetarians can endorse. Nachmanides argues that 'Scripture will not permit a destructive act that will bring about the extinction of a species, even though it has permitted the ritual slaughter of that animal for food' (Perelmuter 1994). Clearly the vision of the commentary moves in the direction of ecological responsibility.

Two Jewish scholars from the modern era, Samson Raphael Hirsch and Umberto Cassuto, further corroborate this classical Jewish perspective. Hirsch, a giant among nineteenth-century Jewish scholars, insisted that the prohibition of purposeless destruction of fruit trees around a besieged city is only to be taken as an example of general wastefulness. Under the concept of *bal tashhit* ('do not destroy') spoken of above, the purposeless destruction of anything at all is taken to be forbidden. As a result, these various rabbinic commentaries rooted in the Scriptures become comprehensive warnings to human beings not to misuse the leadership position God has given them in terms of the governance of creation (Pelkowitz 1976). According to Cassuto,

> Legal cases recorded in the Torah . . . show important points in which Israel's conduct was to be different and superior to their contemporaries in this regard to emphasize the importance of the protection of the environment in a civilization where such considerations were not accepted. (Freudenstein 1970)

An analysis of the Jewish liturgical tradition will yield similar results to the rabbinic commentaries. The major festivals all show a definite ecological bent.

Now that Christian leaders such as the Ecumenical Patriarch Bartholomew and Pope Benedict XVI have situated ecological concern at the centre of Christian Spirituality the Christian and Jewish traditions can become a mutually enriching source for both religious communities. Christians will need to repudiate decisively the misinterpretation of the Genesis creation text by many members of the church throughout the ages. And with the help of the Jewish rabbinic commentaries and understanding of the Jewish liturgical tradition, they can in fact see these texts as a basic foundation for Christian Spirituality today and undercut the exaggerated interpretation of them by Lynn White and company.[2]

The Turn Towards History

Another area where the Jewish tradition can prove helpful for contemporary Christian Spirituality is the historical anchor it brings to the development of such spirituality. There is no question that Christian Spirituality in the past sometimes fled from history and created the impression that spirituality only has to do with the world beyond. No one would deny that there is, and must be, a transcendental dimension to prayer and liturgy but there is also a serious need to connect them with the world around us.

Christian scholars such as David Tracy and Rebecca Chopp have spoken of 'a turn towards history' as a major feature of contemporary Christian theology. By connecting with the Jewish spiritual and liturgical sources as part of the inherent Christian bonding with Judaism, members of the church can avoid the temptation to 'flee from history' in their personal prayer and in the liturgical celebrations of the church year. The presence of the 'flight from history' can generate a pessimistic spirituality that has dangerous implications for the Christian presence in the world. As the Austrian Catholic philosopher Friedrich Heer once wrote after the Second World War, such an approach to spirituality can undergird support for Nazi ideology and for nuclear destruction. Heer remained convinced that only a return by Christianity to the biblical roots of the Hebrew Scriptures can cure this dangerous tendency that has afflicted Christian consciousness on more than one occasion in the church's history (Heer 1970).

Mysticism

Another area that has not received much attention in the Christian-Jewish dialogue is that of the two respective mystical traditions though a few scholars from each community such as Bernard McGinn of the University of Chicago and Moshel Idel of the Hebrew University in Jerusalem have interacted on this topic. The Jewish mystical tradition which flourished in such places in Safed (now in Israel), Spain and Poland is not well known in Christianity nor for that matter in contemporary Judaism. As spirituality over against institutionalized religious practice has risen in both communities, a growing interest has in fact developed of late, one that certainly has significant positive potential for Christian Spirituality in particular. Bernard McGinn, for one, has tried to draw out such potential (McGinn 1996 and see chapter above).

Classical Christianity and Judaism have both experienced the need on occasion to reassert a transcendental connection between the human person and the Creator God. Trying to reach this goal often involved thinking 'outside the box' as contemporary parlance would put it. But as we examine the mystical traditions of both religious communities we tend to see an important difference, at least in degree. The Jewish mystical tradition has never sought to bind itself permanently to the transcendental realm whereas in Christian mysticism one sometimes encounters this temptation. For Christian Spirituality permanent divine contemplation without any interference with worldly activities was often presented as the ideal for Christians even though it was recognized that only a select few members of the church would ever hope to achieve such mystical union on a permanent basis. For the Jewish mystical tradition, on the contrary, the 'return' to the world was as crucial as the experience of divine union. As Rabbi Nachman put it, 'with us, the problem is not the r'tzo, the going out, but the *shuv*, the return' (Weiner 1969). In saying this Rabbi Nachman put his finger on a central characteristic of Jewish mysticism, a characteristic that carries an important lesson for Christian mysticism. Here is another area where the church's renewed sense of bonding with Judaism can indeed make an important contribution for a sense of authentic balance in the practice of Christian Spirituality.

In Judaism there is a genuine concern that the mystical experience not degenerate into vague emotions and visions. Rather, experience must become the foundation for active celebration of the more formal Jewish ritual as well as the performance of *mitzvahs*, good deeds, in history. This emphasis has on occasion given the impression that Judaism did not have strong interest in spiritual depth but only 'this worldly' activities. While this has been a danger in Judaism overall, its mystical tradition on the whole aimed at tying heaven to earth. In the light of the Second Vatican Council, particularly its declaration *Gaudium et Spes* on the church in the modern world, this would now seem to be an upfront goal in the church as well. A serious study of the Jewish mystical tradition's struggle to meet this goal can benefit the same necessary effort in Christianity where its continued use of the mystical tradition must also exhibit a serious preoccupation with 'the return'.

One Hassidic mystical writer in Judaism phrased the ideal of Jewish mysticism in the following striking image: 'Not the transient upshot of a straw flame but the well-cooked heart' (Weiner 1969). And a modern Jewish commentator on the value of the Jewish mystical tradition Rabbi Herbert Weiner puts it this way:

> Not only a way of going out but a tested and quite effective system of return. A way from preventing the ecstatic flame from consuming the soul. A way of using every high so that it lifted the lows. The desire to tie heaven to earth is not, to be sure, an exclusively Jewish goal, but the stubbornness, energy and measure of success which accompanied this attempted unification in Judaism is perhaps singular in the history of religions. Its secrets, in an age which as seen in the bankruptcy of so many attempts to balance spirit and flesh, its exits and reentries, would seem worthy of serious consideration. (Weiner 1969)

Conclusion

As I bring to a close this discussion regarding Judaism and Christian Spirituality I should mention the issue of the Christian Liturgy. For a number of Christian denominations, especially the Orthodox, Roman Catholic and Anglican, the liturgy should be the primal source of growth. Recent scholarship has shown that early Christian worship owed much to the Jewish ritual of its day.[3] This understanding becomes vital for authentic reform of Christian eucharistic celebrations. Understanding the Jewish basis of early Christian Liturgy, including the liturgical practice of Jesus himself who clearly remained within the Jewish community of his time, can prove extremely valuable in the process of cleansing liturgical celebration from unnecessary and unhelpful accretions over the centuries (Tracey 2011). And insofar as I have identified creational spirituality as central for Christian Spirituality today, contact with Jewish tradition can help restore a creational element to the Christian Liturgy. Unfortunately a by-product of Vatican II reforms has been the virtual elimination of such a creational element, something that stands, as I have indicated above, at the heart of Jewish Liturgy.

Hopefully the preceding analysis will reveal the potential significance of reflecting on Christian Spirituality in the light of Jewish spiritual tradition. This may in fact be the primary benefit of the new encounter between Jews and Christians engendered by the Second Vatican Council's *Nostra Aetate* and similar documents in various Protestant churches.

Notes

1 The Anglican Lectionary does offer optional readings from the Hebrew Scriptures.
2 For more on this debate see the chapter below 'Christian Spirituality and Creation'.
3 See opening chapter of this volume.

Bibliography and Further Reading

Cohen, Jeremy (1989), *Be Fertile, and Increase, Fill the Earth and Master It*. Ithaca, NY: Cornell University Press.

Frankfurter, David (2003), 'Beyond "Jewish Christianity": Continuing Religious Subcultures of the Second and Third Centuries and Their Documents', in Adam H. Becker and Annette Yoshiko Reed (eds), *Ways that Never Parted. Jews and Christians in Late Antiquity and the Early Middle Ages*. Texts and Studies in Judaism #95. Tubingen, Germany: Mohr Siebeck.

Freudenstein, Eric G. (Fall 1970), 'Ecology and the Jewish Tradition', *Judaism and Human Rights*, ed. M. R. Konvitz, New York: Norton, pp. 265–74.

Gordis, Robert (1986), *Judaic Ethics for a Flawless World*. New York: Jewish Theological Seminary.

Heer, Freidrich (1970), *God's First Love: Christians and Jews Over Two Thousand Years*. New York: Weybright and Talley.

Holmgren, Fredrick C. and Schaalman, Sherman (eds) (1995), *Preaching Biblical Texts: Expositions by Jewish and Christian Scholars*. Grand Rapids, MI: William B. Eerdmans.

McGinn, Bernard (1996), *Mystical Union in Judaism, Christianity and Islam*. London and New York: Continuum.

Meier, John P. (2001), *A Marginal Jew: Rethinking the Historical Jesus. Volume 3: Companions and Competitors*. New York: Doubleday.

Noth, Martin (1966), *The Laws in the Pentateuch and Other Studies*. Edinburgh: Oliver and Boyd.

Pawlikowski, John (2001), *Christ in the Light of Christian-Jewish Dialogue*. Eugene, OR: Wipf and Stock (2nd edn).

Pelkowitz, Ralph (1976), *Danger and Opportunity*. New York: Shengold.

Perelmuter, Hayim G. (1994), 'Do Not Destroy – Ecology in the Fabric of Judaism', in Richard N. Fragomeni and John T. Pawlikowski (eds), *The Ecological Challenge: Ethical, Liturgical and Spiritual Responses*. Collegeville: Liturgical Press.

Saldarini, Anthony J. (1996), 'Jews and Christians in the First Two Centuries: The Changing Paradigm'. *SHOFAR*, 10.

— (1999) 'Christian Anti-Judaism: The First Century Speaks to the Twenty-First Century'. The Joseph Cardinal Bernardin Jerusalem Lecture. Chicago: Archdiocese of Chicago, The American Jewish Committee, Spertus Institute of Jewish Studies and the Jewish United Fund/Jewish Community Relations Council.

Scroggs, Robin (1986), 'The Judaizing of the New Testament', The *Chicago Theological Seminary Register*, 75 (1).

Sherman, Franklin (ed.) (2011), *Bridges: Documents of the Christian-Jewish Dialogue*. Volume One: The Road to Reconciliation (1945–85). New York: Paulist Press.

Tracey, Liam OSM (2011), 'The Affirmation of Jewish Covenantal Vitality and the Church's Liturgical Life', in Cunningham, Philip et al. (eds), *Christ Jesus and the Jewish People Today: New Explorations of Theological Interrelationships*. Grand Rapids, MI and Cambridge, UK: W. B. Eerdmans.

Weiner, Herbert (1969), *9 and a Half Mystics: The Kabbala Today*. New York, Chicago and San Francisco: Holt, Rinehart and Winston.

22 Christian Spirituality and Islam

Christian Troll

Islam

The word 'Islam' is derived from the Arabic verbal noun *islām*. It indicates the act of submission or surrender to the sovereignty of the one God and his will (see Qur'an 2: 130–2). 'Islam' with a capital 'I', however, normally today designates the socially defined religion of which the Qur'an is the foundational text and Muhammad the prophet.[1]

Currently, in many parts of the world, public discussion of Islam is dominated by political aspects and even by concern with forms of Islamic political extremism. In this situation it is of great importance not to lose sight of the fact that Islam, although in its multidimensional totality it encompasses religious, cultural and political elements, in the first place is a religious phenomenon. None of its various dimensions can be appreciated properly without taking into account the act of faithful submission to the one, transcendent God who has revealed his will in the Qur'an. This personal act of faith forms indeed the kernel of Islam and is its distinctive and pervasive feature.

God is the first and fundamental object of Muslim belief and, ultimately, its only one. In other words, Islam is radically centred upon God. Muhammad figures as its second object, since he was sent to convey the authentic and final revelation of God's guidance. The total ordering of the human being towards God expresses itself in the attitudes of adoration, submission to his will and respect of the 'rights of God'. The Muslim is first and foremost a servant-worshipper, *'abd*, and Muhammad is precisely in this regard 'an excellent model' (Qur'an 33: 21) for the believers. Obedience in faith is essential for Muslims, so that their actions may be in total correspondence with the will of God.[2]

One cannot fail to notice evidence of a strong faith in God in the lives of Muslims as well as in Muslim societies. One is also struck, and at times shocked, by the all-encompassing nature of their faith commitment. The faith of contemporary Christians, on the other hand, would seem to be characterized by more questioning and searching. Christians and Muslims would do well to cherish both the certitude of faith, which is a gift of God received in prayer and humility, and the need for faith to grow and mature by ever new questions of a theological nature.[3]

Islam is one of the great religions of the world. For more than fourteen hundred years the Islamic faith and the values anchored in it have enabled countless people to lead a life rich in human and religious terms and to find meaningful answers to life's deepest questions.

On the normative level two basic features of Islam are of outstanding and lasting significance. On the one hand the foundational scripture of Islam, the Qur'an, which according to Islamic faith is the word of God himself, and on the other the life and teaching of Muhammad, the founder. Both the Qur'an and the body of Islamic custom and practice based on Muhammad's words and deeds, called the *sunna*, from the beginning and throughout the centuries, have been interpreted in very different historical and regional contexts leading to a great deal of variation. Both Qur'an and *sunna* have profoundly shaped Muslim belief and life throughout the centuries.

It is well known that the career of the Prophet as well as the 114 suras of the Qur'an belong to two distinct periods, the Mekkan (610–22) and the Medinan. They are united, and at the same time divided, by the *Hijra*, that is the emigration or flight of Muhammad and his small community of believers from Mecca to Medina. In Mecca Muhammad preaches the message, warns people of the imminent Judgment Day and asks them to convert to One God serving him alone. In Medina, the Prophet in obedience to God's call effectively translates the revealed message into reality by all the diplomatic, political and military means at his disposal. Here Muhammad knows himself commanded by God not only to preach the doctrine of the one God and of His divinely revealed will (which later finds its binding expression in the jurisprudential development of a comprehensive corpus of laws, the *shari 'a*) but also to give it through the rule of the Muslim community (*umma muslima*) political authority and supremacy.

Historically speaking Islam has found expression in the most diverse local and regional cultures, their customs, legal concepts and life worlds. Thus, in the course of time, a new and broad range of local and regional variations of Muslim life have formed. In this process frequent compromises were made with regard to the practical application of the *shari 'a*. In other words, besides the corpus of laws held in faith to be revealed because they are deduced from the divine commands of Qur'an and *sunna*, in some areas the local customary law was also in force.

When we look at Islam as a whole we can make out, roughly speaking, three main currents:

- a cultural, moderate Islam of the middle way;
- an Islamist (or fundamentalist) Islam focused on the text;
- an Islam undergoing radical interpretation according to the spirit of the text.

Two further, relevant distinctions within the total reality of Islam should be mentioned here. First, there is the division between Sunnis and Shi'ites, but each of these two major traditions is further subdivided into many other groups. Second, there is the inner or mystical dimension of Islam, also designated by the term Sufism. By this is indicated the 'inner' path (*tariqa*) of Islam – complementary to the 'outer' path, indicated by the *shari'a* – which in its countless expressions in ritual and teaching has led ever anew to an interiorization of Muslim believing and acting, guided throughout by the exemplary life of the prophet as well as by the 'friends of God' (*awliya' Allah*). All Muslims in their teaching and life to this day remain shaped, more or less strongly and in diverse ways, by this inner, 'spiritual' dimension of Islam.

Spirituality

The use of the term 'spirituality' is notoriously vague and far from precise. In a wide sense, regarding all monotheistic religions, the term spirituality indicates 'the comprehensive act of faith in response to the experience of the saving reality of God' (E. Heyen).[4] In other words, it indicates the basic attitude on the part of the believer of living submission to God and His cause. Etymologically speaking, the noun 'spirituality' is derived from the New Testament term *pneumatikós* ('gifted with the Holy Spirit') and thus qualifies Christian life as a life in and out of the Holy Spirit. 'Since spirituality puts the accent on the concrete realization of the faith, it constitutes a multiform reality just as human life and the relations of the human with God are multiform' (G. Greshake).[5]

Consequently, in this chapter we do not intend to depict the history, or only certain phases of the history, of Muslim Spirituality,[6] trying thus to show, how – either with regard to ritual or to doctrinal accentuations – the shape of lived Muslim faith in the course of the centuries has been modified as a result of the encounter with Christian believers and their faith and practice. Also, we are not going to try to offer a succinct summary of the history of the encounter of Christian Spirituality with Islam,[7] nor do we intend to demonstrate to which particular forms and accentuations in Christian Spirituality this encounter has led.[8] Rather, we shall try to indicate succinctly which aspects of Christian Spirituality are likely to gain special relevance in the worldwide encounter of Christians with Muslims today.

Basic Features of a Christian Spirituality in Encounter with Islam Today

A Challenge that Cannot be Evaded

The Second Vatican Council (1962–5) was marked significantly by the consciousness of the Church being called to be attentive to the 'signs of the times'. The new global presence of Islam and of Christianity and, in consequence, the encounter of Christians and Muslims in almost all parts of the contemporary world, including those traditionally shaped by the Christian tradition, constitute a development that calls believing Christians to a renewal of their faith and to a Gospel-inspired spiritual attitude towards Muslims and Islam. Muslims and their Islam not only question Christian faith and life but question them radically.

More than 1 billion people profess Islam worldwide, and their number grows steadily. This is a fact that cannot leave Christians untouched. The spectacular expansion of Islam consequently concerns the Christian spiritually. Each Muslim who does not explicitly negate Islam as religion, professes faith in the One God, Creator and Judge, Almighty and All-Merciful. Christians, who in faith also relate to the One God, are spiritually challenged to relate in one way or other to the Muslims as fellow believers in God and to understand them and their societies with an open heart and critical mind.

Openness and Willingness to Know and to Understand

If Christians take their faith seriously and therefore strive for the ideal that every one of their thoughts and acts should be shaped by the love of the one, who is 'the Way, the Truth and the Life' (Jn 14.6), then they are challenged first of all to get to know and to understand the witness of Muslims. The ruling principle of any Christian believer in approaching Islam follows from the Golden Rule, as expressed by Jesus in the Sermon on the Mount (Mt. 7.12). This principle of ethical behaviour states that we should do to others as we would have others do to us. This would seem to include the demand: try to understand Muslims, and to describe Islam, as you would like Muslims to understand Christians and to describe Christianity. Hence, in describing Islam, Christians are asked to present its ideals and standards, its history and development while holding as closely as possible to the way in which Muslims themselves describe it. That is the way Christians would like Muslims to present the Christian faith when they have occasion to describe it. We would be disappointed, if Muslims chose to dwell on some of the petty and unworthy aspects of the Church's history. We would consider it best for Muslims to describe Christianity in terms of the highest and noblest ideals, the way it wants to be known to the world. Thus it is essential for Christians who wish to establish relationships with Muslims and develop dialogue with them to gain an understanding of the type of Islamic outlook held by

Muslims. This means encountering the Muslims themselves, listening to them and also studying the programmes and literature published and distributed by the mosque communities and the Islamic umbrella organizations. Christians should then, of course, analyse such information and try to assess it with an open and yet also critical mind, taking realistically into account the realities on the ground. Whether Christians live with Muslims, within Muslim majority societies or as members of a Christian minority that shares national life with Muslims in minority status or as members of a minority of immigrants in one of the Western secularized societies, in each case they are asked to be ready to know, understand and critically assess the situation in which their Muslim partners live and the ideals for which the different groups of Muslims strive.

Readiness to Encounter

However, real and deep knowledge of Muslims will not be possible without readiness to encounter the Muslim neighbour in person, taking real interest in him, as an individual and as member of a collective. The Christian will have to make a serious effort to overcome the inner and outer hindrances to such encounter.

Muslims and Christians live in a great variety of different social constellations and normally today they live together with non-believing citizens or at least with citizens alienated from organized religion. As believers in God and adherents of a religion they share the divine call to co-shape and to promote the common good of their societies. They are thus spiritually challenged to develop and foster societal dialogue without which harmonious and just living together (*convivencía*) cannot be achieved and maintained. Such dialogue and collaboration implies Christian respect of Muslims in their distinctiveness and otherness, eschewing contempt or violence in any of its forms.

Need for a Properly Critical Analysis

However, the considerable differences in Christian and Muslim outlook and practice in no way are to be denied or disguised. Christians (as well as Muslims) in any given situation, and especially in situations of tension, will be tempted in two ways: either to deny reality and its frequently complex and harsh face, painting a rosy picture or to give in to the temptation of exaggerating, generalizing, employing inflationary, popular terms and also of failing to distinguish between, say, vexation, discrimination, mobbing, injustice and persecution.[9] Courage and intelligence are needed in the effort of identifying the concrete problems, analysing them and thus preparing lasting solutions. To isolate the religious factor from the concrete context and thus from all the various social, psychological and possible further elements that may play a role in a given situation, falsifies the picture and renders difficult finding adequate solutions. The objective should be to arrive at a view that focuses on complementarity rather than on oppositeness.

The Basic Spiritual Quality Needed: Inner Freedom

The relationship of Christians to Muslims is often marked either by an almost passionate sympathy that lacks differentiation – and can be bitterly disappointed when confronted with fact and reality – or by a fierce, unqualified rejection that does not see anything good in the Muslims and/or in Islam. The spiritual quality of inner freedom is of capital importance here. It will make the person willing and able to enter a shared process of reflection and exchange that can lead to the healing of memories (a psychological as well as spiritual process) by which the person experiences the personal love of God as liberating from resentment and rejection. The healing of the memory facilitates an unobstructed view of the other and opens the heart to accept the person who has done the hurt.[10]

Such spiritual freedom also will enable the person to understand the religious convictions and traditions of the other with a positive presupposition. To give the other person, in our case the Muslim, such a positive 'benefit of the doubt' would seem to be the essential condition of a successful relationship. The famous 'presupposition', formulated by Ignatius of Loyola right at the beginning of the Spiritual Exercises (n. 22) with the aim of assuring 'that both he who is giving the Spiritual Exercises, and he who is receiving them, may more help and benefit themselves',[11] very much also applies to Christian-Muslim relations. Ignatius considers such a presupposition the necessary condition of the success of the spiritual retreat. At the same time he states that a positive presupposition should characterize all human relations. As long as we do not have proof of the contrary, we should be ready to put a good interpretation on another's statement rather than condemning it as false. If an orthodox interpretation cannot be put on a proposition, the one who made it should be asked how he understands it, and if possible misunderstanding has occurred, it should be cleared up with Christian understanding. So, too, if actual error seems to be held, the best possible interpretation should be presented so that a more correct understanding might develop. Anyway, what is of central importance here is the ability to recognize the facts instead of basing oneself on mere suppositions.

Considering One Another Sisters and Brothers in God

In so far as the faith of the believer in God is a real personal act and not simply a social inheritance taken on without thinking, and provided that, and in so far as, Christians and Muslims seek to live their relationship with God out of deepest conscience, they can also be together where they are different. This can be said because, and in so far as, they believe in the one God, and in this belief perceive the mystery presented by each person's journey with God. In this understanding Christians and Muslims are brothers and sisters in God. Thus Blessed John Paul II said to the Muslim representatives in Davao in the Philippines on 20 February 1981:

> I deliberately address you as brothers . . . we are especially brothers in God, who created us and whom we are trying to reach, in our own ways, through faith, prayer and worship, through the keeping of his law and through submission to his designs.[12]

In other words, real and profound differences in faith do not have to mean absolute separation as we stand together before God. Of course, if talking about God turns out to be a tournament or a battlefield, so to speak, very soon there is the danger of no longer talking about the living God who is, for all of us, first of all ineffable mystery. The mystery invites us: not to eschew understanding, but to surpass what understanding can reach with its own power. Mystery is given through grace, through disinterested love. The mystery of divine love is in fact the real mystery, into which we enter by gift. It invites us to build a community of life with God Himself, which transcends every human idea about community and relationship.

In Christian faith Jesus Christ opens to us and shares with us the mystery of this love 'to the end'; better, 'to completion' (Jn 13.1). The mystery of God's triune life invites us to share in the divine life – a life of connectedness and endless love – in which the unity itself is the absolute unity of absolute love.

Muslims, following the Qur'an and their whole religious tradition, constantly emphasize that it is not given to the human being to enter into the intimate life of God; the human being is not allowed to fathom the 'inner' life of the divine Being. However, the area in which Muslims come nearest to the mystery of God is undoubtedly where they try to follow God's unsearchable will according to the model of Abraham. The Abraham of the Qur'an was ready at God's command to sacrifice his own son, without being able humanly to understand God's decision in any way. Through his submission and dedication, supported by believing trust, Abraham became the absolute model of the Muslim.

Obligation to Dialogue – Obligation to Prayer[13]

Islam and Christianity differ with regard both to attitudes in prayer and in content of prayer. From this it is understandable that Christian and Muslim prayer are not the same or interchangeable. This difference is to be respected. However, it is certainly true that along with the possibility of an encounter in faith in the one living God there is also the possibility of such encounter in prayer. Further, the obligation of Muslims and Christians to recognize one another before the one Creator and Judge, to share with one another and, in short, to encounter one another in dialogue, is constantly likely to evoke the desire and perhaps to arouse awareness of the obligation – precisely in a world which largely forgets God – to witness to this common task: glorifying together before God and constantly asking God for help to know our common responsibility.

It is no easy matter to hold the two ends of this paradox together somehow – the difference in views in faith and attitudes to prayer, on the one hand, and the commitment to encounter one another in prayer on the other. But simply to make a contradiction out of this tension and paradox is inadmissible and highly damaging. This is even more true today as the predominant tendency is to present Islam and Christianity as fundamentally opposed to one another, even as completely and essentially in conflict with one another.

Spiritually it seems of central importance that Christians desire encounter with Muslims before God and in prayer. No difficulty should prevent Christians from knowing themselves to be responsible before God jointly and mutually with Muslims. Nor should anything prevent them from finding themselves together – wherever there are meaningful opportunities – for common supplication of God, for praise of the one whom both faith-communities confess as their Creator, Preserver and Judge, by whom they know themselves called in common responsibility.

Notes

1 For a sensitive, basic introduction to Islam see C. T. R. Hewer (2006), *Understanding Islam. The First Ten Steps.* London: SCM Press.
2 Christian W. Troll (2011), 'Catholicism and Islam' in Gavin D'Costa (ed.), *The Catholic Church and the World Religions. A Theological and Phenomenological Account.* London/New York: T&T Clark International, p. 72.
3 Ibid., p. 93.
4 E. Heyen (1987), art. 'Spiritualität 2. Christlich', in Adel Theodore Khoury (ed.), *Lexikon religiöser Grundbegriffe. Judentum, Christentum, Islam.* Graz/Wien, Köln: Styria, S. 997.
5 G. Greshake (1988), quoted in Christian Schütz, 'Spiritualität, Christliche Spiritualität', in Christian Schütz (ed.), *Praktisches Lexikon der Spiritualität.* Freiburg: Herder, S. 1170f.
6 See C. E. Padwick, *Muslim Devotions. A Study of Prayer-Manuals in Common Use.* London: SPCK, 1961; A. Schimmel (1975), *Mystical Dimensions of Islam.* Chapel Hill: University of North Carolina Press; S. H. Nasr (ed.) (1987), *Islamic Spirituality. Foundations.* London: Routledge & Kegan Paul; J. Renard (ed.) (1998), *Windows on the House of Islam. Muslim Sources on Spirituality and Religious Life.* Berkeley/Los Angeles/London: University of California Press.
7 See J. M. Gaudeul (2000), *Encounters & Clashes. Islam and Christianity in History.* I. Survey; II. Texts. Rome: Pontificio Istituto di Studi Arabi e d'Islamistica; H. Goddard

(2000), *A History of Christian-Muslim Relations*. Edinburgh: Edinburgh University Press.

8   Ali Merad (1999), *Christian Hermit in an Islamic World. A Muslim's View of Charles de Foucauld*. New York/Mahwah, N. J. Paulist Press; M. Borrmans (2009), *Prophètes du dialogue islamo-chrétien. Louis Massignon, Jean-Mohammed Abd-el-Jalil, Louis Gardet, Georges Anawati*. Paris: Cerf.

9   Christian van Nispen tot Sevenaer (2004), *Chrétiens & musulmans frères devant Dieu?* Paris: Les Éditions de l'Atelier, p. 111. On a number of points we follow here this remarkable work.

10 Ibid., p. 115.

11 David Fleming, S. J. (1978), *The Spiritual Exercises of St. Ignatius. A Literal Translation and a Contemporary Reading*. St. Louis, Missouri: The Institute of Jesuit Sources, p. 20.

12 *Interreligious Dialogue: The Official Teaching of the Catholic Church from the Second Vatican Council to John Paul II (1963–1995)*. ed. F. Gioia. Boston: Pauline Books and Media, 1997, n. 363.

13 The following paragraphs take up with light modifications passages of the following essay: Christian W. Troll, 'Can Christians and Muslims Pray Together?' in *The Way* (Oxford), January 2011, pp. 53–70, here esp. pp. 66, 70.

Bibliography and Further Reading

Nasr, S. H. (ed.) (1987), *Islamic Spirituality. Foundations*. London: Routledge & Kegan Paul.

Padwick, C. E. (1961), *Muslim Devotions. A Study of Prayer-Manuals in Common Use*. London: SPCK.

Pontifical Council for Interreligious Dialogue (1990), *Guidelines for Dialogue between Christians and Muslims*, prepared by M. Borrmans. Trans. from French original (publ. 1981) by R. Marston Speight. New York: Paulist Press.

Renard, J. (ed.) (1998), *Windows on the House of Islam. Muslim Sources on Spirituality and Religious Life*. Berkeley, Los Angeles and London: University of California Press.

Schimmel, A. (1975), *Mystical Dimensions of Islam*. Chapel Hill: University of North Carolina Press.

Troll, Christian W. (2005), *Muslims Ask*, Christians Answer. Anand (India): Gujarati Sahitya Prakash (U.S. American edition [2012]: New City Press, Hyde Park, NY 12538). See online version: www.answers-to-muslims.com

— (2011) 'Can Christians and Muslims pray together?' in: *The Way* (Oxford), January 2011.

Part V
Christian and Indigenous Spiritualities

23 Christian Spirituality in Africa: African Traditional Religion and the Spirituality of the African Initiated Churches

Celia Kourie

Introduction

The vast continent of Africa, the spirituality of which predates history, is rich in its diversity of peoples, customs, language and religion. Its powerful spiritual heritage is reflected in many spiritualities and multiple religious traditions, including African Traditional Religion, Hinduism, Buddhism, Christianity and Islam. While acknowledging the vast array of ethnic groups, each with their own spirituality, particular customs, beliefs, practices, this chapter will attempt to elucidate various general themes that are held in common, first with respect to *African Traditional Religion*, and second, in the analysis of the *African Initiated Churches*, the particular area of investigation for this study.[1]

Concerning the nature of spirituality in the wider sense, it refers to the deepest dimension of the human person, and the meanings and values to which s/he ascribes. These values can be religious or secular, 'Spirituality is not restricted to any one religion, but can be found variously in all religions and cultures. It is determined in the first place by the basic worldview of the persons . . . concerned. It is also shaped by their life context, their history, and the various influences that enter a people's life.'[2] This is particularly true with respect to African Spirituality, due to the vast changes that have taken place on the African continent, especially during the twentieth century. Historical, political, geographical, linguistic, sociological, religious and other changes, including urbanization, have impacted upon Africa, effecting modification of former traditional ways of life, and bringing new configurations to the spiritual and religious traditions of the continent. Thus, 'African Spirituality (refers) to the way African people have undertaken to view and understand the physical and spiritual world around them. This understanding will incorporate a socio-cultural, philosophical, political and religious setting of African people'.[3] This statement applies equally to African Christian Spirituality, as will be seen later in this chapter. In order to understand the latter, a brief survey of the spirituality of African Traditional Religion is now undertaken.[4]

The Spirituality of African Traditional Religion

It is not really possible to speak about African Traditional Religion in the singular, due to its cultural and religious heterogeneity. However, there are sufficient areas of similarity to enable a survey of the predominant themes. For present purposes, the following will be briefly considered: the *holistic nature* of African Spirituality; some *concepts* of the Divine; the role of the *Ancestors*; and the importance of *community*.

African Traditional Religion witnesses to the profound religious nature of the African people. As an oral religion, its myths, legends, proverbs, art, rites and symbols illustrate the fact that the Divine permeates all of reality: there is no bifurcation of the sacred and the secular – each and every aspect of life is saturated with God's presence. The interpenetration of the sacred into daily life results in the interrelatedness of religion, culture and society.[5] As a result, the sense of the mysterious prevails. 'The African experience of God is one in which the sacred and the profane tend to be symmetrical. The ordinary human experience is mimetic of the transcendent and the sacred.'[6] This can be seen as *mystical*, since it relates to 'an experience of the invisible world, which is distinct from that which concerns the visible world, although the one is not more "cognitive" or "emotional" than the other. It can even be said that the mystical life of an African is based on a more cognitive experience than that which underlies the ordinary and practical life'.[7] Zahan makes the point that in Africa, one is not born a mystic, but rather becomes one; in this connection initiatory rites have an important role: 'One sees the human body as the starting point of religious and mystical feeling. . . . the body becomes, in a way, the authentic symbol of the elevation of the human being to the heights of spirituality. . . . the mystical in African religion does not remove the human being from the earth; on the contrary it allows him to live there again and again on an indefinite basis'.[8]

The deeply entrenched secularism and philosophical scepticism so prevalent in Western society, although present in some areas, particularly with the rise of urbanization and technological expertise, does not feature strongly in traditional African society. So on the whole, the negative elements of modernism have been rejected, and the positive elements of postmodernism have been welcomed:

Africa associates itself more freely with the post-modernist worldview, which is more open, incomplete, changing. . . . This world is not closed, and not merely basically substantive, but it has great depth, it is unlimited in its qualitative varieties, and is truly mysterious; this world is restless, a living and growing organism, always pregnant with new developments. . . . Action, event, and change are emphasized more than substance and fixity.[9]

African Spirituality is deeply existential; it impacts upon the totality of life. 'Belief in Africa is not an epistemological issue, not *fides* (belief) but rather *fiducia* (trust), a non-epistemological activity. It is not based on propositions but on relationships.'[10] The person in his/her totality is involved; it is a holistic approach, not merely cerebral, but encompasses mind, body and spirit.

The *Supreme Being* is the Great One, *Unkulunkulu* (Zulu, South Africa); *Mulungu* (Akamba, Kenya); *Olodumare* (Yoruba, Nigeria); *Molimo* (Basuto, Lesotho).[11] The divine is described in both masculine and feminine terms, for example, *Cuita dada*, Father, and *Ciuta mama*, Mother.[12] God inhabits the 'upper level' in African Spirituality, which indicates a certain 'distance' from humanity.[13] This does not prevent the depiction of God in anthropomorphic terms, as *Parent, Father, Mother, Grandfather, Friend,* etc.,[14] but 'the distancing of him is undoubtedly the most widespread and the most firmly rooted in the beliefs of Africa'.[15] Since direct access to the divine is not possible, intercession is made to the spirits and ancestors. 'God is only formally a *Deus Absconditus* but not existentially such. He reflects himself through various mediators who transfer His gifts to the human being, such as healing, well-being, and so on . . . the emphasis in the African traditional religion is on the relationship with the ancestors who are concerned with practical needs and on upholding the deep sense of community.'[16]

The *ancestors* (*ambuyafwi*)[17] are those who have passed through death, and become important members of the invisible world. They are the 'living-dead' and are held in high esteem; their customs, instructions, directives and wisdom are essential for those still living in this dimension. They are closer to God than those on earth, and they can intercede with the divine for the living. Intimately concerned with the happenings of the daily life of those whom they have left behind, they become models, guides and inspiration for the community, and can in fact be punitive if those still living do not adhere to the accepted way of living. Ancestors are invoked, particularly at important moments of life, both individual and community, via prayer, invocation, and often with offerings of food and drink. The ancestors, on their side, often communicate with the living via dreams, visions or strange happenings, which need interpretation by those qualified to do so.[18]

275

Community is central to African Spirituality. The newly born is immediately incorporated into the life of the family, the clan and the larger community. As he or she grows up, there is support and acceptance. A Zulu proverb power-fully expresses this reality: *Umuntu ngumuntu ngabantu: A person is a person through other persons.* Each one is dependent on the other/s; the interrelated-ness of all members of the community is paramount. Co-operation, instead of competition is emphasized, and the needs of the other become one's own. Participation in the community is practised, *inter alia*, by undergoing various rites of passage, for example, circumcision, marriage, etc. 'Unity, harmony, mutual respect, especially respect towards the elders, are virtues which the rites of passage seek to cultivate in a person . . . the community to which the African belongs . . . includes the ancestor world. Therefore, being-in-relation, belonging, represents the essential characteristics of being truly human.'[19] Traditional African religion considers ontological harmony to be particularly important: 'The ontology of classical Africa is basically anthropocentric. The person is the centre of existence – not as an individual, but as family, as com-munity.'[20] Consequently, moral and ethical values are of prime importance, and many of these values are the basis for traditional laws and customs.[21]

In the light of the foregoing, we will now consider certain aspects of African Christian Spirituality, with particular reference to the *African Initiated Churches*.

African Christian Spirituality

Without doubt, much of the early missionary activity on the continent (from the late fifteenth century to the middle of the twentieth century) did not recognize or appreciate African Traditional Religion or Spirituality. The rich heritage of the African peoples was generally regarded as 'sim-ply misguided and riddled with errors'.[22] Western missionaries encouraged Africans to abandon their 'primitive' and 'traditional' religion, in order to accept Christianity which was seen to be superior, and civilized. The under-valuation of the religious and cultural heritage of Africa, and the attempt to impose Western intellectual and cultural constructs led to a dire situation. Africans were torn between the new religion and their historical traditions.[23] Fortunately, such colonial approaches have not prevailed and appreciation for cultural diversity in Christianity has greatly increased.[24] This has resulted in a greater sensitivity to the existing spirituality of African peoples, and a more open approach to enculturation in the mainline churches. In addition to the latter, the spirituality of the *African Initiated Churches* deserves atten-tion, particularly with respect to its connections with African Traditional Religion.

The Spirituality of the African Initiated Churches

African *Independent*, or *Indigenous* churches, now more commonly known as *African Initiated Churches* are a break-away from the historic mission churches.[25] Since this break thousands of different AICs have arisen, with over 6,000 in South Africa alone. The major characteristic of these church communities is a 'spirituality that liberates us from dependence'.[26] The need for these Christian communities to experience a spirituality more in line with their African traditional beliefs and practices effected a new way of being African Christians. The structures, ideology and practice of many Western churches in Africa, and their imposition of these values on indigenous African communities are major reasons for the break-away of many members and the burgeoning of the AICs.[27]

African Initiated Churches (AICs) often gather in the open air for their worship services, and also in small dwellings and shacks in urban areas. This is not necessarily merely due to poverty, but more importantly, the deep-felt need for community and sharing in small-scale churches which reflect the extended family system.[28] Instead of retreating from the 'world', AIC spirituality '. . . develops in the congested urban areas where modern industrial stress is the order of the day. Small and overcrowded dwellings are the temples, monasteries and retreat houses for spiritual renewal and healing. It is here where hopelessness is transformed into the joy of living'.[29] The importance of *community* cannot be over-emphasized: the small communities offer support to each other, particularly to those migrating to the cities from the countryside, immigrants, the poor and the marginalized. Social and political issues are addressed in these communities, and efforts to help their members in the details of everyday life witness to the profound understanding of the true message of the Gospel, namely to love one's neighbour. Central to Jesus' message is liberation from 'social deprivation, materialism, disease and *cold, formalised worship*'.[30]

The ecumenical, Pentecostal, prophetic and apostolic nature of the AICs emphasizes the importance of the Holy Spirit in the proclamation of the Gospel. Healing services, visions, dreams, elaborate rituals, flexible modes of worship – all witness to a vibrant and spontaneous spirituality. Joyful dancing and singing characterize the liturgy. The wonderful aptitude for dance and rhythm so often prevented by early missionary 'zeal',[31] is clearly manifest in these church gatherings. This caring, joyful, healing spirituality is solace for many, and allows for freedom of expression and connection with the deeply rooted African religious spirit. Spiritual and physical healing services are common, accompanied by fervent and charismatic prayer, and a great compassion for those who are sick. The role of women in the healing ministry is pronounced, giving status to those who are denied this in several of the historic churches. In many instances, Jesus is seen as the Healer, the great

Ancestor, the Chief and the Liberator. The debate concerning inculturation continues at many levels, especially in the historic mainline churches.[32] Within the AICs themselves, certain practices are allowed in some of the churches, for example, polygamy, with recourse to the Biblical Patriarchs. Such adaptations vary within different communities. Although diverse practices take place in different communities, nevertheless, the underlying spirituality is of prime importance. 'It is incumbent upon the AICs to demonstrate that the multiplicity of denominations can be outlived by spirituality. In other words, spiritual experience and commitment are more important than denominations. The realm of spirituality is wide enough to allow complementary services.'[33]

Conclusion

African Traditional Religion exhibits a *holistic spirituality* which has been taken up *par excellence* by the members of African Initiated Churches. Remaining true to their African heritage, these communities exhibit a powerful *communitarian spirituality*, with care for one another as the primary constituent of their practice. As such, the social, psychological, spiritual and humanitarian care that is given to one another is a shining example of what *church* is meant to be: a community of those, who following the example of Jesus, manifest the warmth and love which is the heart of the Gospel message. This is particularly noticeable in the dynamic, spontaneous and joyful worship services of the AICs, not limited to Sunday services, but often taking place many times during the week. In such a manner, community ties are strengthened, and self-centred individualism is abrogated. In South Africa, in particular, given its painful history of apartheid, and its present challenges with respect to poverty, crime, unemployment, political corruption, secularization, etc., the AICs are instrumental in retrieving the values of *ubuntu* with its emphasis on solidarity, and interdependence. As a result, it can be argued that African Christian Spirituality, particularly as expressed in the African Initiated Churches, can be a catalyst for continual transformation in Africa. In South Africa, two decades after liberation and the first democratic elections, transformation, nation-building and social re-construction are crucial. Returning to the roots of African Spirituality and incorporating vital elements into African Christian Spirituality, it is clear that the AICs have a great service to render to the continent.

Notes

1 In Sub-Saharan Africa.
2 P. Kalilombe (1994), 'Spirituality in the African Perspective', in R. Gibellini (ed.), *Paths of African Theology*. New York: Orbis Books, p. 115.

3 A. Kasambala (2006), 'African Spirituality and Pastoral Theology', *St Augustine Papers*, 7(1), 30.

4 Certain issues pertaining to the overall theme have been briefly considered in M. Karecki, C. Kourie and L. Kretzschmar (2005), *African Spirituality*, in P. Sheldrake (ed.), *The New SCM Dictionary of Christian Spirituality*. London: SCM Press, pp. 92–4.

5 J. Olupona (2000), 'Introduction', in J. Olupona (ed.), *African Spirituality. Forms, Meanings and Expressions*. New York: The Crossroad Publishing Company, p. xvii.

6 J. Olupona (1991), 'Major Issues in the Study of African Traditional Religion', in J. Olupona (ed.), *African Traditional Religions in Contemporary Society*. New York: Paragon House, p. 28.

7 D. Zahan (2000), 'Some Reflections on African Spirituality', in Olupona, *African Spirituality*, p. 20.

8 Zahan, 'Some Reflections on African Spirituality', pp. 20–1.

9 G. Oosthuizen (1991), 'Traditional Religion in Contemporary South Africa', in Olupona (ed.), *African Traditional Religions*, p. 36. Oosthuizen makes the important point that the cold rationalist approach, so prevalent in modernity, does not resonate with African religion. Postmodern thought is reclaiming the place of intuition, and the non-rational and trans-rational (perhaps more accurately, the supra-rational) is once more gaining acceptance. Therefore, 'Africa's sensitivity at the non-rational level . . . could make a valuable contribution to humanity's contemporary search for depth', p. 39.

10 Oosthuizen, *Traditional Religion*, p. 40.

11 J. Mbiti (2006), 'Aspects of African Heritage and Spirituality', *St Augustine Papers*, 7(1), 5. Mbiti has collected 1,700 names for God, from diverse language groups.

12 Kasambala, 'African Spirituality', pp. 46, 47. These terms are to be found among the Tonga and Tumbuka-speaking peoples of Malawi.

13 Kasambala, 'African Spirituality', 33. Whereas God and the spirits, including the ancestors, inhabit the *upper level*, the *lower level* is the place for humans and nature. The distancing of the Divine has been compared to the *apophatic* tradition in Christianity, for example, J. Wiseman (2006), *Spirituality and Mysticism*. New York: Orbis Books, p. 189.

14 Mbiti, 'Aspects of African Heritage', p. 5.

15 D. Zahan (2000), 'Some Reflections on African Spirituality', p. 5.

16 Oosthuizen, 'Traditional Religion', p. 40.

17 A Malawian Tonga term for ancestors. This honorific title is bestowed on those who contributed to society, and it is believed that they continue to exert a positive influence. Kasambala, 'African Spirituality', p. 50.

18 Kalilombe, 'Spirituality in the African Perspective', pp. 126–7. It is important to note that in order to qualify as an ancestor, the recently deceased has to be highly commended by the community. It is necessary for the whole clan of the particular ethnic group to approve. 'There is no short-cut to ancestry; one has to live a full and good life among the people, so that when they pass on, they continue to serve their people from a different world.' Kasambala, 'African Spirituality', p. 43.

19 L. Pato (2000), 'African Spirituality and Transformation in South Africa', in C. Kourie and L. Kretzschmar (eds), *Christian Spirituality in South Africa*. Pietermaritzburg: Cluster Publications.

20 Oosthuizen, 'Tradition Religion', p. 41.

21 Mbiti, 'Aspects of African Heritage', p. 7.

22 Wiseman, *Spirituality and Mysticism*, p. 192.

23 Catholic missionary approaches are reflected in Church documents of the time, for example, Pope Pius XI's declaration, in *Rerum Ecclesiae*, that missionaries should

withdraw 'pagans . . . from the darkness of superstition' and instruct them in the 'true faith of Christ' so as to snatch them from the 'mouth of hell', quoted in C. Isizoh (ed.) (2001), *Christianity in Dialogue with African Traditional Religion and Culture*. Vatican City: Pontifical Council for Interreligious Dialogue, p. 6. Both Catholic and Protestant missionary activity was tainted with their involvement in the slave trade and their support for the imperialistic ambitions of the European countries, coupled with the desire to have a 'Europeanized Africa'. See A. Adogame and J. Spickard (2010), *Religion Crossing Boundaries. Transnational Religious and Social Dynamics in Africa and the New African Diaspora*. Leiden: Brill, pp. 3–5.

24 See in this connection, P. Sarpong (2002), 'Interreligious Dialogue in the Light of the Post-Synodal Exhortation, Ecclesia in Africa', in D. Isizoh (ed.), *Milestones in Interreligious Dialogue*. Rome: Ceedee Publications, pp. 232–45.

25 The earliest record of the provenance of the AICs is in 1862 in Ghana. There are several thousand AICs in Africa, with variants of belief and practice. *Inter alia*, in South Africa there are: Ethiopians, Zionists, Apostolics, Millenarians and Nazarites. As with African Traditional Religion/s, in spite of the various differences, there are sufficient general themes in common to allow an overall survey.

26 S. Tshelane (2000), 'The Spirituality of the African Initiated Churches', in C. Kourie and L. Kretzschmar (eds), *Christian Spirituality in South Africa*. Pietermaritzburg: Cluster Publications, p. 138.

27 Oosthuizen points out that 'the organization of the church as institution became more important to missioners than the traditional inborn sense of fellowship and mutual caring and sharing that are basic in traditional African religion', 'The Task of African Traditional Religion in the Church's Dilemma in South Africa', in Olupona, 2000, *African Spirituality*, p. 278.

28 Oosthuizen, 'The Task of African Traditional Religion', p. 278.

29 Tshelane, 'The Spirituality of the African Initiated Churches', p. 142.

30 Ibid., p. 143 (italics mine).

31 Early missionary liturgies used European hymns, translated into African languages. Concerning isiXhosa, a new musical terminology was developed to *prevent* rhythm. 'In traditional isiXhosa, *ukombela* means to sing with clapping; in mission church IsiXhosa, *ukucula* means to sing without clapping or dancing.' D. Dargie (2010), 'Xhosa Zionist Church Music: A Liturgical Expression Beyond the Dreams of the Early Missionaries', *Missionalia*, 38(1), 32–53.

32 B. Tlhagale (2001), 'Bringing the African Culture into the Church', in Isizoh, *Christianity in Dialogue with African Traditional Religion and Culture*, 43–59. Cf. C. Ugwuanyi (2011), 'Voices of Inculturation in Africa: In the Past, in the Present and the Future', *Asian Horizons*, 5(1), 81–95.

33 Tshlane, 'The Spirituality of African Initiated Churches,' p. 154.

Bibliography and Further Reading

Abraham, K. and Mbuy-Beya, B. (eds) (1994), *Spirituality and the Third World: A Cry for Life*. Maryknoll, NY: Orbis Books.

Adogame, A. and Spickard, J. (2010), *Religion Crossing Boundaries. Transnational Religious and Social Dynamics in Africa and the New African Diasporsa*. Leiden: Brill.

Dargie, D. (2010), 'Xhosa Zionist Church Music: A Liturgical Expression Beyond the Dreams of the Early Missionaries', *Missionalia*, 38(1), 32–53.

Isizoh, C. (ed.) (2001), *Christianity in Dialogue with African Traditional Religion and Culture*. Vatican City: Cedee Publications.

Kalilombe, P. (1994), 'Spirituality in the African Perspective', in R. Gibellini (ed.), *Paths of African Theology*. New York: Orbis Books.

Karecki, M., Kourie, C. and Kretzschmar, L. (eds) (2005), 'African Spirituality', in P. Sheldrake (ed.), *The New SCM Dictionary of Christian Spirituality*. London: SCM Press.

Kasambala, A. (2006), 'African Spirituality and Pastoral Theology', *St Augustine Papers*, 7(1), 28–53.

Kourie, C. and Kretzschmar, L. (eds) (2000), *Christian Spirituality in South Africa*. Pietermaritzburg: Cluster Publications.

Masuku, F. (2007), *Exploring the Nature of the Encounter between Christian and Traditional African Spirituality in Malawi*. Lewiston: The Edwin Mellen Press.

Mbiti, J. (1991), *Introduction to African Religion*, 2nd edn. Nairobi: Heinemann Kenya Ltd.

— (2006), 'Aspects of African Heritage and Spirituality', *St Augustine Papers*, 7(1), 4–28.

Mugambi, J. and Nasimiyu-Wasike, A. (eds) (1999), *Moral and Ethical Issues in African Christianity*. Nairobi: Acton.

Olupona, J. (1991), 'Major Issues in the Study of African Traditional Religion', in J. Olupona (ed.), *African Traditional Religions in Contemporary Society*. New York: Paragon House.

— (ed.) (2000), *African Spirituality. Forms, Meanings and Expressions*. New York: The Crossroad Publishing Company.

Oosthuizen, G. (1991), 'Traditional Religion in Contemporary South Africa', in J. Olupona (ed.), *African Traditional Religions in Contemporary Society*. New York: Paragon House.

— (2000), 'The Task of African Traditional Religion in the Church's Dilemma in South Africa', in J. Olupona (ed.), *African Spirituality. Forms, Meanings and Expressions*. New York: The Crossroad Publishing Company.

Pato, L. (2000), 'African Spirituality and Transformation in South Africa', in M. Karecki, C. Kourie and L. Kretzschmar (eds), *Christian Spirituality in South Africa*. Pietermaritzburg: Cluster Publications.

Sarpong, P. (2002), 'Interreligious Dialogue in the Light of the Post-Synodal Exhortation, Ecclesia in Africa', in C. Isizoh (ed.) *Milestones in Interreligious Dialogue*. Rome: Ceedee Publications.

Shorter, A. (1978), *African Christian Spirituality*. New York: Orbis Books.

Tlhagale, B. (2001), 'Bringing the African Culture into the Church', in C. Isizoh (ed.), *Christianity in Dialogue with African Traditional Religion and Culture*. Vatican City: Ceedee Publications.

Tshelane, S. (2000), 'The Spirituality of the African Initiated Churches', in C. Kourie and L. Kretzschmar (eds), *Christian Spirituality in South Africa*. Pietermaritzburg: Cluster Publications.

Ugwuanyi, C. (2011), 'Voices of Inculturation in Africa: In the Past, in the Present and the Future', *Asian Horizons*, 5(1), 81–95.

Wiseman, J. (2006), *Spirituality and Mysticism*. New York: Orbis Books.

Zahan, D. (2000), 'Some Reflections on African Spirituality', in J. Olupona (ed.), *African Spirituality. Forms, Meanings and Expressions*. New York: The Crossroad Publishing Company.

24 Christian Spirituality in America: Native American Spirituality

Kathy Heskin

Introduction

It is not possible to speak of the Native American peoples as one entity. Over 550 separate nations lived on the North American continent at the time of first contact with Europeans. Each of these peoples had their own beliefs, stories, rituals, language and culture. No word for religion exists in any Native American language. Instead, each tribe or band had a code of behaviour, teachings and spiritual practices that were handed down by the elders and kept sacred within the group. Charles Eastman expressed it this way:

> In the life of the Indian there was only one inevitable duty, – the duty of prayer – the daily recognition of the Unseen and Eternal. His daily devotions were more necessary to him than daily food. He wakes at daybreak, puts on his moccasins and steps down to the water's edge. Here he throws handfuls of clear, cold water into his face, or plunges in bodily. After his bath, he stands erect before the advancing dawn, facing the sun as it dances upon the horizon, and offers his unspoken orison. His mate may precede or follow him in his devotions, but never accompanies him. Each soul must meet the morning sun, the new, sweet earth, and the Great Silence alone!

> Every act of his life is, in a very real sense, a religious act. He recognizes the spirit in all creation, and believes that he draws from it spiritual power.[1]

Each of the tribes understood themselves to have been placed on their land by the Creator, and so the land held their identity and their lives. There are few universal things that can be said of every nation, but one is that the core of life is unity, oneness with all created things. The people know their origins, and tell of them in their creation stories, their songs and their collective memory. 'Through a great variety of ceremonies, songs, and dances, Native Americans expressed their sense that life was a deeply spiritual affair.'[2]

Respect for the animals that were hunted was universal, and a wide variety of rituals surrounded the killing of animals and the harvesting of plants. Much of the spiritual life of the Native peoples is linked to the land on which they live. Thus the cosmology and spirituality of the woodland peoples are quite different from those who dwell in the Arctic north or the deserts of the southwest.

Because my work has been primarily with the Woodland peoples, particularly the Anishinabe, and the Plains peoples including the Oglala Lakota, the Crow, the Blackfeet and the Cree, most of the emphasis in this chapter will be on these peoples, with only brief discussion of the southwest, including the Navajo and Hopi, and the Salish of the Pacific Northwest in the Continental United States. It is important to note that each group, each tribe, could be the subject of entire texts in order to do full justice to each culture. It is also important to remember that because the Native peoples relied on oral tradition, much of what we know of them is from the perspective of Christian missionaries. So it often carries a high degree of bias, perceptions influenced by the religions and cultures of Europe. While many struggled to be accurate in describing what they saw, the missionaries often missed elements such as the importance of the women in society, or egalitarian leadership.

Stories of Creation

If you were to ask a Western European his history, you might be given a timeline. This would be foreign to Native ways, where time is not understood in a linear way, but in a circle. If you were to ask a Native American to tell you her history, she would tell you a story. If you asked about prayer and ritual, there would be another story. For all Native peoples across North America, story is the way meaning, spiritual belief and understanding are conveyed. This is not so different from the Judeo-Christian tradition, which begins with the creation stories in Genesis.

Each individual tribe on the land would have one or more creation stories, some very complex, some simple, but all having a different emphasis. Human beings are typically the last of creation, but not its culmination. In fact they are the least and must learn from all that has gone before them. Instead of human dominion over nature, Native stories emphasize human dependence on the plants and animals, and acknowledge relationships with 'the four-leggeds, the winged-ones and the swimmers':

A presiding characteristic of primal people is a special quality and intensity of interrelationship with the forms and forces of their natural environment. As nomadic hunters or gatherers, or as agriculturists, dependence upon natural resources demanded detailed knowledge of all aspects of their

283

immediate habitat. This accumulated pragmatic lore was, however, always interrelated with a sacred lore.[3]

Only humans and the bear are two-leggeds, and theirs is a special relationship. But the roles of animals and birds are clearly outlined in many of the stories, and in several of the woodland stories, the muskrat saves humans after the Flood. The bear is often depicted as the protector, and teaches about medicines. The wolf teaches about family, in the way wolves care for the young in their packs and in the way they never abandon the old. In stories across the land, the eagle is the one who carries prayers to the Creator.

The lessons the animals and birds teach humans enable them to survive on the earth. The implications of these differences are important. In the Judeo-Christian tradition humans are placed at the top of creation and able to make decisions about how we relate to the other parts of creation. In the Native traditions, placing human beings as the least of creation encourages respect and interaction between humans and all of nature. The Lakota people refer to this as 'Mitakuye Oyasin', which means 'all my relations'.

Creation stories both shape and reflect a culture, and the wide variety of stories of the people who lived in America for millennia before others arrived are fascinating and instructive. The story in Genesis of the Fall and of the enmity between brothers is echoed in many Native creation stories, which often have twins, or brothers, who represent two sides of human nature.

Nearly every Native group refers to themselves in their language as 'First People' or 'Original People'. There is a belief among tribes that the land they inhabit is the land given to them by the Creator, or to which they were led by the Great Mystery. The Anishinabe migration story tells us that the people once lived by the ocean. The Anishinabe people probably began in New England, in Maine, with the Red Ochre people. (The Anishinabe language was identical to the Wabanake of the St Francis band near the border of Canada. They would include the Pennobscat and the Pasamaquati.) As they moved westward their language changed just a little every 100–50 miles, which indicates that the migration took place over a long time. There are 200 to 300 dialects among these people in the United States, and the same number in Canada. At some point the Megis shell, a sacred symbol, appeared to them and said they would journey to a land where food grew on water. They journeyed on from the east coast of the United States to the Midwest and farther west and north, where most of the Anishinabe bands are today.

In the Hopi tradition, when the Creator was giving each group their land, the Hopi people decided to choose last. As a result they were given the least desirable land, but they wanted to claim that land because of their great humility, and because they were able to live with suffering. This was the land they would come to love.

The People of the Land

Love of the land is a universal characteristic of Native peoples. They learned how to walk softly on the land, to treat it with respect, and these are the teachings they passed on to their children and grandchildren. This worldview about the land would bring them into great conflict with the Western Europeans when they first arrived in the New World. Some Europeans came in quest of religious freedom, but others came to establish colonies, to claim land and to settle there. Beginning with the earliest treaties, the 'whites' sought to purchase or in other ways obtain land from the Native peoples. Natives, on the other hand, did not understand the concept of owning land. Land was given for their use, land was their mother. According to Vine Deloria, Jr,

> The essence of the Indian attitude to peoples, lands, and other life forms is one of kinship relationship in which no element of life can go unattached from human society. Thus lands are given special status because they form a motherhood relationship with the people who live there . . . the true meaning of the motherhood of the land is that, like a mother, it shapes and teaches our species, and according to the particularity of the area, produces certain basic forms of personality and social identity which could not be produced in any other way.[4]

You could not sell your mother. So when the Dutch congratulated themselves on the purchase of Manhattan Island for $24 in beads and trinkets, the Natives in that area believed they had been given gifts to allow these people to hunt on their hunting grounds. The next year when the Native people returned, they were hunted themselves.

This shaping of a people by the land is demonstrated in the different ways the peoples in different parts of the continent understood themselves. For the people of the coastal rim of what is now the United States, the land provided game and vegetation. The people were able to provide sufficient food and medicine for themselves, and their spiritual practices were those of gratitude. Their belief in a Creator who cared for them was widespread. The men hunted and agriculture, which appeared around 3,500 years ago, was largely the work of women. As early as 1585 Thomas Hariot observed that the Algonquians of the Carolinas had 'ingenious agriculture, including the use of a graine of marveilous great increase; of a thousand, fifteene hundred, and sometimes two thousand fold'.[5]

The land produced and shaped a people that were open to others, who shared their largesse and believed in the good intentions of the colonists. This worldview led to a transformation of most of the coastal Indians in less than two centuries into small scattered groups, many of whom were forced

to migrate or die. The introduction of diseases by the colonists, both acciden-
tally and deliberately, led to a decimation of Native populations along the east
coast by as much as 90 per cent. What remains is a largely nostalgic view of
a savage people who shared a feast at Thanksgiving prepared mainly by the
'Pilgrims'. The story, the culture and the spiritual beliefs of the people were
obliterated along with the people themselves.

The people of the Southwest occupied a very different terrain, and had
very different contact with the Europeans. The hot arid desert, punctuated by
mountains and pine-covered hills, required strong survival skills, and their
cosmology was shaped by those features. And while the Northeast was populated by a number of essentially similar groups both in language and culture, 'the Southwest was a bewildering mosaic of different cultures living in
sometimes uneasy symbiosis with each other'.[6] Unlike the Northeast, where
the Native presence is remembered largely by the names of towns, in the
Southwest, the Native presence is still strong. Their stories tell of the sacred
mountains and the origins of strange rock formations. The languages were
not obliterated, and the culture today resembles what the first Spaniards must
have seen when they arrived in the sixteenth century.

Most of the Native peoples divide themselves into clans. The names of the
clans correspond to the animals and birds of the region. And so the people who
lived near water or in the woodlands would name clans for the local animals
and water birds – the loon, bear, wolf and crane, while the Pueblo people of the
Southwest had the Snake, Coyote and Parrot clans. Members of clans trace their
lineage matrilineally and do not marry within their clan. Within each tribe the
clans have certain responsibilities, and certain obligations to the group. They
also have specific rituals, dances and songs that pertain to their clan.

Spiritual Beliefs

The Pacific Northwest peoples had a unique belief system. 'For traditional
Coast Salish people, survival depends on acquiring the spirit power of animals such as the salmon. This can occur through inheritance from an ancestor
. . . or through one's own experiential interaction with powerful spirit powers.'[7] An important part of traditional Coast Salish life is the quest for guardian spirits:

After being carefully prepared by the spiritual leaders and elders, individuals
are sent to isolated places such as mountain lakes or waterfalls for several
days of fasting and prayerful contemplation. During this time they tend a
large fire, pray, bathe regularly, and refrain from eating or sleeping. During
these vision quests, some young people receive a visionary experience of
their guardian power and are given a spirit power song.[8]

The guardian spirits are honoured through song and dance, and these rituals are most often practised during the wintertime. It is understood that the summer months are important for gathering and preserving food for the winter months. For the coastal Salish tribes, summer is a time of work, and winter is when ceremonies are enacted, including healing ceremonies that require the spiritual people to journey between two worlds to bring back the soul of a patient for whom the ceremony is held.

The practice of healing ceremonies is almost universal in Native traditions. Certain persons who demonstrate the ability to use the medicines and to heal the people are trained specifically in the wisdom of the tribe. For most of the woodland peoples there is the tradition of the Mide Lodge, where certain skills and wisdom are handed down to those with the gift of healing. In the Anishinabe bands the people in the Midewiwin Lodge, or Great Medicine Lodge, learn about the plants and trees and their medicinal uses, and they become healers for their people. Their wisdom came from thousands of years of careful attention to the world around them. This is why the policies of removal, and the incursion of the Europeans moving westward, disrupted the lore, the practices and the spiritual traditions of the Native peoples.

The Plains Peoples

When we think of 'Indians', the People of the Plains most often come to mind. These are the tribes immortalized by movies and television. Their nomadic lifestyle, their tepees and war bonnets, became the stuff of legend through Buffalo Bill Cody's *Wild West Show*. Separating fact from fiction is now difficult, and distinguishing between the people before and after Christianity is almost impossible but Native peoples were affected most drastically by government policies.

President Thomas Jefferson's impetus towards assimilation was accepted by the tribes of the Southeast. The Cherokee had developed written language, and lived in homes and towns similar to the other colonists by the eighteenth century. As the westward expansion continued, their lands in North Carolina and Georgia became desirable for settlement. The policy of assimilation was changed to removal, and in 1830 the Indian Removal Bill forced the Choctaws, Chickasaws, Seminoles and Creeks to relocate to territories in the Great Plains – the 'Trail of Tears'. That year the Cherokee were likewise uprooted and forced to march to Oklahoma.

Adjusting to the new land, with markedly different vegetation and climate, was difficult. At the same time there arose an increased fervour among Christians to 'save' the Natives:

Missionary activity among tribes native to the plains, and those placed there by treaty, increased after 1830. Protestants and Catholics contacted almost every aboriginal group to acquaint them with the teachings of the gospel and with white civilization. By 1835 most tribes knew that the missionaries wanted to alter their culture with schools, agriculture and Christian morals.[9]

Along with the missionary activity came several epidemics which devastated the Native population, reducing it from 50 to 90 per cent in some areas and making it even harder to resist white influences.

In 1869 President Ulysses S. Grant developed a 'peace policy' promoting assimilation of Native peoples under the direction of the Christian missionaries. While the intent of many of the missionaries was beneficent, there was a general belief that white culture, religion and practice were far superior, and that Native peoples were pagans in need of conversion. Although many Christians failed to notice the deep reverence and prayerfulness of the people they sought to convert, Chief Red Cloud, leader of the Oglala Sioux Indians, brought his band to one of the agencies hoping to help his people to transition to a new way of life. He later petitioned the government to allow the Jesuits to found a school on the Pine Ridge Reservation, and the Holy Rosary Mission was established in 1888. It still serves the people there today.

Culture Wars

While many well-intentioned people believed that educating the Native children would help them to assimilate into the white man's culture, perhaps the most devastating blow for the Native way of life was the removal of the children to boarding schools, sometimes hundreds of miles from their homes. The children were forbidden to speak their own language and were punished, often severely, for doing so. Boys were taught trades and girls homemaking skills, so that they could live in a white world. They had little or no contact with their families, and soon lost their Native skills and traditions. Language carries culture, and when their language was lost, so were the prayers and songs that sustained the people. It wasn't until 1978 that the Indian Child Welfare Act ended the mandatory boarding school experience for Native children. The pain of this policy remains among the people.

The late nineteenth century was a time of great upheaval in the Northern Plains. Many other groups had been eliminated, but tribes on the Northern Plains still lived as they always had. Their spiritual practices were ingrained, and helped them to survive the harsh climate and difficult life. The legend of the White Buffalo Calf Woman was widespread among these people. In the beginning, she had brought their ceremonies and rituals and the pipe to them, and taught them how to honour the Creator, or Great Mystery. This way of life would end, however, with the discovery of gold and silver in the mountains.

Thirst for these metals, and for land, brought thousands of settlers west of the Mississippi to the land that had been promised for all time to the Natives in the treaties that were signed but now broken.

A series of laws was passed in order to bring the bands that still roamed free onto reservations. In 1882 all practice of Native spiritual traditions was outlawed. Those caught participating in ceremonies were imprisoned. Not until 1978, with the passage of the American Indian Religious Freedom Act, were Native peoples again allowed 'the right to believe, express, and exercise traditional religions, and perform ceremonies and traditional rituals'.[10]

The Dawes Act of 1887 broke up the reservations into parcels of 160 acres for a married man and 80 acres for a single man. It was designed to force the Natives to take up agriculture, but it also reserved the gold-rich Black Hills in the territory ceded to the Sioux for use by the Government, and it provided access for the railroads to carry out that gold. The Black Hills were sacred to several of the tribes in the great Sioux Nation. Summer camps were held there and vision quests took place in the sacred hills.

As the last bands were brought into agencies, which were precursors of the reservations, a resistance movement began in the far west. A Paiute man, Wovoka, had a vision of the return of the ancestors and the buffalo. He travelled in order to share his vision, and hope spread as far as Pine Ridge in South Dakota. Many of the people began to gather to perform the Ghost Dance, a ritual that would bring back the ancestors to help them reclaim their land. The Ghost Dancing frightened the whites, who feared an uprising. This led to the massacre at Wounded Knee in 1890, when Chief Little Foot's band was surrounded and slaughtered on their way to the agency.

As told in the book by John Neihardt, the Lakota holy man Black Elk said of this,

> And so it was over.
>
> I did not know then how much was ended. When I look back now from this high hill of my old age, I can still see the butchered women and children lying heaped and scattered all along the crooked gulch as plain as when I saw them with eyes still young. And I can see that something else died there in the bloody mud, and was buried in the blizzard. A people's dream died there. It was a beautiful dream.
>
> And I, to whom so great a vision was given in my youth, – you see me now a pitiful old man who has done nothing, for the nation's hoop is broken and scattered. There is no center any longer, and the sacred tree is dead.[11]

It is almost impossible to believe that people who had undergone so much hardship, dislocation and oppression, would continue to grow. But their spirituality and language were preserved by the elders, and quietly passed down generation after generation to people today. Despite the relocation policies of the 1950s which sought to terminate tribal status and move Native people to large cities, many remained on the reservations and preserved their traditions. When the American Indian Religious Freedom Act was passed in 1978, tribes began to reclaim their past, and again spoke their Native languages, celebrating in ritual and ceremony. People now gather for powwows and Sun Dances, and many Native homes have erected sweat lodges. Tribal elders hold teaching lodges. Pride in their traditions is beginning to change the reservations.

Great poverty and illness still exist everywhere. Native reservations have the highest unemployment, the highest suicide rates and the greatest incidence of diabetes of any segment of the US population. By reconnecting with the land and with the support of broad initiatives in healthcare and ecology, however, these issues are being addressed. One such initiative is being funded by the National Science Foundation. Hopa Mountain has been designed to engage rural and tribal youth by involving them in service-learning activities to create healthier communities.

The Future

Hope is beginning to replace despair, and the spirituality of Native peoples and their connection to the land are at the forefront of recovery. Faith-based organizations are working in Native areas in collaboration with the elders, drawing on the rich traditions and spiritual beliefs. The Red Cloud Indian School on Pine Ridge is one example. Once a forced boarding school where Native children were forbidden to speak their own language, the school's mission now requires that it provide competitive skills for the students while retaining traditional values and culture. In addition to traditional educational curriculum, courses are taught on Lakota religion, culture and language.

The most hopeful sign is the proliferation of immersion language schools all over the United States. From the Eva B. Stokely School in Shiprock, New Mexico, on the Navajo reservation, to the mission school Tsunadeloquasdi in North Carolina, immersion schools are promoting traditional ways, teaching Native language and spiritual beliefs, and helping the young to reclaim pride in their traditions. The diminishing number of fluent elder speakers is being replaced by a new generation of children grounded in their own languages, culture and beliefs.

There is a prophecy among the Anishinabe that after seven generations of living in contact with the Europeans, the people would restore the tradition of stewardship over the earth. This is the seventh generation.

Notes

1 Charles Eastman (Ohiyesa) (1911), *The Soul of the Indian*. Boston and New York: Houghton Mifflin, p. 46.
2 Joel W. Martin (1999), *The Land Looks After Us*. New York: Oxford University Press, p. 39.
3 Joseph Epes Brown (1982), *The Spiritual Legacy of the American Indian*. New York: Crossroad, p. 4.
4 Vine Deloria (1999), *For this Land*. New York and London: Routledge.
5 James Wilson (1998), *The Earth Shall Weep: A History of Native America*. New York: Grove Press, p. 47.
6 Ibid., p. 174.
7 Suzenne Crawford (2007), *Native American Religious Traditions*. Saddle River, NJ: Prentice Hall, p. 50.
8 Ibid.
9 Henry Warner Bowden (1981), *American Indians and Christian Missions*. Chicago and London: The University of Chicago Press, p. 185.
10 Crawford (2007), p. 12.
11 John Neihardt (1979), *Black Elk Speaks*. Lincoln: University of Nebraska Press, p. 207.

Bibliography and Further Reading

Broker, Ignatia (1983), *Night Flying Woman: An Ojibway Narrative*. St Paul, MN: Minnesota Historical Society Press.
Brown, Dee (2007), *Bury My Heart at Wounded Knee*. New York: Macmillan.
Calloway, Colin (2008), *First Peoples: A Documentary Survey of American Indian History*. Boston: Bedford/St Martin's Press.
Deloria, Vine and Wilkins, David (2000), *Tribes, Treaties and Constitutional Tribulations*. Austin, TX : University of Texas Press.
Grinnell, George Bird (1962), *Blackfoot Lodge Tales: The Story of a Prairie People*. Lincoln, NE: University of Nebraska Press.
McClintock, Walter (1999), *The Old North Trail*. Lincoln, NE: University of Nebraska Press.
Nabokov, Peter (1978), *Native American Testimony*. New York: Penguin Books.
Neihardt, John (1979), *Black Elk Speaks*. Lincoln, NE: University of Nebraska Press.
Nerburn, Kent (1994), *Neither Wolf Nor Dog*. Novato, CA: New World Library.
Oswalt, Wendell (2006), *This Land Was Theirs: A Study of Native North Americans*. New York: Oxford University Press.
Ruppel, Kristin (2008), *Unearthing Indian Land: Living with the Legacies of Allotment*. Tucson, AZ: University of Arizona Press.

25 Christian Spirituality in Asia: The Nasranis

Kurian Perumpallikunnel

Introduction

Blessed John Paul II, affirming the glory of Asia, in the opening sentence of his *Ecclesia in Asia*, the Post-Synodal apostolic Exhortation,[1] stated:

> The Church in Asia sings the praises of the 'God of salvation' (Ps 68:20) for choosing to initiate his saving plan on Asian soil, through men and women of that continent. It was in fact in Asia that God revealed and fulfilled his saving purpose from the beginning . . . In 'the fullness of time' (Gal. 4:4), he sent his only-begotten Son, Jesus Christ the Saviour, who took flesh as an Asian! . . . Because Jesus was born, lived, died and rose from the dead in the Holy Land, that small portion of Western Asia became a land of promise and hope for all mankind.

John Paul II regarded Asia as 'a land of promise and hope for all mankind'. Yet Christianity, in its homeland, in spite of its glorious past, still remains a minority. Is there a future for Christianity in Asia? This question may be unsettling in the minds of many. However, the dream of the late Pope need not be brushed aside as an utopian idea since in this land characterized by high thinking, varied religious quests and different cultural heritages, if nurtured properly, Christianity can contribute greatly to its own faithful and even to humanity as a whole. Obviously it should have something original, unique and outstanding to contribute, which of course it does have. Then why even after two millennia does Christianity remain a marginal minority in Asia, its birthplace?

This chapter is an attempt to evaluate the Asian Church, its values and woes, by taking the history of a small group of Oriental Christians called Nasranis[2] as an example of wider trends at work in the whole continent. The trials and tribulations they had to face and the unassuming, non-competitive, down-to-earth spirituality they developed in their struggle for survival and preservation of their identity provide us with ample normative guidelines of how Asia may truly become a land of promise and hope for all mankind. The Christian missionaries from the West arrived in India with the typical Western triumphalistic mentality. They were ready to bear the 'whiteman's burden'[3] of educating, fulfilling, saving and winning the inferior cultures and civilizations for Christ. Their self-complacency, ignorance, and patronization caused untold miseries to the Nasranis. Our search will expose the need of developing a non-domineering spirituality among Christians to achieve the aforesaid goal. We need to uphold a culture of charity, where everyone accepts the other with openness and admiration. Everybody requires the basic freedom of self-expression so that unity does not become uniformity and friendly bonds do not degenerate into enslavement. We call for a Christianity that respects and integrates genuine cultural values of every civilization into its way of life while upholding and disseminating what is authentically Christian towards the further evolution of humanity towards its ultimate goal.

The Story of the Nasranis

It was the publication of *The God of Small Things,* a semi-autobiographical novel by the 1997 Booker prize winner Arundhati Roy, that brought to the attention of the wider public, the existence of Christians in the Indian subcontinent prior to the missionary activities of the Portuguese, the Dutch and the British.[4] With the discovery of the Hippalus wind, a ship leaving the mouth of the Red Sea could reach Cranganore,[5] on the Malabar Coast, within 40 days. Following this route of the Arabs, the Romans and the Jews, St Thomas too took ship to Cranganore in around 52 CE. Malabar was well known to the Phoenicians, Romans, Greeks, Arabs and Alexandrians of the ancient world, and the names of *ivory, peacock,* and the domesticated *monkey* used in the Pentateuch are Tamil names which the Phoenicians had taken along with the wares. There is a hypothesis that the Dravidians are the descendents of the old Assyrians who colonized South India.[6] The community that originated as a result of the evangelization mission of St Thomas identified itself as Nasranis or Marthoma Nasranis announcing their apostolic origin. This community still survives at the southernmost tip of the Indian peninsula in spite of all vicissitudes.

The meteoric rise of Islam in the seventh century CE in Saudi Arabia and the Islamic conquest that followed resulted in the elimination or conversion to Islam of thousands of Christian communities in the Orient, in northern Africa and to a certain extent in the Occident. Away from the epicentre of this event, the tiny Christian community of South India survived throughout. However, they too had their share of trials and hardships, this time not from the Muslims but from their Christian brethren from the West. Though insignificant in number[7] as well as in extent[8] they have an amazing story to recount – an incredible legacy of their enduring struggle for survival and self-preservation. The spirituality they developed and the strategies they employed in their struggle of survival in their given circumstances are not only edifying and intriguing, but also an inspiration and a paradigm for minorities elsewhere who struggle for their survival and identity.

In the cast-ridden social framework of India, Nasranis are considered forward caste.[9] As per the latest census (2001), a quarter of the Christians in India are from Kerala. Of the total 32 million people in the province of Kerala, the Christians constitute around 20 per cent, that is, 6.5 million. The Nasranis numbering about 5 million, spread across various denominations, is the largest ethnic group among Christians. The Nasranis, during their 2,000-year long existence, developed an independent style which according to Placid J. Podipara, was 'Hindu in Culture, Christian in Religion and Oriental in Worship'.[10] Many of the historical records of the Nasranis were destroyed by the Portuguese at the behest of Decree XVI passed in the synod of Diamper which commanded all books written in Syriac to be delivered up to the Portuguese college at Vapincotta to be corrected or destroyed. However, a paradox here is that the records of the proceedings of the synod as well as its decrees give us an excellent insight into the *Marthoma Margam*,[11] and the social and religious customs practised in an unadulterated form at that time.[12]

The Synod of Diamper: A Window to the Ancient Customs of the Nasaranis

In 1599 CE, Alexis Menezes, Archbishop of Portuguese Goa, arrived at Cochin on a mission to 'cleanse' the faith and customs of the Nasranis.[13] This mission culminated with the Synod of Diamper on the 20th of June, 1599 at Udayamperur (Diamper).[14] The synod was an assembly of 640 representatives of churches across Kerala as well as 63 Nasrani priests presided over by Archbishop Alexis Menezes with the Nasrani Archdeacon Geevarghese in meek attendance. Dr Scaria Zacharia in his *The Acts and Decrees of the Synod of Diamper 1599*[15] considers the synod as the first organized attempt to Westernize Kerala society as part of the Western colonial project. The Portuguese colonialists blinded by their history and socio-religious experience tried to impose upon a church far more ancient than their own and pluralistic in outlook, their own imperialistic notions of Christianity and Christianization. The apostolic church of Kerala was compelled to imitate Western concepts of social and cultural conducts as well as embrace the Latin Rite, rituals and the administrative system.

The decrees of the Diamper Synod are a mirror into that past which catalogue numerous practices, beliefs and features unique to the Nasranis. Session III, Decree IV accuses the Nasranis of accepting the Hindu belief of transmigration of souls, fate and predestination. Another accusation against the Nasranis found in the very same Decree, was the insistence of the Nasranis that everyone may be saved in his own law and conscience.[16] This 'heresy' came as a bolt out of the blue to the Portuguese who obviously believed that only their version of truth and faith could ever lead one to the Kingdom of heaven. The Nasranis of that time believed like the average Hindu, that different faiths were only different paths to Heaven.[17] It was with this open-mindedness that the Nasranis allowed the racially and liturgically diverse Portuguese into their churches and participated in their holy liturgy, little knowing that all this would later be held against them.

Session III of Decree XIV condemns many Syrian books, forbids Nasranis from reading them and commands that they be destroyed. This decree condemned and ordered several Syriac books to be burnt. Following the style of Inquisition Courts, emissaries were sent out to every church to gather the books for scrutiny and correction. Most parishes willingly brought their books for verification and authentication. When missionaries found the scrutiny and correction of books time consuming and impossible due to their lack of knowledge of Syriac language they conceived an easy way out. They heaped the books they managed to gather in the courtyard and set fire to them. It is said that this 'final solution' continued non-stop for days. Afterwards the missionaries magnanimously gave permission to translate the Latin liturgical texts into Syriac language for the use of the Nasranis.

Session III, Decree XII forbids the Nasrani children from attending Hindu schools if they also have to take part in the Hindu rituals. The synod recommended the Nasranis to send their children to the parish priests for education instead of sending them to such idolatrous heathens. It is evident from this decree that Nasrani children used to frequent schools run by non-Christian teachers and obviously like their other non-Christian classmates, they also partook in the Hindu ceremonies held in the schools of those days which could have been rituals like *Guruvandana*[18] and paying obeisance to the Goddess of learning, *Saraswati*. In fact even to this day, the majority of the Nasrani families observe *Vidyarambham*[19] ritual for their children, an initiation into education when the child is old enough to learn to read and write, a ritual which is strictly Hindu in origin. The Portuguese would have been alarmed at these customs and practices and wanted to thwart such 'unchristian' rituals. Session III of Decree XIII forbids the Christian schoolmasters from setting up idols in their schools for their heathen scholars. Schoolmasters were instructed to remove all heathen idols and other objects of worship from their schools upon pain of excommunication from the church. From this Decree it is evident that the Nasrani community had no objection to the Hindu children worshipping their own gods in their schools.

As elsewhere around the world, keeping of slaves was prevalent also in the Kerala society. The Tarisapally copper plates[20] as well as the Iravi Kortan plates[21] of 1320 CE disclose various castes made subservient to the Nasranis by the ruling kings of that time. A serious accusation the missionaries made against the Nasranis was not their practice of keeping slaves but not baptizing their slaves into Christian faith. Session IV of Decree IX insists that the children of infidel slaves be baptized, and the slaves to be instructed and exhorted to receive baptism.

The Nasranis followed an age old custom of giving Old Testament and New Testament names along with certain names which they shared in common with their compatriots to their children. Session IV of Decree XVI wanted Nasranis to discontinue this practice and give the names of Christian saints instead. It seems the name 'Eesho' (Jesus) was very common among the Nasranis. The missionaries thought the name of Jesus was too holy to be used. However, in spite of the missionary caveat, Old Testament names and names in common with the Hindus are still in use among the Nasranis. Though the Decree insisted on calling children by their baptismal names the Nasranis have not heeded this decree till today.

The missionaries wanted to impose strict laws and regulations on the religious practices of the Nasranis. Session V of Decree II made the reception of sacraments obligatory at least once a year for all those who are above the age of 14. For the Nasranis participation in the Eucharist and other sacraments was never obligatory. Session VI of Decree I cautions that the neglect of the sacrament of confession is a mortal sin, while noting that many among the participants of the synod had never confessed in their lives at all. Session V of Decree IX.XII made it compulsory for every faithful to attend mass and not attending mass on Sunday was declared a mortal sin. Archbishop Menezes exhorted the Nasranis to take sacraments compulsorily at least once a year. He went further to advise the vicars to instruct their parishioners to do it more often. Since the Syrian mass is too long to celebrate daily, Session V of Decree IX.IV made a provision and recommended to translate the Roman missal into the Syriac language and say it daily.

Hindu musicians playing in churches during church festivals is a common practice among the Nasranis even to this day. But Session V of Decree IX.XIV forbids heathen musicians and other pagans to remain in church when the sacrament is administered. The decree also maintains that no non-Christian should be allowed in the church or even near the doors or windows of the church at the time of the holy sacrifice. Prior to the synod, it seems, the Nasranis were very flexible about allowing anyone inside their holy places irrespective of their faith.

Session VII of Decree XI dissuades Nasrani priests[22] from eating and drinking with 'Mahometans, Jews and heathens'. The priests were to be temperate and sober and not to eat with anybody other than Christians, nor in a public house. The decree exhorted the priests to be an example to their people. Session VII of Decree XIII forbids the clergy from engaging in secular business. This decree observed that very few priests among the Nasranis dedicated themselves particularly to the service of God and the divine worship and most engaged in 'merchandize', that is individual businesses of their own. Such errant priests were asked to renounce those businesses. Session VII of Decree XV warns against priests receiving payment for military service. It is well known that the Nasranis made excellent soldiers and were given the right to carry the 'curved sword' since the decree of the Iravi Cortan copper plates in the ninth century CE. Following the Eastern tradition, priestly celibacy was never imposed on the Nasrani priests. However, the bishops, who were chosen from among the religious, were celibates. Session VII of Decree XVI imposed celibacy on all the Nasrani priests. All the Nasrani priests were commanded to remain unmarried or if married, as the majority were, to put away their wives. This decree was not followed to the last letter for obvious reasons and contemporary accounts speak of women being separated from their husbands and forced to stay apart so that their husbands may not lose their position in the church. However the decree mentioned that an allowance would be paid to all such wives for their maintenance and their children. The priestly training among the Nasranis was called *Malpanate*, following the Indian system of *Gurukula*,[23] under each *Malpan* (Priest's teacher) 10 to 20 candidates were trained. The candidates were taught Syriac and Sanskrit languages along with various theological and allied subjects. The missionaries took steps to put an end to this age-old system of *Malpanate* and introduced the European system of giving seminary training to the aspiring candidates through establishing seminaries under their watchful eyes and patronage.

Session VIII of Decree XXXVII instructs the Nasranis to forgo their local customs and practices and conform to the universal (Catholic) Latin customs of the Church of Rome. For instance, following the Oriental custom, the Nasranis used to make the sign of the Cross from the Left to the Right and not vice-versa. The synod instructed the Nasranis to follow the Western custom. Session IX of Decree IV forbids Nasranis from attending heathen festivals like *Onam*.[24] The Nasranis used to partake enthusiastically in celebrations like *Mamankam*[25] where people playfully fought against each other with bows, arrows and other weapons, in which some used to get wounded or even get killed. The synod urged the Christians to abstain from such heathen festivities and to observe only their own festivals. The missionaries considered that heathen celebrations were festivities devoted to the honour of the devil.

Session IX of Decree XVII gives instruction to the Nasranis to differentiate themselves from heathens by their dress and their way of life. When the missionaries landed in India, they found the Nasrani community enjoying the social privileges equal to that of Nampoothiris (Brahmins) and following most of their customs. Starting with *Jathakarma* (giving honey mixed with ghee and gold to the newborn), *Namakarana* (name giving), *Annaprasana* (first feeding), *Vidyarambha* (initiation into studies), *Upanayana* (substituted by Baptism), *Vivaha* (marriage) and *Pulakuli* (purification after death) almost every Hindu ritual was incorporated into the Nasrani way of life. The decree notes that the Nasranis cannot be distinguished from their heathen neighbours by appearance and dress and asks them to dress differently from the heathens and not to pierce their ears like them. Even the churches of the Nasranis were constructed in the model of Hindu temples and it was the presence of the St Thomas Cross that distinguished them.

Thus the decrees of the Synod of Diamper give us a glimpse of the Nasrani lifestyle in Kerala towards the end of the sixteenth century CE. In his *History of the Church of Malabar* (London, 1694) J. F. Raulin, indicates that up to the sixteenth century, the Nasranis did not use any other image except the St Thomas Cross in their Churches. The Nasranis called their eucharistic celebration the Holy *Qurbana*, which is derived from the Hebrew *Korban* (קרבן), meaning 'Sacrifice'. *Qurbana* was always said in the Syriac language until 1962.[26] The melodies also used by the Nasranis in worship were remnants of ancient Syriac music. Baptism is still called by the Hebrew-Syriac term *Mamodisa* and follows many of the ancient rituals of the ceremony. Boundaries between Christians and Hindus are blurred in the cultural spheres such as house building, astrology, birth and marriage.

The Repercussions of the West's March into the East

The arena of conflict between the Portuguese and Nasranis of Kerala was in the following fields – administrative (Portuguese domination vs national administration), social (Indian culture vs European customs) and Liturgical (Indigenous and historical Syrian Rite vs Latin Rite of the Portuguese). Administrative forms (Archdeacon of Malabar vs Archbishop of Goa) and several issues concerning social customs and the maintenance of the indigenous Syrian Rite were the points around which the battle raged. As already indicated, the early contacts of the Portuguese with the Nasranis were characterized by friendliness, understanding and mutual acceptance of sacraments. It was only later on, when the Portuguese revealed their motive of subjugating the local Syrian rite and substituting Latin Liturgy and Jurisdiction for the Syrian rite that had been prevalent for centuries, that the trouble started. Almost all the Syrian bishops of the Malabar church were frequently arrested, sent to Goa, Portugal and Rome for trials, kept in prison for long periods and were subjected to terrible mental and physical tortures.[27] Blinded by prejudice, made inept by ignorance and arrogant by domination, the missionaries dragged this ancient church of St Thomas through four centuries of suffering, dreadful waste and fatal loss of identity.

The irony of this struggle was that it was not the Hindus or the Muslims but the Nasranis who put up the first moral fight against foreign domination which had on its side, ecclesiastical authority, military might and the weight of the native Rajas. The withdrawal of the Jesuit missionaries from Portugal as a result of the *Koonan Cross oath*[28] was a great relief to the Nasranis. But the Carmelite missionaries who replaced the Jesuits were no better and some-times, even worse.[29] Their aim was also Latinization and they successfully prevented the grievances of the Nasranis from reaching Rome.

The tragedy of the European Christian mission to India was that it was the Portuguese model of the notorious Inquisition and its unchristian and nega-tive spirit that deeply permeated their contacts with people and their church administration. It was the spirit of injustice, cruelty, untruth and selfishness that reigned supreme. The Schismatic group leaders made sincere and ear-nest efforts for reunion but they were all foiled by the intransigent attitude of the Carmelite missionaries. Those who remained in the Catholic Church also strenuously worked for reunion, under various leaders, but could not succeed due to the foul play and opposition of the missionaries. The astonishing efforts of Mar Joseph Kariattil and his colleagues and the daring journey they made to Lisbon and Rome and the sad end of their efforts are all part of the history.[30]

Though the colonial powers vanished from the scene, the basic colonial power structure that had been imposed on the Nasranis remained the same and causes friction between the Oriental rites and the Latin rite Christians even to this day. Even now in India and elsewhere the Nasrani church is confined to narrow territories by the Latin Church under the pretext of 'one territory one jurisdiction'. Though the right of self-rule for Oriental rites is envisaged in Vatican II, which is a natural and fundamental right of any community on earth, the Latin Church continues its stubborn denial of this minimum demand.

Conclusion

In 1599, which was nearly a century after the arrival of the Portuguese mission-aries, the Oriental Jurisdiction was suppressed completely and the Nasranis were put under Latin Hierarchy. This was indeed a triumph of ecclesial coloni-alism. This situation continued for nearly 300 years until in 1896, the Nasranis were given three Apostolic Vicars of their own rite and nationality under the Propaganda Congregation. In the year 1923 Rome re-established the Oriental Hierarchy with the official name: the Syro-Malabar Rite. A few years later Rome further extended the Syro-Malabar jurisdiction to parts of Karnataka and Tamilnadu states. In 1965 the Vatican II promulgated its decrees which guaranteed equal rights to all rites not only in theory but also in practice.

In 1962 the Syro-Malabar Church was given its first mission in North India (Chanda). Seeing the miraculous missionary prowess of the Nasranis[31] in 1968 three more mission Exarchates, Satna, Sagar and Ujjain were given to the Syro-Malabar Church. In 1972 two more mission Exarchates, Jagdalpur and Bijnor were given to them. In 1977 all five existing Syro-Malabar mission Exarchates were raised to be dioceses and one more mission diocese, the diocese of Rajkot in Gujarat, was also given to the Syro-Malabar Church. In 1984 the Diocese of Gorakhpur was entrusted to the Syro-Malabar rite. However, the section of Nasranis who remained loyal to the Roman Catholic Church are still legally forced to confine themselves geographically to 0.47 per cent of the Indian subcontinent. Thus, despite the establishment of the Syro-Malabar Hierarchy, the basic existential right of the Catholic wing of Nasranis continued to be denied. It still continues to be an oppressed Church, a Church in fetters, kept so for the convenience of and domination by a few in the Church. The power-structure of the Latin jurisdiction keeps the Nasranis under them and exploits their personnel for their own survival in India. In India the Latin Church lacks personnel, especially for mission work. They recruit personnel from the Nasrani community and these are Latinized. Many Latin congregations, Latin dioceses and Latin missions in India survive on account of the vocations from the Nasranis.

From this analysis of the *Marthoma Margam* on the basis of the information gathered from *the Acts and Decrees of the Synod of Diamper* the non-competitive and non-domineering spirituality practised by the Nasranis is clear. The evangelization method pursued by the Nasranis was their edifying presence. Only such archetypal *margam* and edifying presence can be the channels of evangelization in a globalizing world. The Nasranis had evolved such a *margam* (lifestyle)[32] in their original and old pluralistic world of religions and cultures. This could be the most effective paradigm for the present world. A return to the communitarian, unassuming spirituality once practised by the Nasranis, which is quite evident in their lifestyle is the hope and future of the Christian Church in Asia. The Nasrani church sets before the universal church a *margam* which is powerful, practical, unassuming, down-to-earth, non-domineering, non-competitive, tested and verified through the 2,000-year long survival of its effectiveness. If only the wider Church could learn some lessons from the Nasranis, Blessed John Paul II's dream regarding Asia as '*a land of promise and hope for all mankind*' could well come true.

Notes

1 Given at New Delhi, in India, 6 November 1999.
2 It was in Antioch the followers of Jesus of Nazareth were named Christians (Acts 11.26), while elsewhere they were mentioned as Nazarenes (Acts 24.5). Following this tradition those who were converted in India by St Thomas the apostle were

known as Nasranis. In the Arabic-speaking cultures Nasrani is the term commonly used to denote a Christian.

3 See in this connection the poem by Rudyard Kipling: 'The Whiteman's Burden' on 'The Whiteman's Burden' [http://public.wsu.edu/~wldciv/world_civ_reader/world_civ_reader_2/kipling.html].

4 Roy, Arunthati (1998), *The God of Small Things*. New York: HarperPerennial, p. 17.

5 Cranganore is a port in Kerala, South India. In the ancient days this port was known as 'Muziris'.

6 Philologically, similarities are found in basic Assyrian and Dravidian words. *Abba* – father (Syriac) *Appa* (Tamil); *Emma* – mother (Syr) *Amma* (Tml); *Ena* – I (Syr) *En* (Tml); *Rmp* – great (Syr) *Rampa* (Tml) etc. point towards this possibility. The excavations of Harappa Mohenjo Daro also suggest possible links between these civilizations.

7 As per India's official census data (2001) the Christian population in Kerala was 6.06 million. About 75 per cent of them (4.5 million) are St Thomas Christians though coming under different denominations.

8 As far as St Thomas Christians are concerned the arrival of the Western missionaries was disastrous. Through their Latinization attempt (forcing Nasranis to follow the Roman rite) they created havoc among the Nasranis which led to divisions. Those who refused to leave the Catholic communion were confined by the missionaries to a small territory (0.47 % of their land) and the rest of India was brought under Latin Rite jurisdiction. (Ref. V. F. Vineeth (1983), *Justice and Reconciliation: The Sad but Living Story of a Church in Fetters*. Bangalore: Dharmaram Publications).

9 The Hindu caste system is comparable to class structures in other countries, except for its religious overtones and rigidity. The four main castes are Brahman, Kshatria, Vaisia and Sudra. Below them are untouchables. The first three castes are treated as 'forward castes' while Sudras and outcastes (untouchables) are treated as backward castes. Although Nasranis and Nairs do not belong to this system in its strict sense, since they were holding a social and financial position equal to that of the higher class Hindus they too came to be treated as forward castes. Nasranis constituted the largest forward caste community in Kerala, accounting for 16.0 per cent of the total population against 14.5 per cent for the Nairs. In this perhaps, they can be accused of not having followed the strict tenets of their faith and doctrine, which emphasized the equality of man. They found their status within the caste system from the tradition that they are converted Brahmins. Even to this day they follow many Hindu traditions and customs.

10 http://en.wikipedia.org/wiki/Placid_J._Podipara

11 The Christian way of life (*Nasrani Margam*) that resulted from the preaching of St Thomas in India came to be known as *Marthoma Margam*, due to the influence of *Margas* in India.

12 Nidhin Olikara, *The Heathen and the Syrian – Syrian Christian Ritual and Tradition pre 1599 A.D.* http://nasrani.net/2011/05/19/the-heathen-and-the-syrian-syrian-christian-ritual-and-tradition-pre-1599-a-d/

13 Many missionaries were under the impression and of the opinion that they belonged to the Nestorian heretics.

14 See Bp. Jonas Thaliath, *The Synod of Diamper* (1958), also Paul Pallath, 'The Synod of Diamper: Valid or Invalid?' in *The Synod of Diamper Revisited* (2001), ed. George Nedungatt S. J. Rome: Pontifico Instituto Orientale.

15 Scaria, Zacharia (ed.) (1994), *The Acts and Decrees of the Synod of Diamper*. Indian Institute of Christian Studies: Hosanna Mount.

16 The Nasranis tried in vain to convince the missionaries that the 'Law of Thomas' is different from the 'Law of Peter' and therefore, they should not try to force their laws upon the Nasranis, which obviously infuriated them.

17 *Ekam sat vipra behudha vananti* (Reality is one, the learned speak of it differently) is a generous and enlightened teaching of Rigveda (1:164:46) that allows space for others.

18 *Guruvandana* is a ritual practiced by students giving homage to their teacher.

19 *Vidyarambham* is a Hindu ritual by which a child is initiated into education.

20 Special privileges granted to Nasranis by Ayyanadigal, the king of Venadu, in 880 AD/CE.

21 Nasranis were often granted special privileges by the ruling kings for various services rendered. Nasranis maintained an army of their own under the leadership of their Archdeacon.

22 A Nasarani priest was called *Kathanar* while a missionary priest was known as *Paadiri*.

23 *Gurukula* is the ancient Indian system of education in which students stay with the teacher's family.

24 *Onam* is essentially a harvest festival though there is a Hindu folklore associated to it.

25 *Mamankam* is a playful battle celebrated in Thirunavaya, Malabar coast, South India, in the present-day state of Kerala from the time of Kulasekharas (Cheras) in every 12 years until the eighteenth century, mostly remembered for the bloody battles that occurred during the festivals. The Mamankam festival was a great trade fair from the Sangam period where traders from around the world came through Ponnani Port by ships and barges.

26 From 1962 onwards Qurbana has been said in the local language of Kerala, Malayalam. But now the Qurbana text is translated into many other Indian languages such as Hindi, Kannada, Tamil, Telugu, Guajarati, etc., including English.

27 N. A. Thomas (2011), *One Territory – One Bishop? Or Shall the Syrian Rites Die?* Vidyanagar: Denha Services, pp. 76–7.

28 The Coonan Cross Oath, taken on 3 January 1653, was a public avowal by the Nasranis that they would not submit to Portuguese dominance in ecclesiastical and secular life. The swearing of the oath was a major event in the history of the Nasrani community and marked a major turning point in its relations with the Portuguese colonial government. The oath resulted directly in the formation of an independent Malankara church, with Mar Thoma I as its head, and the Syrian Catholic Church, with Parambil Chandy as its head and ultimately to the first permanent split in the community.

29 Fr. N. A. Thomas, a Nasrani historian, in his book, *One Territory – One Bishop?* . . . makes the following evaluation of the Carmelite legacy, 'The Carmelite missionaries ever remained the outdated fossils of a crude bureaucratic missionary colonialism that had not even once proved a period of usefulness to its credit' (p. 69).

30 *Varthamana Pusthakam* is the breathtaking description of the historic journey of Mar Joseph Kariattil and Paremakkal Thoma Kathanar to Rome to represent the grievances of the Nasranis recorded in 1785 by the latter. It is an impressive travelogue of an eight-year journey to Rome and back in order to gain freedom for Nasranis from 'Latin' Bishops, written in 562 pages of lucid prose. It argues strongly for the independence of Indians from foreign domination.

31 It was to Carmelites of Mary Immaculate Congregation, the first Indigenous Religious Community in India founded by Bl. Kuriakose Elias Chavara, the mission of Chanda was entrusted. The credit goes to the CMI Congregation for giving leadership in all significant movements and achievements the Nasranis accomplished ever since its foundation.

32 Evaluating the *Marthoma Nasrani Margam* (the lifestyle of St Thomas Christians) from the perspective of 'wayfarer spirituality' is both intriguing and delightful but beyond the scope of this essay.

Bibliography and Further Reading

Aerthayil, James (1982), *The Spiritual Heritage of St Thomas Christians.* Bangalore: Dharmaram Publications.

Every, George (1978), *Understanding Eastern Christianity.* Placid Lecture series 1, Bangalore: Dharmaram Publications.

Mundadan, Mathias A. (1989), *From the Beginning up to the Middle of the Sixteenth Century (up to 1542). History of Christianity in India,* vol. I, Bangalore: Church History Association of India.

Podipara, Placid J. (1979), *The Rise and Decline of the Indian Church of the Thomas Christians.* Kottayam: Oriental Institute for Religious Studies.

— (2007), *Collected Works of Rev. Dr. Placid J. Podipara CMI.* ed. Thomas Kalayil, CMI, Mannanam: Sanjos Publications.

Thomas, N. A. (2011), *One Territory – One Bishop? Or Shall the Syrian Rites Die?* Vidyanagar: Denaha Services.

26 Christian Spirituality in Europe: The Celtic Tradition

Thomas O'Loughlin

Introduction

Few movements in spirituality in recent decades have had such eager and well-resourced devotees as those who claim to follow the 'Celtic Way', to celebrate 'a Celtic liturgy', or to view Christianity from within a 'Celtic vision',[1] In the 'shopping mall' of contemporary spirituality the 'Celtic' variety seems to meet many modern demands and offer exciting possibilities.[2] To some it has that 'authentic feel' of antiquity and a tradition of saints, texts and liturgies. To others it is an alternative to what is seen as the rationalist sterility of modernity. And, for some it is a positive evaluation of the rare, the delicate, the exotic and a system of church life and ritual that is immune to the controversies of the Reformation and the divisions/factions found today. The 'Celtic' seems to provide an historical canvas where desires can be expressed and to provide a space where new patterns of practice can be adopted with comparative safety. Unlike many other contemporary experiments in spirituality and liturgy which stress their novelty – new ideas for new situations – and modernity, those who pursue the Celtic find comfort in its apparent antiquity, which they see as self-authenticating. Combined with this there is the thrill of finding 'lost treasures' that can unlock today's problems, the excitement of encountering a native wisdom that confronts a spirit-less sophistication, and the pleasure of being seen as opting for the distinctive 'alternative'.[3]

This pursuit of Celtic spirituality is a genuine part of today's landscape in spirituality. It is a valuable index of contemporary spiritual hungers; and, indirectly, an indicator of the inadequacy of what is offered in many contemporary churches with regard to liturgy and spiritual inspiration. However, it is worth noting that many of its historical claims are more the product of wishful thinking, and the agenda of romanticism with its search for 'the simple', than of historical reconstruction of the practice and theology found in Ireland, Wales and Brittany in the early medieval period.[4] Indeed, the very fact that devotees of 'Celtic spirituality' combine materials from these diverse cultures – 'Celtic' is a linguistic category and the product of comparatively recent studies in linguistics – and from over a very wide time span is sufficient proof that it is a contemporary 'pick-n-mix' rather than a past being imitated.[5]

However, the mere act of demonstrating that a religious claim to history is not historically grounded does not dismiss the claim's authenticity. Every religion – in so far as a religion implies a tradition of practice from the past into the present – looks back at its past and draws and redraws its history in terms of its present. It looks back, sees some elements in its memory it values as representing the core of its best practice, and tacitly drops those elements that are seen to have failed or which seem to have distracted it from its mission, charism and inspiration. It is worth noting that the Church is always remembering and always forgetting its past. Put another way: Christians, as part of their continual theological development, adapt themselves to their moment while recycling their past for their present and future. Moreover, it is the *theological quality* of the new recycled past, rather than the historical verisimilitude of the product, which is the key issue. The historian may, from the perspective of an academic methodology's access to the truth, point out discrepancies between the presented image and the past facts; but the authenticity of the recycled past is a matter of its theological worth not of its historical mimesis. It is in this light that I propose to examine Celtic spirituality here.

However, the notion that Christians recycle their past as a way of introducing some ideas and eclipsing others might seem a bold claim. If it does, then just consider the example of the Deuteronomistic history.[6] Whatever the relationship between the past events and Israel's image of Moses and his history (and it is far from being a matter of 'simple record') as found in Exodus, Numbers and Leviticus, there were deliberate recyclings of the past to produce new histories. One of these resulted in the history presented in the Book of Deuteronomy, and related texts, which invented a new past which was grafted onto the earlier 'Mosaic' books, and which produced a very different image of what it was for Israel to live the life of the covenant. Yet it was this 'new past' that forms the immediate background to Jesus's presentation of the new covenant, and it stands directly behind the spirituality and practice of the earliest churches.[7] Similarly, the significance of 'the Last Supper' plays a far mightier role in the Christian memory that offers an understanding of the Eucharist than is the case with an historical study of either those texts[8] or the actual historical practice.[9] So, by extension, while it may be that Celtic spirituality is another case of rewriting the past, that does not mean that it may not be a genuine, and valuable, spirituality, or, expressed in explicitly theological terms, a genuine manifestation of the Spirit.

In short, Christians constantly recycle their past as a way of making sense in the present and generating a vision of the future and this is the work of memory, remembering and memorialization – all that is captured in the term 'anamnesis', But the work of memory is not identical with the work of historians, the connection is that both share a common linkage to the past. Memory is part of the creative theological imagination that is concerned with what should constitute Christian discipleship and seeks to encompass, as a theological discourse should, the ineffable. Such a relationship to the past is very different from attempts to reconstruct for our observation a 'back then' in the foreign country of the past. Memory, and remembering, is akin to taking the next step in the tradition, which, as Picasso remarked, is the action of producing a baby rather than wearing your grandfather's hat. Viewed from this perspective, what can we say about 'Celtic spirituality'?

Locality

One of the most striking motifs in this spirituality is that it rejoices not in some abstract name, but in a notion of locality: 'Celtic'. Celtic is thought to refer to region, and the people of that region, and to have a particular, as distinct from a global or international, character. While all movements start somewhere (think of the 'German Mystics', the 'French School', the 'Azusa Street Revival' or the 'Toronto Blessing'), they usually make claims that their message has universal significance. This claim, by contrast, stresses what a single 'area' has to offer, the uniqueness of the area is seen as giving a dimension of appreciation and rootedness. It hints that perhaps what is seen as 'the common', the general inheritance, is not the best of all possible spiritualities; whereas the local is the spirituality that fits 'here'. Since the 'Celtic' is, for most of those who pursue it, the 'other', there is a notion also that one must recover forgotten voices, see the value in those cultures that have not achieved political dominance. This new awareness of the forgotten, small 'Celtic' cultures forms a counterpoint to the global brands, their loss of specificity and their impersonal banality. Someone who is concerned with the local, earthed quality of Celtic spirituality is probably someone who also appreciates hand-made local produce as representing an economy where human scales and values are paramount. Indeed, not least among the benefits of Celtic spirituality is that it has given a theological expression to this notion of human-sized economics and respect for the given-ness of situations, times and seasons. Just as many social and economic movements today reject globalized production values and brands – even in such a simple manner as being concerned to count 'food miles' – so this spirituality rejects Christianities that are presented as global products or which glory in their multinational brands with standard defined products for every situation. The specific, the non-standard, the tailored to the situation, the individual and the local are all seen as desirable qualities in a spirituality. Linking them with 'Celtic' seems appropriate as the 'Celtic' is the alternative to the dominant, global standard, the very small and local, and captures an image of 'craftspeople' each seeking excellence and beauty in their own work. The resulting diversity and uniqueness is seen as a gift of the Spirit who can still be heard in those small-scale, out of the way places.

This notion of the Celtic as somehow embodying the 'small', the 'personal', the 'alternative' is perhaps the most contested aspect of this whole movement. First of all, it is seen as simply a new version of colonial stereotyping: it is not groups who might call themselves 'Celts' that adopt this vision, but others who declare it to be a quality inherent in them or their inheritance. As such, this image of 'them' is as much a failure to encounter other human beings of a different culture as equals, as the colonial stereotypes of 'the Irish' who are a feckless, jolly, talkative lot who like drink and parties. One then does not encounter an individual, but someone who is 'typically Irish' (or not). The stress on individuality that is claimed as a value by the devotee of this spirituality is then not something granted to those who belong to the 'group' that are admired!

A close ally of such stereotyping is the replacement of a real assessment of the people with a romantic construct of 'them' and 'their world'. But the small-scale world of hand-production that is so elegant in an Aran sweater sold in a tourist outlet is rather different from the small scale of subsistence farming on the west coast of Ireland with a memory of the Great Famine, of a village in Wales that once had a slate quarry and now has high unemployment, or of crofting in the Scottish Highlands where the empty solitudes are a result of The Clearances. Such people do not need to be romanticized in a spirituality in the same way they may be packaged by the tourist industry. The cosy images that suffuse this spirituality abound with latent colonialism and ignorant romanticism. Such qualities are inimical to any movement of the Spirit that might promote the *conversio morum* towards a more just human society that should be inherent in a Christian spirituality.

The notion that there is a well-defined 'Celtic' area is, moreover, questioned. Where was it? When was it? And, what linked its parts together? Historically, no such region existed for the term is – apart from classical usage[10] – derived from comparative philology which can show that Irish and its related language belongs to the same branch of the Indo-European family as Welsh and its related languages.[11] At no time in the historical past did those various groups of language users recognize that they had even this linguistic affinity – and so the notion of a common culture is no more than a construct by which coincidences are raised up to being distinguishing marks. Likewise, there was never a religious entity known as the 'Celtic Church'.[12] This notion that has its origins not in the first millennium but in Anglican apologetics; those early churches were Latin-using from the start, and saw themselves as part of the Christianity of the Western Empire. Seeing 'the Celtic Church' as representing an alternative to the divisions that fracture contemporary Christianity is simply an imaginative projection. However, while noting that the 'Celtic Church' is a chimera, one should not ignore its value as forming a bridge for many people to a more ample liturgical experience for whom words like 'Catholic' or 'High Church' would simply produce allergic reactions.

Community

One of the paradoxes of contemporary life is that while we are terrified of any diminution of our individuality, we are in search of community. We want to belong, and we want a church that is both open and welcoming, but also one where we have choice and voice combined with the experience of working/ sharing together. This may be a dream, but it is not an ignoble dream and it is one that many pursue with fervour. We may be committed consumers, but we also want belonging, and this is not the enforced community/collaboration of the village of pre-industrial agriculture, but the result of choice and decision. We want to be able to join a community which shares belief and vision, and in which we feel comfortable. The elective nature of these contemporary communities makes them fluid, self-selecting and club-like, but their inspiration is genuine in the face of contemporary isolating materialism. That Christianity can even be considered in this way – monasticism and its variants apart – has probably only been the case in the first two centuries (where to become a Christian was, for the most part, a decision to 'opt in' to a distinct group in society) and in Western culture today. And, for many who express this desire for community in ecclesial terms, the 'Celtic' promises just such a welcoming community. This takes the form of communities that are almost analogous to religious orders in that the members live in physical communities of one sort of another; to communities that are associations of 'friends'; to groups that meet and share their common spiritual endeavour.

That the desire for community is a spiritual quest close to the heart of Christianity cannot be doubted – the *Didache* which presents Christian discipleship as a community's rule is, after all, older than most of the texts in New Testament[13] – and the history of Christianity cannot be understood without the contribution of monasticism and religious movements that were offshoots from it. Equally, there is the legacy of monasticism across the British Isles in the first millennium – it was not coterminous with Christianity in the period, but most of what we know about it comes either from monks or is mediated through monastic eyes. We should keep Bede's opening comment in his *History of the English as a Church* before our eyes:

> At present there are five languages in Britain . . . all devoted to seeking for and proclaiming the one and the same wisdom, that is the highest truth and the most sublime knowledge. These languages are English, British, Irish, and Pictish, along with Latin; and, through the study of the Scriptures, Latin is in common use among them all.[14]

And he saw monasteries, the home of Latin in these islands in the eighth century, as places where the Christian life was lived in its fullness.

The new quest for community raises two issues for Christians. First, why are existing Christian groups not seen as offering an experience of community? Many who embrace 'Celtic communities' declare that 'the church structures' are too concerned with 'maintenance' rather than 'mission' or with providing a standard 'one size fits all' product, or engage in similar criticisms of the present systems of church life. All such criticisms follow a pattern and need not be taken as detailed critiques, but they do point to underlying problems that large, highly structured religious organizations need to keep in mind: in a lonely age, the churches that fail to form real communities are failing in a fundamental task for which the Church exists. Likewise, those churches which seek to build 'communities' as a by-product of their own structures – one has but to think of the Catholic Church which seeks to produce 'communities' as a derivative-function of its dwindling numbers of professional clergy – have failed to see that community, as the basis of being church, derives from actual human gatherings and desires, rather than as a result of an exercise in logistics.

Second, those who seek out community often confuse what they seek with the minimalism of the club of shared interests or the exclusivity of a salon where the similarly enlightened can display their spiritual sophistication. Community in the Christian tradition is the commitment to the covenant established in the Christ – and it makes demands as a way of living together. Again, one but has to recall the *Didache*: acceptance is not tested by creedal affirmations but a willingness to embrace 'the Way of Life'.[15] It is a community that while bonded in the Anointed is radically open to all who come to him, and so it is a grouping that breaks the boundaries of human divisions and must model the justice of the coming Kingdom. Any community that becomes either indifferent to the needs of those who are poor or which views itself as a sect or which causes division within the larger Christian body may satisfy the desires of its devotees as a community, but cannot claim to be a church. The same consumerist society that makes us seek real communities also makes commitment to such communities more difficult than ever.

Celebration

One of the positive features of 'Celtic spirituality' is, it is said, its joyfulness and willingness to celebrate. It rejoices in the creation, it greets human growth with joy, it is sensitive to the celebration of the seasons, and embraces a cheerful worship. It could be argued that any expression of Christianity that does not fulfil these criteria has somehow lost its way, but the fact remains that these are not qualities that one can automatically expect from one's nearest parish. Between the staid dullness of many churches' worship and the apparently free-flowing enthusiasm of evangelical and 'seeker' churches,[16] the 'Celtic' appears as the middle ground. It appears to present the tradition, but be flexible enough to take in an awareness of the creation, and, in particular, our existence in relationship to the environment.

While this aspect of Celtic spirituality can often produce the greatest outbursts of derision from those who see it as a pastiche of wishful thinking and a devotion to current fads, this reaction does not do justice either to some of its basic inspirations nor to what other Christian groups might learn from it. The situation with regard to what constitutes a successful liturgy is changing within contemporary Western society far faster than most churches with formal liturgies can keep pace with developments. At the very least, the desire for new liturgies found in Celtic spirituality should alert churches to this phenomenon of our times. Likewise, for many the Christian calendar – and liturgy linked to times – either did not exist or had become a token affair; and this sense has been recovered by this movement. This is a development that others should learn from and extend: Christianity emerged within a liturgical religion in which the calendar was central, from its own beginning it developed a liturgical day, week and year, and its main traditions of spirituality are often incomprehensible apart from that sense of religious time. By contrast, modern Western societies have an impoverished time-scape that marginalizes religious time by making people immune to time as vehicle of religious recollection. Lastly, while there is an ever-increasing concern within our culture over the destruction of the environment, this concern and humanity's relationship to the planet is still not on the liturgical agenda of most mainstream churches – while it is eschewed as irrelevant by some forms of evangelicalism.

That leaves a question: has this concern with celebration much in common with the praxis of Christianity in the early medieval period? The answer is rather disappointing! While there is a body of religious poetry and theology that read cosmos as a creation and sought in it the footprints of God (*vestigia Dei*) this is no more than can be found in any other church, east or west, at the time.[17] The creation had been deformed by Adam's Sin as could be seen in pain, sweat and hunger, and further damaged by human sinfulness which required penitence for past sins and asceticism as a training against future wrong, and the preaching of this message was a far cry from the jolly optimism of many contemporary spiritual guides.[18] By contrast, those early cultures in the British Isles had a deep awareness of movement of time through its cycles, and regulated their lives around its alternations of ordinary and stressed times.[19] That said, in its structures their liturgical year was remarkably close to the calendar still followed in the Roman Rite, and one of the most obvious features of its celebration of time was the attention it gave to fasting. All who want a richer calendar should bear in mind that in the Irish language the word for Friday is *Aoine* which means 'Fast' (coming from the Latin word for 'fast': *ieiunium*), while the word for Wednesday is *Céadaoin* which means 'first fast'. In this they were following the pious Jews of Jesus' time who fasted twice a week,[20] and in direct continuity with the earliest communities of Christians which fasted on Wednesdays and Fridays.[21] If one wants to have a rich calendar, the feasts have to have their counterpoint in fasts.

This sense that the patterns of celebration, however new and aimed at the situations Christians find themselves in today, must have a basis in the tradition of Christian Liturgy, and must be in continuity with a communion of people in the past who worshipped (even if the boundary of that 'Celtic community' is largely a product of their own myth of identity), sets them apart from other 'alternative worship' movements.[22] In their invocation of that communion of saints – the Celtic saints – within the Communion of Saints there is scope for a richer ecclesiology and understanding of what is involved in liturgy than is often the case with other contemporary spiritualities and styles of liturgy. However, this is an opportunity those churches which are committed to a high view of liturgy have been slow to build upon.

Diverse Themes

Unlike a spirituality which comes from a single text (or well-defined set of texts) or a structured group like a religious order/movement, it is impossible to draw the lines around what constitutes 'Celtic spirituality'. It has many origins, many teachers and exists in many different cultural situations. What constitutes a 'Celtic liturgy' for someone working with an Irish, formally Catholic, group of young people visiting an ancient monastic site is very different from that which inspires a group of North American Presbyterians to adapt a handful of rituals (what they would refer to as 'worship forms') for possible use on Sunday morning. Indeed, one is sometimes tempted to see the label 'Celtic' as simply a brand that is adopted to give a flavour of authenticity and invent a tradition for otherwise new developments. Less critically, one might see it as an aesthetic style (by analogy with the way we use the term 'baroque' to describe an approach to liturgy) where certain images and language unite an otherwise diverse set of phenomena. However, there is a genuine link which suggests that there is something more than a brand or a style: all these groups make appeal to the history of Christianity and want to see themselves within a tradition of faith. This common appeal (whether it is an appeal to the past simply as an ideal or to the past as explanatory of the genetic code of Christianity) sets this movement apart from many others in the contemporary scene, and as such draws them far closer into the ambit of the mainstream churches than those other movements.

However, that said, there is no adequate point to stop in picking out the themes that might be described here or there as 'Celtic'. No matter how many such symptoms were identified, a common pattern – which you may have already noticed in the three themes examined above – would manifest itself. First, the phenomenon would be seen as 'relevant to the situation today' – and possibly be something that the mainstream churches have forgotten or ignored. Second, the phenomenon would have deep origins. The origins would be seen to lie within the human psychological make-up, often within human nature as ritual beings, then within the depths of the primal responses to God, and, giving shape to all the rest, within the religious insights and experience of 'the Celts'. Sometimes this would include a specific appeal to 'Celtic' Christian experience as in an appeal to a holy place that was/is a site of pilgrimage, or it might be more general to a site or practice that is presented as both 'numinous' and 'Celtic' but without any history of explicit links with Christianity. Third, the Celtic claims – of whatever sort – of the phenomenon would be found to have very little or no factual basis in what scholarly history can state regarding the people/places invoked as 'Celtic'. Lastly, the structure of the claims may act as a guide to those aspects of spirituality that are not receiving sufficient attention within church structures.

Notes

1 For a fuller treatment of this topic, see T. O' Loughlin (2002), '"Celtic Spirituality", Ecumenism, and the Contemporary Religious Landscape', *Irish Theological Quarterly*, 67, 153–68; idem, '"A Celtic Theology": Some Awkward Questions and Observations', in J. F. Nagy (ed.), *Identifying the 'Celtic'* [*Celtic Studies Association of North America Yearbook* 2], Dublin 2002, pp. 49–65; idem, '"Things New and Old": Contemporary Cultural Tensions and the Tradition of Liturgy in Ireland', in J. Egan and T. R. Whelan (eds), *City Limits: Mission Issues in Postmodern Times*, Dublin 2004, pp. 140–59; and idem, '"Celtic Spirituality": A Case Study in Recycling the Christian Past for Present Needs', in U. Agnew, B. Flanagan and G. Heylin (eds), *'With Wisdom Seeking God': The Academic Study of Spirituality*, Leuven 2008, pp. 143–61.

2 I take the image, and the notion of consumer-focused religious products, from B. D. Spinks, *The Worship Mall: Contemporary Responses to Contemporary Culture*, London 2010 which examines 'Celtic' inspired worship on pp. 159–81.

3 These features are examined in T. O'Loughlin (2000), *Celtic Theology: Humanity, World and God in Early Irish Writings*, London, pp. 3–24; many of these themes have their roots in the nineteenth century: see P. Sims-Williams (1998), 'Celtomania and Celtoscepticism', *Cambrian Medieval Celtic Studies*, 36, 1–35.

4 Writers on 'Celtic' spirituality rarely state when was this 'Celtic' period/society which they invoke; but it seems to be very early, before the Normans or even before the Angles and the Saxons. So, in effect, it is in a period between the passing of Roman civilization and the Germanic invasions (both rather loose as termini); moreover, this is a period for which our sources are very limited, and what sources we do have are rarely adequate (in extent or clarity) to answer modern religious questions.

5 See O'Loughlin, '"Celtic Spirituality": A Case Study in Recycling the Christian Past for Present Needs'; and for a far more hard-hitting criticism of all such historical claims, see D. E. Meek, *The Quest for Celtic Christianity*, London 2000.

6 See S. L. McKenzie, 'Deuteronomistic History', in D. N. Freedman (ed.), *Anchor History of the Bible*, New York 1992, vol. 2, pp. 160–8 for an introduction.

7 See T. O'Loughlin (2010), *The Didache: A Window on the Earliest Christians*, London, pp. 28–45.

8 See X. Léon-Dufour (1987), *Sharing the Eucharistic Bread: The Witness of the New Testament*, Mahwah, NJ, pp. 117–56.

9 See P. F. Bradshaw (2009), *Reconstructing Early Christian Worship*, London, pp. 3–19.

10 See J. J. Tierney (1959–60), 'The Celtic Ethnography of Posidonius', *Proceedings of the Royal Irish Academy* 60C, 189–273.

11 See the works of Sims-Williams and Meek already cited.

12 See W. Davies (1992), 'The Myth of the Celtic Church', in N. Edwards and A. Lane (eds), *The Early Church in Wales and the West: Recent Work in Early Christian Archaeology, History and Place-Names*, London, pp. 12–21.

13 O'Loughlin, *The Didache*, pp. 23–7.

14 Bede, *Historia ecclesiastica gentis anglorum* 1, 1.

15 See O'Loughlin, *The Didache*, pp. 28–45.

16 See Spinks, *The Worship Mall*, pp. 63–90.

17 See T. O'Loughlin (2010), 'Salvation and the Liturgy: Some Examples from Early Christian Ireland', in D. Vincent Twomey and Dirk Krausmüller (eds), *Salvation according to the Fathers of the Church*, Dublin, pp. 123–42.

18 This is a point stressed, perhaps too strongly, by Meek.

19 See P. M. Rumsey (2007), *Sacred Time in Early Christian Ireland*, London.

20 See Lk. 18.12.

21 *Didache* 8; and cf. T. O'Loughlin, 'The *Didache* as a Source for Picturing the Earliest Christian Communities: The Case of the Practice of Fasting', in K. O'Mahony (ed.), *Christian Origins: Worship, Belief and Society* [*Journal for the Study of the New Testament: Supplement Series 241*], Sheffield 2003, pp. 83–112.

22 See Spinks, *The Worship Mall*, pp. 31–62.

Bibliography and Further Reading

Meek, D. E. (2000), *The Quest for Celtic Christianity*. London: Handsel Press.

O'Loughlin, T. (2000), *Celtic Theology: Humanity, World and God in Early Irish Writings*. London: Continuum.

— (2000), *Journeys on the Edges: The Celtic Tradition*. London: DLT.

— (2005), *Discovering Saint Patrick*. London: DLT.

— (2008), '"Celtic Spirituality": A Case Study in Recycling the Christian Past for Present Needs', in U. Agnew, B. Flanagan and G. Heylin (eds), *'With Wisdom Seeking God': The Academic Study of Spirituality*, Leuven: Peeters, pp. 143–61.

Sims-Williams, P. (1998), 'Celtomania and Celtoscepticism', *Cambrian Medieval Celtic Studies*, 36, 1–35.

Spinks, B. D. (2010), *The Worship Mall: Contemporary Responses to Contemporary Culture*. London: SPCK, pp. 159–81.

27 Christian Spirituality in Oceania: An Australian Perspective

Anthony Kelly

Introduction

Oceania as a geographical area includes Melanesia, Polynesia, Micronesia, Australasia, Pacific Islands, and so takes in the countries of Australia, New Zealand, Papua New Guinea, Solomon Islands, Vanuatu, Fiji, Samoa and Tonga.[1] While the United Nations is happy to include Australia, for example, within Oceania, that only raises the question of whether it is largely a European concept meaning little more than a huge geographical aggregation of various regions in which nothing much seems to happen.

In terms of the spiritualities of this region, it is important to keep in mind that the present countries of Oceania are mainly products of nineteenth-century European colonization, predominantly by France and Britain (Tonga is the exception, never having been formally colonized). A sense of national identities came with independence in the twentieth century: Australia (1901), New Zealand (1907), Samoa (1962), Fiji (1970), Papua New Guinea [PNG] (1975), Solomon Islands (1978) and Vanuatu (1980).

Along with that sense of national identity came a growing awareness of the indigenous populations as a link to a much larger past, as with the Aboriginal (Australia), Melanesian (PNG, Solomon Islands, Vanuatu, Fiji, Australian Torres Strait Islands) and Polynesian (New Zealand, Samoa, Tonga). While Australasia's population is mainly of European descent, all other Pacific nations are predominantly indigenous. Moreover, the most recent census figures show that all the countries of Oceania are predominantly Christian, though secularization in one sense or another has increased from the 1960s and has had an eroding effect on the percentage of Christians in Australia (64 %) and New Zealand (54 %). The outcome is a growing number of those claiming no religious identity. Still, among the other countries listed, the Christian population is as high as at least 90 per cent, except for Fiji with its large Indian (Hindu) population (44 %). The ecumenical movement is well-established and productive especially in the field of theological writing and education.[2]

Obviously, too, 'Oceania' suggests what is overwhelmingly ocean and sea, rather than land.[3] Any understanding of spirituality must take that into account – most clearly for the populations of the Pacific island countries, but even for coast-hugging, beach-loving Australians. This is not to deny that the symbolism of the land and its ecological features appear strongly in the national consciousness – and conscience. In New Zealand/Aotearoa, writers such as Neil Darragh[4] have been notably productive in connecting the Gospel to Indigenous (Maori and other Polynesian) traditions from different perspectives including prayer and spirituality.[5]

There is a hermeneutical question to keep in mind as we ponder the meaning of spirituality in this region. How different would things be if the Gospel had moved more quickly into the Pacific area, and made contact with its indigenous cultures in a more rapid and immediate fashion – in the way it moved into the Greco-Roman world and to the Europe of the Roman empire? What forms of Christian community, art, ethical priorities, festivity and liturgical rituals might have resulted? Today, missiologists are enthusiastically reconsidering how the Gospel message is related to indigenous cultures. This brings the lament of being too little, too late. The inhabitants of Oceania are, to some extent, the 'poor relatives' in the distribution of pastoral and academic resources since major energies are more likely to be given to the immense classic cultures of Asia, and now to the many peoples of Africa. Moreover, it cannot escape notice that the cultural forms of Oceanic Christianity have been shaped by the British, Irish, French and German cultural presuppositions. Yet history takes strange turns, and while it is to some degree a record of regrets and a long list of 'what might have beens', there is room for surprises – as with new awareness of particular regional or cultural spiritualities underlying the religious life of different peoples.

Nonetheless, there is a common experience of struggle among indigenous cultures. A runaway globalization with its standardized technology and transnational organization is experienced as a threat even to the classic cultures of Europe and Asia. All share a sense of being dragged into something new and even dreaded. A settled sense of self nourished by a culture of community, bodily experience, festivity and belonging to nature tends to be disrupted by a rampant individualism and the consumerism that, *pace* Karl Marx, is now revealed as 'the opium of the people'.[6]

In the Pacific Island communities, the values and priorities that once informed European life have become deeply interwoven with indigenous cultures – so that in any given cultural context it is all but impossible to disentangle the two strands, and strange confusions result. Take, for example, sexual ethics. The native wisdom, earthiness and bodiliness of a Pacific Island integration of sexuality into human life are caught between a prim Jansenistic/ Victorian Puritanism and the erotomania of the West following the 'sexual revolution'. I suspect that the healthy sexuality of indigenous cultures, once derided as pornographic, now has a positive contribution to a more integrated sense, individual and communitarian, of the sexual dimension of human existence.

Spirituality

If Oceania is not without its geographical vagueness, a similar indeterminacy is connoted by the term, 'spirituality'. It can mean a lot of things, as has been pointed out in this volume. In these times of rapid secularization, it can suggest a zone of strategic retreat for those who have been disaffected from Christianity. For capitalist enterprise, it has even opened up new commercial opportunities.[7] As is well known, 'Spirituality' was an all but exclusively Catholic term — but has now taken wings,[8] into other religions, cultures and regions. The 25 volumes of the Crossroad project, *World Spirituality: An Encyclopaedic History of the Religious Quest*[9] has only 3 volumes devoted to Christianity. For our present purposes, the term suggests the discerning effort to integrate more fully the cultural and historical inheritance of whole peoples, together with the psychological experience of individuals and their personal history, into their basic and ultimate commitments. In some ways, that is what has been left out in the nineteenth-century colonial period of the Christian mission to the indigenous populations. It is being regained, now that these former native populations have matured in the Christian faith they inherited and now profess as a vocation – a calling to contribute to the larger world of Christian experience. The challenge to integrate the spirituality of people, region and religious background into the life of Christian faith is presented in the memorable words of Vatican II, 'The joys and the hopes, the griefs and the anxieties of the people of this age, especially those who are poor or in any way afflicted, these are the joys and hopes, the griefs and anxieties of the followers of Christ. Indeed, nothing genuinely human fails to raise an echo in their hearts' (*Gaudium et Spes*, #1). That surely would include the deep meanings and values, the art and sensibilities, the history and regional setting of peoples in their transcendent aspirations, and with the resources of the particular people's heart, mind, soul and imagination. But now with a more catholic understanding of the human condition and the many cultures it manifests, the Church, for example, has awoken to the need, not only of proclaiming clearly articulated doctrines in an objective sense, but also to the necessity of speaking to the cultural consciousness of the hearers of the Gospel. That was hardly a point unknown in the scholastic past, even if not always respected: *quidquid recipitur, recipitur per modum recipientis*, translatable as 'communication must respect the gifts and limitations of those it addresses'.

317

The great medieval theologians made no distinction between their theology and spirituality. But in the centuries that followed, theology was divided and subdivided in various ways, and tended to lose contact with personal experience and religious consciousness generally. Consideration of (elite) contemplative and mystical experience was shunted into a section entitled, 'Spiritual Theology'. The possibility that grace, for example, occurred in human consciousness, whether in its personal, communal or even cultural dimensions, did not attract critical attention. But in these later, more attuned psychological times, to say nothing of this period of expanding interfaith dialogue, an integration is well underway, and theology and religious education have learned to re-configure their methods so as to be firmly embedded in the deep experience of communities and persons.

An Australian Perspective[10]

Maybe there is a certain irony in the phrase, 'Australian Spirituality'. To some it may even appear as an oxymoron. It is true that we Australians are hardly the repositories of one of the world's classic cultures, the way, say, China or India or Europe might be thought of. On the other hand, the emerging global reality would not be attractive if it were populated by standardized humanity, formed by a technological culture and cut off from any particular history. Any people is quite justified in being conservationist in regard to its own distinctiveness within the ecology of humanity. Only in that way, can each culture offer its unique witness to the wider world. Some early attempts to map the Southern hemisphere designated the big landmass in the antipodean regions as *Terra Australis de Spiritu Sancto*, 'The Southern land of the Holy Spirit'. Its continental shape is now clear, but what has not yet been revealed is its occupancy by the Holy Spirit in any manifest sense; but that history is still unfolding . . .

The readiness to witness from the heart of one's culture is crucial in this era of globalization. Such witness contrasts with the desperate effort to defend a real or imagined cultural uniqueness against the homogenizing globalizing influences at work. When a new world is coming into being, the question is, what do we want to contribute to it, from the experience – and indeed, from the experiment – of being who and what we are? There is, after all, something distinctive in living on this continent. Here, Easter is in autumn, Christmas in summer and the South wind blows cold. Here, two centuries of European occupation, with its inauspicious and tragic beginnings, are being awkwardly confronted by the uncounted millennia of Aboriginal prehistory, while being increasingly in contact with the teeming, ancient worlds of Asia.

This is to say that Australia has its own point of view, from 'Down Under', as we imagine what lies ahead. This singular little history is entering a new stage, perhaps to fizzle out as an experiment that failed, perhaps to die into something more wonderful and more healing than anything we – or the world at large – has previously imagined. In the meantime, we are here. As Australians, we relate to our neighbour, understand ourselves, interpret the world and assume our responsibilities. As Australians we confess whatever faith we have, and experience in our hearts the grace of God. Our land, with all its beauty, bounty and menace, gives our souls symbols for prayer. It is here that we find together the joy and hope of life, or drift separately to some infernal region of terminal conflict, among ourselves and with those about us. There is, then, an opportunity in recognizing this time and place as a unique and irrepeatable factor in what is coming to be.[11]

Nearly 25 years ago, my *A New Imagining: Toward an Australian Spirituality*[12] appeared, in belated homage to the Bicentenary celebrations of the time. The word, 'towards' was significant, since there was no question of thinking that Australians or anyone else 'had' a spirituality as something possessed and exploited to one's advantage, even if a 'spirituality industry' has developed.[13] In an economically driven society, we tend not to be interested in plumbing the depths of life, but rather in the production of new workers and consumers, tranquilly accepting their respective roles. But behind such materialistic barbarism lies a general mutilation of the meaning of human existence, life and personhood. Heirs of a flatly secular culture, Australians now speak a public language stunted to the point of being grotesque. When the only answer to the crises in education is more government-imposed uniformity, when the horrors of youth suicide leave society bereft of any hope-giving wisdom, when the main solution to the plight of the growing number of the poor and homeless in our country is to deregulate the activities of the very rich, something is wrong. Amnesia threatens, and a kind of self-induced Alzheimer's syndrome causes the deeper values latent in our history to be unrecognized and unwanted. Lonergan's lapidary words are ominous: 'a civilization in decline digs its own grave with relentless consistency.'[14] And yet he goes on to say that 'a religion that promotes self-transcendence to the point, not merely of justice, but of self-sacrificing love, will have a redemptive role in human society.'[15] Hence, appealing uncritically to the 'spirituality' of a people is not without its perversions – as with the Nazi appeal to the *Geist* of the German *Volk* united against all enemies in a sense of land, blood and historical destiny.

That is where the challenge of spirituality begins, not only for Christians, but for all who use this term in so many ways. In the book referred to above, I have a chapter entitled, 'Talking Points and Embarrassed Silences'.[16] I made the point that spirituality was not ever waiting on some luminous mystical event or cultivating some precious mode of experience. Its roots are to be found already earthed in the routines of social and cultural experience. The spiritual dimension may be unnoticed or inarticulate, but the business of life is always touching on some 'limits'. There are the 'outer limits' or frontiers to our routine arrangements of life, where words run out and we come to the end of our capacities. And there are the 'near limits' of the uncanny mystery of existence that we share – something given, inviting and involving us in an excess of meaning that can never be fully articulated. Affecting all our awareness of the bounds of existence, are the primal limits of birth, life, guilt, love, creativity, suffering and death, and registered within the history of particular peoples in the symbols, the art, the events, the vocabulary and the preoccupations that shape their identity.

The limits here referred to release deep questions. For instance, how do we belong together, now and in the end? What hope can we share? How do we as a nation belong to the world of peoples? What responsibilities do we have to others? Why care at all? True, such questions, latent in routine conversations about the economy, ecological responsibility, Aboriginal reconciliation, government refugee policy, the 'justice system' and the like, tend to leave us incompetent and exposed. But unless disturbing questions are allowed to surface, the national morality tends to become an oppressive tolerance. It will be always seeking to balance the untroubled conscience of the many with what appears to be the pressure tactics of a monomanic minority.

In the face of such unrealities, the notion of 'limits' is a useful strategy for uncovering the latent spiritual dimension in our social and cultural life. Limit-language favours an escape from the flatness of routine interaction into the horizon of life's deepest meanings and values. The overloaded world of mere information yields to a realm where the moral and personal imagination can move and breathe in an atmosphere of wonder, and hope, where the whole truth can be spoken in some way. It may hurt but also it can heal.

There is, therefore, a cutting edge to the notion of 'spirituality', felt in the embarrassed silences where deep questions stir. It can provoke, disturb and speak with a discordant voice. Spirituality is not to be thought of as some form of harmonious inner ecology undisturbed by sharp-edged incalculable events and personal witness. Certainly, the spiritual dimension of human life is about self-realization in the sense of becoming a self in a fuller, more richly realized way. But self-realization means self-transcendence; and that can make it fragile, and vulnerable to organized repression on the part of the reigning cultural idols. Greed, power and absurdity demand human sacrifice – the violence of all ideologies. But a genuine spirituality exists in openness to something more, and is capable of revealing the violence implicit in all convenient self-images. It moves, not towards a greater management of the future, but in openness to the unimaginably new. But that means the embarrassment of naming and confronting the evils embedded in our history, past and present. To this degree, spirituality is not a fragile form of self-realization, but an intentional, compassionate solidarity with others, at the point of what appears as a shared hopelessness. It is formed in the face of the self-serving forces that would mutilate human existence in whatever way.

The 'limit situations' suggested a quarter of a century ago have not changed so much as intensified. There are still the embarrassed silences – and the call to a deeper spiritual self-realization. Isolation, for instance, is a feature of Australian experience. In terms of our European history, we were a long way from home, namely, the British Isles, and originally cast off as displaced persons into a strange, vast uncultivated place. A continent it may be, but it is also a defenceless coastline. Even Heidegger's notion of existential *Geworfenheit* has to be intensified to communicate something of the Australian 'thrownness' and contingency. Some have suggested that this explains our national urge to travel and to make contact with the really important places and people! It seems that from the beginning we occupied the underside of history: what international sense of responsibility does that inspire now?

One aspect of that isolation was the Aboriginal presence which white Australians are only beginning to understand and appreciate. Indigenous Australians occupied this land 40,000 years at least before the arrival of European settlers. They were not just a problem for white arrivals 200 years ago, for they stand at a special limit to our sense of humanity. The 'Ab-original' peoples stand witness to a largely unknown, mysterious dimension of our present history. The breadth of European experience is challenged by the depth of another way of being in the world, its freedom from material possessions, its sacramental sense of the land and the 'dreaming' that pervades all existence.[17]

Then there is a limit that is touched through the arrival of waves of migrations, of peoples attempting to escape the restrictions and even oppression of other times and places, in order to find new hope *here*. Can this really be the place where people are liberated from the destructive elements of their particular past histories? How might a new hopeful humanity be possible among us? How is our vision of the future hospitable to all the stories of suffering and hope so that this country can be a land of promise?

Such, then, are three examples of the 'limit situations' that inspire the deeper questions out of which might arise reflection on what spirituality can mean, and so inspire a conversation on 'where are we going?', and, 'what is it all about?'[18]

Speaking of the experience of limits, an intriguing aspect of the Australian Spirituality is the poetry the culture has produced in reaction to the routine and the superficial.[19] There is a voice within a cultural history that makes 'the heart/ Kindle and quicken at the mystery' (A. D. Hope).[20] Les Murray refers to it as 'wholespeak' compared to all other limited kinds of language. Murray and Kevin Hart, acclaimed Australian poets in their own right and both Catholic converts, have compiled collections of Australian religious poetry, a rich resource when it comes to stimulating reflection on the spiritual dimension of life.[21] Murray, out of his experience of compiling his anthology of Australian religious verse, provocatively observes:

> It was striking how much of the decent religious poetry in this country dated from the period since World War II; this is where the preponderance lay, and I left readers to mull over possible reasons why. I hesitate to give my opinion even now, though it is hard to resist the speculation that a decline in religious certainty has provoked an upsurge in searching and questioning – and a decline in an odd sort of anti-religious hectoring, which required a firm opponent to batter against. Things have arguably gone too far for that now, and the near total divorce of State from any underlying religious ethic has produced not 'freedom' but a terrifying void against which comfortable old Enlightenment audacities are meaningless. It is generations since being an agnostic involved any daring, and atheism tends to put one into coercive rather than generous company. More seriously, whether we believe in the soul or not, neither of these positions feeds it; we feel its hunger as a matter of experience, and have nothing to feed on but our own selves. At bottom, we cannot build a satisfying vision of life upon agnostic or atheist foundations, because we can't get our dreams to believe in them.[22]

Murray could not have foreseen the emergence of the quasi-scientific atheism of more recent years, but his general point is valid – the 'terrifying void' of the nothingness, if not nihilism, at the heart of our sensate, extravert culture. Relativism devours any sense of moral character, and with the loss of moral commitment and even moral literacy, an endless proliferation of regulations is the only way left to govern. It is often observed with some humour that Australians are descendents of convicts; but, more obviously, they are also the descendents of their gaolers and overseers, given the super-regulated society that governments try to engineer.

Conclusion

By way of conclusion, the relation of poetry to spirituality comes to expression in a remarkable passage from David Malouf's novel, *The Great World*.[23] The good Mr Warrender, a poet of some standing, has died. One of his eulogists reflects on the hidden dimensions of life that poetry brings to light:

> He was speaking of poetry itself, of the hidden part it played in their lives, especially here in Australia, though it was common enough – that was the whole point of it – and of the embarrassment when it had, as now, to be

brought into the light. How it spoke up, not always in the plainest terms, since it wasn't always possible, but in precise ones just the same, for what it deeply felt and might otherwise go unrecorded: all those unique and repeatable events, the little sacraments of daily existence, movements of the heart and intimations of the close but inexpressible grandeur and terror of things, that is our *other* history, the one that goes on, in a quiet way, under the noise and chatter of events and is the major part of what happens each day in the life of the planet, and has been from the beginning. To find words for *that*; to make glow with significance what is usually unseen, and unspoken too – that, when it occurs, is what binds us all, since it speaks out of the centre of each one of us; giving shape to what we too have experienced and did not till then have words for, though as soon as they are spoken we know them as our own.

It would be hard to find a more evocative statement of the relation between poetry and spirituality and its role as a 'hidden part' in Australian life even if any attempted disclosure of such depths occasioned embarrassment. But there is a language which deals with 'all those unique and repeatable events', 'the little sacraments of daily existence', 'movements of the heart and intimations of the close but inexpressible grandeur and terror of things', which takes us into 'our other history', that moves forward from 'the centre of each one of us'. Even if in this present context, such phrases are hardly more than a glossary of terms useful in discussing Australian Spirituality, they point to the possibilities of conversation, within this and other countries of Oceania and beyond, concerning the spiritual dimension of life, and the perils of neglecting it, especially in the over-stimulated electronic cultural milieu of today.

Notes

1 Handy references here are Gerard V. Hall, SM, 'Practical Theology in Oceania', in Bonnie J. Miller-McLemore (ed.) (2011), *The Wiley-Blackwell Companion to Practical Theology*. Chichester: Wiley and Sons, and David Pascoe, 'The Church in Oceanic Perspective', in Gerard Mannion and Lewis Seymour Mudge (eds) (2008), *The Routledge Companion to the Christian Church*. New York/Oxford: Routledge, pp. 346–67.

2 This has brought an awareness of national identity and culture and, in recent decades, produced such works as *Living Theology in Melanesia* (D'Arcy May); *The Gospel is not Western: Black Theologies from the Southwest Pacific* (Trompf); *Discovering an Australian Theology* (Malone); *Rainbow Spirit Theology: Towards an Australian Aboriginal Theology* (Rainbow Spirit Elders).

3 Mikaele Paunga, 'Dreaming the Land (Ocean): Resistance and Hope in Pacific Islands Practical Theology', *Australian eJournal of Theology* 5, August 2005.

4 For an annotated bibliography, see Neil Darragh, 'Contextual Theology in Aotearoa New Zealand', in J. England et al. (eds) (2002), *Asian Christian Theologies*. Maryknoll, NY: Orbis Books, pp. 541–98.

5 Henare Tate (2004), *Traditional Maori Spirituality in Encounter with Christian Spirituality*. Auckland: Accent Publications.

6 Philip Gibbs (2009), 'Forces of Death and Promise of Life in Papua New Guinea.' *Australian eJournal of Theology*, 14 August.

7 For an incisive exposition of the commercialization of spirituality, see Jeremy Carrette and Richard King (2005), *Selling Spirituality: The Silent Takeover of Religion*. London: Routledge.

8 The biblical origin of the word is found in the Pauline neologism *pneumatikos*, 'Spirit-ual' – any person or reality (charisms, blessings, hymns, conduct) under the influence of the Spirit (cf. 1 Cor. 2.14–15). Gradually, the word came to refer to the mystical and contemplative aspects of Catholic faith, above all as these were represented in various traditions and emphases, for example, a Marian or eucharistic spirituality, or to the classic traditions of various religious orders, say, a Benedictine, or Jesuit or Carmelite Spirituality.

9 Ewert Cousins (ed.) (1985–), *World Spirituality: An Encyclopaedic History of the Religious Quest*. New York: Crossroad.

10 For background, see Anthony Kelly, 'From Cultural Images to Historical Reality: Questions Arising', in Peter Malone (ed.) (1999), *Developing an Australian Theology* Strathfield, NSW: St Paul's, pp. 65–83; Peter Malone (ed.) (1988), *Discovering an Australian Theology*. Homebush, NSW: St Paul's; Gideon Goosen (2000), *Australian Theologies: Themes and Methodologies in the Third Millennium*. Strathfield, NSW: St Paul's; Rainbow Spirit Elders (1997), *Rainbow Spirit Theology: Towards an Australian Aboriginal Theology*. Blackburn: HarperCollinsReligious; Paul Cashen, MSC (2006), *From the Sacred Heart to the Heart of the Sacred: The Spiritual Journey of Australian Catholics*. Kensington, NSW: Nelen Yubu Productions.

11 For works of continuing influence, see David Tacey (1995), *Edge of the Sacred: Transformation in Australia*. Melbourne: HarperCollins, and David Tacey (2000), *ReEnchantment: The New Australian Spirituality*. Melbourne: HarperCollins.

12 Anthony (Tony) J. Kelly (1990), *A New Imagining: Towards an Australian Spirituality*. Melbourne: Collins Dove; 'Spirituality: An Australian Accent', *The Way Supplement* 73 (Spring 1992): 87–97 which specified nine features of spirituality related to Australian history and culture.

13 Carrette and King, *Selling Spirituality*.

14 Bernard Lonergan (1972), *Method in Theology*. London: Darton, Longman and Todd, p. 55.

15 Ibid.

16 Kelly, *A New Imagining*, 25–35.

17 Joan Hendriks and Gerard Hall, 'The Natural Mysticism of Indigenous Australian Traditions', in K. Acharya et al. (eds) (2008), *Fullness of Life*. New Delhi: Somaiya Publications Pvt. Ltd, pp. 491–518. See also chapter on Native American Spirituality above.

18 Other 'limits' mentioned suggested questions as to the significance of being a 'Commonwealth', the meaning and value of leisure and sport, the Australian experience of sexuality, and the possibility of the Bicentenary being a new beginning. Of course, the value of this kind of listing consists above all in getting people to suggest how they are in fact experiencing 'limits' in their own experience.

19 For theological and philosophical background, see Karl Rahner (1966), 'Poetry and the Christian', *Theological Investigations IV*. Baltimore: Helicon, pp. 357–67; Martin Heidegger (1971), *Poetry, Language and Thought*, trans. Albert Hofstadter. New York: Harper and Row; and Andrew Greeley (1996), *Religion as Poetry*. New Brunswick, NJ: Transaction.

20 From A. D. Hope (1970), 'Invocation', *Selected Poems*. Sydney: Angus and Robertson, p. 51.
21 Useful collections here are Les Murray (ed.) (1986), *Anthology of Australian Religious Poetry*. Melbourne: Collins Dove, and Kevin Hart (ed.) (1994), *The Oxford Book of Australian Religious Verse*. Melbourne: Oxford University Press.
22 Les Murray (1997), 'Embodiment and Incarnation', in *A Working Forest: Selected Prose* Sydney: Duffy and Snellgrove, pp. 319–22.
23 David Malouf (1990), *The Great World*. London: Chatto and Windus, pp. 283–4.

Bibliography and Further Reading

Cashen, Paul (2006), *From the Sacred Heart to the Heart of the Sacred: The Spiritual Journey of Australian Catholics*. Kensington, NSW: Nelen Yubu Productions.
Darragh, Neil (2002), 'Contextual Theology in Aotearoa New Zealand', in J. England et al. (eds), *Asian Christian Theologies*. Maryknoll, NY: Orbis Books, pp. 541–98.
Gibbs, Philip (2009), 'Forces of Death and Promise of Life in Papua New Guinea', *Australian eJournal of Theology*, 14 August.
Goosen, Gideon (2000), *Australian Theologies: Themes and Methodologies in the Third Millennium*. Strathfield, NSW: St Paul's.
Kelly, Anthony (Tony) J. (1990), *A New Imagining: Towards an Australian Spirituality*. Melbourne: Collins Dove.
— (1992), 'Spirituality: An Australian Accent', *The Way Supplement*, 73 (Spring): 87–97.
Pascoe, David (2008), 'The Church in Oceanic Perspective', in Gerard Mannion and Lewis Seymour Mudge (eds), *The Routledge Companion to the Christian Church*. New York and Oxford: Routledge, pp. 346–67.
Tacey, David (1995), *Edge of the Sacred: Transformation in Australia*. Melbourne: HarperCollins.
— (2000), *ReEnchantment: The New Australian Spirituality*. Melbourne: HarperCollins.
Tate, Henare (2004), *Traditional Maori Spirituality in Encounter with Christian Spirituality*. Auckland: Accent Publications.

Part VI
Contemporary Issues in Spirituality

28 Women and Spirituality

Bernadette Flanagan

Introduction

It is widely recognized that a turn to spirituality is of global dimensions in recent decades. In this chapter I wish to reflect on one of the distinctive forms of this turn for women, the production of a great range of spiritual autobiographies. I will not do this in the abstract, but rather will proceed by considering women's own writings regarding how the turn to spirituality is working itself out in their individual lives. Indeed, in a manner similar to a previous era when another turn to spirituality was democratically led by the Beguine movement, so today the flourishing of women's own account of the spiritual journey is again notable.

As well as a historical pattern being reflected in the contemporary turn to creating personal narratives of spiritual unfolding, the current abundance of texts of spiritual autobiography also manifests the significance of narrative for spirituality today.[1] With the postmodern deconstruction of meta-narrative, personal narratives have assumed greater significance. Individual narratives provide inspiration and guidance for those who undertake the spiritual journey today. Since the journey is being undertaken in a great diversity of settings such as the workplace, the counselling room, the marketplace and the family living room there is demand for narratives that tell stories of authentic spiritual seeking in manifold forms. As spiritual autobiographies by women emerge from these new settings, so more are encouraged to tell their personal story of authentic spiritual unfolding.

Eat, Pray, Love

One example of this contemporary writing which has achieved extensive publicity is Elizabeth Gilbert's popular film-novel, *Eat, Pray, Love*.[2] This autobiographical account presents, in today's idiom, the inner spiritual journey precipitated in the 30-something author when she confronted the profound meaninglessness that was assaulting her life. In a manner that is iconic of the spiritual quest of a generation of women in the Western world who today have incredibly busy lives, she cried out with the fervour of a contemporary psalmist on her bathroom floor in the middle of the night. Writing about this event in retrospect in her novel she realized:

> This little episode had all the hallmarks of a typical Christian conversion experience – the dark night of the soul, the call for help, the responding voice, the sense of transformation. But I would not say that this was a religious conversion for me, not in that traditional manner of being born again or saved. Instead, I would call what happened that night the beginning of a religious conversation. The first words of an open and exploratory dialogue that would, ultimately, bring me very close to God, indeed.[3]

The ancient theme of pilgrimage, in a new manifestation, fills the remaining chapters of the novel. Gilbert leaves her everyday involvements and sets off on pilgrimage so as to learn more about this 'voice' which is calling out to her for attention. She follows a three-phase path. First, she leaves her familiar and hectic schedule, with its highly programmed agenda. By immersing herself in the Italian appreciation of life, she allows dimensions of herself that have been anaesthetized to come to life. Her appropriation of new values is signified in the two stone in weight that she allows herself to acquire during this time. Having been liberated in her body from cultural orthodoxies she then moves to India to spend time with a spiritual guide, in the company of other spiritual seekers. Here she willingly learns to embrace practices that are foundational and characteristic of living with a more alert spiritual consciousness. She parallels her efforts to give an account of her encounter with divine mystery with that of Teresa of Avila, Rumi and Hafiz. In doing this she has broken through a barrier which divides mystics from contemporary everyday people. Her description of awakening to mystical consciousness invites contemporary women readers to consider their own alertness to the divine.

> Simply put, I got pulled through the wormhole of the Absolute, and in that rush I suddenly understood the workings of the universe completely . . . I was inside God. But not in a gross, physical way – not like I was Liz Gilbert stuck inside a chunk of God's thigh muscle . . . 'All Know that the drop merges into the ocean, but few know that the ocean merges into the drop' wrote Kabir – and I can personally attest now that this is true.[4]

Something of the same utterly unexpected character of awakening to the hidden and unknown dimension of the spiritual core of the person is evident in the story of Jill Bolte Taylor, as told in her autobiography, *My Stroke of Insight.*[5] Jill was a brilliant neuro-anatomist. However, at the age of 37 she suffered a disabling stroke when a blood vessel in her left brain burst. This resulted in significant loss of her left-brain based ability to speak and to understand speech. While her left-brain analytical function closed down, her right brain function survived intact. Her book describes how her right-brain intuitive way of processing information awakened her to a mystical perception of reality. Her recovery brought her on a journey into a new way of being in daily life and to the discovery of the importance of the practice of presence in particular:

> If I want to retain my inner peace, I must be willing to consistently and persistently tend the garden of my mind moment by moment, and be willing to make the decision a thousand times a day.[6]

Tenzin Palmo

In less dramatic circumstances other contemporary women have experienced the global rising of a new spiritual consciousness. Diane Perry lived a very ordinary life as the daughter of a fishmonger in the East End of London. She and her brother were brought up by her mother, a spiritualist, after her father died when she was 2. At 18 her intuitive attraction to learning more about living with pure simplicity was fanned into a flame when she read, during an airport delay, a book by John Walters with a Buddha on the cover that was entitled *Mind Unshaken.*[7] The title attracted her because she had found living in the middle of the city a busy and crowded experience, one where she had been learning implicitly how to live with a 'mind unshaken' in the hustle and bustle of daily life.

Today Diane Perry is more commonly known by her Tibetan name, Tenzin Palmo. Her personal journey from London denizen to Buddhist nun has been inspiringly told in her biography, *Cave in the Snow.*[8] After her awakening in the airport waiting room Diane felt she needed to find a personal mentor so as to grow in an attitude of unshaken mindfulness. In 1960s London it was not easy to find such a mentor, so she concluded that it would be necessary to spend some time in India. After spending some further time in her library job so as to put together some savings, she made her way at the age of 20 to India. Eventually she moved to the area north-east of India and there, in Tibet, she met her dreamed-for guru in the person of the eighth Khamtrul Rinpoche. Having studied with her guru for six years she became one of the first few Westerners to be ordained a Tibetan Buddhist nun. She then moved to a small monastery in the Tibetan Himalayan valley of Lahaul for more intensive practice. After a while this intensive practice led her to the decision to seek more seclusion in a small cave in the Himalayas, where she stayed for 12 years, the last 3 in strict retreat.

In this isolated spot she inevitably faced a diversity of challenges ranging from plummeting winter temperatures, melting ice floods in spring and
attendant rock-falls. In all this she almost died twice. Her routine involved
meditating 12 hours each day, taking care of the daily chores of survival, giving lots of time to reading, painting and calligraphy, replying to her large
volume of mail deliveries and sleeping for 3 hours each night while sitting
upright in a meditation box. The core purpose of this intensive practice was
'to become a quantum physicist of inner reality'.[9] In other words, she believed
that a person is called to live beyond the isolated self created by an imprisoned solitary ego, and to embrace all living reality. For Tenzin, this attitude
was very simple and was eminently depicted for her in St Thérèse of Lisieux's
image of the little flower growing by the wayside, unnoticed but beautiful in
itself.[10]

When, in 1988, Tenzin Palmo finally came out of her retreat unexpectedly
because of visa problems she felt drawn to reconnect with Western culture.[11]
Initially she chose Assisi in Italy as the location to start exploring founding
a nunnery which took the spiritual education of women seriously, in line
with the dream her guru had encouraged her to develop. However, it wasn't
until she returned from Italy to India to attend the first Western Buddhist
conference in 1993[12] that she began the project which countered the linger-
ing view that it was not possible to achieve enlightenment in a female body.
She founded the Dongyu Gatsal Ling Nunnery with a focus on giving spiritual education and training opportunities to women from Tibet and the
Himalayan border regions.[13] In her view it takes 15 to 20 years of meditation
retreats, usually alone, to achieve monastic *Togdenma* (meaning 'a realized
one'), which is the foundation for building a pool of qualified female meditation teachers in the Tibetan tradition. In this journey Tenzin Palmo illustrates
one key aspect of the turn in women's spirituality: that women are seeking to
train as spiritual teachers today and wish to have women spiritual teachers
available to them.

Elaine MacInnes

The emergence of women as spiritual teachers is not solely confined to monastic settings however. Sr Elaine MacInnes is a spiritual teacher[14] who works in
an environment that contrasts enormously with the solitude and peace of the
foothills of the Himalayas. Her spiritual journey has unfolded in the context
of prisons. Elaine grew up in New Brunswick, one of Canada's three Maritime
provinces, and joined a fledgling Canadian Catholic religious congregation,
Our Lady's Missionaries in 1953. In 1961 her first missionary assignment took
her to Japan. Influenced by her earlier reading of Francis Xavier's appreciation of the Japanese spirit she eventually went to live with an order of Rinzai

Buddhist nuns at Enkoji in Kyoto for eight years. She then moved to the Sanbo Kyodan order which had a more specific focus on spiritual practice in daily life, in contrast to the other two schools of Rinzai and Sōtō Zen which focused more on training for temple services. In 1980 she became a Roshi (old teacher) in the Sanbo Kyodan group.

During her training in the practices of Zen Elaine was transferred to the Philippines and there she began teaching what she had learned in Japan. She received a request from Bago Bantay prison in Quezon City, through the prison underground communication system, that a prisoner there wanted to see her. These were the worst years of the Marcos regime and the prisoner who requested to see her, Horacio (Boy) Morales had been a former friend of the Marcos government who had become an enemy when he joined the underground resistance movement. He longed to recover inner peace and balance as a result of the devastation of his spirit through torture and he believed from what he had heard about her classes that she could help him. She visited him every Friday for four years, despite the personal danger of such an undertaking during the Marcos regime. The positive outcome of these visits gave Elaine a new mission in life: to bring the inner peace evoked by Zen meditation practice to prisoners around the world. Soon eleven more Bago Bantay prisoners were also experiencing the healing power of Zen silence. Since then her life has been devoted to enabling prisoners to become the human beings they are called to be, through bringing them into that silent space in themselves where they can be liberated. *Freeing the Human Spirit* is a charity founded in 2004 by MacInnes, which today works in 22 prisons across her native Canada. Elaine shares the emerging global conviction that everybody has the capacity to be a mystic and she has led in the way in establishing the truth of this conviction through her work in an environment that would truly test it. Her spiritual autobiography has been captured in the documentary *The Fires that Burn*.[15] The title arises from the assertion she makes in the documentary that: 'Your spirituality is what you do with the fires that burn within.'

However, prisoners are not alone in struggling to embrace a spiritual practice that can run counter to the culture of their environment. In a recent article Claire Wofteich has eloquently articulated the challenges of spiritual practice in the midst of the school run, the piling laundry and the relentless intrusions of mobile communication systems.[16] She contends that women's autobiographical writings are privileged resources for providing a window on daily spiritual practice in the lives of women. Women who have written their spiritual biography have noticed, discerned, named and told the story of their own spiritual awakening and unfolding. Many cross new thresholds into the land of the Spirit on the journeys which they undertake.

Kathleen Norris

Among the writings that Claire commends are those of Kathleen Norris. Her style and interests have been compared to Thomas Merton and Hildegard of Bingen,[17] but unlike these writers her work does not carry the association of a global religious community which might bring it to wider international notice. Three of her works are particularly important for women's journey today. *Dakota: A Spiritual Geography*[18] invites the reader to reflect on the portals of mystery within the ordinariness of the space where 'home' is located. For Norris, South Dakota was a place where she had spent many summers with her grandparents. It also became the space within which she and her poet-husband lived their creative callings. *Amazing Grace: A Vocabulary of Faith*[19] is a personal exploration of returning to spiritual resources that had been abandoned in early adulthood because of the perception that they were just something for children and of finding therein sustenance for living the struggles of adult existence.

Kathleen Norris' *Cloister Walk* is a piece of writing that provides unique assistance to women who wish to be part of the new awakening of spiritual consciousness which is happening today. The text has the format of a one-year journal running from September to August. It was written while Kathleen held a residency at St John's Abbey, Collegeville, Minnesota. The liturgical calendar and practices of the Abbey provide a framework on which she hangs her thoughts about living with a mindful rhythm. She reflects on the coincidence between the ancient belief in the healing power of chant and the contemporary scientific confirmation of this wisdom.[20] The prophetic power of writing, of giving voice to and providing words for often unspeakable suffering also receives attention in Kathleen's reflections.[21] She questions why the tales of brave women in the Christian tradition, such as the early martyrs – Ss Agnes, Agatha, Barbara, Catherine, Cecilia, Dorothy, Lucy, Margaret – have been muted so that the power of these stories to inspire women who confront new forms of violence has been neutered. In this view she is in solidarity with those of the radical feminist Andrea Dworkin, who reflecting on the sexual exploitation of young women in contemporary culture, has commented that the current demand on women extends well beyond the virginal violations of early Christianity and is now 'not the blood of the first time (but) the blood of every time'.[22]

The Harvard Professor of Ministry, Stephanie Paulsell, has also drawn attention to the theme of the body in women's spiritual autobiographies in the past 20 years. She contends that despite the differences in these texts, it is possible to detect a common quest among the authors to discern the body as a neglected terrain of spiritual awakening, spiritual insight and spiritual commitment. Paulsell has made her own contribution to this discernment in her publication, *Honoring the Body*. She grounds her discernment in the conviction that bodies are made in the image of God's own goodness and are the dwellings of divine presence. Paulsell writes, 'The practice of honoring the body challenges us to remember the sacredness of the body in every moment of our lives.'[23]

Neglected moments of revelation are drawn to the reader's attention in her hymn to unfolding incarnation. Bathing, for example, is retrieved as a moment of encounter with the compassionate heart of Jesus who bathed the feet of his friends (Jn 13). Compassionate touching, is also a Gospel act and the tenderness and care with which the gift of touch is shared in our lives is challenged by the life of Jesus. Adorning the body can be a moment of evocation of the deeper protective presence surrounding us in God. The act of adornment also evokes a connection with the beauty and distinctiveness with which each plant blooms. Paulsell crosses a threshold to the neglected terrain of the body as locus of divine encounter.

Conclusion

In an equivalent manner, the threshold of intimate friendship has receiving focused attention in the spiritual autobiographical writing of Cynthia Bourgeault which is entitled *Love is Stronger than Death: The Mystical Union of Two Souls*.[24] The book tells the story of the spiritual partnership between a hermit monk at Snowmass, Colorado and the author who was in residence on the monastery grounds. In particular, she explores the continuing journey of spiritual and personal transformation with a soul friend beyond the grave, a conviction which she came to hold subsequent to the death of Br. Raphael Robin, the hermit monk. In exploring this journey she draws on inter-spiritual resources which can enlighten its contours such as the Sufi tradition of 'dying before you die',[25] a phrase which echoes the teaching of Jesus that 'whomsoever loses their life will find it'.[26] While she recognizes the possibility of accusations of subjective bias or narcissism in her narrative, the sincerity with which she presents her experience has its own power of conviction.

Finally, the selection of writings profiled above also reveal a new turn within women's spirituality. Twenty years ago Carol Christ's *Diving Deep and Surfacing: Women Writers on Spiritual Quest* revealed how the writings of Kate Chopin, Margaret Atwood, Doris Lessing, Adrienne Rich and Ntozake Shange could inform women's search for spiritual renewal. The current menu of writings is more intimate. They reveal the joys and excitement, the struggles and pain of those who intentionally and consistently embark on the soul's journey. In this turn to personal narratives of spiritual unfolding there is an ongoing invitation to each reader to consider how one's own narrative of the journey might be told. In this respect they have become resources of empowerment and guidance for present and future generations of women.

Notes

1 J. Ruffing (2011), *To Tell the Sacred Tale: Spiritual Direction and Narrative*. New York: Paulist.

2 E. Gilbert (2006), *Eat, Pray, Love: One Woman's Search for Everything: One Woman's Search for Everything Across Italy, India & Indonesia*. New York: Bloomsbury has been published in over 30 languages and sold more than 7 million copies worldwide. In an interview on Beliefnet www.beliefnet.com/Video/Beliefnet-Interviews/Elizabeth-Gilbert/Elizabeth-Gilbert-Bringing-Spirituality-Back-Home.aspx Gilbert explains that she now arranges her life so that she sets her day against the forces that try to accelerate life. She feels the need to protect herself from the searing pressures of contemporary culture in order to cultivate the light which has been lit in her inner self that is an anchor of peace. Moving slower, saying 'no', choosing contentment are essential to her current spiritual practice.

3 E. Gilbert, *Eat, Pray, Love*, p. 26.

4 Ibid., p. 209.

5 G. Bolte Taylor (2008), *My Stroke of Insight: A Brain Scientist's Personal Journey*. London: Hodder & Stoughton.

6 Ibid., p. 154.

7 J. Walters (1961), *Mind Unshaken: A Modern Approach to Buddhism*. London: Rider.

8 V. Mackenzie (1998), *Cave in the Snow: A Western Woman's Quest for Enlightenment*. London: Bloomsbury.

9 Ibid., p. 115. Tenzin Palmo attributes this phrase to Dr Robert Thurman, professor of Indo-Tibetan studies at Columbia University.

10 V. Mackenzie, *Cave in the Snow*, p. 122.

11 Ibid., p. 145.

12 Ibid., p. 153.

13 H. Hart (2003), *The Unknown She: Eight Faces of an Emerging Consciousness*. Inverness, CA: Golden Sufi Center, pp. 193–225. Tenzin Palmo's books include *Reflections on a Mountain Lake: Teachings on Practical Buddhism*. Ithaca, NY: Snow Lion Publications, 2002 and *Three Teachings*. Singapore: KMSPKS Monastery, 2000.

14 E. MacInnes (2003), *Zen Contemplation for Christians: A Bridge of Living Water*. Lanham, MD: Rowman & Littlefield.

15 *The Fires That Burn – The Life and Work of Sister Elaine MacInnes* is a 1-hour documentary on her life produced by Vision TV in 2004. See http://visiontv.com/DVD/VisionTVDVD_FiresThatBurn.html, Production Company: The May Street Group Film, British Columbia, Canada (2005).

16 C. Wolfteich (2010), 'Standing at the Gap: Reading Classics and the Practices of Everyday Life', *Spiritus: A Journal of Christian Spirituality*, 10/2, 251–6.

17 K. Haueisen (2008), *40-Day Journey with Kathleen Norris*. Minneapolis: Augsburg Books, p. 19.

18 K. Norris (2001), *Dakota: A Spiritual Geography*. New York: Mariner.

19 K. Norris (1999), *Amazing Grace: A Vocabulary of Faith*. New York: Riverhead.

20 K. Norris (1996), *The Cloister Walk*. New York: Riverhead, p. 329.

21 Ibid., pp. 214–15.

22 A. Dworkin (1987), *Intercourse*. New York: Free Press, p. 151.

23 S. Paulsell (2003), *Honoring the Body: Meditations on a Christian Practice*. San Francisco: Jossey-Bass, p. 6.

24 C. Bourgeault (2001), *Love is Stronger than Death: The Mystical Union of Two Souls*. Great Barrington, MA: Lindisfarne Books.

25 Ibid., p. 106.

26 Mt. 16.25.

Bibliography and Further Reading

Bolte Taylor, Gill (2008), *My Stroke of Insight: A Brain Scientist's Personal Journey*. London: Hodder & Stoughton.

Bourgeault, Cynthia (2001), *Love is Stronger than Death: The Mystical Union of Two Souls*. Great Barrington, MA: Lindisfarne Books.

Gilbert, Elizabeth (2006), *Eat, Pray, Love: One Woman's Search for Everything: One Woman's Search for Everything Across Italy, India & Indonesia*. New York: Bloomsbury.

LeClaire, Anne D. (2009), *Listening Below the Noise: A Meditation on the Practice of Silence*. New York: HarperCollins.

MacKenzie, Vicki (1998), *Cave in the Snow: A Western Woman's Quest for Enlightenment*. London: Bloomsbury.

Monk Kidd, Sue (1996), *The Dance of the Dissident Daughter: A Woman's Journey from Christian Tradition to the Sacred Feminine*. New York: HarperCollins.

Norris, Kathleen (1999), *Amazing Grace: A Vocabulary of Faith*. New York: Riverhead.

— (2001), *Dakota: A Spiritual Geography*. New York: Mariner.

Paulsell, Stephanie (2003), *Honoring the Body: Meditations on a Christian Practice*. San Francisco: Jossey-Bass.

Schiller, Verena (2010), *A Simplified Life; A Contemporary Hermit's Experience of Solitude and Silence*. Norwich: Canterbury Press.

29 Men and Spirituality

Richard Rohr

Introduction

The very idea of a spirituality particularly for the males of the species probably strikes some as unnecessary, trendy or even redundant, considering the hegemony that males have had in the Christian world and church history up to now. Was that all 'male spirituality'? Because of this very confusion, we must try to present what might be truly good and helpful about a specific and healthy spirituality for men. As we have already seen, women have done the same, with great insight as in the previous chapter.

I must admit that I believe typical Sunday religion is much more 'neuter' than either healthily masculine or healthily feminine, although it often has elements of both, depending on the denomination, culture and specific event or liturgy. You will have to draw or reject this conclusion for yourself if my attempts at description have any truth about them. And of course, what is the definition of 'healthy masculine' or 'healthy feminine' to begin with? We are in new territory here, and I have almost no 'authoritative' documents to quote. Yet, would it not make sense that it would take much of history for the 'sacrum commercium' or the great marriage of gender to take place on a broad scale? As John Donne said 'We two being one – are *it*!'

Certainly the last 30 years have told us that anything anybody says about gender is highly subject to criticism, newer studies, personal and cultural opinion. I wonder if it can be anything else, this *mystery* of gender and sexuality? I am very aware that any attempt to deal with issues of gender is like tiptoeing through a mine field. The agenda, backgrounds, hurts, opinions and cultural differences are so many and so deep in every culture or church where I have worked or visited.

Let me start, nevertheless, by differentiating masculinity from patriarchy. The 'rule of the fathers' that is called *patriarchy* is describing a deteriorated masculinity and the oppressive male control of groups, governments, institutions and most recent history. It is largely accepted as a negative term today. Masculinity is not the same as patriarchy, however; just as femininity is not the same as matriarchy. We must start on a fair and positive foundation and define masculinity as surely an original blessing more than an original sin or inevitable problem.

What we are searching for in any authentic male spirituality is the good and healthy meaning of maleness, one half of that mystery of God that Genesis says men represent (1.26–7). What might that be? What does that look like? Is there any essential or cross-cultural nature to this *one half of the image of God* that we call masculine? And do men approach enlightenment, transformation, conversion and spirituality by a different path than women? From different starting places? Or with different symbols that fascinate? My studied opinion is that *we do have quite different entrance points, and 'fascination' points, but we nevertheless end up much the same, because the goal is identical – union and even divine union.* At that point, neither male nor female energy is steering the ship, but we are being guided by One who is neither male nor female, but 'all in all' (1 Cor. 15.28). There, in short, is much of my conclusion at the very beginning.

Initiation

My first strong hint that there is a different *entranceway* for men came from my years of study of the rather universal phenomenon of the initiation of males.[1] It seems we cannot find many pre-axial civilizations that did not deem it culturally necessary to 'initiate' the young male, usually between the ages of 13 and 17. This was not true for the young female, who usually had *puberty* rites and *fertility* rites, with a very different goal, method and function. These patterns continued in many cultures until the last Christian millennium when the 'sacraments of initiation' (Baptism, Confirmation, Penance and Eucharist) tended to replace the pre-Christian rituals in the West, although an amalgam of both continued in most parts of Africa, Asia, many island nations, Native Americans and even in some rural areas of Europe. The very notion of the 'godfather' and even Jewish circumcision seem to be leftovers from ancient initiation rites, as is the anointing with ashes on Ash Wednesday and the 'slap' that used to accompany the Sacrament of Confirmation.

The studies of anthropologists seem to suggest that the majority of male initiation rites were concerned with leading the young male on journeys of *powerlessness.* Whereas female fertility and puberty rites had the exact opposite function, which was to sign the young girl with emblems of *power and dignity.* They gave them both what they needed to get started, and it seems they had almost completely opposite starting places. That is, *the male could not be trusted with power unless he had made journeys of powerlessness, the female would not even know she had power unless she was told about it and encouraged to trust it.* The young male was the loose cannon in the social fabric and he needed to be safely brought into the world of relationship, vulnerability, interiority and community (all of which he resists). Left to himself, the young male had little impulse control and far too much autonomous ego and willfulness (Now, of course, we would say the same about young girls in developed countries and middle-class societies!).

This might seem shocking or even incorrect until a Christian reads the four Gospels and notes Jesus' consistently different attitude towards the two genders. He is invariably calling the woman *upward*. For example, the exhortations of 'Go your way, your faith has restored you to health!', Lk. 8.48, 'Neither do I condemn you', Jn 8.11, and to a woman who has just spoken 'up and back' to Jesus, he says 'Woman you have great faith!', Mt. 15.28, and to the young girl he says *talitha cum* 'Get up', Mk 5.41.

Conversely, he is consistently calling the males in general, and the disciples in particular, *downward*. For example, 'Zaccheus, Come down!' in Lk. 19.5, 'You must first drink of the cup that I drink' to James and John, Mt. 20.23, 'If anyone wants to be first, he must be last' to the Twelve, Mk 9.35, and 'Get behind me, Satan' to 'the prince of the apostles' who wants to avoid suffering, Mk 8.33. It is really rather amazing, and a bit of selective memory, that we have not noted this rather clear pattern in the Scriptures that we profess to study and obey. Could that be what we mean by patriarchy? It is these kinds of recognitions that have become a starting point for any Christian masculine spirituality starting with how Jesus related to males.

Much renewed male spirituality is building on honest and trans-denominational Jesus scholarship today. Of course, there is some resistance from some groups who believe in female subordination – and with some very badly needed adjustments for males who have, in effect, been put on the 'feminine' path by reason of poverty, discrimination, sexual orientation, abuse or handicap. In other words, there are some male programmes that still want to exalt the male in his position of superiority and dominance,[2] and there are male spirituality programmes that are counterproductive because they try to 'defeat' an already defeated male. I saw this especially in my years of prison chaplaincy where there was a lot of 'taught and learned helplessness' in the chaplaincy department, in lieu of any authentic Gospel. None of these are what I am talking about here.

There are also a good percentage of male spirituality programmes that seem to have as their focus getting men to come back to church, usually sponsored by individual pastors or bishops. If men return to church attendance that is fine; but this should not be the primary concern of a Christian Spirituality. *Belonging systems and belief systems are not the same as transformational systems.* You can return to 'church as attendance', and not be initiated in any sense that the ancient rites, baptism itself or Jesus were ever talking about. Jesus' invitation was clearly to *leave* security, career and family systems (see Mt. 4.22) for something much larger. Again, it seems amazing that we have missed this, and it might partly explain why our churches and ministries tend to be filled with women. Men do not tend to like being penned inside of any 'white picket fences', unless it has a good ego payoff for them (career, promise of eternal life, affiliation needs, etc.).

Asking Questions

The Christian message up to now has been almost entirely studied and transmitted by a rather small but selective group (educated, very secure, white and largely celibate men till after the Reformation). *This group could not see what it was not told to look for, or had no felt-need to look for.* We clergy were not encouraged to ask or even notice questions of privilege, position and personal advantage in our interpretations of the Gospel, nor in our roles in the churches. In what some call 'Mark's Catechism' (8.22–10.52), the author makes it blatantly clear that Christian leadership had to be servant leadership or it would end up being job security and careerism, thus creating its own kingdoms and its own problems. I will let the reader decide if that is what has happened, but we can see in Mark's Catechism that Jesus surely saved some of his strongest and most sarcastic comments for this predictable phenomenon. It *always* happens in any religion if there is not some in-depth spirituality.

It took until the end of the twentieth century for us to begin to differentiate between what might be the male and the female perspectives on spirituality, even though Jesus had already pointed out the necessary paths of ascent and descent. Now is perhaps the first time in Christian history that we have had the structural freedom to enjoy other perspectives than the male clerical one. Now we have laymen, laywomen, non-celibates, non-whites, the poor, the 'blue collar' worker, the gay person, the non-professional and even the outsider all having their late moment in the sun. It feels a lot more like the heterodox perspective that Jesus trusted in his empowerment of a 'team of rivals': fishermen, a zealot, a tax collector, Judas, Samaritans, non-Jews, 'sinners', women friends, and maybe most especially the 'apostle to the apostles', Mary of Magdala.

In other words, we are finally free to talk about other perspectives and 'reads' on the Gospels than 'churchy' ones. This immediately and strongly attracts men, which I now know by experience. If it is too churchy, males always suspect we clergy are merely feathering our own nest. Naturally the questions of gender are one of the first, the most foundational, and maybe one of the most important perspectives to consider, after so many centuries of pure and unquestioned patriarchy. We tend to identify as a boy or girl almost earlier than any other strong ego identity, and there is so much energy at that level which we must surely gather for both male good and female good – and Gospel good.

Agency Versus Relationship

Something that I find intrinsic to a spirituality for men is what is called the *agentic* character of most males. Men love to move things from here to there, and experience themselves as 'agents' of change somehow. Just watch any little boy. I know there are many exceptions, but I nevertheless have found this general distinction among some teachers of gender and social psychology to be largely true. They say that most males, starting as children, prefer to experience themselves as initiators of movement, fixing, rescuing, speed itself, bodily competence, power games of various types, even destructive ones, building up and tearing down the world. Males like to test and try their embodiment against the pressures and invitations of reality. They like to be agentic (*agere* = to act or do), and 'superheroes' are often their favourite action toys.

Healthy men also don't really trust or admire a process, a group or a religion if it does not ask a lot of them. They like to push but they also respect being pushed back in the right way. Even though they fight it, they love it too! Thus we see men's common inclination towards fundamentalism, athletic training, the rules of the game, clubs and closed groups with high ideals and forbidden things, absolute opinions and war itself; yet they are also inclined towards a most lovely and beautiful heroism whenever possible. Men's need to be 'change agents' creates men at their best and men at their worst.

This agentic quality is in counterpoint to the *relational* preference of most women. Yes, there are plenty of exceptions, but it is no surprise that women prefer circles of sharing to pyramids and hierarchies, they prefer conversation to construction, they will usually choose nurturance and empathy over mere competition and climbing, they will normally choose connection over simple performance games. No wonder it has been said that 'Men are from Mars and Women are from Venus', even though I would admit that Mars and Venus are largely culturally determined and developed.

If there is any truth in this analysis of agentic energy versus relational energy, then you perhaps see why I say that organized religion *is largely neuter – until it leads to, or comes from, in-depth spiritual encounter.* In my opinion, most organized religion does neither gender very well, neither agentic service nor relational nurturance. It usually gives men little to do, move or build since the medieval cathedrals and pilgrimages. And on the other hand, it puts a very special kind of male, often educated in philosophy and theology, in charge of the nurturing, action-oriented and relational world of Christianity, asking of them a kind of pastoral work which they are frequently not gifted for or even inclined towards. We end up with lots of preaching and very little healing. We end up with the 'edifice complex' instead of a house of hospitality, and with religion as spiritual 'worthiness contests' instead of ministries of reconciliation, peacemaking, home, prison or hospital visitation, bereavement ministries, etc. If our Trinitarian God is *relationship itself*, then how can we live inside of this Mystery without deep capacities for relatedness, connection and mutuality?

Being Precedes Gender

It seems as though everyone loses out unless there is eventual and real Encounter for both genders and at that point it is God who takes over, and God who gives the male or female soul what only God knows that it needs. Gender cues and gender biases are now of little help, and probably just get in the way. But the dance of gender is still necessary to get us all started, engaged, on the path and in the search.

In the end, however, a true male spirituality is one that affirms men at the level of their deepest identity, their true selves in God, an objective and ontological ground, actually much deeper than mere gender, which is always in cultural flux anyway. Ironically and paradoxically, this non-gendered and theological foundation is what most deeply affirms them precisely as males and as men in the long run! The questions in the second half of life are not usually 'psychological', but much more metaphysical, philosophical and cosmological. How am I a part of the whole? How can I connect with The Centre? What evokes my sense of primal wonder, awe and humility? What is the pattern that connects me to the Whole? 'How can I let go?' much more than 'How can I hold on?'

A man must first and foundationally know who he is 'hidden with Christ in God' (Col. 3.3), how he is a 'son of God', and then he can – almost by accident – know that it is also good, even wonderful, to be a man, a male, a one gendered half of this larger mystery of God. The category of human precedes the category of gender. The category of human is deeper than any cultural definitions of male gender. The category of pure holiness is broader than any male or female examples of the same; in fact, they start looking very similar towards the end. *Yet we have to start with what fascinates, allures and draws!*

Ironically, calm and secure male identity is what makes mature partnership between males and females possible. Men and women are most alike at their most mature and soulful levels. Men and women are most different only at their most immature and merely physical levels. It is very telling that almost all male initiation rites and female fertility rites included rather rigid demands that included extended solitude in nature, silence, prayer, ritual, fasting: many of the same and essential elements of sacrament and religious retreat! I believe historic cultures wanted to *assure the possibility* of deep inner experience, *to assure the possibility* of Divine Encounter, to make likely the encounter with what Thomas Merton and others would call one's 'True Self'.

Once you touch upon your true self, your gender does not need to carry the whole weight of your identity (Nor does your job, your looks, your education or your sexual orientation, etc.).

The True Self, who you objectively are in God, is previous and superior to any issues of gender, culture or sexuality, which are all 'accidental' to one's foundational core as a child of God (Which is why it is pure heresy to call a transgendered, gay or lesbian person 'intrinsically disordered'). The intrinsic foundation of the human person is given by God and untouchable by any human intervention whatsoever, good or bad. Gender is a combination of biology, psychology and personal history, which are all good and necessary entrance points, but spirituality is not just the gateway to the temple, it is learning how to live in the temple itself (1 Cor. 3.16–17).[3] What makes spirituality precisely 'spiritual' is that it connects us with the Core and the Centre and not just the circumference, with the essence and not just the accidents.

But What Gets Us There?

This is the unique area of male spirituality, as far as I can see: *the symbols, the stories, the images, the rituals, the metaphors, that get us to enter the temple, are usually different for men and for women.* We must honour the need for action, movement, building, fixing, repairing, rescuing and heroic hardship that men love and follow. We must honour the community, the relationships, the empathy, the intimacy, the vulnerability, the healing, the caring that women love and follow. We know, however, that the eventual concern is to get men and women *to love and live both of these.* That is the final spiritual question and the goal. But first we must get them on a serious spiritual path.

My limited experience says this: I find that 'male stories' tend to be more black and white, action-packed, clear good and evil, grand drama, almost always needing a win/lose scenario of some type. We love the clear hero and the clear villain. We men appear to need – or desire – a 'whomp on the side of the head' to get the point. We tend to prefer the brutal, the raw, the earthy, the heroic, the bloody, the sexual to keep our attention. (Only in male poetry, both in the writing and the reading, and in some music, do we seem to change the rules and suddenly give ourselves permission to feel more subtle and tender emotions.) The very fact that we talk of 'men's movies' and 'women's novels' tends to speak for itself. There is a pattern here that religion and spirituality would do well to look at. We live inside very different narratives of valuation, energy and self-importance. Men for centuries read various versions of *The Quest for the Grail*,[4] women tended to read lives of the saints and spiritual memoirs.

I know the success of our *Men's Rites of Passage* has largely been based on the power of raw and honest rituals, and not in the cleverness of the speakers or the teachings themselves. (Just as the church once discovered with Sacraments!) The structure of the days insist on what we call 'hot edges', which tell the men we are taking it very seriously, and thus they should too – and they do! The military and athletic coaches have understood this for millennia, with a resultant loyalty, clear effect, idealized memory and 'romance' that often defies critical analysis. Many conservatives are probably trying to regain these hot edges for the Sacraments, and they are not all wrong.

All things being on course, the genders tend to be much more alike than different by the second half of life.[5] This is much of my lived experience working with men of varying ages for over 40 years now. Men tend to start hard and get softer, whereas women tend to start soft and get harder, hopefully we meet somewhere in the middle, but not usually much before our mid-50s. In between, it can often be a quite difficult dance of missteps, mis-interpretation and mutual hurt.

I end this chapter where you did not expect me to end, but maybe in a place that will also give you hope. Perhaps you imagined that I would draw out huge differences between male and female spiritualities, but I cannot, except in their starting points, style and their fascinations along the way. This is saying a lot, however, and has huge pastoral implications: *Men will and must be challenged in the world of doing. Women, on the other hand, will and must be challenged in the world of relating.* But the object and goal of all spirituality is finally the same for both genders: union, divine love, inner aliveness, soul abundance, generous service to the neighbour and the world. In these essentials and in the Great Whole 'there is no distinction . . . between male and female' (Gal. 3.28). Mature Christian Spirituality, or any true spirituality, always leads us towards universals and essentials, or it is no spirituality at all.

Gratefully, Christ 'holds all things in unity . . . the fullness (the *pleroma*) is found in him, and all things are reconciled through him and for him, everything in heaven and everything on earth' (Col. 1.17, 19–20). Including everything *sexual* that seems to have been split (*sectare*) into halves and parts.

Notes

1 Richard Rohr (2004), *Adam's Return.* New York: Crossroad.
2 'Promise Keepers' is probably the strongest American example of this. There are many other church and prison programmes for men which I would prefer not to name, and hopefully give them freedom to grow.
3 *'Spirituality and Sexuality'* (A recorded conference, 1991, available at the Mustard Seed, www.cacradicalgrace.org)
4 Rohr, Richard (1994), *Quest for the Grail.* New York: Crossroad.
5 Rohr, Richard (2011), *Falling Upward: A Spirituality of the Two Halves of Life.* New York: Jossey-Bass.

Bibliography and Further Reading

Arnold, Patrick M. (1991), *Wildmen, Warriors, and Kings: Masculine Spirituality and the Bible*. New York: Crossroad.

Boyd, Stephen B. W., Merle Longwood and Mark W. Muesse (eds) (1996), *Redeeming Men: Religion and Masculinities*. Louisville: Westminster, John Knox.

Campbell, Joseph (1949), *The Hero with a Thousand Faces*. Princeton, NJ: Princeton University Press.

— (2001), *Thou Art That: Transforming Religious Metaphor*. Navato, CA: New World Library.

Gilmore, David (1990), *Manhood in the Making: Cultural Concepts of Masculinity*. New Haven, CT: Yale University Press.

Herdt, Gilbert H. (1982), *Rituals of Manhood: Male Initiation*. Berkeley: University of California.

Moore, Robert L. (2001), *The Archetype of Initiation: Sacred Space, Ritual Process, and Personal Transformation*. Philadelphia: Xlibris.

Oliva, Max (1997), *The Masculine Spirit: Resources for Reflective Living*. Notre Dame, IN: Ave Maria Press.

Pable, Martin, OFM, Cap. (1996), *The Quest for the Male Soul: In Search of Something More*. Notre Dame, IN: Ave Maria Press.

Rappaport, Roy A. (1999), *Ritual and Religion in the Making of Humanity*. Cambridge: Cambridge University Press.

Rohr, Richard (1994), *Quest for the Grail*. New York: Crossroad.

— (2004), *Adam's Return*. New York: Crossroad.

— (2011), *Falling Upward: A Spirituality of the Two Halves of Life*. San Francisco: Jossey-Bass.

30 Art and Christian Spirituality

Mark Patrick Hederman

Introduction

Coming from Judaism, and being a proscribed religion in Rome, early Christianity had very little art. Prior to 100 CE there is no surviving art that can be called specifically Christian. In Rome the Christian dead were buried in underground chambers connected by narrow passages known as the catacombs. 550 miles of these underground burial sites still exist in Rome today. The art discovered there is borrowed from the late classical style. There is nothing original or specifically Christian about it.

From the beginning, at a theological level, Christianity rejected the religious image, especially any requiring veneration.[1] Popular religion, however, hankers for images to help cultivate devotion. Early Christianity did develop its own images of Jesus Christ, the Virgin Mary and many popular angels and saints. Such images were sometimes attributed to St Luke who had a reputation for being an artist and who had personal acquaintance with the subjects he was supposed to have painted. However, it was not until the sixth century that popular practice began to make inroads into theological austerity.

Two events were of fundamental importance to the development of a unique Christian art. The emperor Constantine gave his official support and legalized Christianity in 313 through the Edict of Milan. This allowed public Christian worship to take place and led to the development of a monumental Christian art. The later declaration of Christianity as the state religion of the Empire in 380 changed both the status and the style of the Christian Church. Constantine moved the capital of his Empire to Byzantium, mostly because sophisticated Roman society found his promotion of Christianity too vulgar for their tastes and eschewed any attempt to baptize their capital city architecturally or artistically.[2] Constantine therefore chose the small town on the sea of Marmora, which he called Constantinople after himself, where he created a great new artistic centre for the eastern half of the Empire. This blossomed into a specifically Christian artefact. It was here that a more abstract aesthetic replaced the naturalism previously established in Hellenistic art. Classical art mostly attempted to create representations as close to reality as possible. Byzantine art favoured a more symbolic approach. Its style was hieratic, meaning that its primary purpose was to convey religious meaning rather than accurately to depict objects and people in the natural world. Byzantium was where Greek and Roman art met other influences which helped to introduce the essentially Christian Byzantine art characterized most particularly by the icon.[3]

Icons

The word 'icon' comes from the Greek for an image, and echoes the words used in the Bible to describe the creation of man and woman in the image of God. Christians who venerate icons believe that the Spirit guiding their creation is the same that guided the creation of the universe. Artists who 'write' icons subject themselves to a regime of prayer and fasting and submit their artistry to a rigorous code of established canons for the exercise of their ministry.[4] They are regarded as instruments of the Holy Spirit which is why they rarely sign their works. Authorship of icons resides elsewhere.

Not all Christians venerate icons. It took a very long time for Christianity to accept and embrace this possibility. As dutiful heir to the Jewish tradition, the early Church inherited the belief in a God who is, and must always be, beyond our imagining and our powers of description. This remains a constant bedrock of all Judeo-Christian teaching and is the natural attitude of a religion which came from a tradition, founded several thousand years before Jesus Christ was born, forbidding any images of God, even images formed in the mind, even the use of the name of God. Such prohibitions are enshrined in the Decalogue: 'You shall not make yourself a graven image or any likeness whatever . . .'[5]

It is easy to understand, therefore, how the history of the icon is intimately bound up with the history of Christianity in the first centuries after Christ's death, as the community of Christians tried to work out the precise meaning of the tradition they had inherited: where it was the same as the Jewish tradition and where it differed. The basic difference was, of course, the fact that God had come on earth in the person of Jesus of Nazareth. It took a very long time for Christianity to understand the full implication of this reality of incarnation. But, essentially, it meant that if God was incarnate as a human being then it must be possible to depict this person in a work of art.

One of the most important moments in this history of discovery of their authentic profile was the iconoclastic crisis.[6] This has been compared with the later crisis in Christendom occasioned by what has become known as 'The Reformation' in the sixteenth century.

Iconoclasm means in Greek 'the smashing of images'. A general council of the church that met in Elvira in 306 stated in its 36th canon that 'the hanging of paintings in churches shall be forbidden, since the object of veneration and worship does not belong on a wall'.[7]

We first hear of the church's use of images in the sixth century, the imperial family playing an important role in this development. An image of the Virgin Mary, said to have been painted by St Luke, was moved from Jerusalem to Constantinople. The cult of images could no longer be ignored. Theologians on both sides began to articulate their positions. John of Damascus (680–749) was one of the first champions of images, issuing the important distinction that 'the image is a likeness that expresses the archetype in such a way that there is always a difference between the two'.[8] Jesus Christ was the archetype from whom all 'types' (as the icons were referred to) derived their venerability.

Any person who prayed before an icon, which was usually of Christ, His Mother or certain saints, nearly always looking out at you, was encountering the presence of whomsoever was depicted there. Devotees were not venerating the icon itself. The eyes of the icon were the vortex through which the eyes of the beholder were suctioned to meet the presence of the original, beyond the depiction, in eternity. The Damascene's subtlety and enthusiasm were not shared by the opposing movement of iconoclasts, whose reform gathered momentum around 725. In this phase of the battle, icons were destroyed as pagan idols, incompatible with Christian belief as well as being a scandal to both Jews and Muslims.

The Emperor Leo III embraced the iconoclastic movement in about 726. He had political reasons for doing so, but it seems that his basic motivation was to institute a religious reform which would bring Christianity back to its roots of worship in spirit and in truth. Leo III had a number of remarkable military successes against the hitherto irresistible advance of Islam. These he took as confirmation from the Almighty of the direction he had initiated. So, his son, in turn, the Emperor Constantine V, something of an amateur theologian, decided to copperfasten his father's endeavours by calling a Church Council which would endorse the principles of iconoclasm.

It was this Constantine V who best expressed the difficulty of icon painting: 'We ask you how is it possible to depict our Lord Jesus Christ who is only one person of two natures, immaterial and material, through their union without confusion?'[9] In other words, he was posing the dilemma for the defenders of icons that if they said the icon was depicting Christ as man only, they were guilty of Nestorianism, the great heresy which separated the human element from the divine; if they said the icon represented Christ as both God and man, they were guilty of the monophysite heresy which refused to separate the incomprehensible divinity from the humanity.

There were 338 bishops at the council which met in Constantinople from 2 February to 8 August 754. Afterwards, it was suggested that the emperor put undue pressure on those bishops present, but whether he did or not, the council ratified the iconoclastic charter.

Later, iconoclasm was defeated, the above Council declared heretical, and icons, images, and representations of Christ, the Virgin Mary, the saints and angels, were not just allowed back into Christian churches and dwelling-places, but were declared to be an essential part of the Christian heritage.

This war was not won without a great deal of struggle, time, argument and even bloodshed. It took centre stage as the most important battle in Byzantium for nearly a century. Two Councils of the Church were devoted to it entirely until eventually in 787 the movement of iconoclasm was definitively defeated and icons were restored to their rightful place in the Christian scheme of things at the Second Council of Nicea.[10] So great a victory was hailed by the Church as a new feastday: the feast of Orthodoxy, which to this day is celebrated in the Orthodox Church on the first Sunday of every season of Lent.

And most denominations of Christianity are involved in this declaration, including Roman Catholicism, because it was pronounced by what was the Seventh Ecumenical Council, held in Nicea from 24 September to 23 October in 787 and gained recognition from the five great patriarchates of the time: Alexandria, Antioch, Constantinople, Jerusalem and Rome:

> We retain, without introducing anything new . . . the representation of painted images . . . because of the belief in the true and non-illusory Incarnation of God the Word, for our benefit. For things which presuppose each other are mutually revelatory.
>
> Since this is the case, following the royal path and teaching divinely inspired by our Holy Fathers and the Tradition of the Catholic Church – for we know that it is inspired by the Holy Spirit who lives in it – we decide in all correctness and after a thorough examination, that, just as the holy and vivifying cross, similarly the holy and precious icons painted with colours . . . should be placed in the holy churches . . . on walls, on boards, in houses and on roads, whether these are icons of our Lord and Saviour, Jesus Christ, or our Spotless and Sovereign Lady, the holy Mother of God, or the holy angels and holy and venerable saints.[11]

This milestone in the evolution of Christianity links the icons to the incarnation. If Jesus Christ actually became man and lived an historical life on earth then it must be possible to depict that life and represent his features in pictorial form. Just as the evangelists were able to write down an account of his life and his person in books which have become the definitive scriptures of Christianity, so, too, it must be possible for visual artists to describe Him in paint.[12] The Eighth Ecumenical Council (869–70) goes so far as to say: 'The icon of Our Lord and Saviour Jesus Christ should be venerated with esteem equal to that afforded to the book of the holy gospels.'[13]

The art of the icon was the creative response to the dilemma posed by the Incarnation: how can humanity and divinity be represented in an artefact? If it is possible to depict this mystery, no method of artistic representation which existed to date could do so. It was necessary to invent one appropriate to the challenge, which is what happened in Byzantium. Byzantium devised an art form in the icon capable of incorporating two completely different natures in one hybrid form. It is almost as if the art form devised was a visible defeat of two of the three laws of logical thought: both the principle of identity and the principle of non-contradiction: Everything is what it is and cannot, at the time, be something else. And a thing, 'A', cannot be both 'A' and 'not A' at the same time. Icons are both what they are and what they are not at the same time. This is not just a magical trick or an ancient form of *trompe l'oeil*. It is a unique and *sui generis* art form which incorporates the paradox upon which Christianity is founded, namely the mystery of the Incarnation, whereby a fragment of the created world becomes the embodiment of a world beyond.

Of course the artists must use the same materials and methods that other artists use. In fact, icons owe a great deal to the contemporary artistic methods used for making effigies of emperors and other funereal monuments both in ancient Egypt and in Rome.[14] However, this does not mean that the iconographers of Byzantium did not succeed in doing something entirely new with these same materials even while using such contemporary models. The icons of Byzantium forced artistic expression to perform a religious deed which had never been as delicately encompassed in a work of art before that time. They fashioned out of wood, paint, lines and colours a way of encountering the face of Christ who is God in human form.

The 'East-West Schism' of 1054 split Christianity into two major divides almost immediately after it celebrated its first millennium. Henceforth, churches remaining in communion with the See of Rome (the diocese of Rome and its bishop, the Pope, as first patriarch) have been known as 'Catholic', while the Eastern churches that rejected the Pope's authority have generally been known as 'Orthodox' or 'Eastern Orthodox'. One of the results of this division was an alternative art form adopted by the Roman Church.

The Renaissance

The Renaissance was the rebirth of Greek and Roman styles of art and even though the themes and personalities were still borrowed from the Hebrew and New Testament Bibles, the style was entirely natural and human. This was the classical style, embodying the ideal forms of Plato and providing an aesthetic of perfect human and natural beauty. This movement started in Italy in the fourteenth century and spread to Northern Europe flourishing until the sixteenth century.

Whatever the merits or the results of this new kind of church art, it sprang from a very different kind of theology. A new age was being born, one which was interested in emotional expression, psychological reality, and in how real people looked, felt and conducted their lives. The technique of oil painting allowed Christian art to take on the most dramatic and picturesque expressions and settings. Raphael, Leonardo da Vinci and Michelangelo expressed a beauty and a realism that were stunningly impressive, but, at the same time, part of that Renaissance which eventually led to a world around us sufficient in and to itself. This world had fewer and fewer windows open to a divine reality of entirely different proportions, perspectives and perceptibility. Caravaggio (1573–1610) carried this realism to its most startling and exquisite perfection.

Such a development can only be understood in terms of the parallel history of the papacy which accompanied the lives and works of the artistic geniuses who adorned nearly two centuries of Roman history. Two popes who were probably the most influential in their support for the fruitful cross-fertilization between the Church and the great artists of the Italian Renaissance were Julius II (Pope from November 1503 to February 1513) and Leo X (March 1513–December 1521). Julius was a forceful, ruthless and violent ruler who set out to extend the Papal States. Historians allow him high marks for military prowess but less for spiritual stature. As patron of the arts he sponsored Michelangelo and Raphael among others. He laid the foundation stone for the new St Peter's and arranged for the costs to be defrayed by selling indulgences.[15] His successor, Leo X was recklessly extravagant. He sold ecclesiastical offices and even cardinals' hats to pay for his projects. The huge expenses of St Peter's were met by renewing the indulgences authorized by Julius and arranging for these to be promoted by preachers throughout Christendom. In January 1517, John Tetzel began his preaching outreach to Germany. It might be said that art was one of the causes of the Reformation as Tetzel provoked a very understandable iconoclasm in Martin Luther (1483–1546).

We who were brought up on the compelling wave of Renaissance art have to become aware of the prejudices of our own culture and education. Most of us expect a painting to look like the thing it is depicting. We like to see on the canvas or in the picture an exact representation of what we see around us. And this preference is not 'natural'. It is, in fact, the result of a direction taken by the great masters of European art from the thirteenth to the sixteenth century especially when the extraordinary geometrical device of perspective was developed. In the art of the Renaissance the spectator is the centre of the composition. The world is on display for your benefit, from your perspective as consumer. By drawing lines in a deceptive way on a flat piece of paper or a square of canvas, artists were able to fool us into thinking that we were looking at an exact representation of the reality we saw around us. And so fooled were we that we came to identify these paintings with reality, and these artists with the only possible way to be a painter.

Vasari, who was Michelangelo's contemporary and one of the first to write biographies of great artists of his time, gives us a very revealing account of how Cimabue discovered Giotto, who is sometimes identified as the person in whom and through whom Western European painting took this 'naturalistic' turn:

> [Giotto] while his sheep were grazing, was sketching one of them in a lifelike way with a slightly pointed rock upon a smooth and polished stone, without having learned to draw it from anyone other than Nature. [H]elped by his natural talent and Cimabue's teaching, not only did the young boy equal the style of his master, but he became such an excellent imitator of Nature that he completely banished that crude Greek style and revived the modern and excellent art of painting.[16]

We would not see Giotto as the epitome of the 'modern and good style of painting' nor would we see the Byzantine style as 'crude', however this commentary shows the change of direction which was taking place. The incredible burgeoning of genius during this period provided the appropriate artists to carry the movement to unprecedented heights of originality and excellence. The Dominican Fra Angelico (1400–55) remained in the contemplative tradition while adopting the new naturalistic style. Vasari tells us that he would never retouch or redo his paintings, leaving them always just as they had been painted. That, he used to say, was how God wanted them. It was also claimed that he would never take up his brushes without a prayer. Whenever he painted a crucifixion the tears would stream down his face.[17]

Botticelli (1445–1510) conquered the practical difficulties of depth perspective which removed from his rooms and spaces the awkwardness with regard to depth which we still find in Giotto. He, like many of his contemporaries, was obsessed by 'the investigation of difficult and impossible questions of perspective' to quote Vasari once again.

Leonardo Da Vinci (1452–1519) must be one of the most famous artists of all time. His *Last Supper* and *Mona Lisa* are two of the most discussed artworks ever painted. However he did not consider himself to be a painter in the first place. 'He is entirely wrapped up in geometry and has no patience for painting'[18] the head of the Carmelite order in Florence wrote in 1501 to Isabella d'Este, wife of Francesco Gonzaga, one of the cultured mercenary dukes of Mantua, when she wished to have her portrait painted.

Michelangelo (1475–1564) is probably the most famous of them all. He was almost 90 when he died and the amount of work he carried out in every branch of artistic endeavour is phenomenal. Vasari waxes eloquent:

The most benevolent Ruler of Heaven mercifully turned His eyes towards earth, and witnessing the hopeless quantity of such labours, the most fervid but fruitless studies, and the presumptuous opinion of men who were further from the truth than shadows from the light . . . decided, in order to rid us of so many errors, to send to earth a spirit who, working alone, was able to demonstrate in every art and every profession the meaning of perfection in the art of design . . . He wanted to bequeath to this spirit, as his native city, Florence, the most worthy among all the other cities, so that the perfection Florence justly achieved with all her talents might finally reach its culmination in one of her own citizens.[19]

Raphael (1483–1520) provided the synthesis of order and science which gave the Western medieval church a formula for a predictable and insulated aesthetic. Raphael's paintings of the Madonna became almost standardized: the recognized and acceptable face, shape and arrangement of the mother of God. Such endorsement of one particular art form had a double effect. Autonomous sources of creative endeavour were marginalized while mainstream art within the Roman Catholic Church became imitative and derived. With the passing of time and the development of artistic reproductive technologies these original, and in themselves, outstanding models became weaker and paler, until they eventually turned into the mass-produced 'holy pictures' which today clutter the stalls and shrines of popular Catholic religious imagination.

The pride of sight developed by perspectival representation reached its triumphal heights in the sixteenth century. The Reformation questioned once again the use of images for genuine religious purposes. The old battle was fought on new ground. The Council of Trent reiterated the teachings of Nicaea II, condemning superstition and excess and reiterating well-worn theories about icons:

Images of Christ, the virgin mother of God, and the other saints should be set up and kept, particularly in churches, and that due honour and reverence [*honorem et venerationem*] is owed to them, not because of some divinity or power [*divinitas vel virtus*] as reason for the cult, or because anything is to be expected from them, or because confidence should be placed in images as was done by the pagans of old; but because the honour showed to them is referred to the original which they represent . . . The holy council earnestly desires to root out utterly any abuses that may have crept into these holy and saving practices . . . All superstition must be removed . . . all aiming at base profit etc.[20]

Towards the Modern World

The Romantic era, an artistic, literary and intellectual movement originating in the second half of the eighteenth century in Europe, sought to express the 'sublime' which was the presence of 'the divine' in the natural world. 'Sublime' meant for them: awe-inspiring, savage grandeur, a natural world revealing evidence of the power of God. Romanticism was reacting against the scientific rationalism of the Age of Enlightenment, on the one hand, and the Industrial Revolution on the other. Painters and poets sought for new ways to express the religious transcendent. In Friedrich's *Monk by the Sea*, for instance, we are still the spectator, represented by the monk within the picture, gazing at a panoramic representation of the sublime in terms of sea and sky.[21]

The twentieth century introduced us to the contrived nature of all such representation, to the trickery of art. As inheritors of the Renaissance and as educated citizens of Europe, we have received an inborn bias in favour of an art which is naturalistically real. Two new realities helped us to unveil this prejudice and readjust our way of seeing things. The first was the invention of the photograph; the second was the new art which was being foisted upon us by the artists of our own times. The camera showed that the long and dedicated move from Giotto to Caravaggio – this perfection of perspectival geometry and natural realism – could now be reproduced by a machine. The art we had come to admire was no more than a well-disguised trick.

Cezanne showed us the difference between seeing and recognizing. He tried to slow down the process of seeing so that we could become aware of colour impressions or sensations before the mind closes in to complete the picture. He taught us not so much how to see but rather how to see what prevents us from seeing.

A contemporary artist, Bridget Reilly, paints abstract canvasses of vertical stripes or interlocking diamonds. Her aim is to convey to us pure sensation before the mind takes over: what you see in a split second out of the corner of your eye before you focus attention and label the experience. She and other artists claim that we are essentially killers of reality. It is the mind that sees not the eye. Artists show us how the mind destroys what is presented to our eyes. The eye is simply used by the mind which short-circuits all our perceptions for its own selfish and greedy purposes. We only see what we already know. Experience is killed by recognition. The reality outside us is always transformed by what we are supplementing from the inside.

In the 1960s when art was influenced by a limited drug culture, people were suggesting that all kinds of visions were to be had as a result of certain 'hallucinating' substances. Aldous Huxley in his book *The Doors of Perception*, produced a startlingly contrasting theory.[22] These drugs did not add anything to our normal vision. Instead they removed the natural censorship and filtering systems which chaperone our eyes. We have in-built customs and excise barriers around our visionary processes which make us concentrate only on data which is useful for survival. Most people, Huxley claims, most of the time, know only what comes through the reducing valve of their perceptive faculties. The function of the brain, the nervous system, the senses, is mainly eliminative, blotting out everything that is happening everywhere in the universe, except the particular booty upon which I am now focusing. We are protected from a plethora of sense impressions, all vying for our attention, so that we can concentrate upon 'that very small and special selection which is likely to be practically useful'.[23] We are equipped as eliminators of all that is not useful to us from the outside world.

Art and Religion

So, when we talk about the connection between art and religion, the first possibility, at the most basic level, is not showing us visions of God, but rather clearance of our own vision; revelation of all that comprises our somewhat limited capacity to see. Art teaches us, or tries to teach us, how to see what is, rather than what is real for us. It tries to dispel innate blindness of vision. In this way, some artists are prophets. Our normal vision is like a telescopic lens on a double barrelled shotgun, if fixes our sights on what we have targeted. Art can educate us to approach things as they are in themselves; it can open both us and the world around us to the dimension of the Spirit.

It was the phenomenological revolution in philosophy during the twentieth century which made us aware that everything we see is interaction between the things themselves and our hidden but sophisticated modes of apprehension.[24] In the twentieth century the whole basis of our self-understanding and the way in which we can know either the things of this world or the realities of a transcendent one have come under severe critical scrutiny. It is suggested that the metaphysical network which our Western-European culture elaborated to ensure some form of almost guaranteed contact with the mystery of God, was more likely to provide a shield against any such access, because it had constructed a 'natural' facsimile of the God it was meant to be reaching. This displaced transcendent energy in the wrong direction, towards a bogus image of divinity which was no more than a projected extension of ourselves. Perspective, as well as being a specific movement in the history of art, is also an exact reproduction on the outside of the way we see as human viewers on the inside. Perspectival art plays into our idiom of seeing. Every one of us sees from a particular and personal point of view which is mounted on the swivel range of our eyes. These eyes are binocular and view in terms of left and right from wherever we are situated. The trick of perspective, brought to such perfection by Renaissance art, gives us the gratifying illusion of depth in what we are viewing, whereas, in fact, these artworks were painted on flat two-dimensional surfaces usually affixed to a wall. The discoveries of phenomenology allow our visual apparatus to become transparent. We now know that we see in ways analogous to the perspectival trick of Renaissance art, which flattered our particular blind-sight.[25]

Contemporary art forces us to deconstruct this familiar Renaissance scenario. It causes artworks to undergo the kind of self-emptying which makes us aware of our own visual prejudices. It thwarts and frustrates our natural vision. In effect, this means that a similar process of self-emptying, which, theologically speaking, is called *kenosis*, and which was undergone by Jesus Christ in his human body, whereby he reduced himself to nothing, and underwent annihilation in order to manifest his glory, happened in the history of Christian art also. Art's self-emptying can also provide access to the divine.

For Christianity, art, like everything else in this world, is being led by the Holy Spirit, through the processes of creation, to the imageless infinity and timeless eternity of God the Father. As in the parable of the Prodigal Son, there seem to have been two journeys for Christian art in this return to the Father: the one who stayed at home and the one who went off into the world. The path of the prodigal has been rich and varied. It has led from grandiose triumphalism to self-emptying abasement. Perhaps the twentieth century taught us at least one lesson: that the human face cannot be flattened into life-preserving taxidermy on any kind of surface. Art has to renounce the presumption of portraiture of any or every human person, but most especially of God's person. Persons, by definition, elude portraiture.[26]

Abstract Expressionist art has taught us how to bear looking into the abyss without comforting figures and familiar furniture. We even have to remove the monk from Friedrich's romantic painting of the sublime and take this place ourselves. We have to place ourselves firmly and squarely in the position once held by that monk facing up to the infinity and the eternity of the 'Other'. Up against 'it' in the here and now. Max Beckmann, the German artist, writing from the trenches during the First World War described 'here and now' as: 'This unending void whose foreground we have to fill with stuff of some sort or another not to notice its horrifying depth.'[27] This void is what contemporary abstract art displays before us, without any of the 'stuff in the foreground' which was the *sine qua non* of the Renaissance. Contemporary art places us outside our spatio-temporal comfort zone on the edge of eternity and infinity.

We have to learn to endure looking at that which is beyond. Naturally, we would rather climb steps or descend into caves, to be on one side or the other, to be anywhere but in the middle of 'it'. But such must be our vision of an unseen God.

Notes

1 Hans Belting (1994), *Likeness and Image, A History of the Image before the Era of Art*. University of Chicago Press, p. 144. Translated by Edmund Jephcott and originally published as *Bild und Kult – Eine Geschichte des Bildes vor dem Zeitalter der Kunst*, Munich, 1990.

2 Martin Goodman (2007), *Rome & Jerusalem, The Clash of Ancient Civilizations*. New York: Knopf.

3 Mahmoud Zibawi (1993), *The Icon, its Meaning and History*. Collegeville, MN: Liturgical Press, translated from the French: *Icône, sens et histoire*, Paris: Desclée De Brouwer, 1993.

4 G. Ramos-Poquí (1990), *The Technique of Icon Painting*. Kent: Search Press Ltd.

5 Exod. 20.1–17: 'You shall not make yourself a carved image or any likeness of anything in heaven or on earth beneath or in the waters under the earth; you shall not bow down to them or serve them. For I, the Lord your God, am a jealous God . . .'

6 André Grabar (1968), *Christian Iconography, A Study of its Origins*, The A. W. Mellon Lectures in the Fine Arts, 1961, Bollingen Series XXXV, 10, Princeton, NJ: Princeton University Press, 1968.

7 Hans Belting (1994), *Likeness and Image, A History of the Image before the Era of Art*. Chicago: University of Chicago Press, p. 145.

8 *Patrologiae cursus, series Græca* (ed.), J. P. Migne, Paris 1857, vol. 94, col. 1337 [De imaginibus oratio, 3, 16]. St John Damascene, *On Holy Images* (Mary H. Allies, trans.), London: Thomas Baker, 1898, pp. 92, 114.

9 The emperor drew up a series of questions for the bishops meeting at the Council of Constantinople from 2 February to 8 August 754. These questions can be found in *Textus byzantinos ad Iconomachiam pertinentes in usum academicum*, ed. H. Hennephof, Leiden, 1969. This particular question is on page 52. Cf. Christoph Schönborn, 'Theological Presuppositions of the Image Controversy', in *Icons, Windows on Eternity, Theology and Spirituality in Colour*, compiled by Gennadios Limouris, Geneva: WCC Publications, 1990, pp. 86–92.

10 *Nicée II, 787–1987: Douze siècles d'images religieuses*, ed. F. Boespflug and N. Losskey, Paris: Les editions du Cerf, 1987.

11 Vittorio Peri (1990), 'The Church of Rome and the Ecclesiastical Problems Raised by Iconoclasm' in *Icons, Windows on Eternity: Theology and Spirituality in Colour*, compiled by Gennadios Limouris, Geneva: WCC Publications, pp. 28–9.

12 Cf Col. 1.15: 'He is the image of the invisible God' (where the Greek word used is 'icon') and Heb. 1.3: 'He reflects the glory of God and bears the very stamp of his nature'.

13 *Enchiridion Symbolorum et Definitionum* (Handbook of Creeds) compiled by Heinrich Denzinger (1819–83). Editio xxxiii, 1965, # 653 p. 218. Can. 3. 'Sacram imaginem Domini nostri Jesu Christi et omnium Liberatoris et Salvatoris, aequo honore cum libro sanctorum Evangeliorum adorari decernimus.'

14 cf. Andre Grabar, *Christian Iconography, A Study of its Origins*, which were the A. W. Mellon Lextures in the Fine Arts at the National Gallery of Art in Washington in 1961 (Bollingen Series, Princeton University Press, 1968).

15 The word 'indulgence' from *indulgeo*, to be kind or tender in Latin, came to mean the remission of a tax or debt. It is explained theologically as a remission of the temporal punishment due to sin, which has already been forgiven. However, in practice, it was open to serious abuse whereby people imagined that they were able to buy their way into heaven. Originally, indulgences replaced the severe penances imposed by the early Church. Penitents could offer money as a substitute for otherwise taxing reparation. On Luther and indulgences see earlier chapter on 'Reform Spirituality – The Lutheran Tradition'.

16 Giorgio Vasari (2008), *The Lives of the Artists*, a new translation by Julia Conaway Bondanella and Peter Bondanella, Oxford: Oxford World Classics, p. 16.

17 Ibid., p. 177.

18 Randall Davies (1914), *Six Centuries of Painting*, London, T.C.& E.C. Jack, reproduced in Affordable & High Quality Paperback Book Edition by Amazon.co.uk., p. 34.

19 Ibid., pp. 414–15.

20 At its 25th session, the Council of Trent (1545–63) translated by Norman P. Tanner, (ed.) (1990), *Decrees of the Ecumenical Councils*, 2 vols. London: Sheed & Ward, 2:774–6. Quoted in Belting, op. cit., pp. 554–5.

21 See Robert Rosenblum (1975), *Modern Painting and the Northern Romantic Tradition: Friedrich to Rothko*. New York: Harper & Row.

22 Aldous Huxley (1970), *The Doors of Perception*. New York: Perennial Library.

23 Ibid., p. 23.

24 See Maurice Merleau-Ponty (1962), *Phenomenology of Perception*. London: Routledge & Kegan Paul; Herbert Spiegelberg (1960), *The Phenomenological Movement*, 2 vols. The Hague: Nijhoff; Quentin Lauer (1965), *Phenomenology: Its Genesis and Prospect*. New York: Harper & Row.

25 See Jean-Luc Marion (2004), *The Crossing of the Visible*. Stanford: Stanford University Press, trans. James K. A. Smith from the French, *La Croisée du visible*. Paris: Presses Universitaires de France, 1996.

26 'I can see a body, in all its nudity, and a face as objects placed in evidence and in a spectacle; I can never see the eyes of another human; or rather, even if I see his iris and so on, I cannot see his gaze, since it comes out of his pupils, which are empty spaces; the gaze alone is not real: it is born from a black hole, which, in the dialogue I look for or flee from, I want to capture or avoid, precisely because its irreal space fascinates me, as the source of the invisible, at the centre of the visible.' Jean-Luc Marion (2004), *The Crossing of the Visible*. Stanford: Stanford University Press, trans. James K. A. Smith from the French, *La Croisée du visible*. Paris: Presses Universitaires de France, 1996, p. 21.

27 *Max Beckmann, Self-Portrait in Words, Collected Writings and Statements, 1903–1950* (1997), edited and annotated by Barbara Copeland Buenger. Chicago: University of Chicago Press, p. 173.

Bibliography and Further Reading

Grabar, Andre (1968), *Christian Iconography, A Study of its Origins*, which were the A. W. Mellon Lextures in the Fine Arts at the National Gallery of Art in Washington in 1961, Bollingen Series, Princeton: Princeton University Press.

Hederman, Mark Patrick (2007), *Symbolism, The Glory of Escutcheoned Doors*. Dublin: Veritas.

Merleau-Ponty, Maurice (1962), *Phenomenology of Perception*. London: Routledge & Kegan Paul.

Rosenblum, Robert (1975) *Modern Painting and the Northern Romantic Tradition: Friedrich to Rothko*. New York: Harper & Row.

Vasari, Giorgio (2008), *The Lives of the Artists*, a new translation by Julia Conaway Bondanella and Peter Bondanella. Oxford and New York: Oxford World Classics.

Zibawi, Mahmoud (1993), *The Icon, its Meaning and History*. Collegeville, MN: Liturgical Press.

Christian Spirituality and Creation: Ecospirituality

Mary Grey

Introduction

Spirituality is the lived practice of faith and the living out of a person's fundamental values: it is how people make sense of self, world and God. Ecological Spirituality (or ecospirituality) includes relating to the earth itself as a chosen focus. For Christianity this means placing ecospirituality within faith in a God who created and sustained the entirety of creation or cosmos and who destines all created organisms for a redeemed and transformed future.

Ecospirituality is at the same time both ancient and new. It is ancient because it flourished – even if not named as such – within Judaism, within early Christianity up until the Middle Ages and appeared irregularly in certain contexts. It has acquired a recent renaissance in the recognition of the ecological crisis since the 1960s and has gathered strength in different forms, making connections with its ancient roots.

The Renaissance of Ecological Spirituality

Concern for the environment has emerged as a specific focus within the last 30 years:[1] it has now become an explicit dimension of Christian Spirituality. Growing awareness of the ecological crisis has awakened Christians not only to a sense of responsibility but to the fact that the forgotten dimension – creation – should have been at the heart of their spirituality in the first place. In 1962, Rachel Carson's book *Silent Spring* shocked many people as to the damage inflicted on the earth through pesticides,[2] and society began to question agriculture's dependence on these as well as its over-reliance on oil. But it was the article of Lynn White Jr in 1967 that specifically implicated theologians in negative attitudes and practices towards the earth.[3] The text blamed for this was Gen. 1.28:

God blessed them and God said to them, 'Be fruitful and multiply and fill the earth and *subdue it*: and *have dominion* over the fish of the sea and over the birds of the air and over every living thing that moves upon the earth'. (*my italics*)

There have been many efforts to show that 'dominion' does not necessarily mean exploitation or domination. There is also a consensus that damage wreaked upon the earth by human beings is relative to political and economic contexts, and that the grave environmental crisis (complicated recently by climate change), is both a product of capitalist expansion that gradually developed since the Reformation, the industrial development of the nineteenth century – especially the springing up of the oil corporations at its end – and the economic system of globalization that maximizes profit whatever the cost to the environment.

Theologians reacted to the challenge in different ways. Some still remain in denial. Yet it is widely recognized that capitalist expansion often relied on religious legitimization, as in the case of the discovery of gold in South America in the sixteenth century – where the Genesis text (cited above) was invoked for ulterior motives. The most influential prevailing attitude is that all created things exist solely for the use and benefit of human beings. This anthropocentrism has penetrated deep within the human psyche and is proving difficult to eradicate. It continues to influence attitudes to the earth, to justify a range of policies from fish farming, experiments on animals, over-extraction of ground water, genetically modified crops, the slaughter of healthy animals in a foot-and-mouth crisis to the ongoing global destruction of the rain forests. And as the poet Gerard Manley Hopkins wrote so sadly about humanity's interaction with the earth:

Even where we mean to mend her,
we end her
when we hew or delve.[4]

Yet within the Churches, an increasing sense of responsibility towards the earth has prompted many Christians to develop attitudes of stewardship. Others realized that even responsible stewardship still considers the earth and its resources to exist solely for the benefit of humanity. Thus more radical attitudes – influenced by secular movements like 'deep ecology' – see the need to value all forms of life within the great web of life.[5] For Christian theology this means that all its central tenets – God/Christ/creation/redemption/eschatology/sin/grace – must be refashioned to include the flourishing of the environment along with humanity. The very word *environment* has come to be seen as inadequate, when viewed under the lens of God's loving care for the whole of creation: it seemed more to imply a backcloth for human activity and thus that the earth was of lesser importance.

The impact on spirituality has been dynamic and is still evolving. At its simplest, ecospirituality means a recognition that Christian spiritual growth takes place in a much more rooted way, linked with place, with awareness of a relationship with soil and trees, with water and the plant world; but more importantly, with the *quality* of interaction between the human and the non-human. Pastoral care now includes this dimension.[6] The link between women and the earth has awakened consciousness that where environmental degradation is acute –in the poorer southern hemisphere, for example – the suffering of women is more severe, since the provision of water, firewood and fodder is mostly their responsibility. This became the starting point for Ecofeminist Spirituality. A third approach developed within Liberation spirituality: just as 'the poor' are the focus of Liberation Theology, so the environment/ nature is now to be understood as 'the new poor' and should be at the centre of responsible action.[7] The World Council of Churches has been particularly active in consciousness-raising, especially in making links between justice and responsibility for the earth. In 1989, it inaugurated a decade entitled 'Justice, Peace and the Integrity of Creation' that had great impact in, for example, Germany and The Netherlands, although less in Britain.

Rediscovering our Roots

The development of Ecospirituality has been fuelled by the rediscovery of ancient roots and traditions. From Jewish Spirituality of 'shalom', to Jesus' own situatedness in the ecology of Israel, and supposed environmentally – friendly figures in Christian tradition[8] such as St Hildegard of Bingen and St Francis of Assisi, the Protestant seventeenth century mystical poet, Thomas Traherne, to the more recent Jesuit theologian Teilhard de Chardin. Christian tradition does not lack prophetic figures, even if our predecessors did not face the same environmental degradation and had a far lighter 'ecological footprint'.[9]

First, Christians will always draw on Biblical inspiration for the way to live: for many, the Creation story begins and ends with Genesis – and we are again confronted with the 'dominion text'. A more helpful method is to begin with the prophet Isaiah: covering the period of the conquest of the Jews by the Persian Empire, exile in Babylon and return to Judah (535 BCE), Isaiah links with our current situation in showing us that we always begin *from the broken web*[10] of ravaged creation. He, like all the prophets, connects devastation of the land with human sin and responsibility. He, more than anyone, appeals to people throughout history with his imaginative vision of *shalom* that embraces the flourishing of people, land and animals. Water springs up in the desert with a diversity of trees (Isa. 39). Lion, lamb, panther and kid feed together in this messianic vision of redeemed creation (Isa. 11). Whether this means a vision of messianic times (the Jewish interpretation) or a prophetic dream of what might be, given our changed behaviour, it nonetheless calls us into something radically different from our limited human imaginings.

The second Biblical feature is the radical otherness of God's vision for creation, revealed, for example, by the Book of Job. Here, in chapters 38–41, we are given magnificent poetry and a cosmology radically different from the normal reading of the Book of Genesis.[11] As opposed to apparently being the summit of creation, humanity is toppled from pride of place and placed alongside the animals and humbler forms of life. Radically different views of freedom, justice, the wisdom of creation and the gratuitousness of God's love are presented. This is no Walt Disney view of creation: its wildness, savagery and ambiguity are poured out before our eyes.[12] Where human beings have looked to conquering the land and taming the wilderness, God, who displays intimate knowledge of the ways of birds, gives us the image of the baby vultures being taught to drink the blood of their prey and a place for the monsters of the deep. Dissonance is revealed not only in the text but also in reality. Otherness, strangeness and the savagery of animals seem to be part of God's creation. Not that the savagery and ambiguities of creation are any consolation to those threatened by earthquake, tsunamis and drought: but a word of warning is given. In the powers human beings now have at our disposal to destroy the world with nuclear bombs, to clone human beings, to manipulate the genetic structures of the plant and animal world, we have taken God's role and challenged God's control of creation. God's words to Job are clear:

Have *you* commanded the morning? (38.12)
Have *you* entered the storehouses of the snow? (38.22)

The seemingly-imperious tones of God recall humanity to a proper sense of humility and place. This God gives new responsibilities in the current threatened situation of creation: a call to respect wildness and the needs of wild animals, not to hunt them to extinction, and an imperative to hear the cries of the victims whose land has turned to desert because of the unjust policies of governments or corporations. The God of Job calls from the whirlwind that we respect the total ecology of place: *ecological* rather than *exclusively economic* objectives must be our priorities.

So from Biblical roots we learn that conversion to the earth needs a radical humility, a sense of responsibility and an awareness of limit. The framework within which this is given is that of covenant, God's covenant with the whole of the cosmos. From the covenant with Noah (Gen. 9) to its constant renewals, and the role of the king in expressing this on behalf of the community,[13] to its renewal in the Jesus' Last Supper, covenant is a profound summons to understand our authentic role in the cosmos. Responding to this may yet bring hope to battered creation.

Speaking within this covenant and within the tradition of the Jubilee laws, calling for justice for the land, Jesus of Nazareth proclaimed his own mission of liberation (Lk. 4.18–30). It has taken more than 2,000 years for ecotheologians to call for the inclusion of the earth herself within this vision. Jesus, a faithful Jew, inherited the prophetic dreams, for example, of Isaiah – including the vision of redeemed creation, to include all animals in the peaceable kingdom. The Jubilee laws of Lev. 25 extend justice to liberating the land, as well as setting free slaves and cancelling debts.

This vision of the flourishing of land, animals and people together is the context for a culture of peace, the ideal that swords be turned into ploughshares, that each shall sit under his/her own olive tree.[14] In Edward Echlin's book, *Earth Spirituality: Jesus at the Centre*, we are given an imaginative picture of the ecology of Palestine in the time of Jesus: he evokes the creatures of the desert, the diversity of birds, dogs and foxes, goats, water creatures and snakes.[15] How did Jesus relate to this richness of creatures, tree, and landscape and how did they shape his faith and his followers' lifestyles? In his time Jesus was addressing poor farmers, hirelings of the Romans, landless people, delighted to have day's work in the vineyard, in the wheat fields, in the olive groves, or being swineherds for the pork destined for the tables of the Roman occupier.

But it is not just the ecological context that is crucial for understanding Christian Spirituality but if, as ecotheologian Sallie McFague suggests, we see *the earth* metaphorically as the Body of God, then Jesus is this body, this dream enfleshed. Jesus is the pattern and embodiment of the Body of God, then body has a Christic shape. Looking closely at his ministry, we see a focus on bodies – their health and well-being matter for Jesus. He wants them to be fed, nourished and healed. Further, the Christic body focuses on the most poor, underfed, vulnerable and rejected bodies. Jesus' concern reaches out also to the non-human – to trees, birds, animals and the lilies of the field. All find a place in his vision. The Christic body through the ages has sought out new situations where the Body is rejected and suffering. Hence, now, the threatened earth herself, the cosmic Body, is the concern for spirituality.

In time Christianity lost its holistic vision, although it lived on in the mediaeval period, since a more organic view of creation persisted until after the Reformation, when a mechanistic world view replaced it.[16] But the Liturgy of the Orthodox Church has never lost its dimension of praise for creation, central to Ecospirituality. This is a tradition that includes the non-human world as capable of praise – a tradition that draws on the Psalms of blessing.[17] Orthodox theologian Elizabeth Theocritoff tells a delightful story still current on Mt Athos: an elder is distracted in his night prayer by the dawn chorus of frogs from a nearby marsh, and sends his disciples to tell them to be quiet until the monks have finished the Midnight Office:

When the disciple duly transmitted the message, the frogs replied, 'We have already said the Midnight Office and are in the middle of Matins; can't *you* wait till *we've* finished?'[18]

To the liturgy of praise must be added a liturgy of lament – almost lost in western liturgy. To lament what has been lost, in terms of species and rainforest, is one way of inspiring that conversion to the earth needed by Ecospirituality.

Remaining within the organic world view of the early mediaeval world, the Celtic Spirituality of Ireland, Scotland, Cornwall and Brittany is frequently drawn on by contemporary Ecospirituality, especially as practised by, for example, the Iona community (Scotland – and dispersed around the world), and the Lindisfarne community in Northumberland.[19] Although Celtic Spirituality is often drawn on in an over-idealized fashion, and the difference in contexts can be ignored, its reverence for the diversity of nature, the beauty of creation and affinity with growing things, the friendship between its saints and animals and the encouragement of a mystical attention to God in nature, are all aspects that continue to influence the development of ecospirituality.

Later in the mediaeval period (the twelfth century), St Hildegard of Bingen and St Francis of Assisi were both inspirational and are increasingly drawn upon today. St Francis, although sometimes called the 'patron saint of ecology', has a wider influence on spirituality as a prophet of peace and social justice.[20] Here Hildegard is depicted as an example of the way contemporary ecospirituality draws on the mediaeval period.

The Importance of St Hildegard of Bingen

Hildegard, born in 1098,[21] was only 8 years old when she entered the monastery of Disibodenberg (in the Rhineland of Germany) to become the pupil of the anchoress, Jutta of Spanheim. She is unique in many ways. Famous in her own lifetime – her visions received the approval of Pope Eugenius III – her creativity was prolific. She travelled throughout the Rhineland on four preaching tours, and included bishops, abbots and even the Pope among her correspondents. She received the call to write at the age of 43, after a serious illness – pain and sickness haunted her entire life – and produced many works.[22] Her understanding of the world included detailed knowledge of plant life – she is sometimes known as the founder of homeopathic medicine – as well as possessing an intuitive psychological understanding of human nature.

Her new understanding of the Scriptures was based not on human learning, but on inspiration from the 'living light' of her visions.[23]

She was also musically gifted, 'and brought forth songs with their melody in praise of God and the saints, without being taught by anyone.' Her vision of 'a world instinct with order, mystery and flaming love' and 'her profound concept of synergy' is at the heart of her creation spirituality.[24] This means that salvation is a joint concept for God and humanity working together. A distinctive contribution is Hildegard's idea of greenness, or *viriditas*: *greening power* which is seen as the power of life, the dynamic energy nourishing the entire creation.

In the *Book of Divine Works*, the loss of greening power because of the Fall is explained. 'Greening power' is the heart of Hildegard's theocentric view of creation. It is a more profound theological concept – it is God's power of life – than any contemporary secular interpretation of 'greenness':

> In these arrangements the eternity of God's perfect power indicates what should occur in the total fullness of creation. It is, so to speak, the greening power of generation in a shoot as it sprouts forth, for heaven and earth were not yet in existence when the gifts of the Holy Spirit poured out this green freshness of life into the hearts of men and women so that they might bear good fruit. (*Book of Divine Works* 10, 2)

What is remarkable is that even before the Incarnation, Wisdom (*Sapientia*) and the Holy Spirit are at work in creation. Greening power is the work of the Holy Spirit drawing all creation into fullness. Within the work of redemption Christ's role is central:

> My Only-begotten . . . came forth into this world as the greenness of integrity. . . . (*Scivias* II 3.6.147)

Jesus himself was the greenwood because he caused all the greening power of virtues (*Book of Divine Works* 24.4). Through Christ's Cross and resurrection, the possibilities of the restoration of the lost greenness is made available. And that is our task – to cooperate in this work:

> Whenever we believers simply go about our work in life, our thoughts are turned to whatever is proper and useful. And so our thinking affects our greening power to bring forth much fruit of holiness. (*Scivias* 4.8.85)

But after the early inspirational days of Christianity, the greening power that Christ embodied became weaker. Here, a dualist vision creeps into Hildegard's thinking:

> This was known as the 'manly age' but afterwards the greening power lost strength and was changed into womanish weakness. (*Book of Divine Works* 10.8)

So we read her visionary texts, mindful that she is of her times, and that her creativity comes to us, manifesting an oscillation between a joyful affirmation of the world and a melancholy distrust of the flesh.

Yet, for all her knowledge of medicinal plants and brilliant nature imagery, Hildegard was not in fact a 'hands-on' ecological theologian as many attempt to be today. Despite her intriguing metaphor of cheese-making in the creation of the human soul (*Scivias* 4.13), there is no evidence that Hildegard herself was involved in any dairy or agricultural activity. She neither milked the cows nor baked the bread. The Benedictine tradition was quite hierarchical and Hildegard, although as Abbess held responsibility for the governance of the foundation, was a choir nun, with the prime duty of singing the Divine Office every day.[25]

Hildegard does break away from the traditional 'womanly weakness' tradition in her specific use of female symbols which are given a positive role in the redemptive process. Her most important figure is wisdom/*Sapientia*. *Sapientia* – who is symbolized as bride, mother queen, is linked with 'the ultimate mystery of God, the link between Creator and creature.'[26]

This weakness when the greening power was lost is associated by Hildegard not only with human wrongdoing but specifically with the corruption of the church. Not only did the greening power of the virtues die away so that justice entered a period of decline, but 'the power of life on earth was reduced in every seed' (*Book of Divine Works* 10.7). So her integrated thinking is very clear. It is this theocentric vision, the Spirit's working out of Christ's redemptive grace in terms of greening power that remains Hildegard's inspiration for contemporary ecospirituality.

Thomas Traherne

After the Protestant Reformation, the theocentric vision of creation was dimmed, together with the strength of medieval mysticism with regard to creation. Yet a strand of creation spirituality has been discovered and increasingly drawn on in the person of the seventeenth century poet Thomas Traherne. His importance for us lies in showing that the medieval theocentric vision of creation was not completely lost, despite the rigours of Puritanism, and in foreshadowing themes crucial for us today.

Thomas Traherne was born in the late 1630s, the son of a shoemaker at Hereford. Educated at Oxford, he became rector of a church at Credenhill, near Hereford, and subsequently chaplain to Sir Orlando Bridgeman, Lord Keeper of the Seals of England. What we discover with Traherne is the recovery of the *mystical way of relating to nature*, offering a healing of both our instrumentalism and our hierarchical anthropocentrism. A remarkable link between Traherne and our times, situated as we are in a late phase of global capitalism with its damaging results on the environment, is his reaction to the economic system of his day, namely, the early days of global capitalism. He is prophetic in his grasp of the dangers of idolizing money and manufactured goods, contrasting these with the gifts of the natural world.

Nature, he writes, is real in a way manufactured goods are not. These can tempt us with false values. So a culture is constructed in a way that exploits nature. This is a theme that permeates his profound work *Centuries of Meditations* (prose-poetry), and throughout many of his writings.[27]

The need for rediscovery of radical awe and wonder, and a deep attentiveness to nature, the Book of Creation, is a primary and constantly stressed theme – also stressed by many contemporary writers. The idea of desire and want, of God wanting, is a deeply mystical idea, picking up by earlier mediaeval writers like Meister Eckhart and Jan van Ruusbroec. The idea at its simplest is that our longing and desires are matched by the longing of God and meet their satisfaction and fulfilment in the simple joys of nature. Several texts speak of this strangeness of the 'wanting of God':

> This is very strange that God should want . . .
>
> It is of the nobility of man that he is insatiable. For he hath a benefactor so prone to give, that He delighteth in us for asking. (*Centuries* 1)

The core of discovering the wanting is to discover the immanence of God in creation: the Human Person holds the entire universe within him/herself:

> You never enjoy the world aright till – the sea itself floweth in your veins, till you are clothed in the heavens and crowned with the stars . . . and perceive yourself to be the heir of the whole world . . . Till your spirit filleth the whole world. (*Centuries* 1.7–8)

Thus Traherne displays a delight in nature and rediscovers a lost connectedness between human and the non-human. But in order to rediscover this connectedness and immanent presence of God, there is an educational task: Traherne anticipated Wordsworth and other poets by thinking, in a neo-Platonic way, that the child still possesses 'original innocence', the knowledge of the presence of God, lost by the Fall:

> I seemed as one brought into the Estate of innocence. I was a little stranger, which at my entrance to the world was saluted and surrounded with innumerable joys. My knowledge was Divine. I knew by intuition those things which, since my Apostasy, I collected again by the highest reason. (*Centuries* 3)

Traherne speaks of unlearning the ways of the world and becoming a child again. He writes of nature as teacher[28] and reimagines immanence and transcendence in a vibrant way:

You never enjoy the world aright till you see how a sand exhibiteth the wisdom and power of God: . . . wine by its moisture quencheth my thirst . . . but to see it flowing from His love. Who gave it unto man, quencheth the thirst even of the Holy Angels. (*Centuries* 1)[29]

All these strands coalesce in Traherne's idea of *Felicitie* (Felicity). It is a key term and includes a family of ideas such as delight, pleasure, happiness, beauty, bounty, enjoyment, blessing, amiableness, satisfaction, contentment, peace, sweetness, treasure and goodness:[30]

I thought the ways of felicity to be known only among the holy Angels . . . till at last I perceived the God of angels had taken care of me and prevented my desires. For he had sent me the book I wanted before I was born . . . I see nothing wanting to my Felicity but mine own perfection. (*Centuries* 4.71, 74)

Traherne's idea of 'Felicity' is at the heart of the contemporary movement of Ecospirituality and it is to this we turn.

Contemporary Currents

Recovering our roots inspires the many-levelled process of 'conversion to the earth' that characterizes ecospirituality. All the dimensions offered by these earlier positive traditions[31] are brought into play as life-practices: a radical humility before creation, the recovery of awe, praise, wonder and lament both personally and in community liturgical prayer. Recognizing our place in creation alongside other forms of life is another part. All cohere in a sense of joy and wellbeing – what Traherne called 'felicity'.

A new awareness of being part of a more ancient earth story undergirds the journey. Ecospirituality focuses on this mystery at the heart of creation. Its emphasis is on all living things created and blessed by God. As such they reveal the wisdom of God immanent in the world.[32] In its current manifestation, Ecospirituality belongs within a wider spectrum of evolutionary thinking about and a changed relationship with the earth. *The need to place the human story within the cosmic story* is an urgent plea. Brian Swimme and Thomas Berry provide inspiration here, as well as insights from Quantum Physics, of the interconnectedness and interpenetration of all dimensions of existence.[33] A creation-centred perspective views the entirety of life as sacred, rejecting any dualistic split between the sacred and profane. In a cosmic perspective, human beings lose their place of privilege, yet still retain a unique responsibility within the vast scheme of things.

In the Creation Spirituality of Matthew Fox, the centrality of the Fall and original sin in the western tradition is challenged.[34] Without denying the reality of sin he makes *original blessing* his central focus. His contribution has been to offer a practice of Creation Spirituality as a fourfold path. These steps are not linear but 'spirally interwoven'. The *Via Positiva* is the practice of awe, gratitude and delight in creation; the *Via Negativa* is the practice of letting the dark be the dark. Instead of conquering pain by asceticism or will power, *letting pain be pain* means allowing ourselves to experience it as well as giving up the will to control; the *Via Creativa* invites humanity to reconnect with our own creative power, to give birth to new ideas and to new expressions of God. The final movement, the *Via Transformativa,* calls us to bring the insights of compassion, wisdom and justice on the three other paths with a view to changing self and society.

An integral part of the practice of this form of Creation Spirituality is the stress on both prophecy and mysticism, the prophet being the 'mystic in action'. There is also a call to recover a cosmology respectful of the earth by paying attention to other cultures remaining more faithful to the earth, for example, indigenous Indians of North America.[35] The principal argument is that Creation Spirituality – as defined by Fox – is the underlying authenticity of Christian faith that has been suppressed by the western Fall tradition, with its overemphasis on guilt: with the loss of 'the cosmic story' has come the loss of *eros* and mysticism, the scapegoating of women and earth alike, culture's loss of childhood innocence and a dysfunctional Church.

While there is much here that is positive, Creation Spirituality needs to be put in a wider framework – and some of Fox's claims modified. It is undeniable that there has been an overemphasis on Fall and guilt, a turning away from the earth, but recovery and 'turn to the earth' involve holding both creation and redemption *together as interwoven concepts.* Original blessing has to be set alongside creation's need for healing and redemption in this 'broken web'. Also, resisting darkness as 'sin' by embracing it as wholly positive in the *Via Negativa,* risks ignoring the whole intricate web of suffering and evil in which many poor communities are trapped.[36]

The path embraced by Ecospirituality includes a new way of seeing as well as of acting. Sallie McFague advocates the practice of 'seeing with the loving eye', as opposed to the 'arrogant eye', that tries to control and dominate.[37] Many such contemplative practices, fostering a caring, responsible attitude to nature, and a sense of relatedness, help to bring about a changed way of living. A new *radical asceticism* is freely chosen, in order to not only to call a halt to the exploitation of nature and demonstrate how humanity can live in harmony with the non-human world, but also to act to save the planet threatened with extinction, as global warming accelerates. Prophetic groups like Christian Ecology link and Operation Noah offer practical examples.[38] Christian Ecology Link uses the Loaf principle to guide choices in buying food.[39] This asceticism draws on the traditional virtues of Thomas Aquinas, which can be given – for example, by eco-theologian Celia Deane Drummond – a new interpretation in ecological terms.[40] The virtues concerned are *prudence, justice, fortitude and temperance. Prudence* is the facet of deliberation, the capacity to make decisions in emergency situations. It is part of wisdom: practical prudential knowledge means knowing how to work in harmony with the earth's regenerative cycles. *Fortitude* is the capacity to stand firm in adversity. *Temperance* is the necessary *ascesis* or living within limits: it is the reordering of our desires towards the whole and invokes moderation within the knowledge of nature's limits. *Justice*, for Aquinas, is informed by charity, the gift of the Holy Spirit, so is theocentric, with God as ultimate arbiter. In Aquinas's ability to link individual, community and global justice, there is a way for justice to include the self-preservation of all life forms and ecosystems.

Conclusion

Ecospirituality is inspired by the gift of imagination, of reimagining a transformed universe, and is nourished by poetry, art and music. At last Christian Churches are awakening both to the gravity of the crisis and to the richness of their own resources in addressing it. For the sacramental churches there is immense potential for spirituality to reconnect their sacramental dimension with all the aspects described here – awe, praise, humility, lament and prophetic action. A mystic of more recent times saw this clearly: the Eucharistic vision of the French Jesuit, Pierre Teilhard de Chardin (1881–1955), included his pan-Christic mysticism, his belief in the Divine transfiguration of matter and its importance for the future of the universe; all are ingredients in what we could call the sacramentality of the entire cosmos. As Ursula King wrote:

> The whole universe 'is seen to be flesh'. The universal, cosmic Christ is the centre of the universe, the centre of humanity, and the centre of each person. This is why he speaks of 'the heart' – the heart of matter, the heart of the world, the heart of humanity.[41]

Teilhard wrote before the awakening to consciousness of the threatened universe. It was another Jesuit, the late David Toolan, who effectively brought Teilhard's vision of transformation to the centre of an Ecospirituality for our planet in peril. With his stirring words, I end:

> In effect, Jesus is saying that the whole work of transfiguring earth stuff in accord with the creator's dream is not his solitary work but fundamentally the work of the Father in heaven . . . Swallow this, Jesus declares, I am God's promise for the elements, the exemplary inside of nature, its secret

wish fulfilled. Swallow my words, let them resonate in the marrow of my bones, and you will tap into the same current of spirit that moves me. Swallow me and you will have taken in what God imagines for matter: that it be spirited, that justice be done to all, according to the vision of the great rainbow covenant.[42]

Notes

1 The environment is the word used to refer to nature and to the interaction of the human with the non-human world. Its meanings include an enormous range of life forms, from forests and plant world to insects and the entire bird and animal world, from agriculture to climate, from pollution of soil, water and air.

2 Rachel Carson (1962), *Silent Spring*. Boston: Houghton Miflin Co.

3 Lynn White Jr, 'The Historical Roots of the Ecological Crisis' in *Science* 155/1967: pp. 1203–77. See also comments on this text in the chapter above: Christian Spirituality and Judaism.

4 Gerard Manley Hopkins (1953), 'Binsey Poplars', in *Poems*. Harmondsworth: Penguin, pp. 39–40.

5 *Deep Ecology* is usually associated with the late Norwegian ecologist, Arne Naess. For Christians, even if its valuing of all life forms is appreciated, the frequent derogatory attitude to human beings is unhelpful.

6 See Howard Clinebell (1996), *Ecotherapy: Healing ourselves, Healing the Earth*. Minneapolis: Augsburg Fortress.

7 This became a new focus, for example, for the liberation theologian, Leonardo Boff.

8 The word 'supposed' is used, not to undermine the inspiration of the person cited, but to emphasize the need to place this person in historical context and to guard against over-idealization.

9 Measuring 'ecological footprint' has become an indication as to the level of consumption of the earth's resources through methods of travel, fuel consumption, heating of buildings and so on. It is used to gauge the sustainability of the lifestyle of individuals and society as a whole. The selection of sources here is geared to what nourishes contemporary spirituality rather than attempting to offer an exhaustive survey.

10 This is the title of Catherine Keller's book (1986), *From a Broken Web: Sin, Separation and the Self*. Boston: Beacon.

11 M. Grey (2003), *Sacred Longings: Ecofeminist Theology and Globalisation*. London: SCM, Chapter 7.

12 See Bill McKibben (1994), *The Comforting Whirlwind*. Grand Rapids: Eerdmans.

13 Robert Murray (1992), *The Cosmic Covenant*. London: Sheed and Ward.

14 For the relevance of Isaiah's vision today, see M. Grey (2000), *The Outrageous Pursuit of Hope: Prophetic Dreams for the 21st Century*. London: Darton, Longman and Todd.

15 Edward Echlin (2000), *Earth Spirituality: Jesus at the Centre*. New Alresford: Arthur James.

16 That is not to say there were no dualistic thinkers. Flesh/spirit dualisms have always been present: they became more pronounced when Christianity encountered Greek culture in the first century CE, yet were not so damaging in their effect, when the prevailing world view was more organic.

17 See John Chryssavgis' chapter above.

18 Elizabeth Theokritoff (2001), 'Creation and Salvation in Orthodox Worship', in *Ecotheology* 10, pp. 97–108.

19 Celtic Spirituality is meant, roughly, as the period after the Roman Empire until the Norman conquest of Britain (1066). Clearly the edges overlap. For the Iona

Community, see Philip Newell (2008), *Listening for the Heartbeat of God: A Celtic Spirituality*. London: SPCK; for the Lindisfarne community, see the many works of David Adam, a former leader, for example, *The Path of Light: Meditations on Prayers from the Celtic Tradition*. London: SPCK 2009; also see John O'Donohue (1997), *Anam Cara: Spiritual Wisdom from the Celtic World*. London: Bantam Press; and Seán O Duinn OSB (2000), *Where three Streams Meet: Celtic spirituality*. Dublin: the Columba Press. In addition, Thomas O' Loughlin's chapter above.

20 Again, there is a need to be historically accurate: both were dualistic in their theology. Francis did not treat his own body very well – 'Brother Ass' he named it. Likewise Hildegard held a derogatory view of women.

21 Or as late as 1100.

22 These were: *Scivias* (*Know the Ways* – visions with a doctrinal emphasis), *The Book of Life's Merits* (here the emphasis is ethical), and the *Book of Divine Works*, in addition to *Natural History* (*Physica*) and *Causae et Curae* (*Causes and Cures*). *Scivias* is unique in being beautifully illuminated in the Abbey workshop, possibly under the supervision of the saint herself.

23 Peter Dronke (1984), *Women Writers of the Middle Ages*. Cambridge: Cambridge University Press, p. 253.

24 Barbara Newman (1987), *Sister of Wisdom*. Aldershot: Scholar Press, p. 17.

25 I have tried to discover the origins of this cheese metaphor. Aristotle used the metaphor of cheese-making to illustrate conception in his *De Generatione Animalium*. But would Hildegard have had access to this a century before Thomas Aquinas made his works well-known? Peter Dronke quotes from an anthropological study of a Basque community in S. France which seems to suggest a whole range of popular beliefs in N. Europe about the development of life from cheese analogies. See the extensive discussion in Barbara Newman, *Sister of Wisdom, op cit.*, pp. 137–41.

26 Newman, *Sister of Wisdom*, op cit., p. 44.

27 *Centuries of Meditations* was discovered in 1896–7 and published in 1908, by Bernard Dobell.

28 Nature as Teacher: 'From when I clearly find how docible our Nature is in natural things, were it rightly entreated . . . Natural things are glorious and to know them glorious . . . The riches of Nature are our souls and bodies' (*Centuries* 3, 64–5). This is also a strong biblical theme (See the Book of Job Chapter 12).

29 Much of what he says here anticipates the work of Sallie McFague cited earlier, for example, 'This visible world is the Body of God'. (*Centuries* 2.36–7)

30 David Ford (1999), *Self and Salvation*. Cambridge: Cambridge University Press, pp. 275–80.

31 Space has limited the selection offered here.

32 As the Biblical Book of Wisdom teaches.

33 B. Swimme and T. Berry (1992), *The Universe Story*. New York: HarperCollins.

34 See Matthew Fox (1983), 'Original Blessing: A Primer in Creation Spirituality'. Santa Fe: Bear and Co.

35 See chapter by Kathy Heskin above.

36 In addition, *letting pain be pain* is in many cases unhelpful – even cruel – advice. Feminist theology has been active in disclosing the mechanism by which guilt and sin of disordered sexuality is projected onto women, a mechanism that eludes any facile categorizing.

37 See Sallie McFague (1997), *Super, Natural Christians: How We Should Love Nature*, Minneapolis: Fortress .

38 See the websites of the organizations for many rich resources: www.christian-ecology.org.uk; www.operationnoah.org.

39 LOAF= Local, Organic, Animal-friendly, Fairly-traded.

40 Celia Deane Drummond (2004), *The Ethics of Nature*. Oxford: Blackwell, p. 140.

41 Ursula King (1997), *Christ in all Things: Exploring Spirituality with Teilhard de Chardin,* London: SCM, p. 156.
42 David Toolan SJ (2003), *At Home in the Cosmos,* Maryknoll: Orbis, p. 212.

Bibliography and Further Reading

Abram, David (1996), *The Spell of the Sensuous.* New York: Random House.

Adam, David (2009), *The Path of Light: Meditations on Prayers from the Celtic Tradition.* London: SPCK.

Boff, Leonardo (1995), *Ecology and Liberation – A New Paradigm.* Maryknoll: Orbis.

Carson, Rachel (1962), *Silent Spring.* Boston: Houghton Miflin Co.

Deane Drummond, Celia (2004), *The Ethics of Nature.* Oxford: Blackwell.

Fox, Matthew (1983), *Original Blessing: A Primer in Creation Spirituality.* Santa Fe: Bear and Co.

Fox, Matthew (ed.) (1987), *Book of Divine Works,* trans. Robert Cunningham. Santa Fe: Bear and Co.

Grey, Mary (2000), *The Outrageous Pursuit of Hope: Prophetic Dreams for the 21st Century.* London: Darton, Longman and Todd.

— (2003), *Sacred Longings: Ecofeminist Theology and Globalisation.* London: SCM.

Hessel, D. and Rasmussen, R. (eds) (2001), *Earth Habitat: Eco-injustice and the Church's Response.* Minneapolis: Fortress.

Hildegard of Bingen (1986), *Scivias,* trans. Bruce Hozeski. Santa Fe: Bear and Co.

King, Ursula (1997), *Christ in all Things: Exploring Spirituality with Teilhard de Chardin.* London: SCM.

McDonagh, Sean (1994), *The Greening of the Church.* London: Geoffrey Chapman.

McFague, Sallie (1993), *The Body of God.* London: SCM Press.

— (1997), *Super, Natural Christians: How we should love nature.* Minneapolis: Fortress Press.

— (2001), *Life Abundant: Rethinking Theology and Economy for a Planet in Peril.* Minneapolis, Augsburg Fortress.

Newell, Philip (2008), *Listening for the Heartbeat of God: A Celtic Spirituality.* London: SPCK.

Radford Ruether, Rosemary (1992), *Gaia and God: An Ecofeminist Theology of Earth Healing.* San Francisco: Harper Publishing.

Santmire, Paul (2000), *Nature Reborn: The Ecological and Cosmic Promise of Christian Theology.* Minneapolis: Fortress Augsburg.

Swimme, Brian and Berry, Thomas (1992), *The Universe Story.* New York: HarperCollins.

Teilhard de Chardin, Pierre (1957), *Le Milieu Divin.* London: Collins/Fontana.

Toolan, David (2003), *At Home in the Cosmos.* Maryknoll: Orbis.

Traherne, Thomas (2009), *Centuries of Meditation.* General books LLC publication.

White Jr, Lynn, 'The Historical Roots of the Ecological Crisis' in *Science* 155/1967, 1203–77.

32 Christian Spirituality and Atheism

Stephen Bullivant

Introduction

A chapter on atheism in a guide to Christian Spirituality may perhaps seem paradoxical. Unlike certain strands of Buddhism or Jainism, Christianity is not commonly regarded as an atheistic religion. Likewise, atheism – which is, after all, either a belief in the non-existence of a God or gods (*positive* atheism), or more broadly, a lack of belief in the same (*negative* atheism) – does not strike many people as being especially 'spiritual'. Thus as Hamlet might say, 'Seems paradoxical? Nay madam, it is'. And indeed he would be right. But that said, 'the way of paradox' is by no means inimical to Christian spiritualities and mystical theologies. And so, it is hoped, this chapter will prove.

There are, in fact, a number of ways that one might profitably approach a title such as this. One could, for example, embark upon a comparative inter-rogation of one or more Christian spiritualities, alongside one or more of the genuinely secular forms of spirituality in evidence in today's world. Just as one might compare and contrast, say, Orthodox hesychasm with Muslim Sufism or Zen Buddhism, so too one might do the same for any number of Christian spiritualities and the myriad gay, eco, feminist, New Age, sporting and other types of spiritualities identified by scholars (see Van Ness 1996), many of which are atheistic in at least the negative sense outlined above. Alternatively, one could focus on the recent emergence of spiritual literature intended explicitly for unbelievers – such as Steve Antinoff's *Spiritual Atheism* (2010) or André Comte-Sponville's *The Little Book of Atheist Spirituality* (2008) – and explore the ways in which these relate to sources from the Christian tradi-tion (see, for example, Saint-Arnaud 2010).

In both of these cases, however, atheism (or rather, specific manifestations of what is in fact a very diverse intellectual and cultural phenomenon) is viewed and studied as something *external* to Christian Spirituality. What I would like to do in this chapter is, however, rather different. I want to explore two forms of 'atheism' present *within* mainstream, orthodox Christian Spirituality and mystical theology: the intellectual 'atheism' of the *via negativa*, and the

experiential 'atheism' of the mystic's feeling of God's absence and/or abandonment. To do this, I will be referring to and quoting from a wide range of
well-known figures from the tradition, although in each case I will concentrate
particularly on one twentieth-century example: the English Dominican philosopher and theologian Herbert McCabe (1926–2001) for the intellectual, and
the Albanian-born foundress of the Missionaries of Charity Blessed Teresa of
Calcutta (1910–97) for the experiential variety of Christian 'atheism'.

The use of inverted commas here is, it must be stressed, of the utmost significance. Historically speaking, the word *atheism* has always carried a range
of meanings, overtones and connotations. In applying this word to the ideas
of McCabe, and to the spiritual life of Teresa, I am of course not deploying it
in the usual, common-speech meanings previously mentioned (Although it
depends, of course, on precisely what one means by the terms 'God', 'belief'
and 'existence'). Clearly, Mother Teresa was not an 'atheist' in the same way
that Richard Dawkins, or Bertrand Russell, or Jean-Paul Sartre is or was! But
that is not to say that the word is a wholly inappropriate one either. My use
of inverted commas is intended to flag up that the word 'atheism' is being
applied in this chapter in a kind of analogical way: there is a real, though quite
specific, sense in which both Teresa and McCabe are 'atheists', and a real, and
more general and obvious, sense in which they are – *of course* – absolutely
nothing of the sort. Needless to say, such deployments of analogical language,
and simultaneous saying-and-unsaying, are likewise no strangers to Christian
spiritualities and mystical traditions.

'The God who is not a god'

In his posthumously published *God Still Matters*, in an essay tellingly titled
'The Trinity and Prayer', McCabe points out:

> Of course we do not know what God is. We do not know what we are
> talking about when we use the word 'God' . . . When Jews and Christians
> came to use the word 'god' it was already lying around meaning something
> else – I mean it meant something that God certainly could not be, a god.
> Whatever we are referring to when we use the word 'God' it can no more
> be a god than it can be model aeroplane or half-past eleven. (2002: 55)

Developing this provocative line of thought earlier in the book, he writes:

> 'God', 'Theos', 'Deus' is of course a name borrowed from paganism; we take
> it out of its proper context, where it is used for talking about the gods, and
> use it for our own purposes. This is quite a legitimate piece of borrowing
> and quite safe as long as it does not mislead us into thinking that the God

we worship (or don't) is a god . . . He is always dressed verbally in second-hand clothes that don't fit him very well. We always have to be on our guard against taking these clothes as revealing who or what he is.

For this reason it is sometimes safer to use clothes that are quite obviously second-hand, words that have been scandalously ripped from their proper context and stretched and bent and distorted to suit our purposes. (ibid.: 3)

Strange though this may sound, McCabe's basic point here is easy to grasp. In its original contexts, 'god' – *theos, deus* – is a description of certain supernatural, superhuman beings. Pluto, Hera and Jupiter Dolichenus may well be powerful, but are also things *within* the universe. Jews and Christians, however, took this description from their Greco-Roman neighbours, but transformed it into a proper name for the creator and sustainer of the universe itself: *God*. In this new context, the word has become a metaphor. There is a sense in which God is *like* the 'gods' (he too is powerful, for example, albeit both far more so, and in a qualitatively different way), just as there is a sense in which God is *like* 'a mighty fortress' (he is steadfast, and protects those who 'dwell within' him). But the Judaeo-Christian God cannot be an actual mighty fortress. And he cannot be, as McCabe reminds, an actual god. To think that God is a god in the same way that Mars or Hera are gods is to commit idolatry.

The same applies, of course to all of our language about God. The human capacity for language has evolved to deal with mundane, everyday realities. This is why so much of our speech, and especially our words for talking about abstract things or concepts, is at bottom metaphorical ('Metaphor', from the Greek words for 'to carry over', is itself a metaphor: the 'carrying-over' of a meaning to apply it to something else). Such language is not well suited to speaking accurately about God. Even human words that we know in some sense to be validly applicable to God (such as, for example, those recorded in the Scriptures from the mouth of the incarnate God himself, Jesus Christ), cannot be so in any naive or straightforward way. As Denys Turner once put it, in his inaugural lecture at Cambridge titled 'How to be an Atheist', 'Negative theology does not mean that we are short of things to say about God; it means just that everything we say of God falls short of him' (ibid.: 11). Whatever it is that we mean, or think we mean, when we say that God is 'good', or 'powerful', or 'wise', there is an important sense in which the true God cannot be these things. This insight is, of course, central to certain, deep-rooted strands of the Christian mystical tradition. St Gregory of Nyssa's fourth-century midrash on Moses' ascent of Mount Sinai, for example, offers up a metaphor for the Christian spiritual life as a journey into an ever-darkening mystery:

This is the true knowledge of what is sought; this is the seeing that consists in not seeing, because that which is sought transcends all knowledge, being

separated on all sides by incomprehensibility as by a kind of darkness . . .
When, therefore, Moses grew in knowledge, he declared that he had seen
God in the darkness, that is, that he had then come to know that what is
divine is beyond all knowledge and comprehension, for the text says, *Moses*
approached the dark cloud where God was. (Malherbe and Ferguson 1978: 95)

Pseudo-Dionysius' fifth- or sixth-century *Mystical Theology*, which betrays the
author's acquaintance with Gregory's work, is even more explicit. Speaking
of God, he writes:

It is neither one nor oneness, divinity nor goodness. Nor is it a spirit, in the
sense in which we understand that term . . . and it is not anything known
to us or to any other being. It falls neither within the predicate of nonbeing
nor of being . . . It is beyond assertion and denial. (Luibheid and Rorem
1987: 141)

For Pseudo-Dionysius – a huge influence on Thomas Aquinas, among many
others – God is a non-spiritual, non-known, non-divinity who does not exist
(though he also does not non-exist either!). Compared to *that*, McCabe's
description of the Ten Commandments, with its opening distinction between
'the Lord your God' and the other 'gods', as 'that great atheist manifesto'
(2002: 32; see also McCabe 1987: 7) appears somewhat conservative.

The idea that, among the very many things that the Christian God is not, he
is not 'a god' – and that Christians are, or should be, 'atheists' in this (admit-
tedly quite specific) sense – in fact occurs in the Christian tradition as early as
the second century. It is well known that the early Christians were distrusted,
and intermittently persecuted, for being *atheists*: their refusal to acknowledge
the State's pagan gods, alongside their refusal to serve in the Roman army,
was tantamount to treason. The second-century convert St Justin Martyr,
addressed this charge in his *First Apology* (c. 150). Prefiguring McCabe, he happily acknowledges: 'We do proclaim ourselves atheists as regards those whom
you call gods'. However, Justin continues: 'but not with respect to the Most
True God' (1948: 38–9). A similar view, albeit less explicitly put, is expressed
by Paul in 1 Corinthians. There he contrasts the 'idols' and 'so-called gods in
heaven or on earth', whom Christians reject, with the fact that 'for us there is
one God, the Father, from whom are all things and for whom we exist, and
one Lord, Jesus Christ, through whom all things are and through whom we
exist' (1 Cor. 8.4–6). Both Paul and Justin preserve the necessary tension inherent in this mode of Christian 'atheism' we have been exploring. The Creator
of the universe, who became incarnate in Jesus of Nazareth, is not one of 'the
gods'. He is not a kind of super-thing, for he is not a thing at all. And as such,
there is a sense in which Christians are rightly regarded as 'atheists', insofar

as they reject the 'idols' and the 'so-called gods'. And yet, the name *God* does indeed refer to a genuine reality – Justin's Most True God – and one which far surpasses, albeit in a literally indescribable way, any of the mere 'gods'. True Christians are not, of course, atheists with regard to this God. Though that does not mean, of course, that Christians are immune from lapsing into idolatry through being insufficiently atheistic towards the (false) gods. This temptation is, as Paul well terms it, 'a stumbling-block to the weak' (8.9).

This realization has profound ramifications for Christian prayer and worship: the Most True God whom we cannot accurately describe or conceive, whose own name (if mistaken as a literal description) falls infinitely and insultingly short of him, can scarcely be a tame or domesticated companion to one's spiritual life. The thirteenth-century Dominican theologian and preacher, Meister Eckhart, wrote famously in one of his sermons: 'let us pray to God that we may be free of God that we may gain the truth and enjoy it eternally' (Walshe 2009: 422). Eckhart is notoriously difficult to interpret (or more to the point, notoriously easy to misinterpret!). But certainly one parsing of this statement would be: let us pray to the true God that we may be free of 'god', that is, of the lesser and idolatrous parodies that our language dupes us into mistaking God to be. On this reading, Eckhart's statement is radical enough to be fully orthodox: an expression of, and desire for, a roughly similar kind of 'atheism' to that expressed by Justin and Paul. For these, and for McCabe too, false gods – whether these are actual demons, mere fictions, or naive theological constructions – are beneath human worship. In the words of McCabe:

> The worship of [the] Creator is the only worship worthy of a human being. The Creator is the reason why there is a universe with or without gods in it. But if there *are* gods in it, it would be degrading for humans to worship them. This, you might say, was the great Hebrew discovery: human beings are such that they worship *only* the mystery by which there is anything at all instead of nothing . . . And this Jewish discovery was surely a turning-point in the history of humankind. It implied, of course, a piece of self-discovery about humankind: the human being is now defined, if you like, as the Creator-worshipper, the atheist with no gods to worship, no gods to petition, no gods to pray to, no gods worth praying to. (2002: 56)

In Dostoevsky's magnificent 1872 novel *Demons* (or *Devils*, or *The Possessed*, as its title has also been translated), in a section that the Russian censor insisted be cut from its original printing, there is a remarkable dialogue between the Orthodox bishop, Tikhon, and the enigmatic Stavrogin. Tikhon informs the unbelieving Stavrogin that: 'A complete atheist stands on the next-to-last upper step to the most complete faith' (2000: 688). The idea here is that the

complete atheist – one who rejects all false gods, including the misrepresenta-
tions so often promoted by believers themselves – is the ultimate anti-idolater;
the only thing he or she is lacking is faith in the 'Most True God'. This basic
idea has proven a popular one in the theological literature on atheism, and it
is worth taking seriously. There are, however, serious problems with taking
it as a straightforward comment on *atheists* themselves (though this chapter
is not the place to discuss them – but see the remarks in: Bullivant, 2012). But
as a comment on Christianity, and especially Christian Spirituality, there is
much here to ponder. Tikhon's metaphor for the spiritual life as the ascending
of a series of steps, or perhaps ladder rungs, is a familiar one, especially in
Eastern Orthodoxy (and contains echoes, of course, of Gregory's imagining
of Moses' climb to the top of Mt Sinai). On this model, the final attainment of
'the most complete faith' presupposes that one has passed through 'the most
complete atheism': the non-worship and non-recognition of the multitudes of
mere 'gods'. Just like the pagan gods of old, these gods may appear to us in
many forms. They may be literal idols or representations of other gods (as for
Paul and Justin), or they may be our own, necessarily mistaken constructions
of who God is (as for Pseudo-Dionysius and Gregory). Alternatively, as for
McCabe, they may be the false gods of modern society, in whom we misplace
our trust and worship:

> It would be tedious to list the well-known gods of this exceptionally
> superstitious twentieth century. Quite apart from surviving old ones like
> astrology, there are a lot of new ones like racism, nationalism, The Market,
> the Leader . . . you name it. (2002: 32)

McCabe continues his essay with a phrase that both nicely parallels Bishop
Tikhon and serves as a neat conclusion to this section: 'So let us leave the gods
temporarily behind and consider the God who is not a god, the God of truth'
(ibid.).

'My God, My God, why have you Forsaken Me?'

I mentioned above that, among the several implications of McCabean intellectual 'atheism', it follows that the Most True God can hardly be a domesticated companion to one's spiritual life. This suspicion is, moreover, confirmed
by even a cursory knowledge of the spiritual lives of the saints – those who
are, surely, nearest to the top of either Tikhon's steps or Gregory's mountain. Nowhere is this more apparent than in the case of Blessed Teresa of
Calcutta.

Revelations of Mother Teresa's spiritual afflictions, 'this terrible sense of
loss – this untold darkness – this loneliness – this continual longing for God'

(Kolodiejchuk 2008: 210),[1] first emerged in 2001, but were only fully disclosed with the 2007 publication of her private writings and correspondence in *Come Be My Light*. In these, Teresa describes to her confessors and spiritual directors how over long periods, ultimately stretching to over 40 years with only fleeting respites:

> Darkness is such that I really do not see – neither with my mind nor with my reason. – The place of God in my soul is blank. – There is no God in me. – When the pain of longing is so great – I just long & long for God – and then it is that I feel – He does not want me – He is not there. – Heaven – souls – why these are just words which mean nothing to me. – My life seems very contradictory. I help souls – to go where? – Why all this? Where is the soul in my very being? God does not want me. – Sometimes – I just hear my own heart cry out – 'My God' and nothing else comes. – The torture and pain I can't explain . . . I long for God – I want to love Him – to love Him much – to live only for love of Him – to love only – and yet there is but pain – longing and no love. (ibid.)

Given these startling and graphic admissions from one who, prior to her death in 1997, was already regarded by millions as a living saint, and whose 2003 beatification was at that time the swiftest in recent history, the level of popular and media interest was considerable. Understandably, Teresa's words have been widely interpreted as proving her to be an atheist, pure and simple.

The truth is, as ever, far from being so straightforward. And yet, there is a qualified, analogical sense in which one can indeed speak of Teresa's *experiential* 'atheism'. This is the 'atheism' of one who acutely, and painfully, perceives God's seeming absence. Somewhat similar experiences, of one sort or one another (we need not suppose them all to be of the same kind or cause), are far from unprecedented within the Christian spiritual tradition. Mark 15.34 affirms that while he was being crucified, Christ despairingly cried out from the cross, quoting Psalm 22: 'My God, my God, why have you forsaken me?' (cf. Mt 27.46). The Catholic saints John of the Cross, Gemma Galgani, Paul of the Cross, Thérèse of Lisieux and Padre Pio all reported periods of spiritual desolation or abandonment. And yet none of them, Christ included, were atheists, except of course in the McCabean sense. As we shall see below, moreover, such *prima facie* 'irreligious' experiences are far from being the preserve of saints or saviours alone.

Among the many striking things about Teresa's 'atheism', particularly noteworthy is quite how early in life she was afflicted by such darkness. While still a Loreto Sister in 1937 – and indeed, a full nine years before 'the call within the call' which would ultimately lead to her founding the

Missionaries of Charity in 1950 – she wrote to her former confessor in Albania:

> Do not think that my spiritual life is strewn with roses – that is the flower which I hardly ever find on my way. Quite the contrary, I have more often as my companion 'darkness'. And when the night becomes very thick – and it seems to me as if I must end up in hell – then I simply offer myself to Jesus. If He wants me to go there – I am ready – but only under the condition that it really makes him happy. (ibid.: 20)

This early statement is far from being as detailed, or as heart-rending, as some of her later ones would be. However, we do see here one of the hallmarks of Teresa's 'atheism', which will endure *alongside* even her most tortured avowals of faithlessness to come: an abiding trust in, and abandonment to, the will of God. Consider, for example, the following statement from 1959:

> Lord, my God, who am I that You should forsake me? [. . .] I call, I cling, I want – and there is no One to answer – no One on Whom I cling – no, No One. – Alone. The darkness is so dark – and I am alone. – Unwanted, forsaken. – The loneliness of the heart that wants love is unbearable. – Where is my faith? – Even deep down, right in, there is nothing but emptiness & darkness. – My God – how painful is this unknown pain. – It pains without ceasing. – I have no faith. I dare not utter the words & thoughts that crowd in my heart – & make me suffer untold agony. So many unanswered questions live within me – I am afraid to uncover them – because of the blasphemy. – If there be God, please forgive me. – Trust that all will end in Heaven with Jesus. – When I try to raise my thoughts to Heaven – there is such convicting emptiness that those very thoughts return like sharp knives & hurt my soul. (ibid.: 187)

This is, arguably, Teresa's strongest and most eloquent statement of her darkness, and of the intense suffering which it caused her. And yet, even here, in the midst of a string of *prima facie* atheistic statements, one cannot escape from the fact that one is reading a text that is consciously, and unmistakably, a *prayer*. This much is especially clear from her concluding paragraph:

> If this brings You glory, if You get a drop of joy from this – if souls are brought to You – if my suffering satiates Your Thirst – here I am Lord, with joy I accept all to the end of life – & I will smile at Your Hidden Face – always. (ibid.: 188)

Hence in the same way that Justin's belief in the Most True God qualifies and contextualizes his avowal of the name 'atheist', and indeed Jesus' address to 'My God, my God' undermines his feeling of having been 'forsaken', Teresa's paradoxical choice of genre undercuts any unthinking identification of her as an atheist (in the usual sense of the word).

This realization is not in any way intended, however, to diminish the force of her harrowing experiences. Having at other times in her life felt Jesus' joyful and loving presence, his subsequent and sustained 'absences' from her interior, spiritual life (what I have termed her experiential 'atheism') were all the harder to bear. The same is true, of course, for some of the other mystics mentioned above. The sixteenth-century Carmelite poet, St John of the Cross, described his own experiences in similarly evocative terms:

> When this purgative contemplation oppresses a man, he feels very vividly indeed the shadow of death, the sighs of death, and the sorrows of hell, all of which reflect the feeling of God's absence, of being chastised and rejected by Him, and of being unworthy of Him, as well as the object of his anger. The soul experiences all this and even more, for now it seems that this affliction will last forever. (Kavanaugh and Rodriguez 1966: 338)

John famously termed his sense of *godforsakenness* 'the dark night of the soul' (though see Tyler 2010: 83–98), a phrase that is commonly applied to all such episodes within the Christian tradition. It is worth noting, however, that while Teresa herself was aware of the concept, she denied that her own, seemingly similar experiences, were accurately so designated (Kolodiejchuk 2008: 218). For Teresa, her own abandonment was not for the purposes of her spiritual purification (as she understood 'dark night' to imply), but was instead both an identification with Christ's passion, and a form of solidarity with the unwanted, unloved, abandoned and bereft (ibid.: 277). What is beyond doubt, though, is that it was her thirst for Christ that motivated and sustained her courageous life of service and devotion: not finding him in her interior life, she sought out Christ both on the altar and 'in His distressing disguise'. Hence as she once put it:

> To those who say they admire my courage, I have to tell them that I would not have any if I were not convinced that each time I touch the body of a leper, a body that reeks with a foul stench, I touch Christ's body, the same Christ I receive in the Eucharist'. (González-Balado 1980: 105)

As Teresa herself once told the Superiors of her communities, without alluding to her own experience: 'It often happens that those who spend their time giving light to others, remain in darkness themselves' (Kolodiejchuk 2008: 248).

I have spoken here of 'irreligious' experiences, and of experiential 'atheism': these inverted-comma phrases ought not to be misunderstood. Clearly, there is a certain measure of contact between the feelings described, and what one might call common-or-garden atheism. In the former, one is dealing with an acutely, and perhaps overpoweringly, *felt* lack of God's presence (or even existence). Certainly, such episodes are compatible with an actual, longstanding lack of belief in the existence of a God or gods, or positive belief in the non-existence of the same. They may even be a key factor in a person's becoming an atheist in either of those two senses (see Bullivant 2008). But such episodes, however graphically described, are clearly not *sufficient* for making somebody an atheist in one of those senses. Indeed, in many cases (though not in others), such experiential 'atheism' serves as the catalyst for a deeper and stronger faith in the Most True God. In the case of Mother Teresa, we see this in her devotion to the 'same Christ' literally present in both the poor and the Eucharist. Recent, unpublished fieldwork among 'ordinary' Christians shows a similar pattern, at least in some cases. In the words of a 27-year-old, female Anglican ordinand:

> Often immediately before or after I've preached or led a service . . . God can feel very absent and I can feel deeply alone in the universe. My own experience is that they have been deeply strengthening for my faith so I think they would be more accurately described as 'masked religious experiences' rather than something which implies that they pull me away from my religion . . . Both in the medium and in the long term the effect has been that I have a stronger relationship with God.[2]

Conclusion

In this chapter we have explored two forms of genuine (and orthodox) Christian 'atheism'. This is, however, not the 'Christian' atheism of those twentieth century, western theologians who pronounced the 'death of God', and yet still felt able to persevere with their Christian language and rituals (and indeed jobs). And nor is it the normal atheism of the large, and rapidly increasing number, of people who either believe that there is not, or do not believe that there is, a god (or even a *God*). Instead, the Christian 'atheisms' we have looked at relate (1) to the specific grammar of theological utterances (God is a name and not a straightforward description), and (2) to the inner, spiritual lives of a significant number of Christians (some, though by no means all, of whom are recognized saints). On both cases, as I hope to have demonstrated, such 'atheisms' are indeed germane to the topic of Christian Spirituality.

I mentioned in the introduction to this chapter that the paradoxical nature of using the word *atheism* in the context of Christian Spirituality, and therefore its necessarily qualified, analogical, both saying-and-unsaying deployment herein. Certainly, this use of the term risks giving rise to a certain amount of confusion. As I have mentioned several times, to almost all normal, straight-up askings of the question 'Were Mother Teresa, Herbert McCabe, Justin Martyr, Pseudo-Dionysius, John of the Cross, Meister Eckhart, or Jesus atheists?' the correct answer is an unhesitatingly emphatic '*NO!*'. But that said, occasional provocative language, even at the calculated risk of misunderstanding, undoubtedly has a vital place in theology (Something has, for example, gone very wrong when we cease to find such fundamental statements as 'that baby is God' and 'God is hanging from a cross' provocative). This applies especially to the theological exploration of spirituality. Among much else, such verbal pyrotechnics may help to remind us that: 'my thoughts are not your thoughts, nor are your ways my ways, says the Lord. For as the heavens are higher than the earth, so are my ways higher than your ways and my thoughts than your thoughts' (Isa. 55.8–9). In their very different ways, McCabe and Teresa, 'atheists' both, might readily agree.

Notes

1 A notable feature of Teresa's writing style is the heavy use of dashes as punctuation. Though initially distracting, these convey something of the urgency and hurriedness of her writing, typically undertaken in stolen moments between her many other duties.

2 Author's unpublished data.

Bibliography and Further Reading

Antinoff, S. (2010), *Spiritual Atheism*. Berkeley, CA: Counterpoint.

Bullivant, S. (2008), 'Introducing Irreligious Experiences', *Implicit Religion*, 11(1), 7–24.

— (2012), *The Salvation of Atheists and Catholic Dogmatic Theology*. Oxford: Oxford University Press.

Comte-Sponville, A. (2008), *The Little Book of Atheist Spirituality*, trans. N. Huston, London: Penguin.

Dostoevsky, F. [1872] (2000), *Demons*, trans. R. Pevear and L. Volokhonsky, New York, NY: Everyman.

Falls, T. B. (ed. and trans.) (1948), *Writings of Saint Justin Martyr*. Washington, DC: Catholic University of America Press.

González-Balado, J. L. (ed.) (1980), *Mother Teresa: In My Own Words*. London: Hodder & Stoughton.

Kavanaugh, K. and Rodriguez, O. (eds and trans.) (1966), *The Collected Works of St John of the Cross*. London: Thomas Nelson.

Kolodiejchuk, B. (ed.) (2008), *Mother Teresa: Come Be My Light*. London: Rider.

Luibheid, C. and Rorem, P. (eds and trans.) (1987), *Pseudo-Dionysius: The Complete Works*. Mahwah, NJ: Paulist Press.

Malherbe, A. J. and Ferguson, E. (eds and trans.) (1978), *Gregory of Nyssa: The Life of Moses*. Mahwah, NJ: Paulist Press.

McCabe, H. (1987), *God Matters*. London: Mowbray.

— (2002), *God Still Matters*, ed. Brian Davies, London: Continuum.

Saint-Arnaud, J.-G. (2010), '"I'm an Atheist, Thank God!" On the Spiritual Life of Atheists', *The Way*, 49(2), 97–109.

Turner, D. (2002), *Faith Seeking*. London: SCM Press.

Tyler, P. (2010), *St John of the Cross*. London: Continuum.

Van Ness, P. H. (ed.) (1996), *Spirituality and the Secular Quest*. London: SCM Press.

Walshe, M. O'C. (ed. and trans.) (2009), *The Complete Mystical Works of Meister Eckhart*. New York, NY: Herder and Herder.

Epilogue: Whither Christian Spirituality?

Peter Tyler

We began this book by asking the questions 'What is Christian Spirituality?', 'Whence does it arise?' and 'What distinguishes Christian Spirituality from other spiritualities?' Drawing on the breadth of wisdom presented in this volume, this concluding chapter will try to suggest a way forward for Christian spirituality. Or, as we may term it, what may be the key elements of a Christian spirituality for the twenty-first century.

The beginning of the Millennium, starting with the terrible events of 9/11 and its aftermath, has challenged us to rethink how we can go forward as people of faith in a time of darkness. Although we may see around us despair and confusion, what arises in the essays of this volume are the gentle words of peace of the Risen Lord that allow us to treasure in our hearts a 'spirit of optimism' intrinsic to Christian faith. In addressing this final question, which is very much a question of futures – our future, the future of our faith and the future of our planet – we would like to suggest some forms a 'Christian spirituality for a New Millennium' may take. To aid this reflection we will divide these characteristics into the following areas: contemplation, engaged social ethic, psychological insight, embodiment, God in the everyday, awareness of creation and ecumenism. In looking at these categories we shall draw in particular on the insight of the visionary twentieth-century American Trappist monk, Thomas Merton, whose life, career and writings foreshadowed so many of the developments of the later twentieth century and still point the way ahead.

Contemplation

As we have seen, from the very beginnings of the Christian tradition *contemplatio* – the contemplation of the soul on the presence of God through the inspiration of the scriptures – has been central to all Christian Spirituality. As we have seen, the Desert Fathers and Mothers saw in *contemplatio* the vision of the 'pure in heart' mentioned in the Beatitudes (Mt. 5.8) and tried to live this through their solitary contemplation. A *contemplatio* taken up by St Benedict and Western monasticism and manifest through the Middle Ages

387

in the traditions of *theologia mystica*, the Mendicant movements of St Francis and St Dominic and the great Spanish Carmelite mystics of the sixteenth century, St Teresa of Avila and St John of the Cross. Thus, as we enter our new Millennium, we do so as heirs to this tradition of contemplation. The tradition is essentially heart-centred – although it is not anti-intellectual (as we have seen some of the greatest exponents of *contemplatio* have been intellectual giants of the Church, for example, St Thomas Aquinas and Meister Eckhart), many proponents of the tradition have sought to place the intellect in context often through a use of teasing paradox or 'shock tactics' that throw a spanner into the restless whirring of the mind. It is succinctly put by the late Dominican scholar, Herbert McCabe:

> Prayer is really a waste of time. The incarnate form of our prayer may be concerned with getting something done, forwarding our plans, and the generosity of God is such that he will let himself be incarnate even in these ways. But the very heart of prayer is not getting anything done. It is a waste of time, an even greater waste of time than play . . . For a real absolute waste of time you have to go to prayer.[1]

Thomas Merton makes the same point slightly differently in one of his last books, *On Contemplative Prayer*, published posthumously:

> We should not look for a 'method' or 'system', but cultivate an 'attitude', an 'outlook': faith, openness, attention, reverence, expectation, supplication, trust, joy. All these finally permeate our being with love in so far as our living faith tells us we are in the presence of God, that we live in Christ, that in the Spirit of God we 'see' God our Father without 'seeing'. We know him in 'unknowing'.[2]

Prayer and contemplation are not, then, an 'add-on' to life, they are at the heart of life. This 'divine unknowing', what the medievals called the *stulta sapientia* (literally: 'foolish wisdom' cf. 1 Cor. 1) is thus the beginning of all wisdom and the heart of Christian contemplation. 'It is the seriousness', Merton reminds us, 'of breathing when you're drowning'.[3] Once we recognize our nothingness and helplessness before God then we can begin to pray. From such a perspective, even a coldness or impossibility to begin prayer is in itself a sign of this helplessness before God – a sign of His grace towards us and the necessity for our dependence upon God's grace. For, as McCabe and Merton remind us in their own ways, ultimately there can only ever be one teacher of prayer – and that is the Holy Spirit.

Such a prayer, such a *contemplatio*, is not a *fugit mundi*, a flight from the world, but leads us back into life, into the arms of the world. Which leads us to our second aspect of a 'Christian spirituality for the Twenty First Century': an engaged social ethic.

An Engaged Social Ethic

One of the most precious insights of Christian contemplatives and writers in the past half century has been that there is no such thing as a Christian contemplation that does not engage with the world. Merton, the deeply contemplative Trappist monk, also engaged in the struggles of the anti-Vietnam protestors, the black rights groups and the anti-nuclear lobby. The ultimate irony was that after his sudden and tragic death in Bangkok in 1968, his body was transported back to the United States in the same aeroplane carrying the bodies of the young men and women killed in the Vietnam conflict.

From Merton's writings we can draw out three aspects of his understanding of such an engaged social ethic:

First, how such an ethic reiterates the essentially Trinitarian nature of Christian Spirituality. As we have seen in this volume, much Christian discourse over the past half century has sought to re-engage with the Trinitarian model at the heart of Christian theology and social anthropology. For the modern theologians we could describe ourselves as *homo relationis* – instead of 'I think therefore I am', our twenty-first century motto could be 'You are therefore I am'. As God is defined in terms of relatedness, then our basic anthropology, as reflecting God's triune life, can also be defined through relatedness.

One of the key characteristics of Christian Spirituality in recent years has been the search for and, indeed, recovery of Christian community. L'Arche, Iona, Taizé, Focolare are just a few of the new movements that have sought to refind Christian community and have proved especially popular with the young. Such communities have all, in their own way, sought to rediscover the essential communitarian, trinitarian basis that lies at the heart of Christian anthropology.

The second aspect of our understanding of the 'engaged social ethic' is our relationship to and analysis of violence in society. In *Faith and Violence* Merton places our First World Western consumerist behaviour in the context of a radical social analysis that still bites today:

> The population of the affluent world is nourished on a steady diet of brutal mythology and hallucination, kept at a constant pitch of high tension by a life that is intrinsically violent in that it forces a large part of the population to submit to an existence which is humanly intolerable . . . The problem of violence, then, is not the problem of a few rioters and rebels, but the problem of a whole structure which is outwardly ordered and respectable, and inwardly ridden by psychopathic obsessions and delusions.[4]

389

The third and final part of our understanding of this social ethic in a way combines our first point with our second: that there can be no social engagement unless it is rooted in deep contemplation and awareness of self. In the famous 'Letter to an Activist' written to Jim Forrest on 21 February 1965, Merton emphasizes the importance of not attaching to the results of activism: 'face the fact that your work will be apparently worthless and even achieve no result at all, if not perhaps results opposite to what you expect'.[5] 'All the good that you will do' he adds, 'will come not from you but from the fact that you have allowed yourself, in the obedience of faith, to be used by God's love'. Along with alcohol, sex, food and consumer goods, it seems we can add social activism to the list of things we use to fill the void that lies at the centre of our aching hearts. 'The great thing' he concludes 'is to live, not to pour out your life in the service of a myth: and we turn the best things into myths'.

Psychological Insight

The past century has seen enormous strides in our understanding of the psyche, its subtleties and forms. Sadly this has not necessarily been matched with a concomitant increase in our awareness of the integration of the spiritual and psychological. For historical reasons, modern psychology grew up with a distrust and wariness towards religion, an attitude which was by and large reciprocated by the churches. Fortunately the past two decades have seen a rapprochement in this attitude with both sides willing to dialogue and learn from each other. There have, of course, been notable exceptions on both sides and from the Catholic tradition both Thomas Merton, and his near contemporary, the British Benedictine monk, Dom Bede Griffiths, stand out.

In a letter written in the 1960s to a friend of his, Dr Mary Allen, a Jungian analyst, Griffiths makes some startling analogies between the psychological insights of the twentieth century and the ancient Christian ascetic traditions of the Desert Fathers and Mothers. For Griffiths the life of prayer is essentially a 'reordering' of the unconscious through the reflection of God's love: 'The point is that though these sins (Pride, Lust etc.) are largely unconscious our *will* has consented to them. This is the mystery of original sin'.[6] Much of the life of prayer then, becomes for Griffiths, a purification of the unconscious on this radical level: 'We are all by nature under the power of these forces of the unconscious . . . these forces may be kept down, to some extent a kind of balance established, and that is the normal human condition, but it is very inadequate'. Struggling with the forces of the unconscious we have two choices – to repress them or to give way to them in an undiscriminating fashion – 'becoming slaves to passion'. The first option, so common in the West, represses these forces so much that we become slaves to them, in which case we are controlled by the all-controlling, all-powerful, all-knowing ego. 'The average Christian' says Griffiths, 'simply represses the unconscious like everyone else and lives from their will and reason'.

However, in baptism in Christ we have entered the deepest depths of the unconscious to allow their purification: 'It is Christ alone who can set us free from the unconscious. Baptism is a descent beneath the waters, a conflict with Satan (in which the soul is mystically identified with Christ) in which the daemonic powers are defeated and the healing powers of the unconscious are realised to give birth to new life'. This, for Griffiths, is what should happen in our Christian life – 'The Holy Spirit should penetrate to the depth of the unconscious to the ultimate root of being, and transform us'.

So many of us, especially in the West, lock up the forces of the unconscious and are terrified of opening up their contents (often with good reason), and alternatively we see around us total unconscious 'acting out' of the destructive unconscious forces of the psyche. The Life of Christ penetrating into the darkest depths of the unconscious can bring liberation and healing in a most unexpected and profound way. The goal, following Griffiths, is to bring about a marriage of the conscious and unconscious, the male and female, animus and anima in which each is preserved and reintegrated in Christ.

Examining the lives of Thomas Merton and Bede Griffiths we see exactly this 'reintegration of the self in Christ' through marriage of different poles of the self. Merton, living from the unconscious as a young man embraces the hard ethical demands of the Christian life when he enters the Trappist monastery of Gethsemani (as does Griffiths when he enters Prinknash Abbey), only with age and experience realizing that the hard edges of ego-control have to be surrendered to allow a softer entrance of the spirit into all aspects of the self, bringing about what Blake calls the 'marriage of heaven and earth'. As we saw above in the chapters written by Richard Rohr and Bernadette Flanagan, it is highly likely that through deepening awareness of the gendered life of the Spirit that Christians will increasingly learn to articulate the spiritual quest in the twenty-first century.

Embodiment

The Christian Spirituality of the new Millennium will not only be psychologically aware but embodied. It takes all aspects of the self seriously, including the erotic. A point observed by Pope Benedict XVI in his encyclical *Deus Caritas Est*. Benedict's encyclical restores *eros* to its rightful place at the centre of Christian life, reinvigorated and renewed in *agape*: 'Man is truly himself when his body and soul are intimately united; the challenge of *eros* can be said to be truly overcome when this unification is achieved'.[7]

The new spirituality is not just a school of the head but a school of the heart and intuition that gives as much importance to the arts, liturgy and embodied expression as it does to scholastic theology. As Merton puts it in *Zen and the Birds of Appetite*: 'In our need for whole and integral experience of our own self on all its levels, bodily as well as imaginative, emotional, intellectual, spiritual, there is not place for the cultivation of one part of human consciousness, one aspect of human experience, at the expense of others, even on the pretext that what is cultivated is sacred and all the rest profane. A false and divisive "sacredness" or "supernaturalism" can only cripple us'.[8]

God in the Everyday

The breakdown of the barrier between the sacred and the secular leads to our fifth aspect of the spirituality for the twenty-first century – the breakdown of the barrier between the ordinary and the extraordinary. It is what the eighteenth-century Jesuit, Jean Pierre de Caussade referred to as the 'sacrament of the present moment'. Merton, again, put it thus: 'There is no longer any place for the kind of idealistic philosophy that removes all reality into the celestial realms and makes temporal existence meaningless . . . we need to find ultimate sense here and now in the ordinary humble tasks and human problems of every day'.[9] Merton himself, following the artistic example of his parents, was a keen photographer and his photographs illustrate the 'quiddity', the 'this-ness' of everyday objects. The essence of the Creator 'shining out like shook foil' in all creation.[10]

Awareness of Creation

This awareness of the present moment – 'the power of now' – leads to a wider cosmic awareness and our own place within creation. Faced with the ecological disasters of the late twentieth century, we are forced more and more to reassess our place within creation and our commitments and responsibilities to the world around us. Merton, in the late 1960s, talked about the need to address those problems 'which threaten our very survival as a species on earth'.[11] How prescient he was in this respect and how pressing now the task which is finally being taken up by contemporary theologians as explored so well above by John Chryssavgis and Mary Grey amongst others.

Ecumenical

The seventh and final aspect of our 'Christian spirituality for the Twenty First Century' is the importance of openness to dialogue between the Christian denominations and the faiths. As we have seen in this volume, in the past decades, following the decrees of *Nostra Aetate* at the Second Vatican Council, the Roman Catholic Church has embraced ecumenical and interfaith dialogue with gusto under the pontificate of Pope John Paul II and now under Pope Benedict XVI. Slowly we talk to each other and slowly we edge towards healing the scandalous divisions of centuries. As we live at this precarious moment in our planet's future the ecumenical imperative becomes even more important than ever. As with all our seven aspects of the spirituality for the new Millennium, Merton was again ahead of his time embracing dialogue with Buddhists, Muslims, Jews, Hindus and Sikhs. The four chapters above have articulated in some depth the perils and promises that this new dialogue will be revealing in the coming decades of the new century.

Conclusion: 'A New Role for Religion'

So then, our personal list of the seven aspects of the 'Christian Spirituality for the Twenty First Century', or better, an 'Engaged Christian Spirituality for the New Millennium' embraces *contemplatio*, an engaged social ethic, psychological insight, embodiment, God in the everyday, awareness of Creation and the ecumenical.

Reading the contributors to this volume there is always a sense of optimism. It is a sense that God the Father, through the Holy Spirit and Jesus Christ is leading us into new paths and new ways that are unknown to us. We live in Meister Eckhart's *Now-Moment*, the place of potential and renewal where the Eternal Creator gives birth to the Eternal Child within us if we will but let it happen. As the great tenth-century Orthodox theologian, St Symeon the New Theologian, reminds us, the natural condition of Christians is to be caught up in the great Cosmic renewal of the *Logos* by birthright from baptism, what is extraordinary is that we have forgotten who we are and how we are related to the cosmos. In this new ecumenical spirit – the great spirit of renewal which blows through our churches at the present time – we are called and challenged once again to respond to the great tradition of 2000 years of Christian Spirituality in a new positive spirit of optimism and humility.

Notes

1 H. McCabe (2002), *God Still Matters*, ed. Brian Davies. London: Continuum, p. 75.
2 T. Merton (1973), *Contemplative Prayer*. London: Darton, Longman and Todd, p. 39.
3 Merton, 'Lectures to Novices', quoted in R. Baker and G. Henry (1999), *Merton and Sufism: The Untold Story*. Louisville: Fons Vitae, p. 154.
4 T. Merton (1968), *Faith and Violence*. Indiana: University of Notre Dame Press, pp. 78–9.
5 T. Merton (1985), *The Hidden Ground of Love: The Letters of Thomas Merton on Religious Experience and Social Concerns*, ed. William H. Shannon. New York: Farrar, Straus and Giroux.
6 B. Griffiths (2005), 'Letter to Dr Mary Allen', reprinted in the *Bede Griffiths Sangha Newsletter*. March 2005, vol. 8: 1.

7 Pope Benedict XVI, (2005) *Deus Caritas Est.* Accessible on www.vatican.va/ holy_father/benedict_xvi/encyclicals.
8 T. Merton (1968a), *Zen and the Birds of Appetite.* New York: New Directions, p. 30.
9 Ibid.
10 See also P. Pearson (2003), *The Paradox of Place: Thomas Merton's Photography.* Louisville, KY: Thomas Merton Centre at Bellarmine University.
11 T. Merton (1968a): 30.

Bibliography and Further Reading

Baker, R. and Henry, G. (1999), *Merton and Sufism: The Untold Story.* Louisville: Fons Vitae.
Pope Benedict XVI (2005), *Deus Caritas Est.* Accessible on www.vatican.va/ holy_father/benedict_xvi/encyclicals
McCabe, H. (2002), *God Still Matters*, ed. Brian Davies. London: Continuum.
Merton, T. (1967), *Mystics and Zen Masters.* New York: Farrar, Straus and Giroux.
— (1968a), *Faith and Violence.* Indiana: University of Notre Dame Press.
— (1968b), *Zen and the Birds of Appetite.* New York: New Directions.
— (1973), *Contemplative Prayer.* London: Darton, Longman and Todd.
— (1985), *The Hidden Ground of Love: The Letters of Thomas Merton on Religious Experience and Social Concerns*, ed. William H. Shannon. New York: Farrar, Straus and Giroux.

Notes on Contributors

Dr Margaret Barker is an independent biblical scholar and former President of the Society for Old Testament Study and a member of the Ecumenical Patriarch's Symposium on Religion, Science and the Environment. She is a Methodist local preacher.

Dr Stephen Bullivant is Lecturer in Theology and Ethics at St Mary's University College, Twickenham. He is the author of *The Salvation of Atheists and Catholic Dogmatic Theology* (Oxford University Press, 2012) and *The Oxford Handbook of Atheism* (Oxford University Press, forthcoming, co-edited with Michael Ruse).

Dr Mark J. Cartledge is Senior Lecturer in Pentecostal and Charismatic Theology and Director of the Centre for Pentecostal and Charismatic Studies at the University of Birmingham (UK). He is an Anglican priest who has studied charismatic spirituality for over 20 years.

Revd Dr John Chryssavgis studied in Athens (Greece) and Oxford (UK). He has taught in Sydney (Australia) and Boston (USA). The author of many books and numerous articles, he currently serves as theological advisor to the Ecumenical Patriarch on environmental issues.

Dr Bernadette Flanagan is the Director of Research at All Hallows College (a College of Dublin City University). Her current research interests are new monasticisms, spiritual capital and research methods for applied spirituality issues. She co-edited *With Wisdom Seeking God: The Academic Study of Spirituality*, Studies in Spirituality Supplements, 15 (Leuven: Peeters, 2008), a collection of papers from the first European conference on the academic study of spirituality.

Dr Martin Ganeri, OP is Director of the Centre for Christianity and Interreligious Dialogue at Heythrop College, University of London. He is Prior of Blackfriars, Cambridge. His main areas of teaching and research are Catholic approaches to other religions, World Christianity and Indian religions.

Prof. Mary C. Grey is D. J. James Professor Emerita of Pastoral Theology, Trinity St David's, University of Wales; Visiting Professor at St Mary's University College, Twickenham and Honorary Professor at the University of Winchester. Her latest book is *The Advent of Peace – a Gospel Journey to Christmas* (SPCK, 2010). She is a founder trustee of the NGO *Wells for India*.

Prof. Michael D. Guinan, OFM is Professor Emeritus of Old Testament and Semitic Languages at the Franciscan School of Theology (Graduate Theological Union), Berkeley, CA. His special interests are Old Testament Wisdom Literature, Psalms and biblical dimensions of Franciscan spirituality. Among his books are *The Pentateuch* (Wipf & Stock, 2003) and *Gospel Poverty: Witness to the Risen Christ* (Paulist Press, 1981).

Abbot Mark Patrick Hederman, OSB is Abbot of the Benedictine monastery of Glenstal in Co Limerick, Ireland. His latest book is *Dancing with Dinosaurs: A Spirituality for the Twenty-First Century* (Dublin: Columba, 2011).

Prof. Kathy Heskin received her MDiv from Loyola University in 1993 and her DMin from St Mary of the Lake Seminary in 1998. A member of the theology faculty of Dominican University, she is the founder and director of the bachelor's programme in pastoral ministry and the master of arts degree programme in family ministry and faith development. Deeply involved in Native American studies, she teaches three community-based learning courses in Native culture and spirituality. She is the author of *Marriage: A Spiritual Journey* (Twenty-Third Publications, 2002) and several articles on family life and ritual.

Fr Gerard W. Hughes, SJ had his first experience of Ignatius Loyola's full *Spiritual Exercises* in 1942 and they have lived with him ever since. Having completed his very long training as a Jesuit, he found he had an increasing dislike of these *Exercises* on which he had tried to build his life. He now lives in gratitude for that crisis, because facing into it revealed a God who is both in all things and in all people: God who is closer to us than we are to ourselves, yet always greater, a beckoning and most attractive God, continuously summoning us out of our self-made prisons, including our religious certainties, into the freedom of unity and peace, love and compassion, which is God.

Dame Laurentia Johns, OSB entered Stanbrook Abbey, Yorkshire, England in the 1990s after studies at Oxford and Harvard and a career in teaching. She has served the community in a variety of capacities including as novice mistress. She contributes regularly to *The Downside Review* and other journals and is editor of *Touched by God: Ten Monastic Journeys* (Continuum, 2007).

Prof. Anthony J. Kelly, CSSR is a Professor of Theology in the Faculty of Theology and Philosophy at Australian Catholic University in Melbourne, having been Dean of Theology previously and President of Yarra Theological Union for 12 years. Since 2004 he has been a member of the International Theological Commission and was made a Fellow of the Australian Catholic Theological Association in 2010. His areas of specialization include the interdisciplinary framework of theological method, trinitarian theology and the Thomistic tradition. Recent publications include *The Resurrection Effect: Transforming Christian Life and Thought* (2008), *Eschatology and Hope* (2006) and *'God is Love': The Heart of Christian Faith* (2011).

Dr Michael Kirwan, SJ is a Jesuit priest lecturing in systematic theology at Heythrop College, University of London. He is the author of *Discovering Girard* (DLT, 2004), *Political Theology: a New Introduction* (DLT, 2008) and *Girard and Theology* (T & T Clark, 2009).

Prof. Celia Kourie is Professor of Christian Spirituality at the University of South Africa, Pretoria. She is the convenor of the postgraduate programme in Christian spirituality at Unisa. Recent research projects include interspirituality, secular spirituality; inter-religious mysticism and Carmelite mysticism.

Prof. Martin Laird, OSA is Professor of Early Christian Studies at Villanova University. Among his writings are *Gregory of Nyssa and the Grasp of Faith*; *Into the Silent Land: A Guide to the Christian Practice of Contemplation*; *A Sunlit Absence: Silence, Awareness and Contemplation* (each from Oxford University Press). He lectures and gives retreats widely throughout the United States, Great Britain and the Republic of Ireland.

Dr Jonathan Linman is Bishop's Assistant for Formation in the Metropolitan New York Synod of the Evangelical Lutheran Church in America where he engages in teaching and oversight ministries related to various educational programmes and processes that prepare people for public ministry in the church. He is also an adjunct professor of Ascetical Theology at The General Theological Seminary of the Episcopal Church in New York City, and author of *Holy Conversation: Spirituality for Worship* (Fortress Press, 2010).

Prof. Bernard McGinn is the Naomi Shenstone Donnelly Emeritus Professor in the Divinity School of the University of Chicago. Recent books include *Doctors of the Church* (Herder and Herder, 2009), *The Mystical Thought of Meister Eckhart: The Man from Whom God Hid Nothing* (Crossroad, 2001) and the first four volumes of the *Presence of God* series (Crossroad, 1991–2005): *The Foundations of Mysticism, The Flowering of Mysticism, The Growth of Mysticism* and *The Harvest of Mysticism in Medieval Germany*. He is also co-editor of two volumes in Herder & Herder's *World Spirituality* series. Prof. McGinn is the Editor-in-Chief of the Paulist Press 'Classics of Western Spirituality' series and a member of the board of trustees of the Eckhart Society, London.

Bishop Gordon Mursell was ordained in the Church of England in 1973 and served successively in Liverpool, London, Salisbury, Stafford and Birmingham. He was made Bishop of Stafford in 2005 and retired in 2010. He now lives in Scotland and is a Visiting Lecturer at the University of Glasgow.

Prof. Gerald O'Collins, SJ is emeritus professor of the Gregorian University (Rome) and adjunct professor of Australian Catholic University. His latest books include *Rethinking Fundamental Theology* (Oxford University Press), *Believing in the Resurrection* (Paulist Press) and *A Midlife Journey* (Connor Court and Gracewing).

Prof. Thomas O'Loughlin is Professor of Historical Theology in the University of Nottingham. His research concentrates on how Christian self-understanding and expression in the first centuries changed and developed through the process of groups seeking to reinvent their present by creating images of an ideal moment in the past – a process that continues in Christianity to this day. His most recent book is *The Didache: A Window on the Earliest Christians* (London: SPCK & Grand Rapids, MI: Baker Academic, 2010).

Prof. John T. Pawlikowski, OSM is Professor of Social Ethics and Director of the Catholic-Jewish Studies Program at Catholic Theological Union in Chicago. He has served as President of the International Council of Christians and Jews and continues to serve on its board as President Emeritus. He is the author/editor of more than 15 books on Christian-Jewish Relations including *Christ in The Light of the Christian-Jewish Dialogue* (Paulist Press, 1982).

Dr Kurian Perumpallikunnel, CMI is a residential staff member in the Faculty of Theology, Dharmaram Vidya Kshetram, Pontifical Athenaeum of Philosophy, Theology and Canon Law (Bangalore). He is the Chief Editor of *Vinayasadhana: Journal of Psycho-Spiritual Formation*. He is a regular contributor of articles to national and international periodicals.

Fr Brian J. Pierce, OP is a Dominican friar of the Province of St Martín de Porres (USA). After 15 years of ministry in Latin America, interspersed with a year and a half in a contemplative Christian ashram, Brian now accompanies the contemplative nuns of the Dominican Order worldwide. His two books in English are: *Martin de Porres: A Saint of the Americas* (New City Press, 2004) and *We Walk the Path Together: Learning from Thich Nhat Hanh and Meister Eckhart* (Orbis Books, 2005).

Fr Richard Rohr, OFM is a Franciscan priest of the New Mexico Province, and the founding director of the Center for Action and Contemplation in Albuquerque, New Mexico. He has written several books on male spirituality and conducted male initiation rites throughout the world since 1996.

Dr Judith Rossall is Vice Principal for Reflective Practice at the Southern Theological Education and Training Scheme (STETS) in Salisbury (UK). Her doctorate focused on Calvin's theology. She is a Methodist Minister and held two Circuit appointments before moving to STETS.

Dr David D. Thayer, PSS is currently a member of the General Council of the Society of Saint-Sulpice and the Director of Intellectual Formation at Theological College, the seminary of the Catholic University of America, where he is also a lecturer in both the School of Theology and Religious Studies and the School of Philosophy. Several of his articles on the French School of Spirituality have appeared in the *Bulletin de Saint-Sulpice*, for which he is the Director.

Prof. Christian W. Troll, SJ is Honorary Professor of the Study of Islam and Christian-Muslim Relations at the Philosophisch-Theologische Hochschule Sankt Georgen Frankfurt am Main (Germany). His most recent publication is *Dialogue and Difference: Clarity in Christian-Muslim Relations* (Maryknoll/NY: Orbis, 2009).

Dr Peter Tyler is Reader in Pastoral Theology and Spirituality at St Mary's University College, Twickenham, London. He is the Director of the Centre for Initiatives in Spirituality and Reconciliation (InSpiRe). His latest book is *The Return to the Mystical: Ludwig Wittgenstein, Teresa of Avila and the Christian Mystical Tradition* (Continuum, 2011).

Dr Benedicta Ward SLG is the Reader in the History of Christian Spirituality at the University of Oxford and is a supernumerary Fellow both of Harris Manchester College and of St Stephen's House. She has written seven books on the Desert fathers and five on the Middle Ages. Her most recent book is *Anselm of Canterbury: His Life and Legacy* (SPCK, 2009). She is a member of the Anglican monastic community of the Sisters of the Love of God.

Prof. Richard Woods, OP is Professor of Theology at Dominican University, River Forest, Illinois. Holder of the Lund-Gill Chair for 2010, he is a member of the Board of Trustees of the Eckhart Society. Recent publications include *Meister Eckhart: Master of Mystics*, (Continuum, 2010), *Eckhart's Way* (Veritas, 2009), *Wellness: Life, Health, and Spirituality* (Veritas, 2008) and *Christian Spirituality: God's Presence through the Ages* (Orbis, 2006) and other books and articles.

Index of Biblical Citations

Index of Names

Index of Subjects